MW01626891

HOW TO SEE
COLOR
AND PAINT IT

HOW TO SEE COLOR AND PAINT IT

by Arthur Stern

Watson-Guptill Publications/New York

Dedicated to all my students—
past, present, and future—
whose painting problems and solutions
are the heart of this book.

First published in 1984 in New York by Watson-Guptill Publications,
a division of Billboard Publications, Inc.,
1515 Broadway, New York, N.Y. 10036

Library of Congress Cataloging in Publication Data
Stern, Arthur, 1916–
How to see color and paint it.
Bibliography: p.
Includes index.
1. Color—Psychological aspects. 2. Color in art.
3. Visual perception. I. Title
ND1495.P8S73 1984 752 83-23545
ISBN 0-8230-2469-5

Distributed in the United Kingdom by Phaidon Press, Ltd.,
Littlegate House, St. Ebbe's Street, Oxford.

Manufactured in Japan

1 2 3 4 5 6 7 8 9 / 89 88 87 86 85 84

Edited by Bonnie Silverstein
Designed by Brian D. Mercer and Bob Fillie
Set in 12-point ITC Garamond

ACKNOWLEDGMENTS

My thanks to Alexander J. Yow, who brought the news of Charles Hawthorne from Cape Cod to Manhattan; to Frederick Henderschott, John Russell, Roger Stevens, and the late Mildred Otto, who permitted me to sit in on their painting group; to Erik Falkensteen, who gave freely of his time, skill, and energy to make the color photographs of the paintings; to Don Stern and Kevin Kennedy, who shot the black-and-white pictures of the setups; to both my editors, Don Holden and Bonnie Silverstein, and to my old friend. Dr. Thomas Lopez, without whose joint unflagging support I would never have completed this project.

And of course I owe a special debt to a man I never knew—Charles Hawthorne—whose teachings, summarized in that remarkable book, *Hawthorne on Painting*, have inspired generations of artists.

CONTENTS

Learning to Paint What You See 9

BASIC INFORMATION **12**

Materials and Work Area 14

Handling Color 19

How the Projects Work 28

THE PROJECTS **32**

1. How Dark Is White, How Light Is Black? 34
2. When Is "Black" Black? 36
3. How Green Can Turn Red 38
4. How Plain Is a Plane? 40
5. When Is an Orange Orange—and Where? 42
6. Color Without Contour 46
7. A New Light on Shadows 50
8. Black and White in Light and Shade 54
9. Light and Shade Are Colors 58
10. Space Influences Color 62
11. Metal Is No Mystery 66
12. What Color Is Wood? 70
13. Surfaces Aren't Scary 74
14. Even Twins Don't Look Alike 78
15. Slicing Bread into Many Colors 82
16. A New Angle on Color 86
17. Seeing Through Translucency 90
18. A Bagful of Color 94
19. A Look at Transparency 98
20. A Glass of Water Isn't Colorless 102
21. The Color of Greenery 106
22. Unstill Life 110

IDEAS FOR INDEPENDENT STUDY **114**

Bibliography 143

Index 143

"Paint what you see, not what you know." CHARLES HAWTHORNE

"Everything that you can see in the world around you, presents itself to your eyes only as an arrangement of patches of different colours. . . ." JOHN RUSKIN

"Don't think of things as objects, think of them as spots of color coming one against the other." CHARLES HAWTHORNE

"There is no model; there is only color." PAUL CÉZANNE

"We must never forget that any painting—before being a warhorse, a nude woman, an anecdote, or whatnot—is essentially a flat surface covered with colors arranged in a certain order." MAURICE DENIS

"The painter has to unlearn the habit of thinking that things seem to have the colour which common sense says they 'really' have, and to learn the habit of seeing things as they appear." BERTRAND RUSSELL

"I work on all parts of my painting at once, improving it very gently until I find that the effect is complete." JEAN-BAPTISTE CAMILLE COROT

"The successful painter is continually painting still life." CHARLES HAWTHORNE

"I will astonish Paris with an apple." PAUL CÉZANNE

LEARNING TO PAINT WHAT YOU SEE

One afternoon, I took several students to Riverside Park, along the water's edge, to look across the Hudson at New Jersey. I pointed to three architectural structures: an apartment house at the very top of the Palisades; a silo or storage tank down at the waterside; and a tall factory further up the river. Then I asked: "What color are those buildings?"

My students all gave me the same answers. The apartments were red. ("Red brick," someone said.) The storage tank was white. And the factory was orange.

But then I handed around some small gray cards, each with a hole punched through it—I call them *spot screens*—and asked each student to hold the card at arm's length and look through the hole at each of the three structures. "Now tell me what colors you see."

They all followed my instructions, but remained silent until one of them finally spoke up. "They're all *blue*, like the rest of the scenery over there when you look through the hole in the card." The other students joined in. The red apartment house, the white tank, and the orange factory building all looked *blue*!

The students had just made a remarkable discovery. When they first looked at the buildings and agreed that they were red, white, and orange, they were truly telling me what they saw—but not what they saw with their *eyes alone*. Their minds had exerted a powerful influence over what they saw. And this calls for some explaining.

When we look at anything in the world for any purpose other than painting, our mind acts as a kind of filter for the eye. That is, the mind seems to filter out the momentary, constantly changing effects of light, weather, distance, and other transitory phenomena—the kind that make red, white, and orange buildings look blue. But this mental filter serves an obvious, practical purpose. When someone arranges to meet you in front of a red building, the mind filters out the blue light that has turned the bricks to violet—so you can *find* the place.

But this mental filter is no help when you're trying to paint a picture of that same building. On the contrary, the mind gets in the way of the eye and makes it terribly hard for you to paint what the eye really sees.

In short, my students were experiencing the basic problem that every painter must face: *The mind stands in the way of the eye*. That's why most beginning painters don't paint what the eye sees, but what the mind *lets* the eye see. They paint what they *expect* to see.

Students expect water to be blue, so they paint a lake blue. But this lake may actually appear red, orange, yellow, and brown because it's filled with the reflections of these autumn trees on the shore. Or students paint clouds white because they expect them to be white—though clouds can actually be yellow, red, orange, or violet, since the color of the sunlight shining on them changes throughout the day, and they also reflect the colors of the land below.

The purpose of the spot screen—like many other devices invented by artists over the centuries—is to turn off that mental filter so you don't paint what you expect to see. Thus, looking through the hole in the spot screen, the students were able to ignore the fact that they were looking at red, white, and orange buildings in a late afternoon shade. They now saw that the buildings were bathed in blue light reflected from the sky and the surface of the river. (Actually, on closer inspection of those objects, you would begin to realize the buildings aren't all the same blue but differ subtly—though you won't be able to see this until your eyes are trained to see more subtle color.)

The purpose of this book is to confront this problem of the mind getting in the way of the eye and train (or re-train) you to paint what your eye actually sees.

THE HISTORY OF COLOR SPOTS

The greatest masters of color in oil painting were the Venetian, Spanish, Dutch, and Flemish masters of the 16th and 17th centuries: Titian, Veronese, Tintoretto, El Greco, Velasquez, Rubens, and Vermeer. They painted the world with extraordinary freshness and brilliance because they saw the world as a vast pattern of interlocking colored areas. That is, they saw and painted the world as a dazzling patchwork of color spots, as they were called by the famed American artist and teacher, Charles Hawthorne, when he taught his celebrated classes in Provincetown, Massachusetts, early in this century. The lesson of the 16th and 17th century masters is essentially quite simple: if you put the right color spot in the right place on the canvas, all those color spots will link up in the viewer's eye to produce a convincing image of nature. This book is based on the methods of those remarkable old masters.

As you read these pages, you'll learn how to identify, mix, and paint those color spots. You'll discover how to turn off the mental filter that gets in your way and tells you what colors *should* be there—but aren't. And you'll learn how to rely on your eyes to observe and record the colors that actually are there—true to nature, yet full of surprises. You'll learn to paint the colors that you *see*, and nothing else!

Above all, you'll learn that there are no rules. Why are there no rules? Simply because colors are so variable and unpredictable! There are too many factors, and one factor tends to overpower another. Let's take an orange as an example. We may start out thinking of what may be called its *object color*, its orangeness, let's say. But this color may be altered in any conceivable way by other factors. One is the color of the *primary light source*—natural sources like the white light of the sun or the light of the sky (which can be almost any color, depending on the weather or time of day); and artificial light sources such as the warm color of an incandescent light bulb or the cool light of a fluorescent tube. There is also a third factor: the influence of indirect light or *secondary light sources*, the light reflected from nearby surfaces: the colors of the dish on which the orange rests, the colors of the surrounding walls, and the colors of other objects on the dish or table—all of which may be reflected in the surface of that supposedly orange orange.

Finally, there's the color of the *atmosphere*: the air, filled with particles of dust, microscopic droplets of water, gases, and the products of air pollution, all hovering between your eye and the object. It can be as little as six feet between your eyes and the orange—or as great as two miles across the river to those buildings.

In short, there's no way of deciding, in advance, what color to paint that supposedly orange orange. You have to look at it without any preconceptions, without any memories of what an orange *should* look like, and just paint the colors that you see.

This is a lot harder than you may think. It takes practice. But it's not a gift or a talent that's bestowed on a handful of geniuses. It's a skill that anyone can master.

HOW THIS BOOK WORKS

The heart of this book is a series of twenty-two painting projects, organized in order of increasing difficulty, with the last one being the most difficult. Each project requires you to paint a still life study of one or more objects of the kind easily found about the house or at some local shop. You will pose these subjects for your studies in a highly specific situation—in a special sort of model stand we call a setup box. (It is actually half of a box—two walls and a floor—which you will line with colored papers.) You're going to illuminate the still life subject and the setup box also in a specific way. I'll give you exact instructions on how to set up and illuminate your subject for each painting project.

Of course, you could learn most of the same lessons by painting portraits instead of still lifes. But the job would be a lot harder. Still life offers many advantages that portraiture and landscape painting lack. For example, you can't always control the light or the colors in portraits or landscapes as easily as you can in still lifes. But the main reason is the essential nature of still life—they are still. Put a still life model where and how you want it and it stays put. And it doesn't get paid by the hour, either.

You're going to paint with simple, inexpensive materials and equipment. Your basic painting tool is the common steel palette knife, with which you can lay down bold flat strokes of paint. Your painting surface should be nothing fancier than a sheet of canvas paper, which costs no more than a sheet of good drawing paper. You don't even need an easel but can work with your canvas paper, backed up by cardboard, resting on a table or your knees—which should be covered by old clothes or an apron. You don't even need a smock.

The projects in this book have been devised as teaching projects, so the student who follows them carefully will learn the essentials of painting by eye and discovering the color in ordinary objects that lie there waiting to be seen and painted. These projects have not been designed so that the studies you paint in the process of doing the projects will give you paintings "suitable for framing." Often your studies will look like just what they are—homework, exercises, lessons. Sometimes, though, they will surprise you with their freshness and power. A few may even strike you as brilliant, bold, even vital. You may want to hang one or two on your wall. Go ahead and do so. But remember, they are still studies—learning tools, not works of art.

Once you have learned what this book has to teach, you will be free to move ahead in any direction. Following the projects, there is a collection of studies painted by my students over the years, some done while they were still students, others painted after they had become professionals. I am exhibiting these paintings not only to show you how far this method can be taken but also as a kind of gallery of ideas, to inspire you to go and do likewise—not in the sense of imitating *what* they have done but rather to take off *as* they have done.

White Tulips by Don Stern.

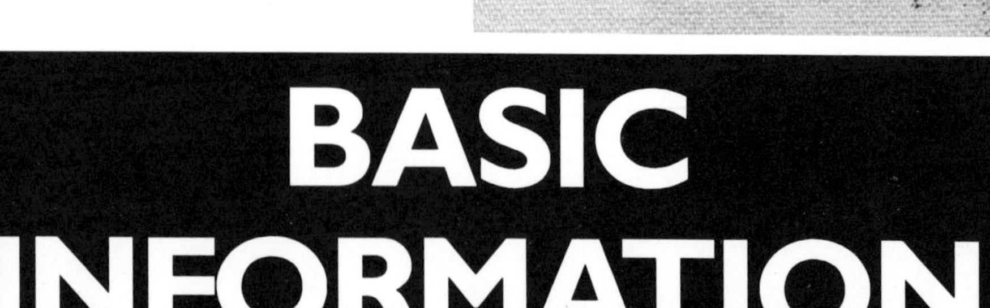

BASIC INFORMATION

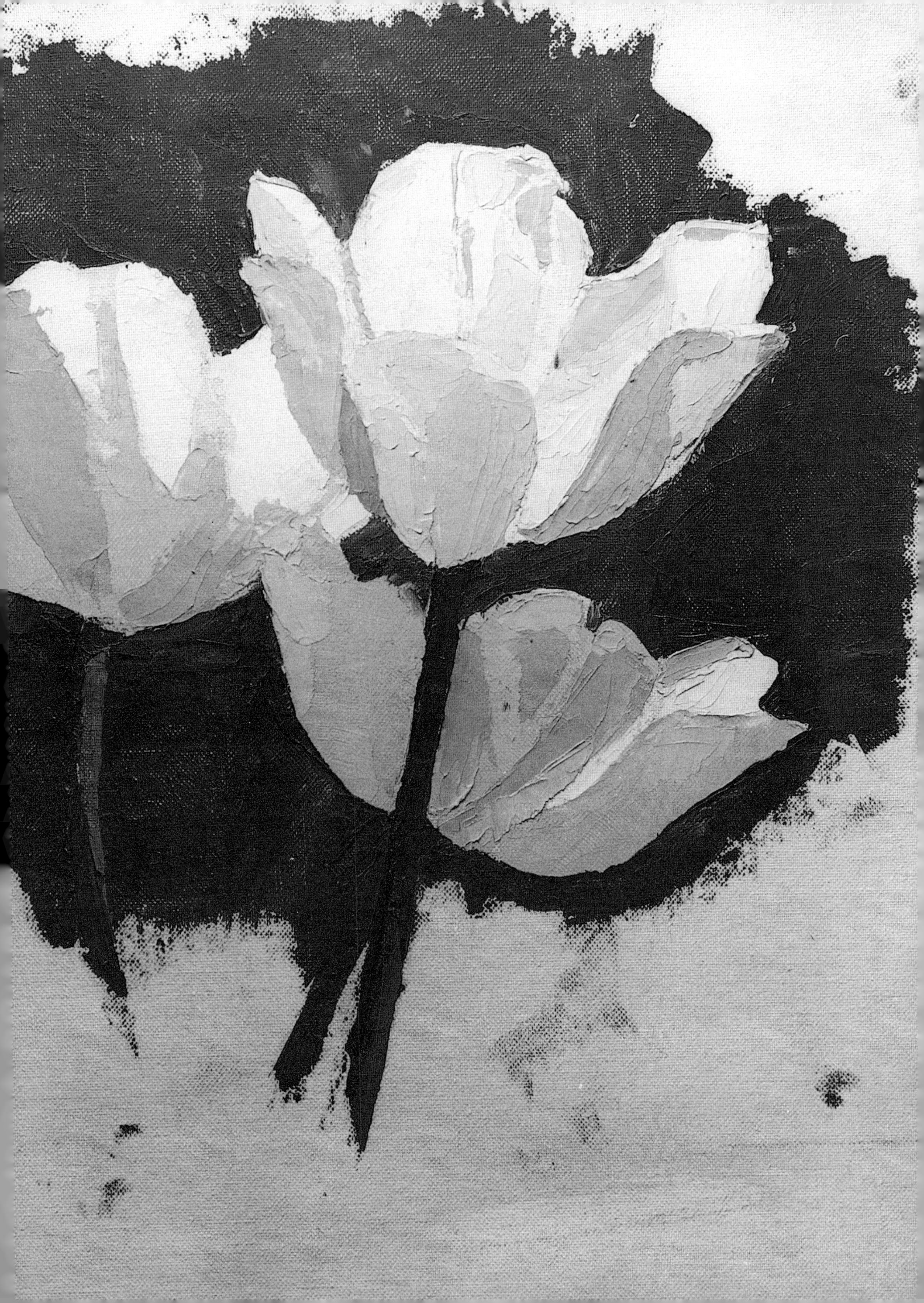

MATERIALS AND WORK AREA

Before I go any further, I'd like to tell you what kind of painting materials, equipment, and other odds and ends you're going to need to paint the twenty-two projects. If you've already done some oil painting, you probably have most of these things already. But if you're just starting out, you'll have to shop for these things at your local art supply store—so I've tried to keep the number of items, and the expense, to the absolute minimum. The list also includes a few simple things that you can make out of ordinary cardboard in no more than a few hours.

OIL COLORS

The projects in this book are all executed with oil paint. Although you'll see dozens of tubes of color displayed in your local art supply store, you won't need more than eight tubes. Working with this limited palette, you can mix all the colors you need. Furthermore, a limited palette will force you to do a lot of mixing instead of simply reaching for another tube of color. I want you to do as much mixing as possible so that you'll learn all you can about color. After all, that's the purpose of this book.

No, you don't have to buy "artist's colors," as they're called, the most expensive grades of paint. You can easily get by with the less expensive grades, such as the London colors made by Winsor & Newton (called Winton colors in the United Kingdom) or the Pre-tested colors made by Grumbacher. Here are the eight colors I want you to work with:

Alizarin crimson	Phthalocyanine green
Cadmium red *light*	Phthalocyanine blue
Cadmium orange	Ultramarine blue
Cadmium yellow *pale*	Titanium white

I must warn you against accepting substitutes. There are no alternatives to these colors. I stress that it be cadmium red *light* rather than any of the other cadmium reds, and that it be cadmium yellow *pale* rather than any of the other cadmium yellows because of the special properties of these two colors.

SOLVENTS AND MEDIUMS

As it comes from the tube, oil paint is a thick paste that you may find slightly *too* thick to mix and spread comfortably. A few drops of solvent will soften the paste and make it easier to handle when you're mixing your colors—and easier to apply to the painting surface with your palette knife. The usual solvent is either rectified turpentine (the very pure form of turpentine that's made for artists) or mineral spirit, which is called "white spirit" in the United Kingdom.

Buy a fairly big bottle of turpentine or mineral spirit—at least a pint—since you'll use it not only for thinning your tube paint, but to clean your knife, palette, and painting surface as well.

Many artists like to dilute their tube paints with something other than turpentine or mineral spirit. You can make a *painting medium* by filling any small, clean bottle with ⅓ turpentine or mineral spirit, ⅓ damar varnish, and ⅓ linseed oil. Cap the bottle tightly and shake the mixture thoroughly. Be sure to shake it again at the beginning of each painting day.

A small glass or plastic bottle that has a tiny neck and an opening that emits just one drop at a time is ideal for storing solvent or painting medium. With this kind of bottle, you can add very small quantities of solvent or medium to the mixtures on your palette.

PAINTING SURFACES

My students normally paint on a stiff, nonabsorbent paper that's manufactured with a texture that simulates canvas. You can buy this canvas-textured paper—which I call "canvas paper"—in 12″ × 16″ (31 × 41 cm) pads. I recommend the brand called CanvaSkin.

You'll need a stiff sheet of cardboard, corrugated board, fiberboard, or plywood—roughly 16″ × 20″ (41 × 51 cm)—to support your canvas paper when you paint on it. Buy a roll of 1″ (25 mm) wide masking tape to tape all four edges of the paper to the board.

Canvas boards are available in the same size as the canvas paper. The board is just a sheet of sturdy cardboard to which the manufacturer has glued thin, white canvas. It's more expensive than canvas paper, and it's just as easy to do the projects on the less expensive canvas paper. Canvas board should also be taped (or tacked) down to the bigger backing board.

PALETTE KNIVES

Your painting tools are just two palette knives. Both should have flexible, springy blades. Buy one with a straight blade for mixing colors on your palette. Then buy another one that has a blade with a bend in it—something like a trowel—that you'll use for painting.

I know that most oil painting books tell you to *avoid* painting with a palette knife and steer you to those specially designed painting knives with their elegant-looking blades in various shapes and sizes. But I really *want* you to paint with a palette knife because it prevents you from being elegant and finicky. The palette knife forces you to work with big, broad, decisive strokes.

If you already own brushes for oil painting, put them aside. When you're working on the projects in this book, you won't need them.

Straight palette knife.

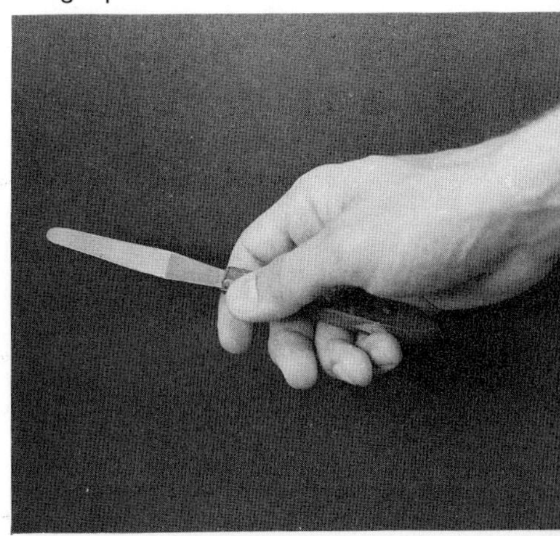

Trowel-shaped palette knife.

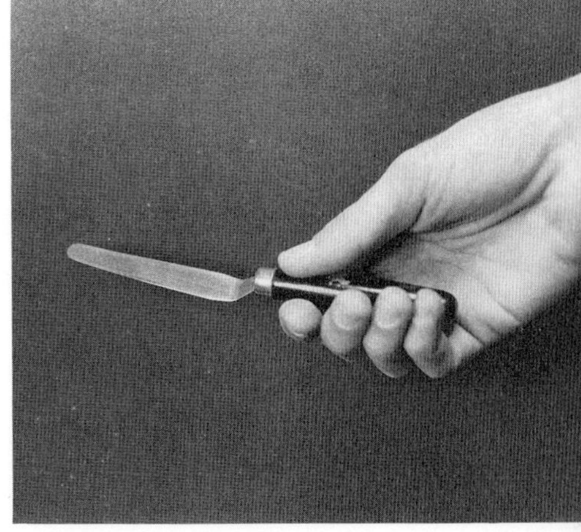

MIXING SURFACE

The traditional surface for mixing colors is a wooden palette that, with age and use, will gradually turn to a deep, glossy "brown." A more modern palette is a pad of white, oil-proof paper that you can tear off and throw away at the end of each day's work. If you already own one of these and you feel comfortable working on it, use it. But I prefer that you switch to a different kind of surface for these projects because the wood or paper palettes tend to distort the colors you mix on them. Therefore I recommend that my students work on a sheet of clear glass taped onto a sheet of paper in some neutral color like gray, brown, or—best of all—the color interior designers call "greige" because it's a cross between gray and beige. I find that color mixtures look most accurate and least distorted on this neutral "greige" tone that comes through the glass.

I should add that the glass is easy to clean by wiping or scraping at the end of the painting day. And even if the oil paint dries as hard as leather on the glassy surface, the dry color is easy to scrape off with the aid of a razorblade. The sheet of glass should be no larger than the canvas paper or board that you're working on.

Palette setup.

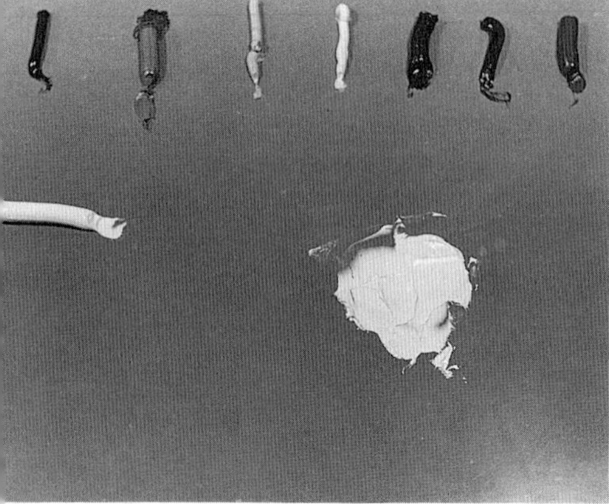

Squeezing out color.

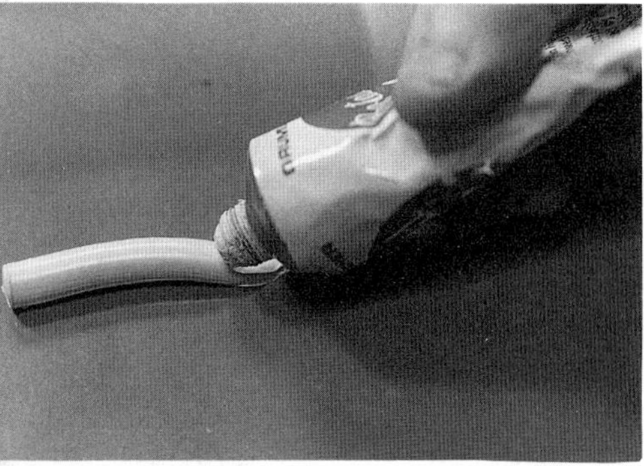

Spot screen.

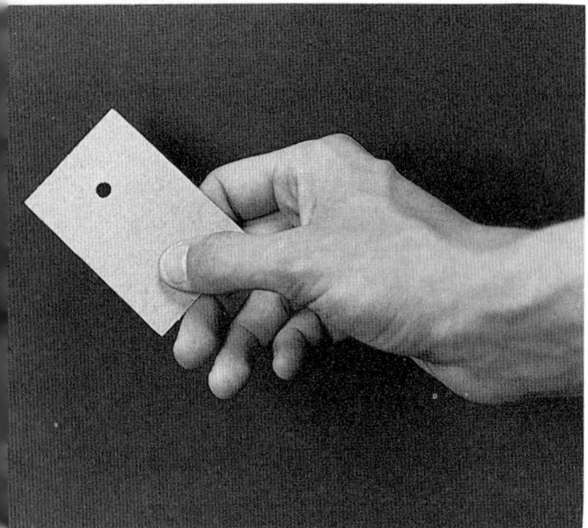

PALETTE SETUP

Over the years, my students have found it convenient to set up their paints on the mixing surface in a specific way.

Let's assume that you're working with the standard 12″ × 16″ (31 × 41 cm) palette. Squeeze out the seven colors, *excluding* white, along the top 16″ (41 cm) edge of the palette. From left to right, the colors are: alizarin crimson, cadmium red light, cadmium orange, cadmium yellow pale, phthalocyanine green, phthalocyanine blue, and ultramarine blue (see photo). If you're right-handed, squeeze out a big gob of white at about the midpoint of the left side. If you're left-handed, that big gob of white ought to be near the midpoint of the right side. This leaves the whole middle of the palette for mixing. And you can use the lower area—along the 16″ (41 cm) side closest to you—for storing your mixtures, ready to use.

When you squeeze the paint out of the tube, don't make little, round puddles of paint. Instead, squeeze out long, slender "worms" of color, starting near the edge of the palette and moving in toward the center. There's a practical reason for this; when you nip off a bit of color for mixing, the rest of that long, narrow squeeze will remain clean.

SPOT SCREEN

In addition to the paint, knives, and other items you must buy, there are three simple objects you will need to make. The first is a spot screen.

To make the spot screen, cut a piece of gray cardboard down to roughly 2″ × 4″ (50 × 100 mm). Turning the card vertically, measure about 1″ (25 mm) down from the top and make a clean, round hole in the card, roughly ¼″ (6 mm) in diameter, with a knife or a hole punch (see photo.) When you actually start to paint the project, you'll be looking through the hole in the spot screen to isolate the colors in your subject. I'll tell you how to do this a bit later on.

VIEWFINDER

A viewfinder is really optional and eventually you may be able to do without one. But it's a convenient device to have on hand, at least when you're beginning to paint.

To make one, you'll need two pieces of gray or black cardboard, 12″ × 16″ (31 × 41 cm) each. With a sharp knife or a razor blade, cut a rectangular window in the center of each card. One window should measure 1″ × 1½″ (25 × 38 mm) to give you a 2:3 proportion. The other window should measure 1½″ × 2″ (38 × 50 mm) to give you a 3:4 proportion. Later on in the book, I'll refer to these as your 2:3 or 3:4 viewfinders.

Landscape painters have used viewfinders for centuries. Surrounded by the overwhelming detail of nature, the landscape painter holds up the viewfinder and looks through it to frame and isolate some small fragment of the world to make a picture. You can use the viewfinder in the same way when you paint the still life projects in this book. Hold the viewfinder at whatever distance seems right to frame your subject and compose a satisfying picture.

SETUP BOX

Nearly all of your still-life objects will be placed on a kind of homemade stage called a setup box. The simplest way to make a setup box is to pick up a discarded packing box from a store. It ought to be made of some kind of sturdy cardboard or corrugated board that you can cut with a sharp knife or razor blade.

As you can see in the illustration, the setup box has a floor and two walls. The floor is 12″ × 16″ (31 × 46 cm) and so is the long wall. The shorter wall is 12″ × 12″ (31 × 31 cm). If the packing box is big enough, you can simply cut it down to the right size, slicing off the top of the box and two of the sides. You can also accumulate several packing boxes of odd sizes and cut them up. Make the floor and walls of the setup box in three separate pieces, which you then tape together at the edges.

You can also start from scratch by buying a big sheet of cardboard, corrugated board, or foam board. You can then cut it into three pieces (for the floor and two walls of the setup box) and tape them together at the folds. Foam board has an additional advantage: it's so thick that you can use ordinary straight pins to hold the setup box together and then pull out the pins when you want to put the box away for storage. I had a carpenter make my own setup box out of plywood.

Typical setup box.

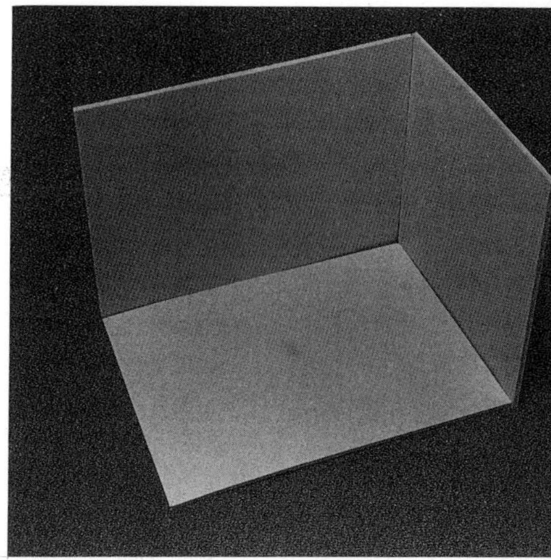

My own plywood setup box, with colored paper pinned to it. Note the position of the lamp. Its long, adjustable arm allows you to swing it down into the box, a necessary position for some painting assignments.

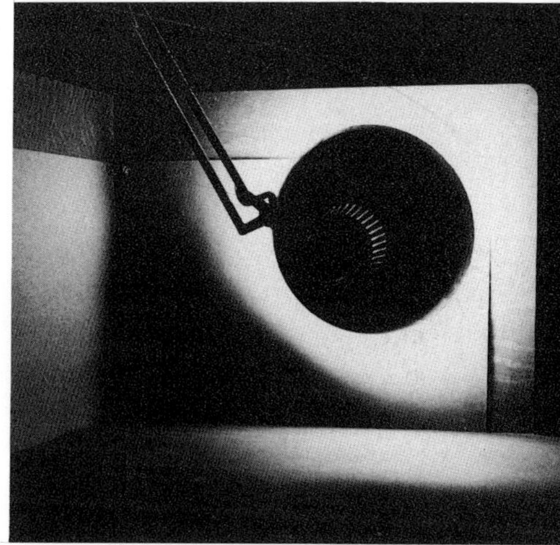

ASSORTED EXTRAS

Here are a few more items you'll need.

COLORED PAPER. To line walls of the setup box, buy a pad or package of inexpensive assorted colored papers—the kind that children use in school. The best size is around 12″ × 18″ (12 × 46 cm).

TAPE. For taping the colored paper to the inside of your setup box and for taping your painting down to the backing board, you'll need a roll of 1″ (25 mm) masking tape, as I mentioned earlier.

CLEANUP PAPER. A roll of white toilet tissue or paper towels—the tissue is cheaper and handier—is a necessity for cleaning your knife blades and painting surfaces, wiping your hands, and generally keeping your work area tidy. White tissues or towels are easiest to work with.

STORAGE BOX. You'll find it convenient to store your paints, knives, bottles, and other gear in a wood or metal paintbox with compartments. But an old fishing tackle box or a cigar box is just as good.

PENCIL. Although I'd rather you paint without any preliminary sketch on the canvas paper, you may find it helpful to draw a few guidelines with a pencil at first. Any ordinary office pencil will do the job. So will the standard HB artist pencil.

WASTE DISPOSAL. You'll also need some sort of receptacle nearby to collect those soiled tissues or towels. It doesn't matter whether this is a paper bag in a metal basket, a plastic container, or just a cardboard box. The main thing is to toss these soiled papers into some sort of container rather than let them accumulate on your worktable or studio floor.

EASEL OR CHAIR

If you want to invest the money in an easel, that's fine, but that big piece of studio furniture isn't really necessary for the projects in this book. You can tape the canvas paper or board to a bigger backing board and rest the whole thing on a table. Or sit in a chair and paint in your lap. These solutions offer several advantages. For one thing, you can maneuver the knife and the painting more easily when it rests horizontally on a table or on your lap. That way, you can turn the picture to the exact angle to receive the stroke of the knife and get at those odd corners.

TABLES

Aside from a chair that allows you to paint on your lap, you'll need two tables: one to hold your palette and other painting equipment, and one for your setup box.

Tables are rarely too high, but they are often too low, which can produce an aching back or neck. However, you can adjust the setup box or your work surface by adding a couple of boards or a large, flat cardboard box.

Lamp for lighting the work area and setup box.

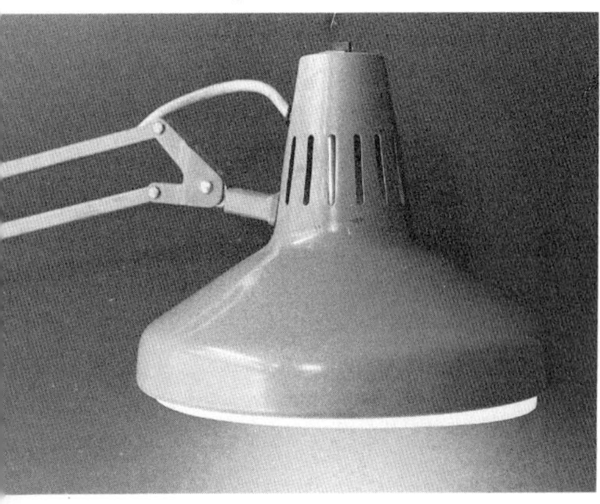

LIGHTING YOUR SETUP

To light your setup box, the ideal light source is an architect's lamp that clamps to the edge of the setup table. The lamp has a long, adjustable neck that allows you to swing it into various positions. Such a lamp has a big hood or reflector that holds both a 60-watt incandescent bulb and a 40-watt, circular fluorescent tube. The main advantage of such a lamp is its approximation to daylight.

LIGHTING YOUR WORK AREA

When you set up your work area—whether it's a corner of a room or an *entire* room that's going to serve as your studio—it's essential to have the right kind of light to work by. If you live in the Northern Hemiphere, the ideal natural light comes through a north window. Conversely, if you live in the Southern Hemisphere, the best light comes from a south window. When I say that this will give you the *best* light, I mean that the light will be as constant and unchanging as natural light can be, making the necessary allowances for changes in the weather. The light should come over your left shoulder if you paint with your right hand, and over your right shoulder if you paint with your left hand.

Obviously, not everyone can find a window that faces north or south. If you live in the Northern Hemisphere and your studio window happens to face east, you'll find that it's best to paint in the afternoon, while if your window faces west, the light is steadiest in the morning. Just the opposite will hold true if you live in the Southern Hemisphere, of course.

If you don't have the right kind of natural light in your work area, buy a second lamp like the kind suggested earlier for your setup. Be sure to get the type that holds a 60-watt incandescent bulb *and* a 40-watt fluorescent tube. This combination of incandescent and fluorescent light will give you just the right balance of warm and cool rays to approximate the feeling of natural light on your painting and on your palette.

CLOTHING

Finally, be sure to wear old clothes that won't be ruined by paint smears. Wear painting clothes that are neutral in color, preferably brown or tan or gray. You don't want the color of your clothes to distract you as you work. I remember one student who was wearing a bright red shirt and kept wondering why her colors always looked so red. She finally caught on: the paint was reflecting the color of the shirt! And by the way, it may seem obvious, but don't wear tinted glasses when you paint!

HANDLING COLOR

Now that you have the materials and equipment you'll need for the projects in this book, let's start talking about the all-important subject of color.

WORKING WITH A PALETTE KNIFE

We'll begin with the use of the knife. As I said before, you'll be *mixing* paint with the straight knife and *painting* with the trowel-shaped knife. Here are some suggestions on how to use them.

MIXING COLOR. Used properly, the straight knife will give you color mixtures of extraordinary smoothness and purity. You begin by picking up a dab of color with the tip of the knife—on the underside of the blade—and laying this color down on the central mixing area of the palette. Wipe the last trace of color from the blade with toilet tissue or a paper towel before you pick up the next color. Then pick up your second color in the same way and work the two colors together on the mixing area of the palette.

The job essentially consists of two operations: spreading the color and then heaping it up until the mixture is smoothly combined.

One important point: each time you add a bit more color to the mixture, wipe the blade clean before you pick up fresh color. In this way, you avoid contaminating the color along the top edge of the palette.

PAINTING WITH THE KNIFE. The trowel-shaped knife is better suited to painting because the bend in the blade keeps your knuckles off the canvas. Use the flat underside of the blade to pick up color from the heaped-up mixtures that you've made with the straight knife. Make big, broad strokes with the underside and smaller strokes with the tip. Always work with the absolute minimum number of strokes. Don't move the knife back and forth, but set it down firmly on the canvas and spread the paint with a single decisive movement, lifting the blade away when the stroke is completed.

If you're painting a shape that has a hard edge at its left side, start your knife stroke at the left and pull away toward the right. You can tilt the blade just a bit so that the left edge presses firmly against the canvas paper. If you're painting a shape that has a hard edge on its right side, simply reverse the process, tilting the blade slightly to the right, pressing down firmly at the right edge, pulling away to the left.

Where two colored shapes meet, it's not necessary to overlap the colors. Start the shapes a hairline apart and move them together so that they just barely touch.

Your goal should be to cover each area with the absolute minimum number of knife strokes. If possible, you should work with a single stroke. For example, if you're painting a flower, each petal should be a single knife stroke. If the petal turns out to have a lighted area and an area in shade, then you should try to do the job with two strokes, one for each color. If it's really impossible to paint an area with a single stroke and you absolutely must do the job with several strokes, then do so. With practice, you can learn how to go back over that area and smooth it out so that it *looks* as if you've done the job with a single stroke. With practice, you'll master the knife and learn how to make one stroke for each color spot.

Painting with the knife.

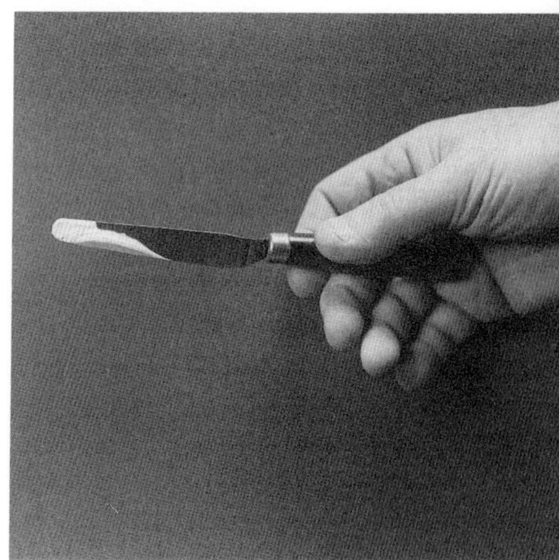

Wiping the blade.

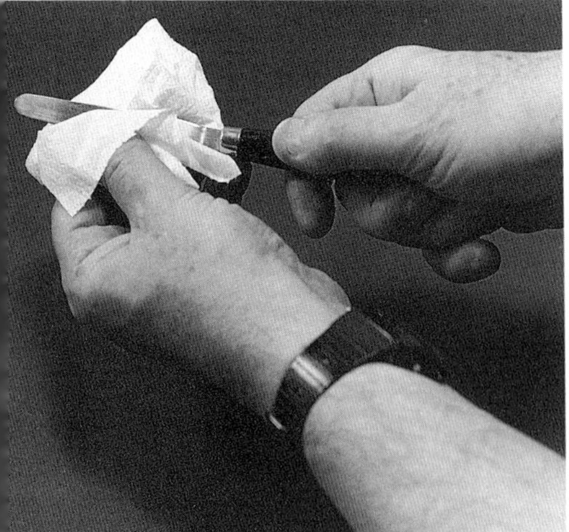

Try to work with short strokes that move *across* the form. For example, if you're painting a long, skinny bottle, don't try to do the job with long, vertical strokes that run down the shape of the bottle. It's a lot easier and more effective to build up your color with short, horizontal strokes that move across the bottle.

Mix a lot of paint and mix it thoroughly so that there are no streaks in the mixture. Be generous with your strokes, applying enough color to the canvas to cover up the grain. Don't be parsimonious.

Don't forget to wipe your knife blade absolutely clean before you pick up a new color. The slightest trace of color on the blade may show up as a streak in the next stroke you make. You don't want muddy colors—you want them to be *clean*!

If something doesn't look quite right, don't try to correct it by piling the right color over the wrong. Scrape off the wrong color. If you can't get off enough color with the knife, wipe the area with a tissue, possibly moistened with solvent. Then repaint the color spot.

Let me emphasize that this book is *not* a treatise on knife painting. There are other books that go into the complex craft of painting with the knife, telling you to buy an arsenal of shiny, shapely painting knives, and showing you how to produce a whole vocabulary of knife strokes in varied shapes and sizes. But that's *not* what this book is about. To execute these painting projects, just learn to move the knife smoothly and decisively across the canvas to make the color go where you want it to go in order to execute these painting projects. The movement of the knife isn't much more complicated than spreading butter on a slice of bread.

MIXING COLORS

Now that you can handle a painting knife, you need to learn how to mix your paints. There are no rules about such things, and there's no way that I can tell you how every tube color behaves when you mix it with every other color on your palette. That's something you've got to learn by actually doing it. But here are some facts that should be helpful.

To begin with, I like to divide colors into two groupings: the six spectrum colors—red, orange, yellow, green, blue, and violet—and the six intermediaries, which fall between the spectrum colors—red-orange, yellow-orange, yellow-green, blue-green, blue-violet, and red-violet.

These twelve colors are normally shown on a diagram called a "color wheel," like the one you see here. The wheel is a convenient reference chart for two reasons. First, you can see how the intermediaries fall between the spectrum colors: yellow-green between yellow and green, red-violet between violet and red, and so on. Second, the wheel gives you an easy way to keep track of *complementary colors*, which are directly opposite one another on the wheel. Remembering the complementary colors is essential in color mixing because the best way to dull any color is to add its complement.

But how do you produce those twelve fundamental colors when you've got only seven colors, not counting white, on your palette? Only a few of your tube colors actually match any of the twelve, so you've got to learn how to mix the rest.

RED. You can produce a spectrum red—and the most brilliant red of all—by mixing cadmium red light and alizarin crimson.

RED-ORANGE. Fortunately, cadmium red light is actually a kind of red-orange. So you already have a good red-orange on your palette.

ORANGE. The cadmium orange on your palette is a good match for spectrum orange.

YELLOW-ORANGE. There's no yellow-orange on your palette, so the way to mix it is by blending cadmium orange and cadmium yellow pale.

YELLOW. The cadmium yellow pale on your palette is reasonably close to spectrum yellow, but needs a hint of cadmium orange to be exactly right.

YELLOW-GREEN. Don't try to find this color in a tube; rather, mix it from cadmium yellow pale and phthalocyanine green.

GREEN. Phthalocyanine green needs a lot of cadmium yellow pale to produce a true spectrum green.

BLUE-GREEN. This color isn't on your palette either. Mix phthalocyanine green and phthalocyanine blue, plus a hint of white to bring out the full richness of the color.

BLUE. To produce a true spectrum blue, mix the two blues on your palette: phthalocyanine blue and ultramarine blue—plus enough white to bring out the full brilliance and clarity of the color.

BLUE-VIOLET. The ultramarine on your palette actually has a slightly violet cast, so this will serve as blue-violet. Add a touch of alizarin crimson and some white to bring out its color.

VIOLET. Your tube colors don't include spectrum violet, so mix ultramarine blue, alizarin crimson, and a touch of white.

RED-VIOLET. Alizarin crimson is a true red-violet, needing just a hint of white.

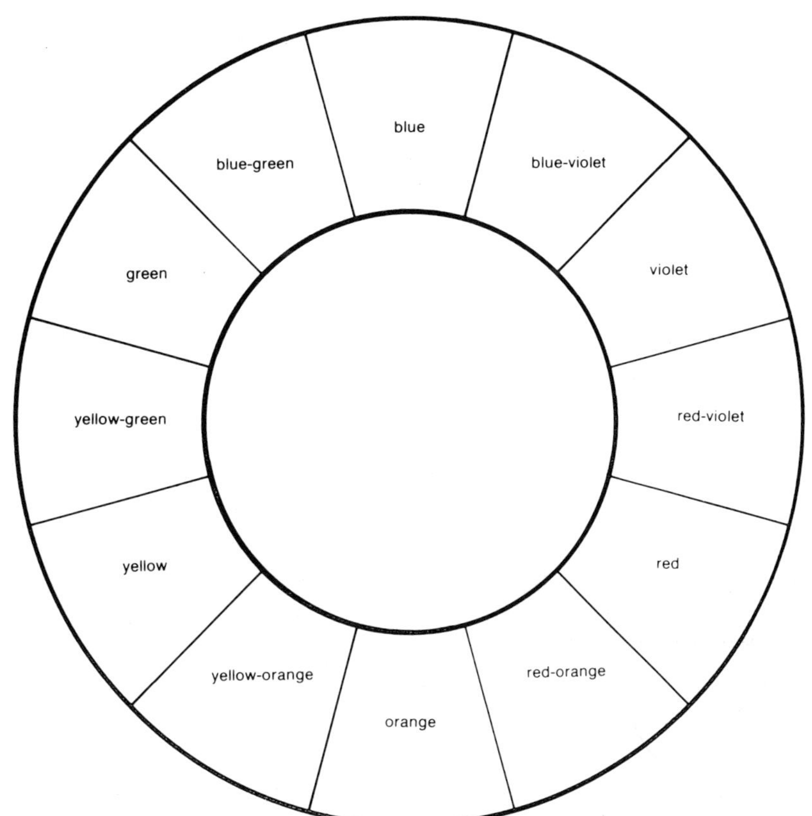

Color wheel.

CONTROLLING COLOR

Now that you know how to make the six spectrum colors and the six intermediaries, it's time to practice what you've learned. Squeeze the paints onto your palette following the arrangement recommended in the materials section and then try these three color-mixing experiments.

MIXING SPECTRUM COLORS AND INTERMEDIARIES. First, do your best to mix all the spectrum colors and intermediaries that you can't get straight from the tube. I've just told you how to do this. Do your mixing with the palette knife and store up all your finished mixtures in little mounds toward the bottom of your palette.

NEUTRALIZING COLOR WITH COMPLEMENTS. Now look at the color wheel to identify the complementary colors, that is, the colors that are opposite one another on the wheel. Now dull each color, one by one, by adding its complement and examine the results. Here's an orderly way to conduct this experiment.

1. Mix the two complements to produce a color that seems to fall midway between the two—a "neutral," as it's called. Thus, if you're mixing red and green, aim for a color that's neither red nor green. You won't arrive at this neutral by mixing equal quantities of red and green. You've got to try various quantities of red and green, and judge the results by what you see.
2. Mix this neutral with the first complement. If the first complement is red, you'll obviously produce a *duller* red.
3. Mix this same neutral—the color you made in step 1—with the second complement. If the second complement is green, you'll create a much duller green.

Repeat this series of three steps with each pair of complements on your color wheel.

LIGHTENING COLOR WITH WHITE. Now perform a similar experiment to learn how each of the twelve colors behaves when you lighten it with white. Again, follow the same three steps.

1. Mix each color with white to produce a color that seems to fall midway between the two. As I said a moment ago, you can't just add equal quantities of each. You must try various combinations until you get one that looks right.
2. Mix the product of step 1 with the original color. If your original color was green, let's say, now you're lightening it with a mixture of green and white.
3. Finally, mix the product of step 1 with white. If the product of step 1 was a blend of green and white, now you're *really* lightening that mixture with white.

When you repeat this same series of steps with each of your twelve colors, you're going to make an unexpected discovery: white not only lightens all twelve colors, but makes other profound changes in six of them. When you add white to red, red-orange, orange, yellow-orange, green, and yellow-green, you change not only their luminosity, but also their hue and intensity. They all tend to become slightly duller and bluer. So when you lighten these six colors with white, you must also add a speck of yellow to restore their original hue and intensity.

RECORDING THE RESULTS

You can perform all these mixing experiments on discarded scraps of canvas paper and then toss them out. But it's more enjoyable to do the whole job in some organized way. Many teachers of painting recommend that you record all of your experimental color mixtures on a series of simple charts. I know this sounds like a formidable job, but making these charts is really fun, and also gives you a visual record that you'll find helpful later on.

Just take a sharp, hard pencil and rule up one of your sheets of canvas paper so that it becomes a checkerboard of 2″ (50 mm) squares. If you're working on a sheet of canvas paper that's 12″ × 16″ (31 × 41 cm), and your boxes are 2″ (50 mm) square, then you'll have forty-eight boxes on the chart. This gives you a lot of room to experiment with color mixtures. Rule up at least two charts: one for the colors that result from mixing complementary colors and the other for mixing colors with white. When you create a mixture, paint a sample in one of the boxes, and then, beneath the sample, write the names of the tube colors used below each mixture—just for the record.

LEARNING TO NAME COLORS. Simply learning to name the colors you see in a setup is an enormously valuable aid in the process of mixing and matching them. But you must be accurate. If you operate within strict rules about learning to name colors, you'll move along more rapidly. Here are some basic terms to help you describe what you see.

It's customary to classify colors according to their three dimensions: hue, luminosity, and intensity. I'll try to define each of these terms.

Hue is simply the common name of the color. Thus, the spectrum is conveniently divided into six hues: red, orange, yellow, green, blue, and violet. Between any pair of the hues I've just listed, you can insert an intermediary hue: red-orange, yellow-orange, yellow-green, blue-green, blue-violet, and red-violet. To identify any color, you start by naming its hue as best you can—naming one of the six hues of the spectrum or one of the six intermediaries.

Luminosity is the lightness or darkness of a color, sometimes called its *value*. For our purposes, it's enough to think about three possible gradations: high luminosity or light value; middle luminosity or middle value; and low luminosity or dark value. Thus, a color can be red-orange in hue, and either high, middle, or low luminosity. So we can call it a light red-orange, a middle-luminosity red-orange, or a dark red-orange.

Intensity is the brightness or dullness of a color, sometimes called *saturation* or *chroma*. Once again, three gradations are enough: high intensity or bright; middle intensity; and low intensity or dull. Going back to that same red-orange, we can then call it a bright red-orange, a middle intensity red-orange, or a dull red-orange.

To describe a color completely, we must bring in all three dimensions: hue, luminosity, and intensity. Thus, we can call it a red-orange of high luminosity and high intensity. We can also say it more briefly by describing the color as a light, bright red-orange. In the same way, a blue-green of low luminosity and low intensity could simply be called a dark, dull blue-green.

To keep the rules of color description as simple as possible, I tell my students to exclude all other words except for *very*. Sometimes it helps to be able to describe a color as a light, *very* bright blue-green.

FORBIDDEN COLOR NAMES

In the interest of accuracy, I also tell my students that there are certain "dirty words" that are absolutely taboo. These unspeakable words are *black*, *white*, *brown*, and *gray*. I discourage the use of these words because dirty words encourage carelessness in seeing and identifying color, and ultimately produce dirty colors.

The word *black* is on the taboo list because it means any hue that's too dark to identify easily. If you've ever hand-laundered a pair of black socks and looked carefully at the rinse water in the basin, you've discovered that the supposedly black dye is merely a very dark green, blue, or violet.

Similarly, the word *white* means any color that's too light to identify easily. If you've ever done any house painting and tried to match an existing white wall, you've discovered that all whites are really "off-whites" as interior decorators describe them, and that white can be "off" in the direction of any hue. White turns out to be a *very* light variation of any hue. (Even very light colors should be described in terms of their hue, intensity, and luminosity.)

Brown simply means a very dull variant of any *warm* hue. Look at all the brown objects around you and notice how much the brown varies. One brown is yellowish. Another is an orange-brown. The third is a red-brown. And a fourth may have a clearly red-violet cast.

Finally, *gray* means a very dull variant of any *cool* hue. The gray objects around us turn out to be dull yellow-greens, dull greens, dull blue-greens, dull blue-violets, and dull violets.

Then how *do* we name the colors we used to call "dirty words"? When you look closely at colors like black, white, brown, and gray, you must try to identify its actual hue and then describe the color in terms of the three dimensions I listed earlier. Thus, "black" can turn out to be almost any hue of very low luminosity; so a particular black might be described as a very dark, very dull green. "White," on the other hand, is likely to be any hue of very high luminosity; so a particular white might be described as a very light, very bright red. "Brown" is likely to be any warm hue of very low intensity; so a particular brown might be described as a dark, very dull yellow-orange. Finally, "gray" is apt to be any cool hue of very low intensity; so a particular gray might be described as a light, dull blue.

Once you call any color by its right name, describing it in terms of the proper dimensions, it becomes a lot easier to mix and match.

MATCHING COLOR

Once you've had some practice in using knives and mixing colors, matching color seems simple. If someone were to hand you a color sample—say a swatch of fabric or a scrap of colored paper—you'd find it no problem. With the color sample in one hand and your palette knife in the other, you'd start mixing the tube paints on your palette until the color of your paint begins to look like the color of your sample. To check the match, you'd pick up some of your color on your knife, bring the sample and the blade together, and quickly ascertain how close the color you mixed came to the original color. To adjust the mixture, you'd add more of this paint or that until you'd matched the sample.

The whole process sounds easy. And it is easy because both the color sample and the color you've mixed are within arm's reach. You can literally hold the sample and the paint-covered knife blade in your hands to check one against the other.

But matching the colors of objects in a setup several feet away isn't that easy. The colors "out there" aren't scraps of paper or fabric that you can hold in your hand. They don't exist by themselves, apart from objects, isolated from the rest of reality. Colors are parts of surfaces. In turn, these surfaces are parts of objects. And the colors of these objects are subject to all kinds of influences, such as light, atmosphere, distance, and the colors reflected from other objects.

Thus, it's extremely difficult to look at some small part of a surface and ascertain its exact color without your being influenced by the total object and its surroundings. That is, it's virtually impossible to isolate that small area of color from the object and from the whole scene of which that color is but a part.

Furthermore, when we look at something, we also recall all the things we know about it. In other words, what we see is distorted by what we know, or at least what we *think* we know and expect to see. We look at the color on the cheek of a young girl and we say to ourselves: "That area can't possibly be as blue as I see it; girls' cheeks are pink!" We look at a bit of summer foliage and we react: "That area can't be blue, even if that's what I see; leaves are green!" And so preconception battles vision—and usually wins.

However, if we want to paint what we really see—not what we *think* we see—then what we see must triumph over what we "know." We can only see a color area accurately if we learn to ignore the object of which that color is a part.

Artists have discovered all kinds of ways to perform this psychological trick. One way is to improvise a frame or a viewfinder with the thumb and forefinger of each hand, as movie cameramen do it, but with this difference: Turn this frame sideways, turn your head with it, and then look at a figure; you no longer see a person, flesh, and clothing. The figure becomes a pattern of color areas.

Another such procedure works especially well when you're painting landscapes—although it may provoke laughter. Simply turn your back on the scene you mean to paint, bend low, and look at the subject through your legs. By turning your view upside down, you easily ignore all the objects that make up the scene, and concentrate only on its colors.

A third way takes more practice. You hold out one hand at arm's length, pointing a finger straight up and partly obscuring the object you plan to paint. You soon discover that you can't keep both your fingertip and the object in focus. So the trick is to keep your fingertip in focus and let the distant object go out-of-focus. As the distant object becomes a blur, all you see is its color.

Any of these procedures will work, but nothing works as well as the spot screen. Looking through the hole in that small gray card, you can isolate the color of any object so efficiently that the object seems to disappear, and all you see is the color itself.

USING THE SPOT SCREEN

Here's how to use the spot screen. Pick up the card in whichever hand is *not* your painting hand. (If you're right-handed, hold the palette knife in your right hand and the spot screen in your left. If

Holding the spot screen.

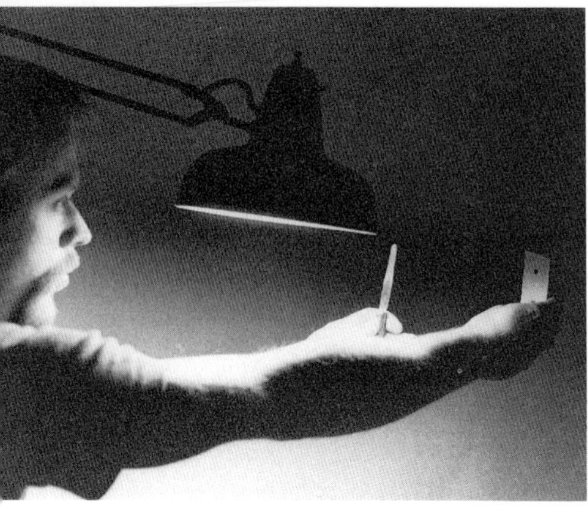

Holding the knife against the spot screen.

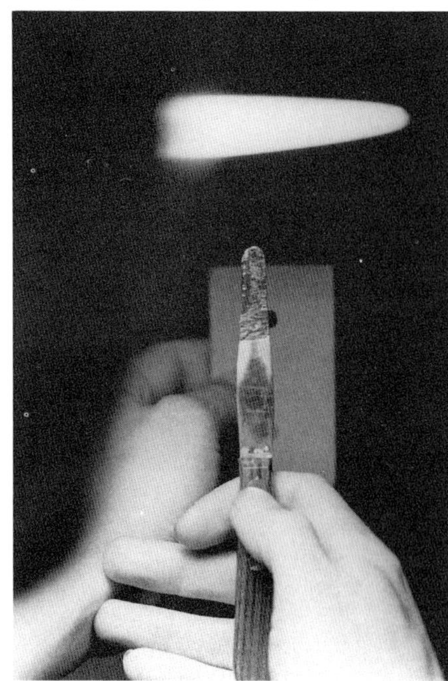

you're left-handed, do the reverse.) Hold the spot screen so that the hole is toward the top and stretch your arm to its full length, pointing toward the subject. *Always* hold the spot screen at arm's length so that you keep a constant distance between your eye and the card. This also keeps the spot screen out of the direct light of your work lamp, which is also essential.

With your "working eye" half closed and your other eye completely closed, look through the hole in the spot screen at the color area you're trying to match. Forget everything you know about the object and simply concentrate on the color you see through the hole. Name the color and describe it by referring to the three dimensions I explained earlier. Call it a "light, bright green" or a "dark, dull violet" or whatever—but be sure to name all three of its dimensions.

Now start mixing the color. As the mixture begins to look right, hold the paint-covered knife blade in front of the spot screen, partly overlapping the hole. Note the differences between the color you see through the hole and the color on the knife. Go back to the palette and adjust the mixture. Once again, bring the paint-covered knife blade in front of the spot screen, slightly overlapping the hole. Compare and then go back to the palette to make further adjustments. Repeat the process of mixing and comparing until you're sure that the mixture absolutely matches the color you see.

The color you mix may—and probably *will*—surprise you. Parts of that orange fruit may turn out to be some totally unexpected color. Don't be tempted to go back and redo the mixture because your memory tells you that the entire orange is *supposed* to be orange in color. Your eyes aren't playing tricks on you. It's your *memory* that's playing the tricks. Be faithful to what your eye sees.

MIXING THE COLOR YOU SEE

Now that you understand how to use the spot screen for mixing and matching colors, let's talk a bit more about the actual process of color mixing.

Having named the color that you see through the hole in the spot screen, ask yourself which tube of paint on the palette is the color closest in hue and luminosity to the color you've seen and named. Pick up some of that paint on your knife—the one with the straight blade—work the color back and forth a bit on the palette, and cover about half the knife blade with the paint, keeping the color as flat and smooth as you can. The smoother the paint on the knife, the less glare it gives off, and the more easily you can see the color.

Hold the paint-covered blade in front of the spot screen, overlapping the hole, as I said earlier. Don't actually touch the blade to the card, but hold the knife a good deal closer to you than the spot screen. When you mix the colors for the project, try to hold the knife so it's just outside the direct light of your work lamp, but still receives some light. The spot screen, further away, should be out of the direct light altogether.

As you compare the color of the paint on the blade with the color you see through the hole, you'll certainly see that the paint color needs altering. Remember those three dimensions: hue, luminosity, and intensity. Any one of these dimensions—or possibly all of them—may have to be changed. Add new colors to the mixture in very small quantities, mixing, comparing, and then mixing again. Don't make sudden, violent alterations in the mixture by adding a big gob of some new color. Close in very gradually on the color you're trying to match.

If you find that you've gone too far in one direction, and the mixture is way off the track, discard it and start again. Repair jobs are often demoralizing because they're more trouble than they're worth. Making a fresh start will energize you because it's more fun.

At the beginning, you'll probably spend a great deal of time mixing a single color. But that's not bad. On the contrary, the more time you spend mixing and matching your first colors, the more quickly your work will go later. I find that students who take hours to observe, name, mix, and match their first colors in the early projects can mix each color in later projects in a few minutes.

Keep reminding yourself to wipe the knife clean before you pick up fresh pigment. That's the only way you can keep your mixtures bright and pure. It's also a good idea to keep your piles of paint as compact as possible, not spread out over the palette. Compact piles of paint dry less rapidly.

HOW THE PROJECTS WORK

Before you begin work on the twenty-two projects that form the course of study in this book, let me explain how each project is arranged.

SETUP

I'll begin by recommending some simple still-life object, most often something that you can find around the house, such as a piece of fruit or kitchenware. Then I'll tell you how to organize the setup box: which colored papers should be taped or pinned to the walls and floor of the box; how to turn the box to the proper angle in relation to your line of vision; where to place the object inside the box; and finally how to light the contents of the box. Then I'll show you a photograph of the setup and give you a diagram that explains the proper position of the box for the project.

POSITIONS OF THE SETUP BOX

There are five possible positions for the setup box in relation to your line of sight. A diagram in each project will indicate the correct position for that particular painting assignment. After lining the walls and floor of the setup box with colored paper, simply turn the box to the correct angle. There's also a detailed explanation of how to arrange the box and lighting. In these diagrams, you'll be looking at the box from directly above, although, when you start to paint, the setup box will be resting on a table top, slightly below your eye level. The dark lines represent the two walls of the box; the dotted line is your line of vision.

FIRST STATEMENT

Next, I'm going to ask you to paint what I call a *first statement*. That is, I'm going to ask you to look carefully at the contents of the setup box, visualize these contents as a few big color areas, identify these colors through your spot screen, and paint them with a few broad, well-placed strokes—which we'll call color spots. The idea of the first statement is to reduce the subject to the minimum number of color areas that will convey the essence of the subject, and paint them as flat, solid color spots. (It's also important to cover the glaring white of the canvas paper as soon as possible since the white of the painting surface tends to make all the colors look too dark.)

Let's see how this works. Say you're painting a single piece of fruit in the setup box. You may be able to see it in as few as six big color spots: three spots for the walls and floor of the box; two for the light and shade sides of the fruit; and one last spot for the shadow of the fruit on the floor of the box. If you paint these six color spots accurately, with the aid of your spot screen, you'll find that you have a very convincing image of your subject, as bold and simple as a poster. (In each project, I'll show you a typical first statement painted by one of my students.)

Painting the first statement is a good time to make use of one of your viewfinders. Hold one of these frames somewhere between your eye and the subject. Move the card back and forth and look through its window to frame a pleasing composition that looks somewhat like the illustration in the book. Make sure you include enough of the walls and floor of the setup box.

If possible, I'd prefer that you start painting directly with the knife, without relying on pencil guidelines. But if you haven't done much painting and you feel uncomfortable about slashing away immediately with the knife, there's no harm in making a few pencil marks on the canvas to position the shapes of those big color spots. But keep these marks to a minimum. One lesson this method teaches is *painting without drawing*. Very soon, I hope you won't need the pencil. With only a little experience, you should be able to visualize where the spots go and paint them in without guidelines.

SECOND STATEMENT

When you're satisfied with your first statement, you're ready to paint a *second* statement. This means that you're going to look even more carefully at each of those big color spots and try to identify the subtle color changes there. For example, as you scan the shade side of a piece of fruit, moving the spot screen slowly over the entire area, you'll probably discover parts of the shade that differ in hue, luminosity, and intensity. In fact, several smaller color spots probably exist within that big color spot. Seeing that, you'll repaint the entire shaded area as *several* flat color spots. You'll do the same with areas in the light and under cast shadows.

If the painting is dry—probably because a number of days have gone by since you completed the first statement—you can paint right over the dry color. (Try to work very smoothly when you do the first statement, so you won't have too many ridges of paint to deal with when you go over it later.) If the color of the first statement is still wet, scrape it off with your knife and wipe off the remaining color leaving just tints of the original colors. The hint of remaining color will help you to paint your second statement.

The second statement should completely cover the first statement. No matter how much you liked the colors of the first statement, don't save any of them. Mix and repaint every area of the study so that the second statement is completely new. Force yourself to do this so you learn to look freshly at every area of the setup *and* on your study. Don't forget to use the spot screen to check and recheck every one of those new color spots.

When you study the completed second statement, you'll see, of course, that the color spots are smaller and far more numerous than the few big color spots in the first statement. You're now beginning to identify the colors *within* colors. And your painting is gaining in richness and accuracy.

THIRD STATEMENT

Some of the projects will require only one or two statements. But most of them can also be carried on to a *third statement*. As you did before, if the colors of your second statement are dry, you can paint the third statement directly over it. But if they're still wet, you'll have to scrape and wipe away the wet color to a ghostly tint and paint over the almost bare canvas. With the third statement, you are searching for greater subtlety and complexity within the colors of the setup, and so you'll find still more delicate shifts in hue, luminosity, and intensity. Your color spots will multiply and become even smaller. Thus, where you may have found three or four color spots within the shadow of the fruit when you painted the second statement, you'll now find many more as you keep scanning the subject through your spot screen. As always, your job is to mix each of these color spots with unerring accuracy, and then lay them down on the canvas paper as a flat knifestroke.

What emerges in that third statement is also a kind of ragged mosaic of colors—ragged because the color spots are different shapes and sizes, as you see them in nature. Just as you observed the hue, luminosity, and intensity of each color spot, so you must observe the shape, size, and position of each spot, too. There's no need to blend or fuse all these color spots so that they flow softly into one another. When seen from normal viewing distance, all those color spots will fuse in the viewer's eye to convey a realistic image of the subject.

Needless to say, the third statement may take more time to paint than the first and second because you must repaint the entire third statement over the second, without preserving any of the underlying color. This means you must force yourself to be ruthless, reexamining and repainting every inch. But the labor will be worthwhile. You'll be very proud of your successful third statement.

ADDITIONAL FIRST STATEMENTS

On the other hand, I don't think there's anything more satisfying—or more instructive—than a successful *first* statement. In fact, I often encourage my students to paint a series of first statements before they go on to the second because the first statement is really the foundation of the painting. There's a very old saying: "Well begun is half done." The more solid the first statement, the stronger will be the second and third statements erected on that foundation. So try painting five or six first statements, each time improving on the one before. Then choose the best as the basis for your second and third statements.

PREMIXING YOUR COLORS

I also encourage my students to try a color-mixing method that was common in the nineteenth century. In fact, Whistler demanded that his students work this way. You may want to try it too. You begin by identifying and mixing all the colors of the first statement—storing them up in little mounds on the palette—before you start to paint. Then, when all the colors for those big spots are mixed accurately, you knife them onto the canvas paper in one swift operation. Obviously, this is easiest to do when you're working on the first statement. As you work on the later, more complex statements, it makes more sense to mix and paint as you go along.

TIPS ON CLEANUP AND SAFETY

At the end of each painting session, it's important to follow a reliable and consistent cleanup procedure. Here are the most important things to do.

Wipe your painting knives thoroughly with toilet tissue, making sure that there's no trace of paint on the blades or handles. It's unpleasant to grip a paint-smeared or encrusted handle. And dried paint on the blade will impede the movement of a knife, whether you're mixing or painting. Be especially careful to get every trace of paint off the sharp edge of the blade—which you must handle with care so you don't cut yourself.

Wipe the neck of each paint tube with a tissue so that the cap will go on or come off easily the next time you paint. (A pair of pliers will help to move a stuck cap.) Then cap all your tubes tightly to prevent the tube color from drying out. Wipe any wet paint off the tube itself so you can see the label clearly. It's no fun trying to identify the contents of a paint-covered tube.

Cap all your bottles of medium and solvent tightly too, after wiping off any sticky stuff that might cover the label or make the cap difficult to remove next time.

Clean the mixing area of your palette with a tissue or a towel, perhaps moistened with some solvent to make the job easier. You can leave the wet piles of paint on the palette if you're going to be working in the next day or two. If you expect a week or more to pass before your next painting session, it probably makes sense to scrape and wipe the remaining paint off the palette so you can start on a fresh surface next time. Some artists find that they can keep paint moist by placing the palette in an airtight plastic box that's sold at art supply stores.

Wipe up all spills and stains with a tissue or towel, moistened with solvent if necessary. I know that you can't keep a painting studio as clean as a hospital room, but the gradual accumulation of paint stains and dribbles can be distracting when you're trying to think clearly about color. Always clean up *promptly*—old, dried paint is hard to remove.

There are also a few safety precautions that every painter must learn to take. Always work in a well-ventilated room, allowing solvent fumes to go out the window, preferably aided by a fan that draws the fumes toward the window and expels them. To avoid getting colors and solvents into your mouth, don't eat, drink, or smoke while you paint. Also try to keep colors and solvents off your skin—and keep a tissue or a paper towel nearby to wipe your hands. At the end of the painting day, get all those paint-stained tissues or towels out of the studio and dispose of them; don't store them up and risk spontaneous combustion. If you're using an extension cord for a lamp, pull the cord out of the wall and wind it up for storage until you go back to work on the painting.

A WORD OF ADVICE

Before you actually start painting, I want to emphasize one final point. Your purpose in painting these projects is not to create masterpieces, but to learn. Hawthorne often used to remind his students that they were painting *studies*, not pictures. So remember that the product of each assignment in this book is a color study, not a painting to frame and hang on a wall. I think you'll be proud of these studies. You may even produce some works you'll want to save. But you'll certainly turn out others that you'll want to throw away when you've learned what you can from them. What really matters is the learning experience. My students hear me say again and again: "What's important is not what we put onto the canvas, but rather what painting the canvas puts into us."

THE PROJECTS

Glass Pitcher and Stirrer by Richard Gleason.

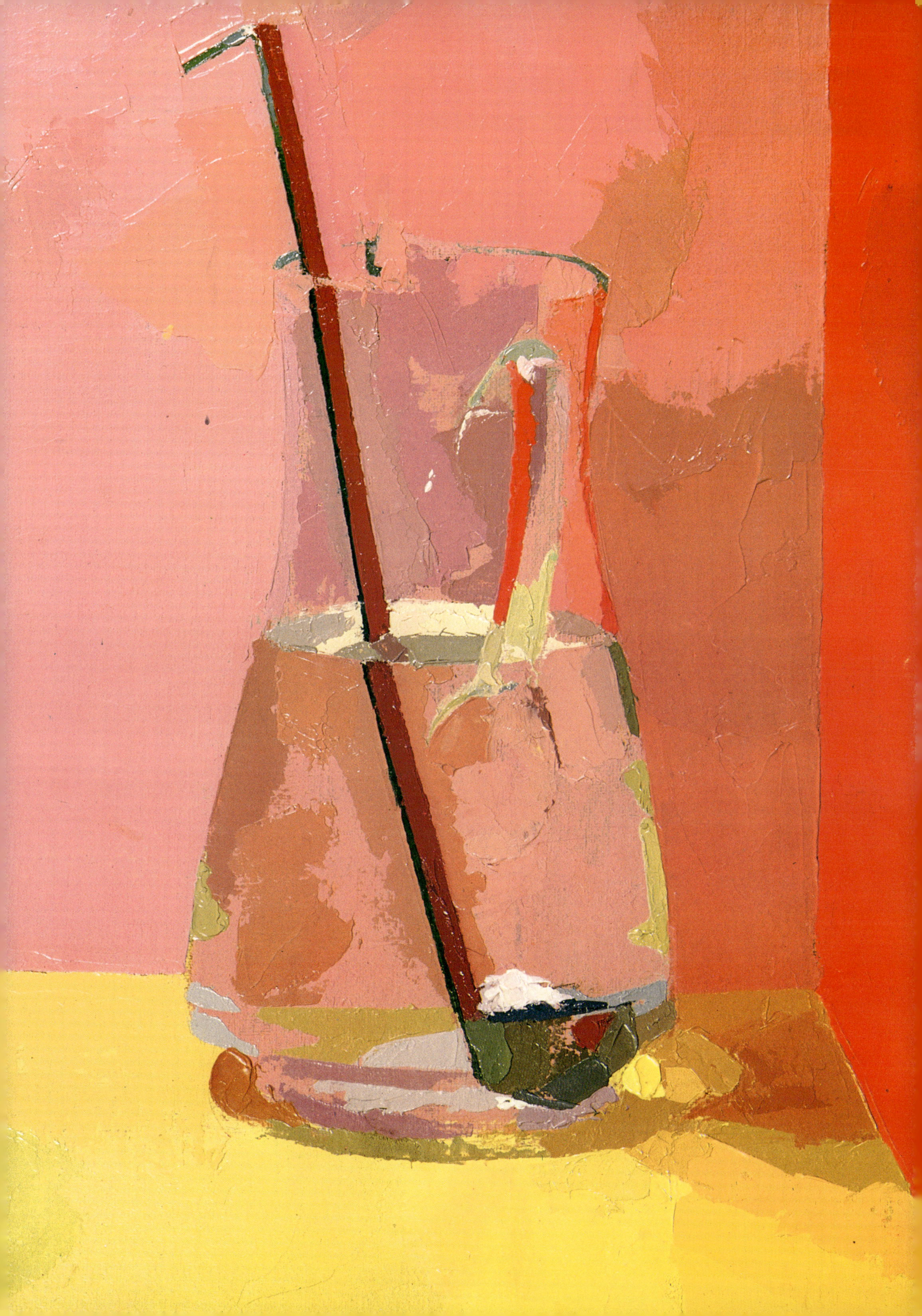

HOW DARK IS WHITE, HOW LIGHT IS BLACK?

SETUP. For your first project, your "model" is a white cylinder—an ordinary roll of white toilet tissue. Line the two walls of your setup box with sheets of black paper. Place a red sheet on the floor of the box. Stand the roll of white tissue on end in the middle of the setup box floor. Place the entire setup sufficiently below your eye level so that you can see the top of the roll from where you work. Arrange the setup lamp carefully. Push it far back and point the lamp at the back wall of the setup box. Only this back wall should receive the direct light of the lamp. No light should fall directly on the roll of tissue; its top should be dimly lit by the reflected light from the back wall, and the face of the roll should be in full shade. If you do all this properly, no direct light will fall on the setup box floor. The area of the floor closest to the back wall will be dimly lit by the reflected light, while the front area of the floor will be in full shade. Study the photo of the setup to see how the whole arrangement should look.

SETUP BOX POSITION 4

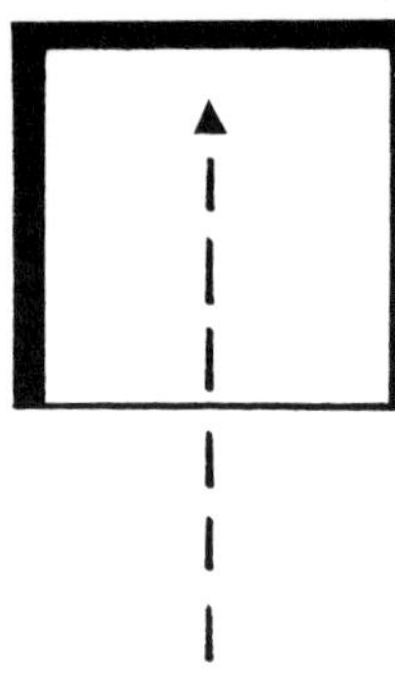

Place the box so its right wall is perpendicular to your line of vision. You're looking straight at the wall. The left wall is parallel to your line of vision, which means that it's off to one side and out of sight. You see only the right wall, which is directly behind your subject.

FIRST STATEMENT. Work on a half sheet of canvas paper, about 8″ × 12″ (20 × 30 cm), held vertically. Look through your viewfinder to compose a vertical picture. This is a first statement, which means that you're going to identify and paint the fewest, biggest, and simplest color spots that represent the subject. Here's what to do. Look at the shaded face of the roll; name the color you see and, with the straight knife, mix it, checking the color on the blade against the color you see through the hole in the spot screen; and then, with the bent knife, lay down the color with a few broad strokes. Don't worry about being neat. The main thing is to place the right color where it belongs. Now repeat this process with each of the big color spots that you see in the setup as listed below. (Ignore the hole in the top of the roll.) You'll probably see a total of nine color spots:

1 for the face of the roll
1 for its top
1 for the light part of the back wall
1 for the dark part
2 for the dimly lighted parts of the floor
2 for the dark part
1 for the shadow of the roll on the floor.

By the way, remember to name the color of each spot as you mix it. That will be a big help.

OBSERVATIONS. If you've followed these instructions carefully, you'll have already begun to grasp the essential point of this book—that you must paint what you *see*, not what you *think* you see. In other words, you can't predict the colors of the light and shade areas of the "white" roll; you just have to observe them carefully, paint them, and then see what happens. The same is true of the light and shade of the wall and floor of the setup box. Look again at your finished painting. The roll of white tissue isn't white at all. In fact, the shaded face of the white tissue roll is actually darker than the lighted area of the black wall. Under the lighting conditions of this project, white looks darker than black!

EXTRA PROJECT

You'll learn a lot by trying this project again, but with different colors. Replace the sheet of red paper with a green one, and see what happens not only to the back wall of the setup box, but to all the colors. See how much the green influences the "black" and "white" parts of the setup.

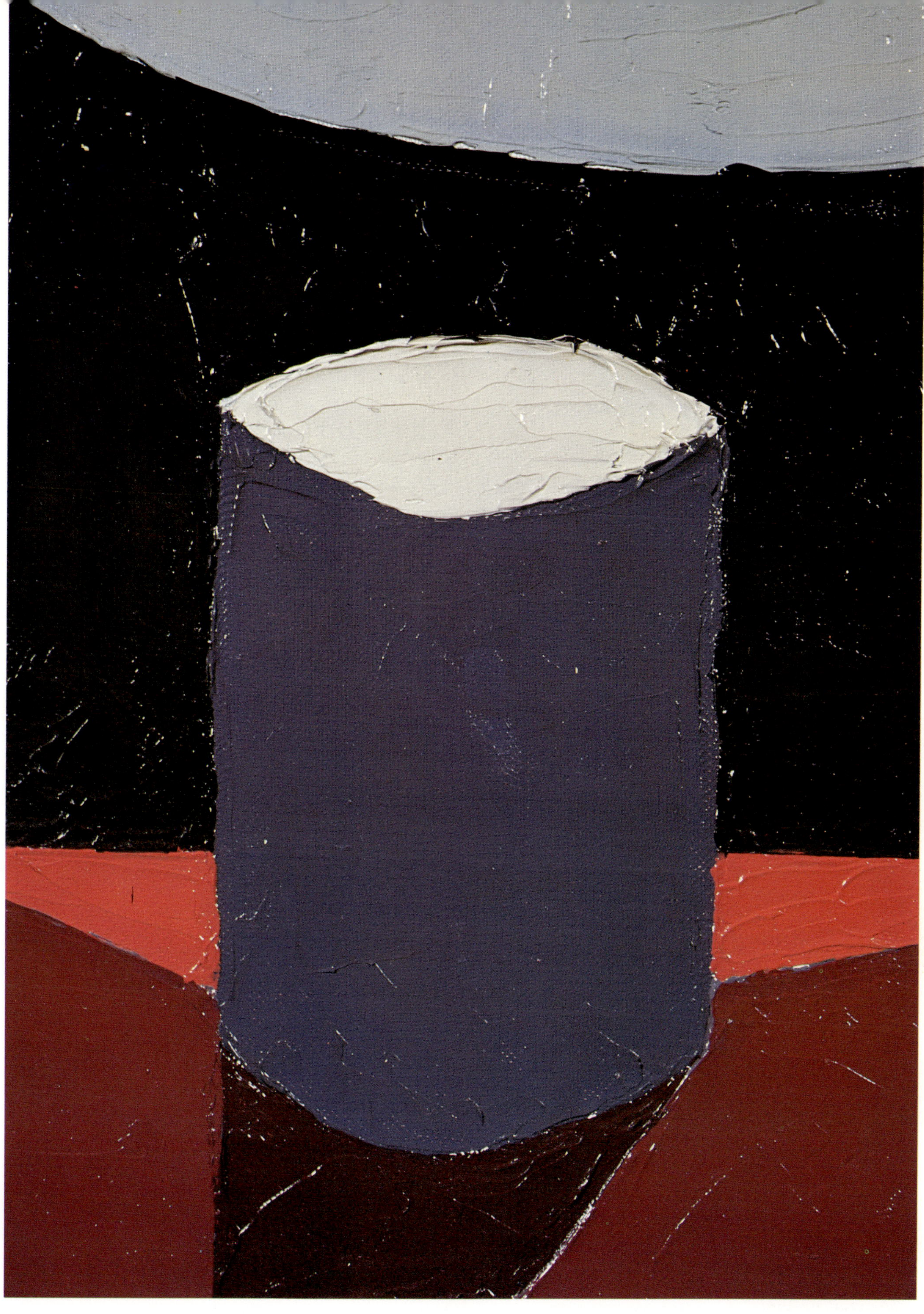

Note: These statements are not to be copied; they serve only as examples of how the projects might look. You must make your own setup, observe the colors for yourself, and see where the color areas begin and end, on your models.

WHEN IS "BLACK" BLACK?

SETUP. You'll have to find or make a cube about 3″ (75 mm) square for this project. A block of wood will do. So will any small cardboard box, cut down to the right size if necessary and reinforced with masking tape. Now cover the cube with a smooth coat of black poster color or with black paper, neatly folded and pasted smoothly to the six planes of the cube. Line the left wall of the setup box with yellow paper, the right wall with blue, and the floor with red. With the setup box in Position 3, place the cube to the left of the setup box corner, as you see in the photograph. Rotate the cube until its left face appears to be about three times as wide as its right face. Place the entire setup box far enough below eye level so that the top plane looks about the same size as the right face of the cube.

Put the lamp toward the front of the box, and high enough so that it may cast a shadow on the floor of the box, but not on either wall. Keep the lamp close to the setup box, however, so you can see the colors clearly.

SETUP BOX POSITION 3

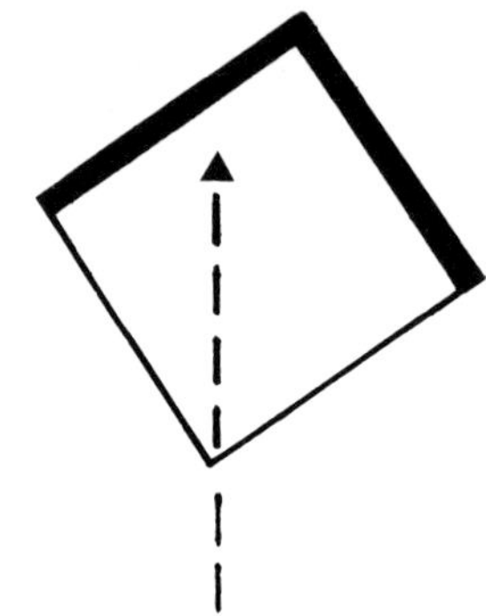

The corner of the box is to the right of your line of vision. You see more of the left wall than the right. The corner of the box is to the right of the cube.

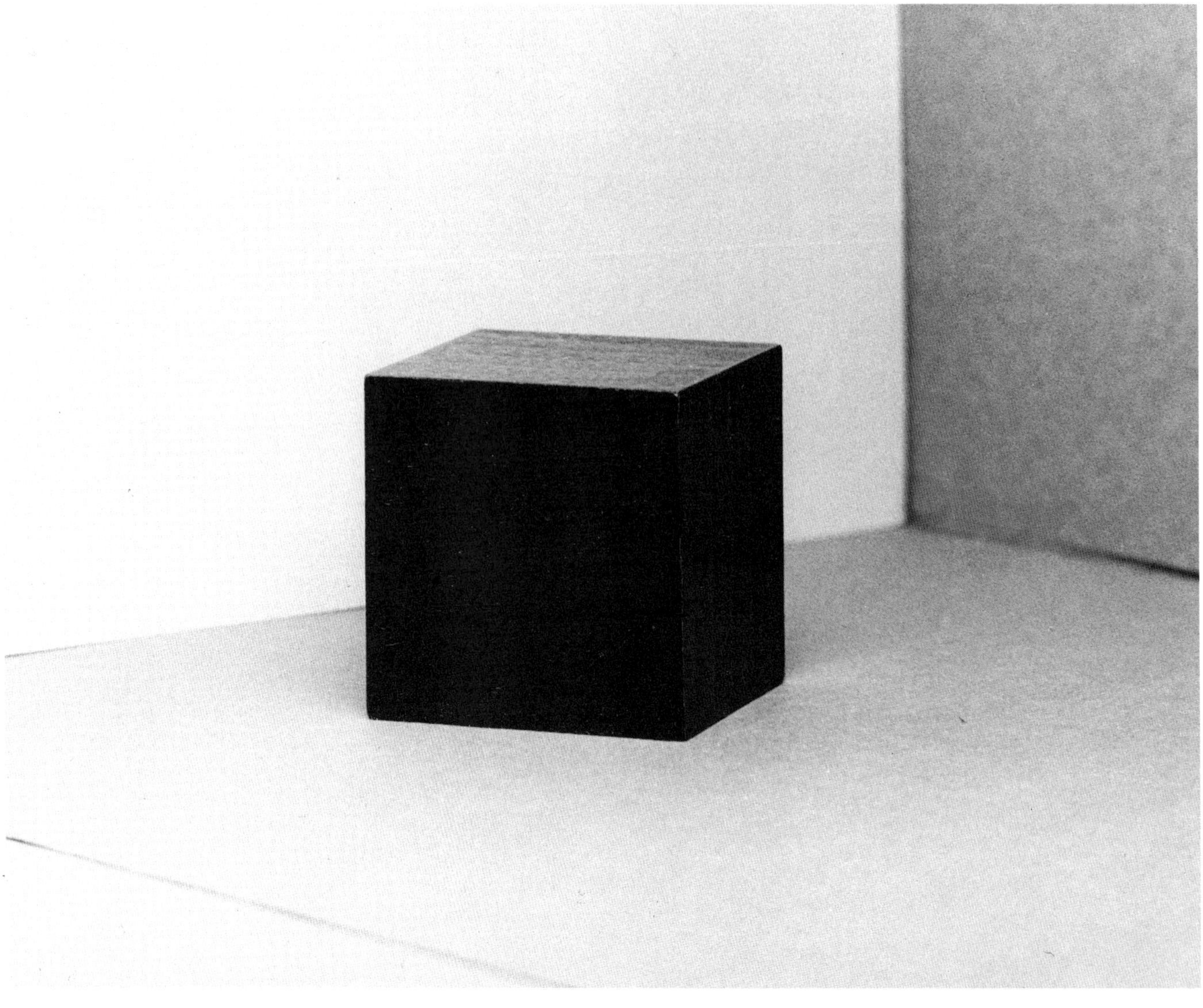

First Statement, Alfred Tyrol.

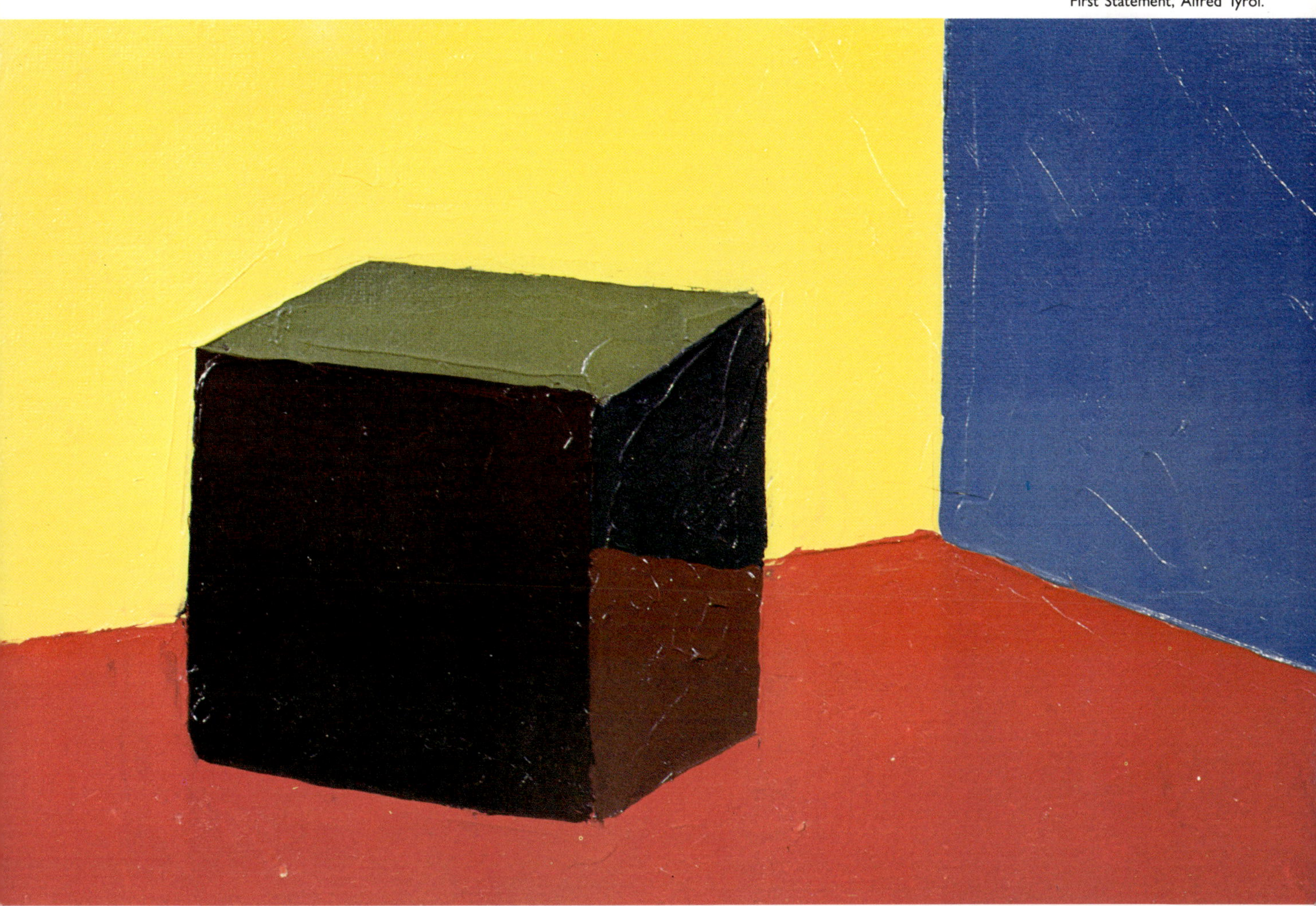

FIRST STATEMENT. This is a fairly small composition, so you can work on a half sheet of canvas paper, 8″ × 12″ (20 × 30 cm), held horizontally. Hold your 2:3 viewfinder horizontally to compose the subject as you see it here. As you did in Project 1, you're just going to paint a simple first statement. I think it's best to start with the big color spot on the dark face of the cube. Begin by naming the color—identifying its hue, luminosity, and intensity. Then use the spot screen and the knife to observe, mix, match, and apply a smooth spot of color to the canvas paper. To make those nice, crisp knifestrokes, rotate the painting to a convenient angle in your lap or on the table, and then work inward from the sharp edges of the color spot to its center. I want you to identify and paint just seven color spots:

1 for the left face of the cube
1 for its top
2 for its right face
1 for the left wall of the setup box
1 for its right wall
1 for the floor.

OBSERVATIONS. Just as Project 1 taught you that there's no such thing as "white," Project 2 will certainly teach you that there's no such thing as "black." Every plane of this supposedly "black" cube turns out to be some colorful mixture—because each plane of the cube is influenced by the colors of the environment. The right face of the cube is particularly interesting because it divides into two color spots that reflect both the floor and the right wall of the setup box. Until you actually paint those two color spots, there's no way to predict the divided color of that plane (or where the division would occur), any more than you can predict the colors of the other two planes of the cube. If you tried to predict the colors of those three planes, I'm almost certain that you'd predict much darker, duller, colors than the rich tones that you'll see in this example.

EXTRA PROJECT

Now find or make a white cube that's about the same size. You can just repaint the present cube if you like, or cover it with white paper. Keep the same colors on the walls and floor of the setup box. Now paint another first statement, showing what happens to those seven color spots when the cube is white instead of black. For additional variations, you can also try transposing the wall and floor colors, lining the left wall with blue paper, the right with red, and the floor with yellow. The cube can be white *or* black.

HOW GREEN CAN TURN RED

SETUP. The same cube, painted green or recovered with bright green paper, becomes a new model. Line the left wall of the setup box with yellow paper, the right wall with red, and the floor with blue.

Place the setup box in Position 1. Pose the green cube close to the forward edge of the setup box—as you see in the photograph—with the left edge of the cube aligning with the corner where the two walls of the setup box meet. Rotate the cube until you see a lot of the left face of the cube, and only a little of the right face. Place the whole setup sufficiently below eye level to let you see the top of the cube, which ought to look roughly the same size as the slender right face of the cube. Keeping the lamp well within the setup box, aim the bulb at the left wall so that not too much light falls on the right wall and on the floor. If you do this correctly, the three planes of the cube will all be lighted differently: the top receives the strongest light; the left face receives much less light; and the right face is in full shade. The cube also casts a shadow on the floor to the right.

SETUP BOX POSITION I

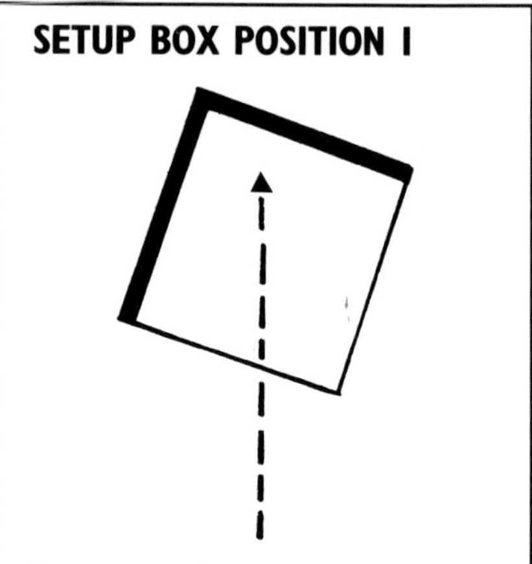

The corner of the box—where the walls meet—is to the left of your line of vision. You see more of the right wall than the left.

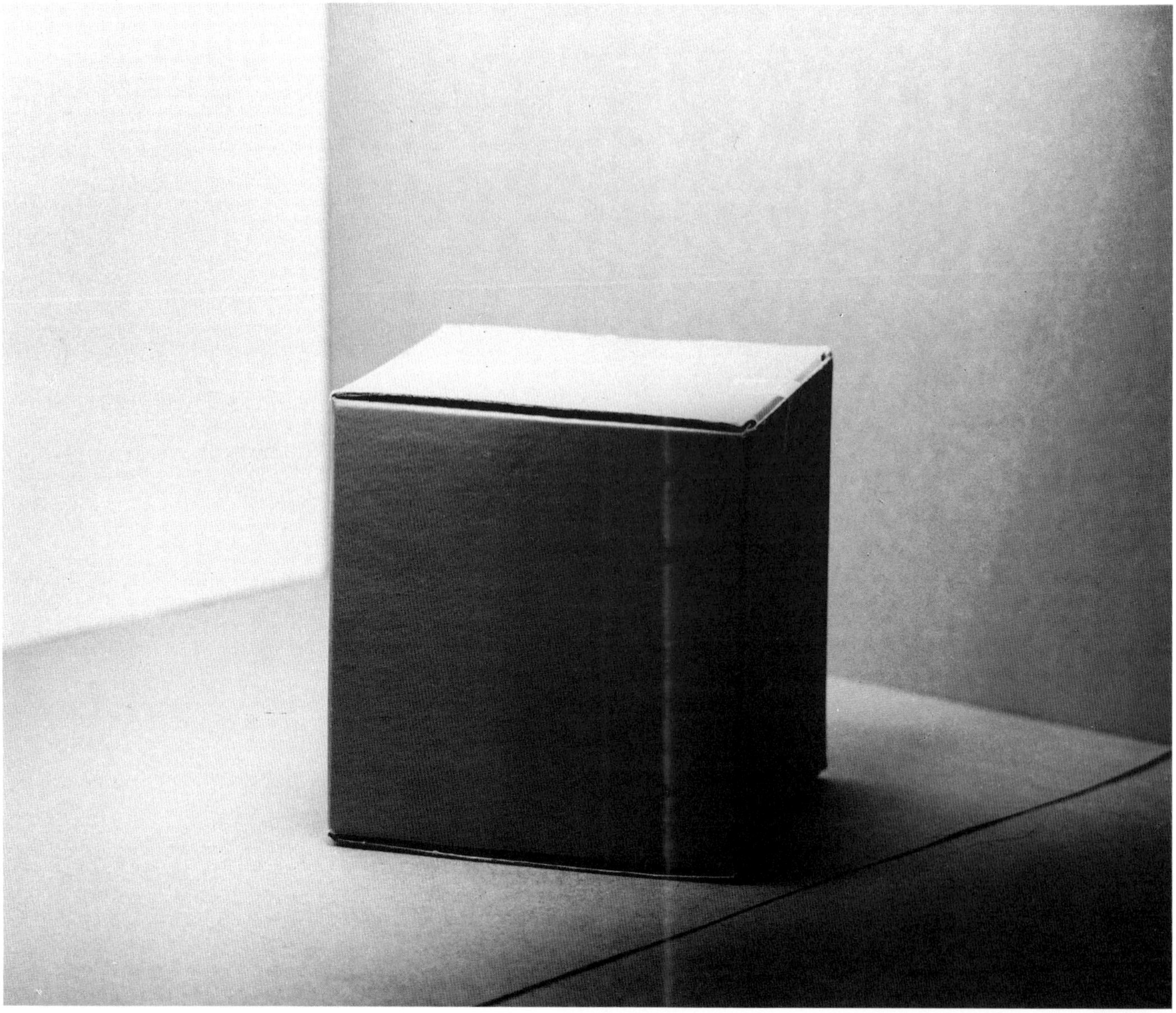

First Statement, Alfred Tyrol.

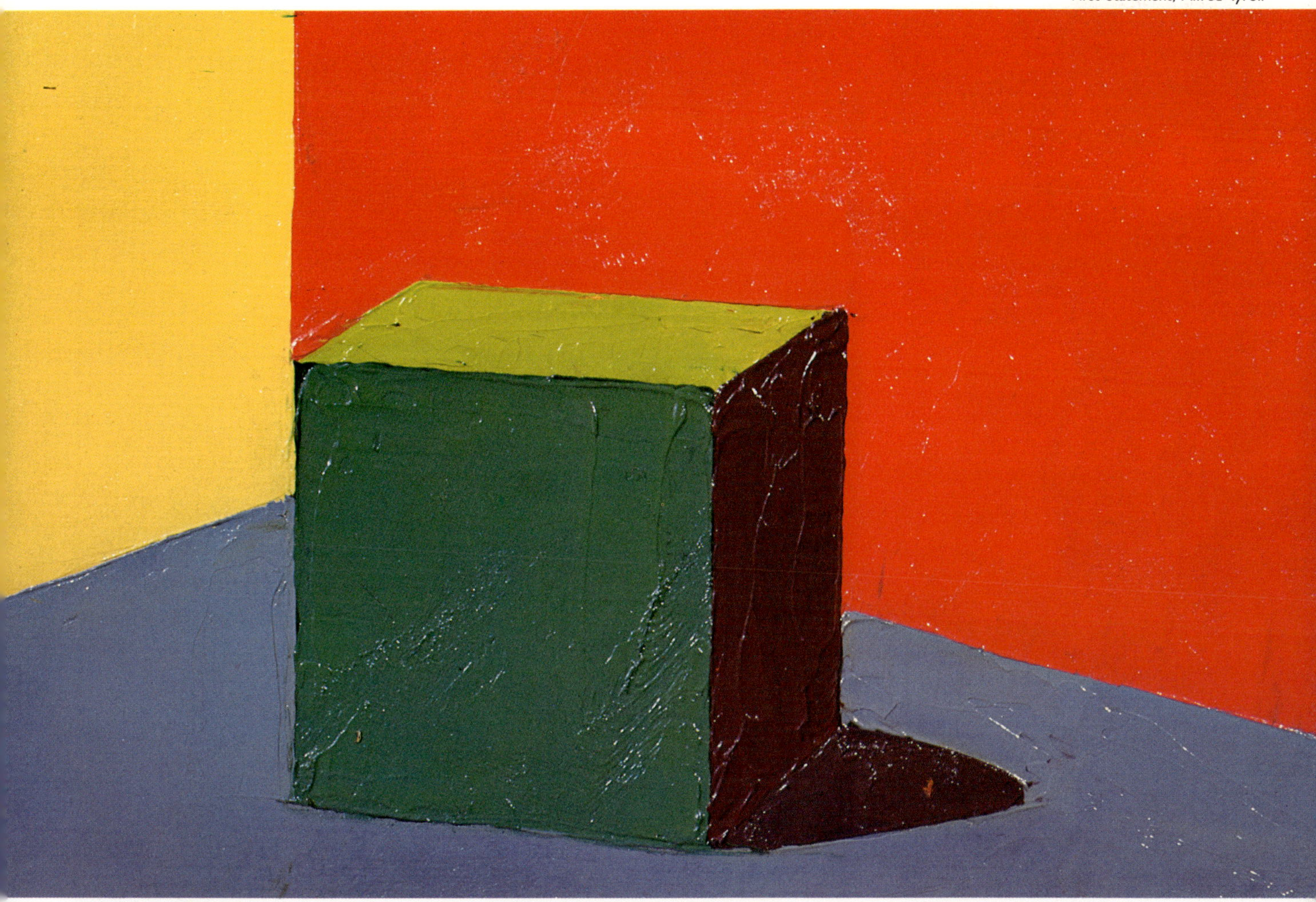

FIRST STATEMENT. As you did when you painted the cube in Project 2, you're going to find that you can capture the form and color of the green cube in Project 3 with just seven color spots. You're going to paint a first statement and stop there. Working on a vertical half sheet of canvas paper that measures 8″ × 12″ (20 × 30 cm), use your 2:3 viewfinder to frame a horizontal composition. You can get fairly close to the cube, eliminating the diagonal front edge of the floor of the box. Just be sure you include enough of the floor and walls. Then start by naming, mixing, matching, and painting the biggest plane of the cube. Then go on to paint the other color spots, exaggerating the shadow of the cube on the floor to create a distinct color area. In the first statement shown here, there are seven color spots:

1 for the left face of the cube
1 for its right face
1 for the top
1 for the left wall of the setup box
1 for its right wall
1 for the floor
1 for the shadow on the floor

OBSERVATIONS. After seeing that white can look darker than black in Project 1, and that black can be full of color (and perhaps lighter than white) in Project 2, you won't be surprised to see green turn into red. The right face of the cube, in particular, is startling. The right wall of the setup box—which you've lined with red paper—exerts an irresistible influence over the right face of the cube; there's no way that that right face can remain green. Likewise, the top plane of the cube is powerfully influenced by the yellow wall at the left. But despite the unpredictable colors of these two planes, if you showed someone this painting and asked the color of the cube, the answer would probably be "green."

EXTRA PROJECT

You can have a lot of fun surprising yourself by painting the same picture with cubes of different colors in the same setup. Keep the same colored paper on the walls and floor of the setup box, but paint first statements of red, blue, orange, and violet cubes. The colors will be so surprising that you won't become bored.

HOW PLAIN IS A PLANE?

SETUP. Now I'm going to ask you to look more closely at the three planes—the two walls and floor—of the setup box itself. Line the left wall of the setup box with yellow paper, the right wall with red, and the floor with blue. Place the box in Position 2. Arrange the lamp to the left, flooding all three planes of the box with direct light, as you see in the photograph. When you do that, the three planes won't be evenly lit; some areas will be more brightly lit than others. Such variations will help you to paint a second and third statement after you've completed your highly simplified first statement.

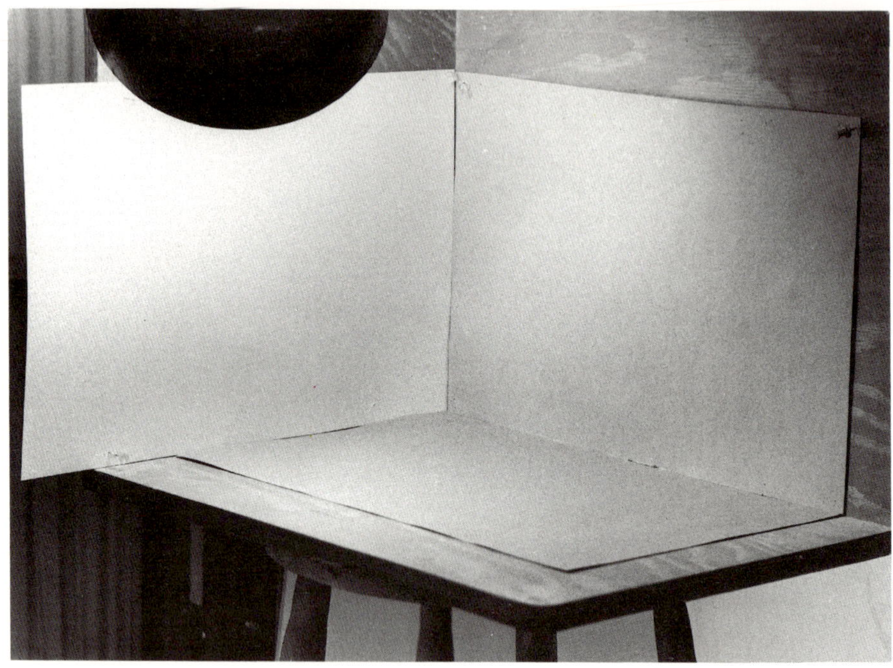

SETUP BOX POSITION 2

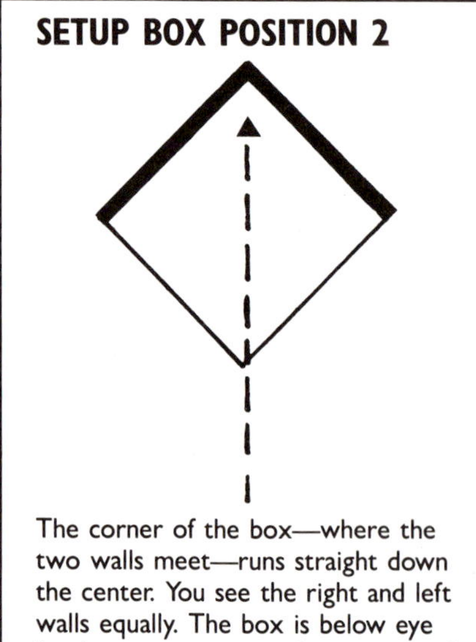

The corner of the box—where the two walls meet—runs straight down the center. You see the right and left walls equally. The box is below eye level, so you can see a fair amount of floor.

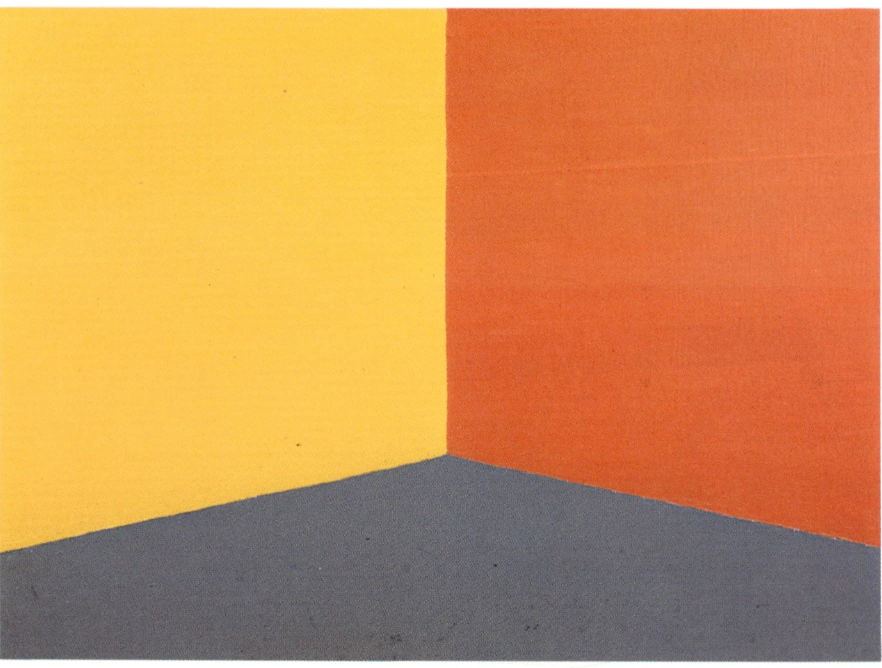

First Statement, Fabio Rincón.

FIRST STATEMENT. You've done this before, so the process should be familar by now. Scan each of the three planes of the setup box with your spot screen and try to mix a color that best represents the overall hue, luminosity, and intensity of the entire plane. So far, you're not looking for subtle variations, but trying to find a kind of "average" color that best represents each big area. You're most likely to find that color somewhere toward the center of each plane. Work on a full sheet of canvas paper that measures 12″ × 16″ (31 × 41 cm) and use your 3:4 viewfinder to create a symmetrical composition like the one you see here. This view of the empty setup box can be represented by just three color spots:

1 for the right wall
1 for the left wall
1 for the floor.

OBSERVATIONS. If you look at each plane carefully, you'll begin to realize that the first statement is an obvious oversimplification. In visualizing any subject as a first statement, you ignore the subtle color variations that will become increasingly obvious as you move your spot screen over the subject to paint later statements. Yet, this simplified view of the subject gives you a powerful and convincing image that's not only satisfying in itself, but forms a foundation for later statements. In fact, the success of your later statements depends substantially upon how clearly you visualize that first statement.

Second Statement, Fabio Rincón.

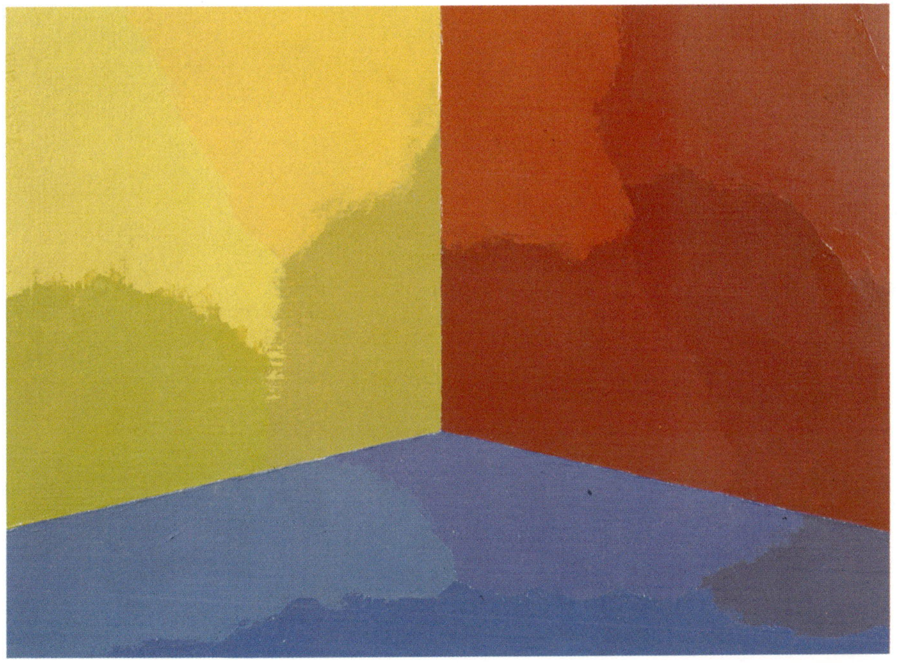

Third Statement, Fabio Rincón.

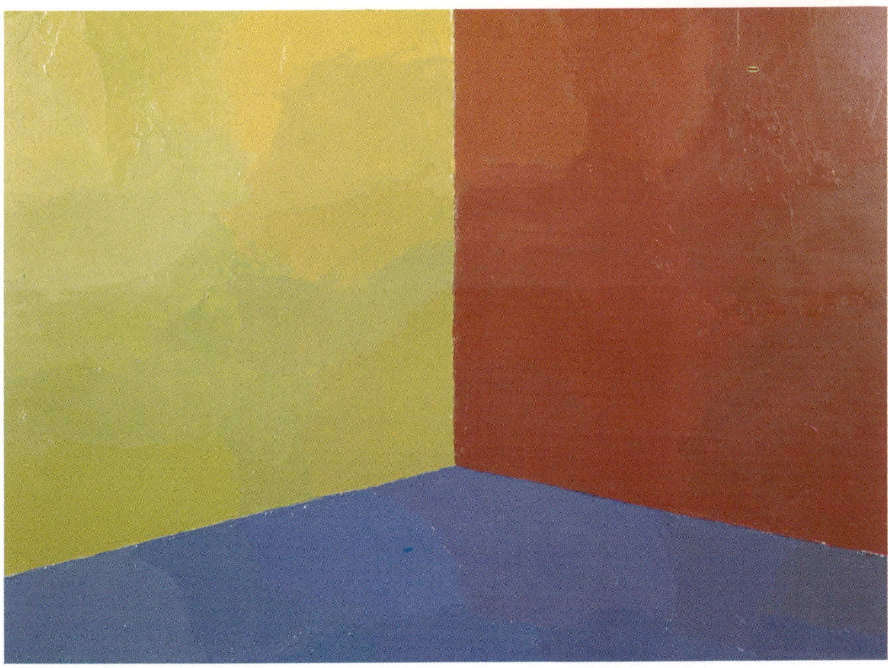

SECOND STATEMENT. Now you're going to paint a second statement right over the first. If the first statement is dry, you can work on top of the dry color. If the paint is still wet, use your knife to scrape it down to a pale ghost of the original image. Now run your eye slowly over each of the three planes, first without the spot screen and then with the aid of the spot screen. Study each plane separately, running your eye along the edges and paying particular attention to the corners. You're going to discover that significant color changes happen in those corners. In fact, each plane is likely to reveal a separate color spot that spreads from the corner to the center of the plane. Now you'll probably see twelve color spots instead of the original three that you painted in your first statement:

4 for the left wall
4 for the right wall
4 for the floor.

OBSERVATIONS. Now you'll begin to see how those three planes are influenced by changes in the amount of light they receive—and by one another. Thus, the lightest of those twelve color spots will be the area of the yellow wall that receives the most light. Conversely, the darker spots will be furthest from the light. However, each plane is also influenced by the reflected color that it picks up from the other planes. That's why such important color changes appear at the edges and corners where the planes meet. You can't predict what colors are produced by these influences. There are no rules. You just have to identify them, mix them, and place them on the canvas.

THIRD STATEMENT. Having painted the empty setup box in twelve color spots, you've already found surprising richness and complexity in those three flat planes. But even more color spots are waiting to be discovered. Now there's no limit. Once again, scrape off the wet paint or work right over the dried paint if you prefer. Scan each plane with your spot screen, looking again at the corners, touring the edges of the planes, and then working toward the center of each plane. Try to find even more subtle variations and then represent these by as many small color spots as you can actually discern. There's no minimum or maximum number of color spots. But don't invent or guess. Paint only what you see. Stop as soon as you feel that you've done justice to your subject.

OBSERVATIONS. Having carried three supposedly simple planes of color all the way to a third statement, you'll learn a lot more about how colors influence one another. Look back at your second and third statements to see how both walls influence each other and the floor and vice versa.

EXTRA PROJECT

You'll learn a lot more by shifting around the colors of the setup box and painting the subject again. So line the left wall with red, the right wall with blue, and the floor with yellow. Or try any other arrangement of these colors—or any other colors—that you enjoy. For example, you can replace the red, yellow, and blue with orange, green, and violet. Paint a first, second, and third statement of each arrangement.

WHEN IS AN ORANGE ORANGE—AND WHERE?

SETUP. After painting all those cubes and angular planes in Projects 1 through 4, I think you'll enjoy painting something round. Line the left wall of the setup box with blue paper, the right wall with red, and the floor with green. Set an orange in the box about 7" (18 cm) from each wall. Place the setup box in Position 3, well below eye level so that you can see plenty of the floor of the box. The setup lamp ought to be at the left so that a good-sized shadow extends to the right of the orange, running across the floor of the box and then up the right wall. Light and shade are divided more-or-less equally on the orange.

SETUP BOX POSITION 3

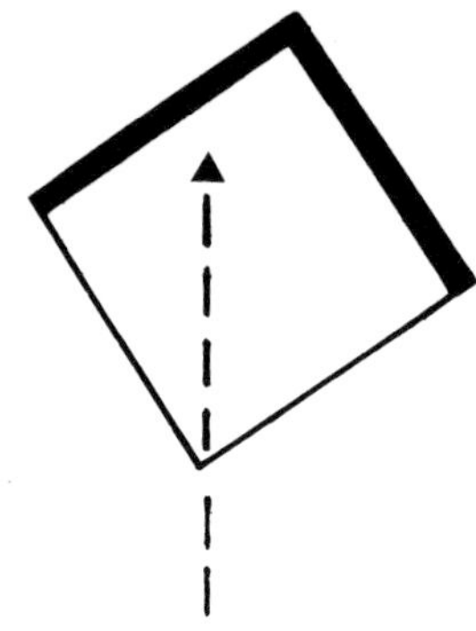

The corner of the box is to the right of your line of vision. You see just a little of the right wall and a lot of the left. The setup box is well below eye level, so that you see equal amounts of the left wall and the floor.

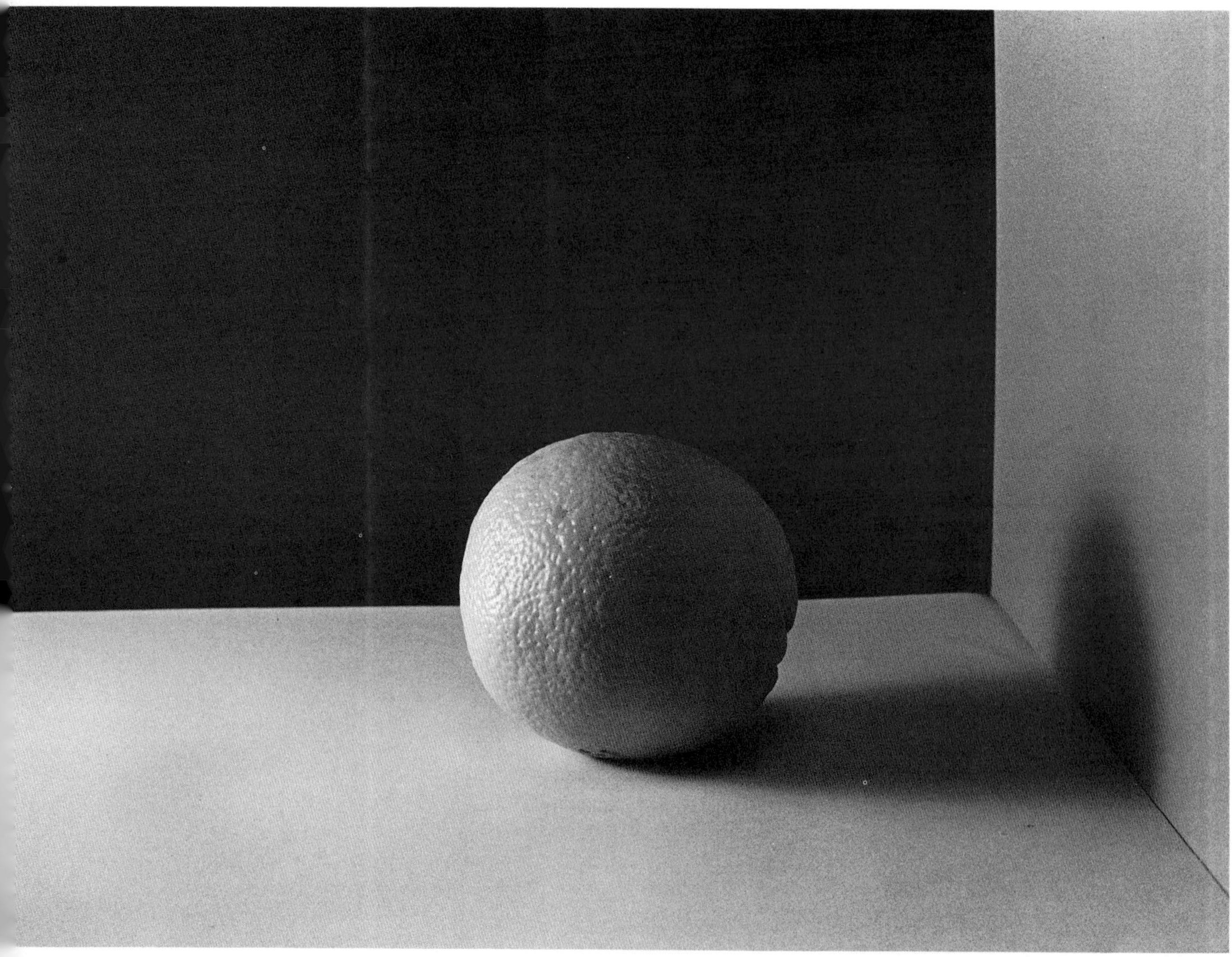

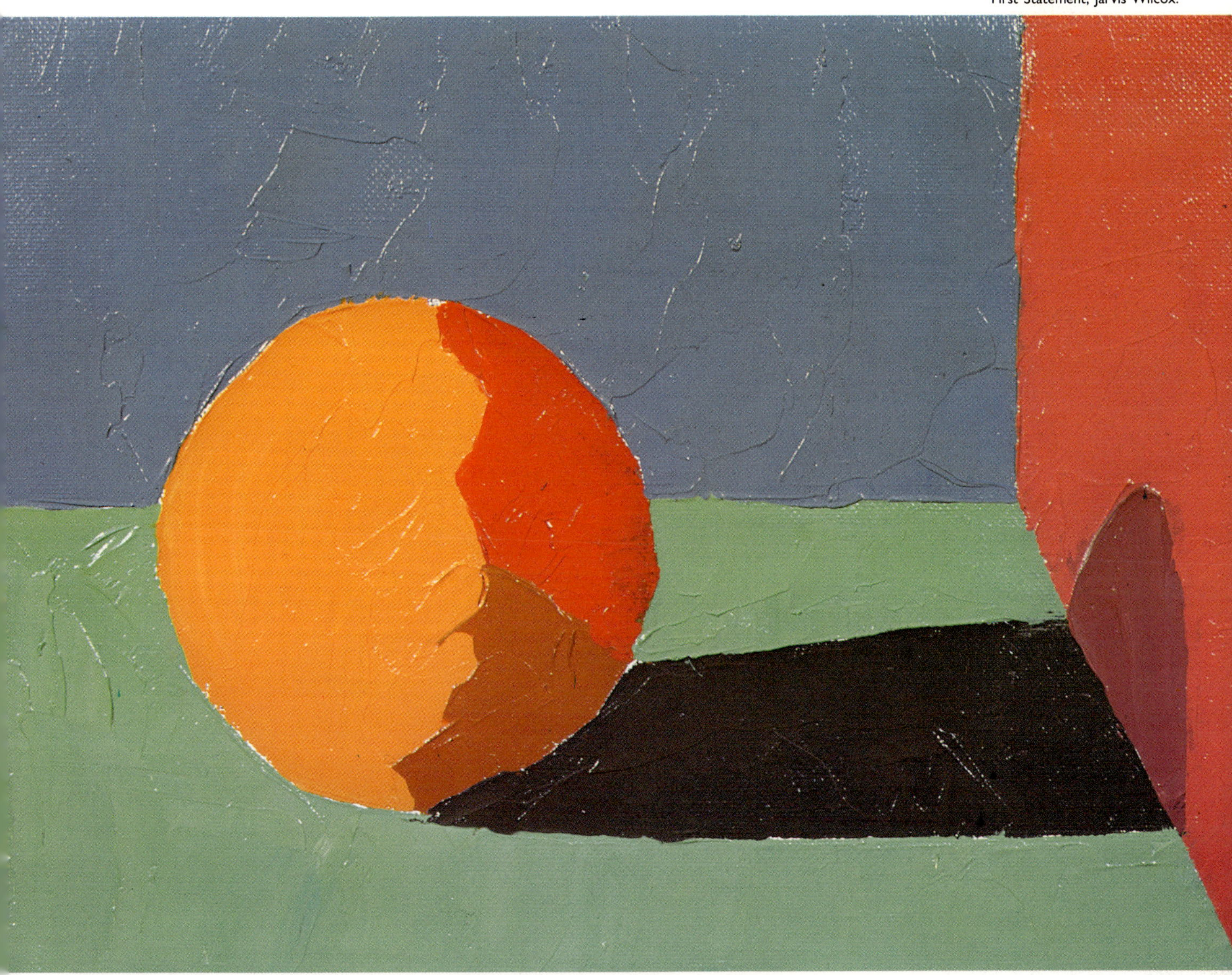

First Statement, Jarvis Wilcox.

FIRST STATEMENT. At this point, some student always sighs: "Ah, a round object—and alive too!" This painting will fit on a half sheet of canvas paper, held horizontally. Use your 2:3 viewfinder to compose a picture that looks something like the one shown here. You should be able to paint this first statement in just nine color spots. As you follow the edge where light and shadow meet on the orange, you'll probably end up with a jagged edge that makes your spherical model look rather angular—or lumpy. Don't fret about this. If the shapes and colors are right, that orange *will* look like an orange. Here are the nine color spots:

1 for the light side of the orange
2 for the dark side
1 for the left wall of the setup box
1 for the right wall
2 for the floor
1 for the shadow on the floor
1 for the shadow on the right wall.

OBSERVATIONS. Despite its roundness, the orange is really no more difficult to represent in flat color spots than the rectangular planes of the cube. The orange also resembles the cube in that its shade side becomes two color spots, one for the upper part and one for the lower. When you look at the color plate you'll see why this happens. And once again, you'll discover that shadows aren't simply dark—and certainly not gray, brown, or black. The cast shadow is one color on the floor to the wall of the setup box and another on the wall!

SECOND STATEMENT. When you have that first statement clearly on canvas, start work on the second statement, painting right over the first. use your spot screen to scan each area separately: the right and left walls, the floor, the light and shade areas of the orange, and the shadow that is cast across the floor and up the wall. Within each of these areas, you will find more color variations. Visualize them for what they are—color spots. It's hard to predict the exact number of color spots you're going to find, but here's what to aim for:

4 for the left wall of the setup box
4 for the right wall
4 for the floor (excluding the shadow)
3–4 for the light side of the orange
4–6 for the dark side
3 for the shadow on the floor
3 for the shadow on the right wall
1 for the orange's reflection on the floor.

Second Statement, Jarvis Wilcox.

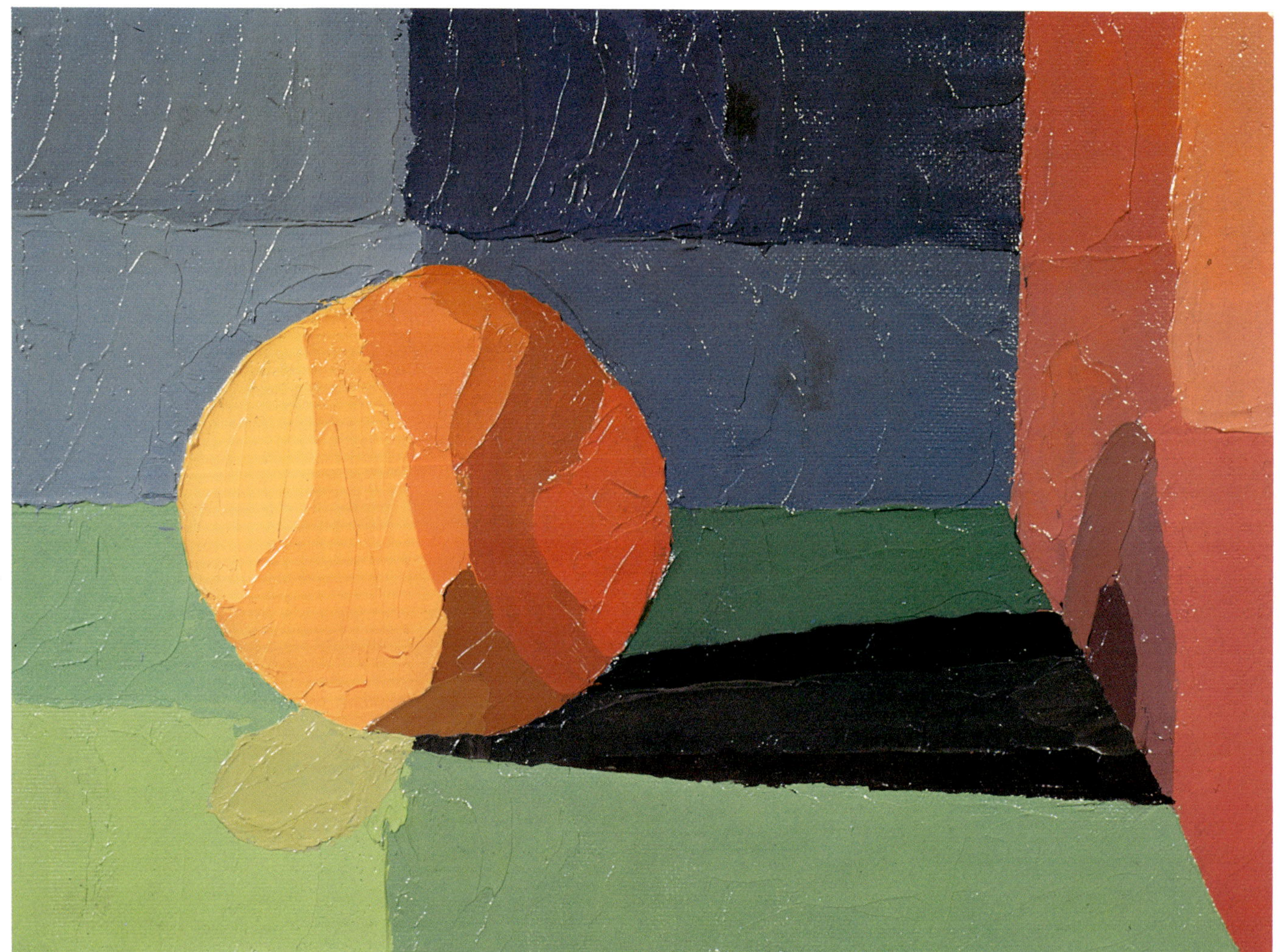

OBSERVATIONS. As the few big, simple color spots of your first statement gradually disappear beneath the smaller, more complex, and more numerous color spots of your second statement, the orange looks less like a polyhedron and more like a spherical piece of fruit. As you discover and lay down more color spots, the *form* begins to change with the color. If this book has any "message," it's that form and color are really inseparable. Form is constructed by placing the right color spots in the right location. This second statement is still an oversimplification, however, particularly where you've represented the varying colors of the wall with big, rectilinear color spots. The walls, floor, and shadow won't begin to look "real" until the third statement. As you scrape out the colors of the first statement and paint in the second, I hope you're remembering to remove and redo just one big color spot at a time.

THIRD STATEMENT. Now you can let yourself go and search for all the color spots that you can find with your spot screen. Identify, mix, and lay down as many color spots as you feel the picture needs to make the orange look spherical and the walls three-dimensional. You can paint thickly if you like, building up your paint, since you won't be going over them again. Remember to use the side of the knife for the big strokes and its tip only for the smaller touches. Place all the subtle colors side by side as separate color spots. Don't blend them! You don't have to fuse those knife strokes to make the orange look round. If your color spots record all the subtle changes that you see in the surface of the orange—and in the setup box walls—then the orange will look solid and the setup box walls will look spacious.

Third Statement, Jarvis Wilcox.

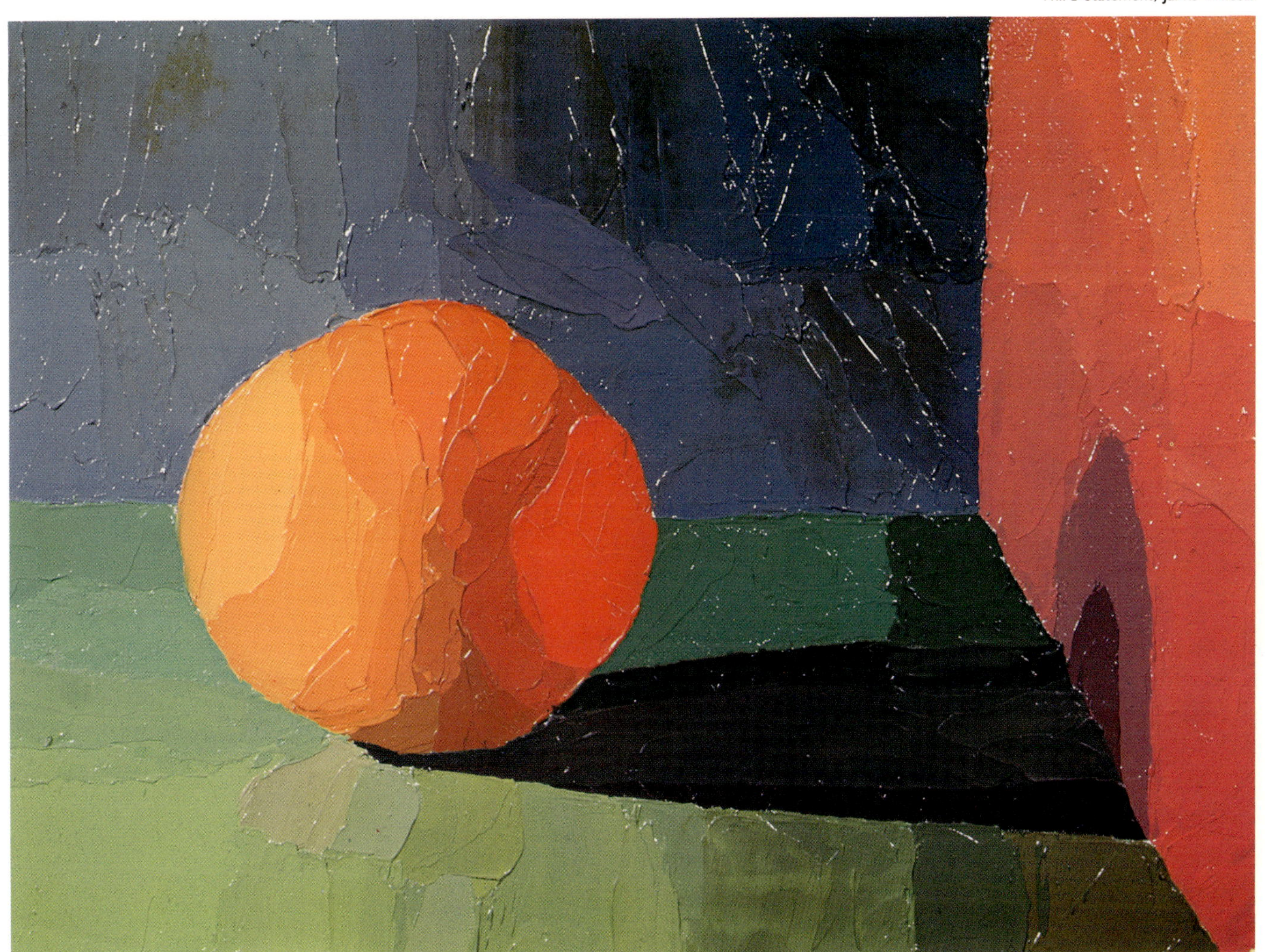

OBSERVATIONS. This is only your second attempt at a third statement, but it should be obvious by now that there are many complexities possible within any simple setup. The simple, round form of the orange can reveal a couple of dozen color spots, influenced by the multitude of color changes that take place in the surrounding walls and floor. And you'll see once again that colors of walls and floor influence one another, too.

EXTRA PROJECT

As a variation on this project, rearrange the colors on the walls and floor of the setup box, perhaps transposing the colors on the two walls and finding another color for the floor. Then substitute a big lemon for the orange. As you paint a first, second, and third statement, you'll see how little of the lemon is really "lemon yellow"!

COLOR WITHOUT CONTOUR

SETUP. Here's another project in which you're going to paint a round piece of fruit—but with a difference. Line the left wall of the setup box with yellow paper, the right wall with light blue, and the floor with green. With the setup box in Position 3, place a large grapefruit well back in the corner, overlapping the point where the walls and floor meet. The grapefruit ought to be near the left wall, but not quite touching it. Place the lamp to the left and in front of the setup box, close enough to the grapefruit to cast a shadow on the floor and right wall. In the photograph of the setup, you can see that there's not much contrast between the pale left wall and the lighted face of the grapefruit—and that's exactly as it should be.

SETUP BOX POSITION 3

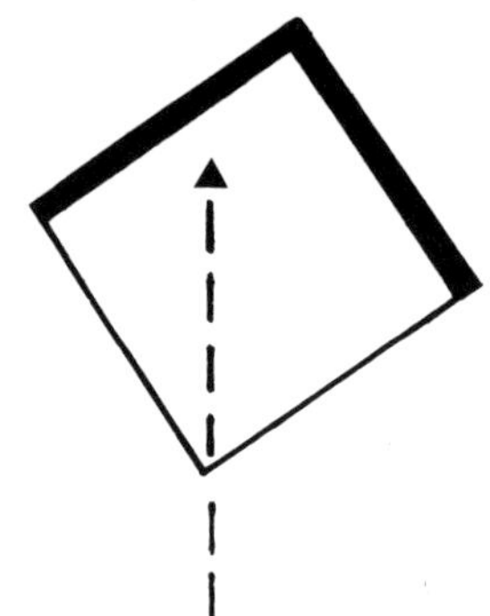

The corner of the box is to the right of your line of vision. You see more of the left wall than the right. The box is below eye level so that you see a fair amount of floor.

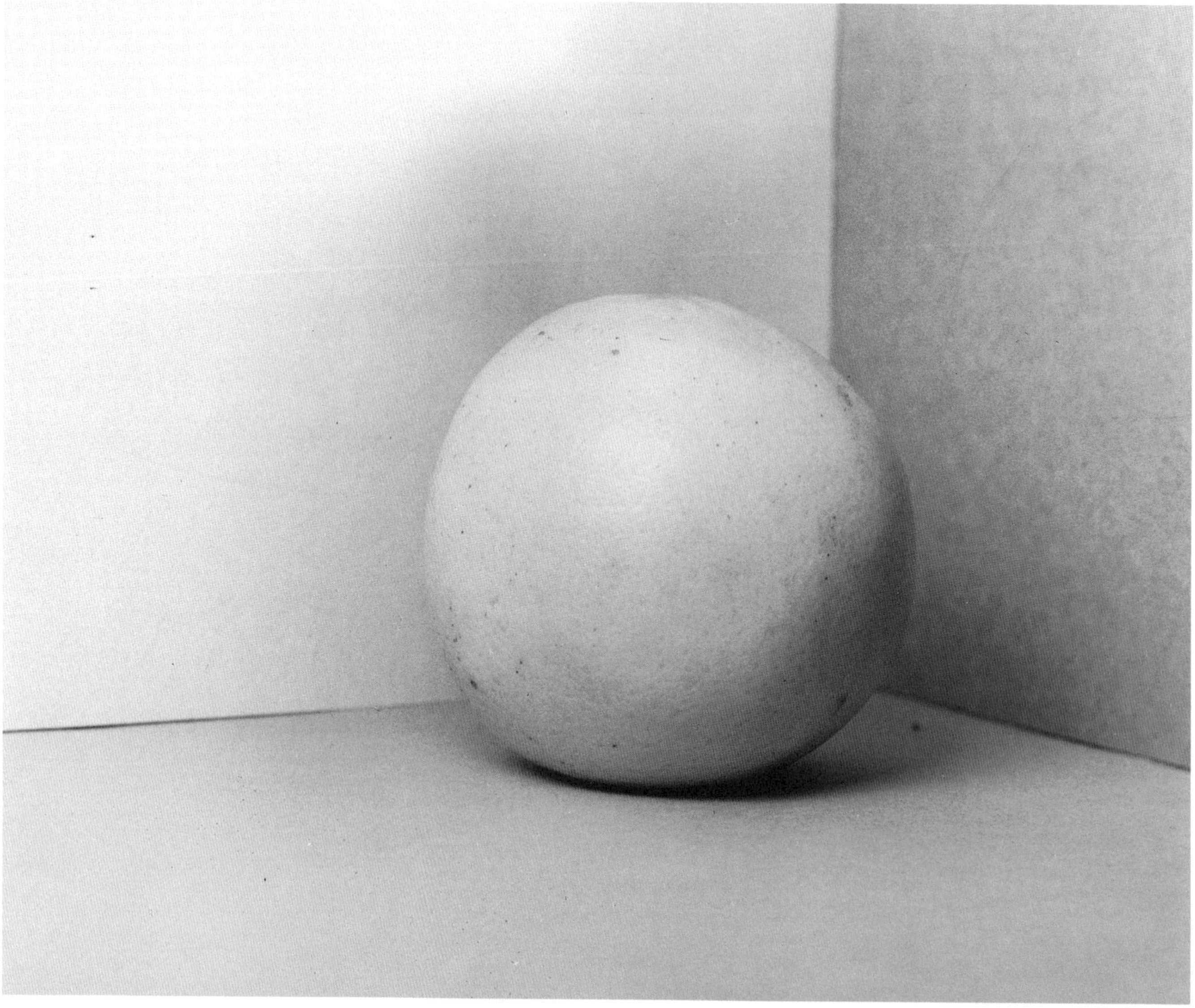

First Statement, Jarvis Wilcox.

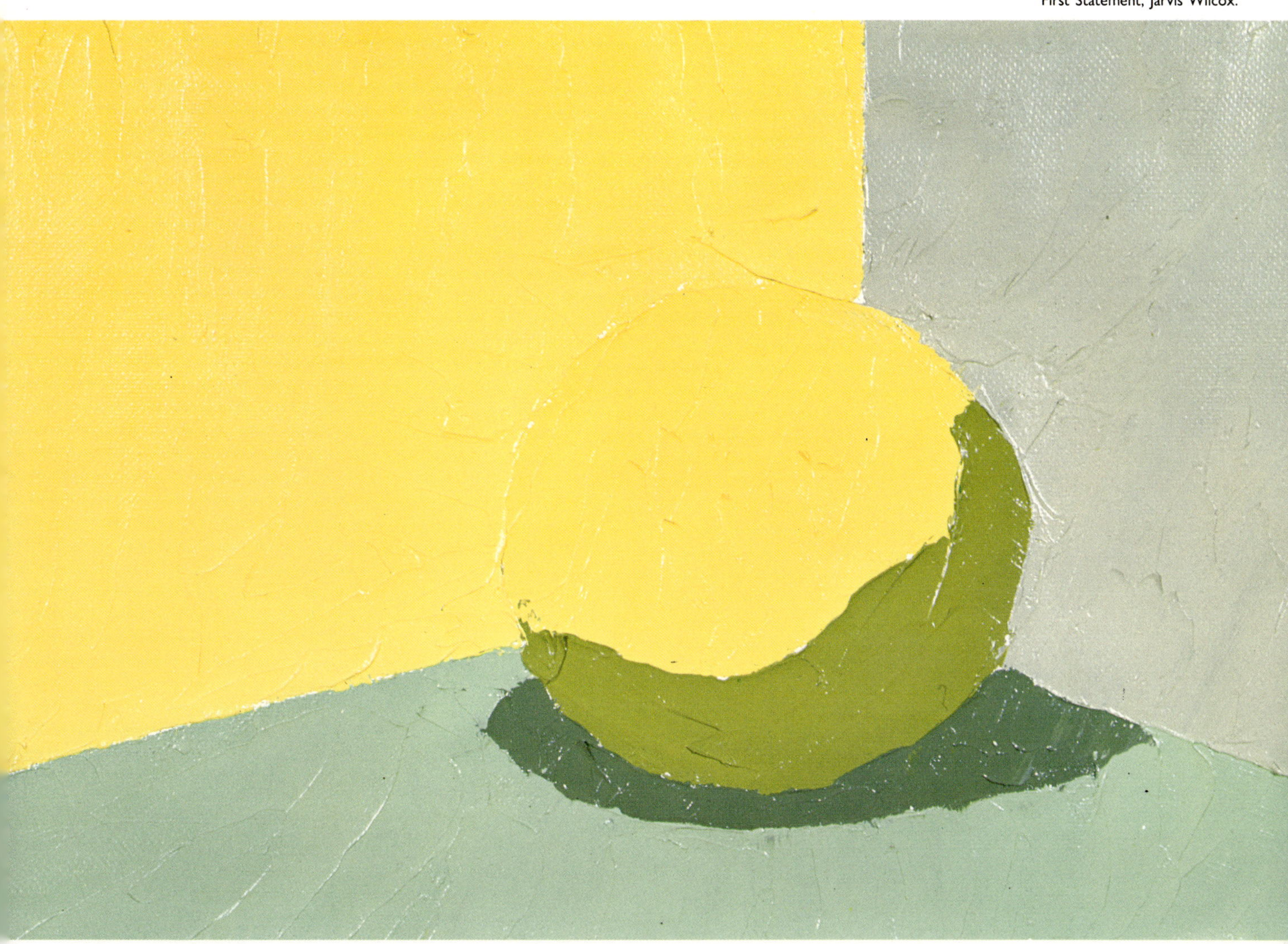

FIRST STATEMENT. This project will easily fit on a half sheet of canvas-textured paper, held horizontally. Don't forget to use your 2:3 viewfinder to frame a composition that looks like the one shown here. Use your spot screen to identify the "typical" color of just six big color spots, which will be enough to summarize the fruit, walls, and floor. Here are the six color spots that you should lay down with your trowel-shaped palette knife:

1 for the left wall of the setup box
1 for its right wall
1 for its floor
1 for the light side of the grapefruit
1 for its dark side
1 for the shadow on the floor

OBSERVATIONS. The most important lesson of this project is that you can't paint contours that you don't see. If you set up the grapefruit, the box, and the light properly, the color spots of the left wall and the light side of the fruit will be so similar that they'll seem to disappear into one another. The contour of the fruit is virtually invisible—except where the color spots of the fruit come up against the contrasting color spots of the right wall, floor, and cast shadow. The lesson here, as you can see, is that contours aren't lines, but contrasts between color spots. You can't re-establish a lost contour by drawing a line. It may strike you as odd, but you can still paint the grapefruit convincingly even without the missing contour. More important, that grapefruit looks real partially because of that missing segment.

SECOND STATEMENT. Go back to work on that grapefruit and see how many smaller and subtler color spots you can find without faking a contour you cannot see. As you scan the grapefruit and the surrounding walls and floor with your spot screen, of course you will discover some areas that suggest slightly more contrast between the light side of the grapefruit and its pale surroundings. But don't be tempted to exaggerate these contrasts in order to "restore" contours that you can't really see. This whole project is an exercise in restraint. I want to encourage you as strenuously as I can to paint only what you see—and to not paint what you don't see. Even if you're annoyed by the absence of a distinct contour on the side of the grapefruit, don't paint one in if you can't see it. I won't tell you to look for a specific number of color spots here. But it's a good rule to look for three or four times as many color spots in your second statement as you found in the first. This student painted his second statement in twenty-two color spots.

Second Statement, Jarvis Wilcox.

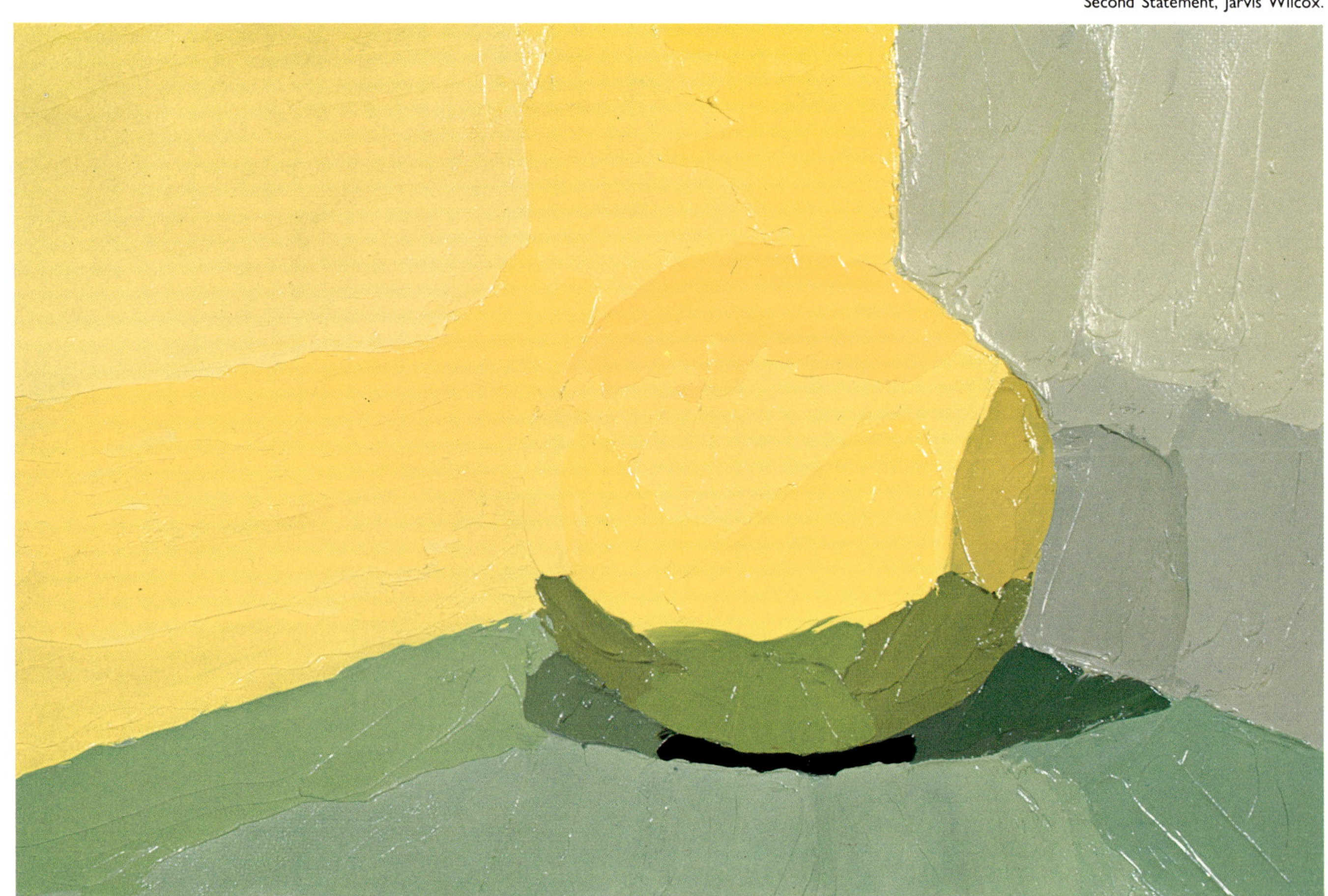

OBSERVATIONS. The most interesting fact about this second statement is that the picture does succeed in reading as a grapefruit despite the lack of a complete contour. You don't really need outlines around things in order for them to look solid and complete. There's just enough contrast between the color spots on the dark side of the grapefruit to suggest a complete, rounded form. And the remaining color spots, delicate as they may be, somehow convey the roundness of the shape without the invention of invisible boundaries.

THIRD STATEMENT. When you develop a third statement, you're not only finding smaller, more delicate, and more numerous color spots—but you're also looking for contrasts you couldn't see in the first and second statements. So, as usual, you should carry this study of the grapefruit to a third statement, as this student has done. Now you'll see more contrasts—which means more color spots—within the light and dark areas of the grapefruit, as well as on the walls and floor of the setup box. Adding more of these contrasts within its form also makes the grapefruit grow rounder. Although this student has found a bit more contrast between the light side of the grapefruit and the light wall behind it, most of that pale contour still remains invisible. I don't know how many color spots appear in this third statement, but I should think there are at least twice as many as the second statement.

Third Statement, Jarvis Wilcox.

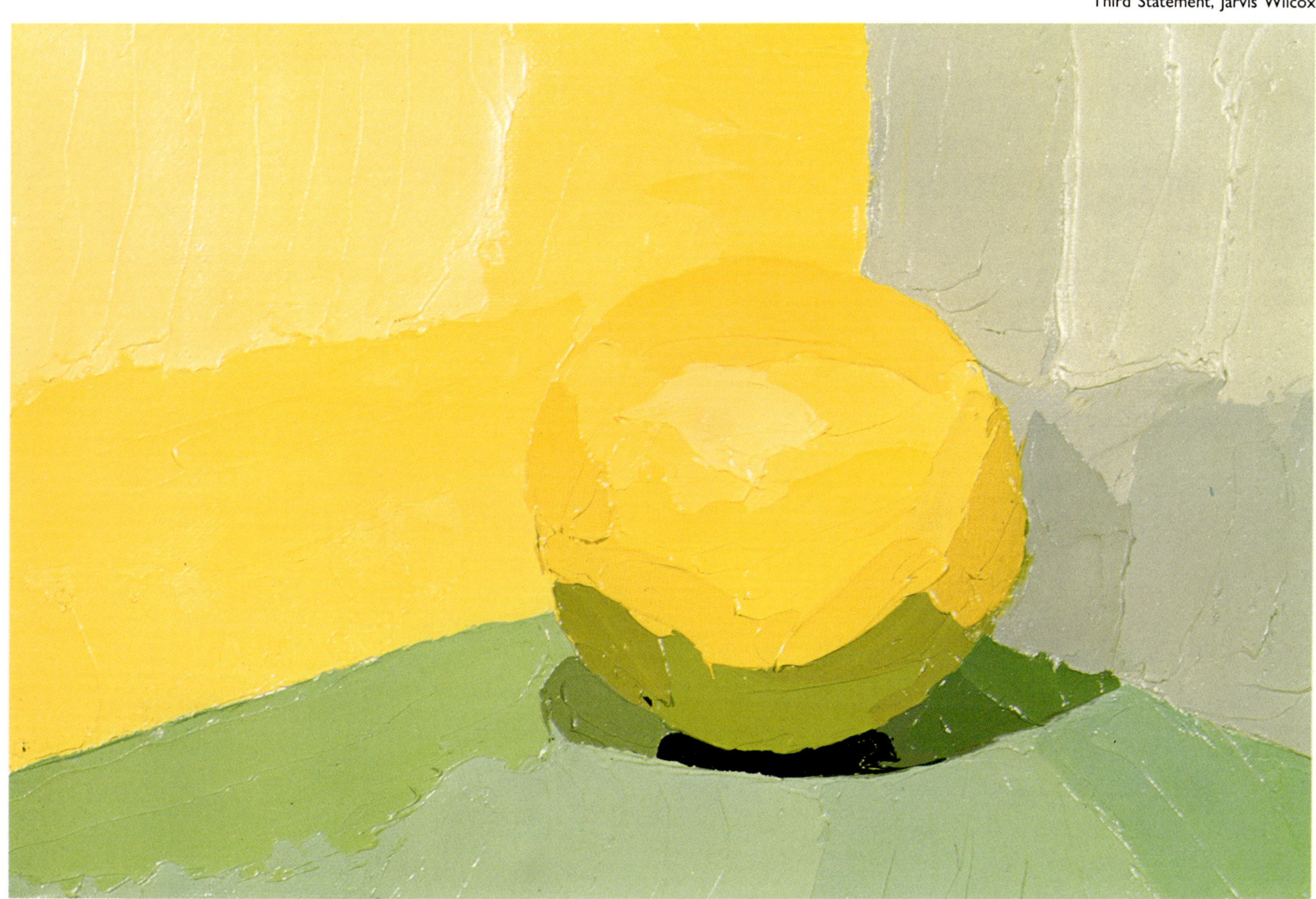

OBSERVATIONS. In this final statement, the grapefruit grows more solid and "real" not because you add any more contrast to its contours, but because you're finding more contrasting color spots *inside* the contours. As you add each new color spot to the grapefruit, the form grows rounder. This grapefruit looks three-dimensional, not because we can follow a complete outer edge, but because of the interaction of the color spots. If the right color spots are in the right places, we can imagine those parts of an object that aren't really visible.

EXTRA PROJECT

Try a similar project with an orange. Line the left wall of the setup box with orange paper, the right wall with violet, and the floor with red. Then put an orange where the grapefruit stood. Do your best to light the setup so that the edge of the orange is partly lost in the background. Then see what you can make of it.

A NEW LIGHT ON SHADOWS

FIRST SETUP. Although I've said that nearly all of these projects will be done indoors within the controlled conditions of the setup box, here's one project that can't be done indoors. Find another orange and get a large sheet of some ordinary white paper that measures about 18″ × 24″ (46 × 61 cm), and wait for a clear, cloudless early morning or late afternoon. Then pose the orange in the center of the sheet of paper, as you see here. Position the orange in relation to yourself and the sun so that the orange casts a big shadow to one side. When you're ready to paint, place yourself far enough above the setup to see the full length and breadth of the shadow. By now, I'm sure you've realized that my photos of the setup—like the one above and also like the other photos you've seen so far—are not something I expect you to duplicate exactly. They're just rough guides to how the setup should look. Everybody's setup will be a bit different, anyway. (If the clear, cloudless day happens to be breezy, find four small stones or other weights to hold down the corners of the paper on which you see the orange.)

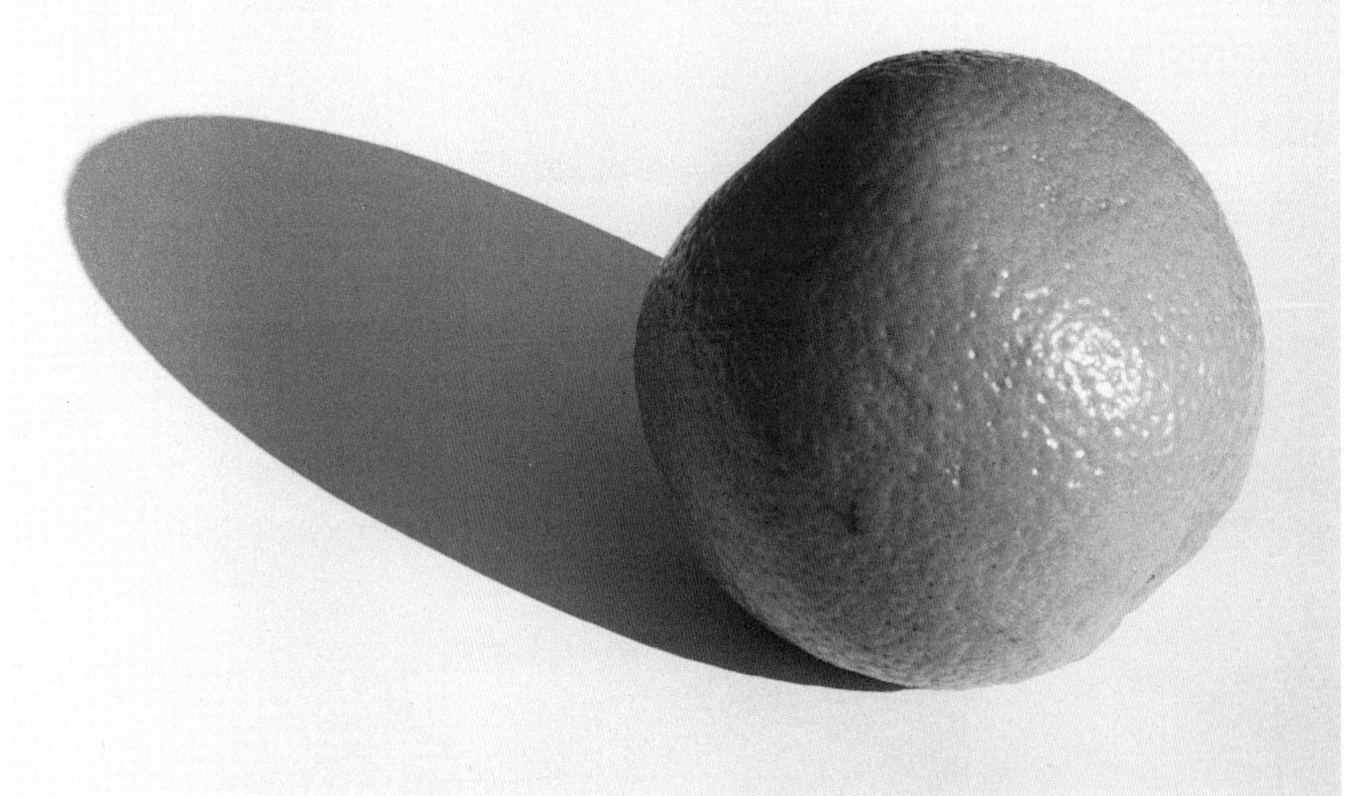

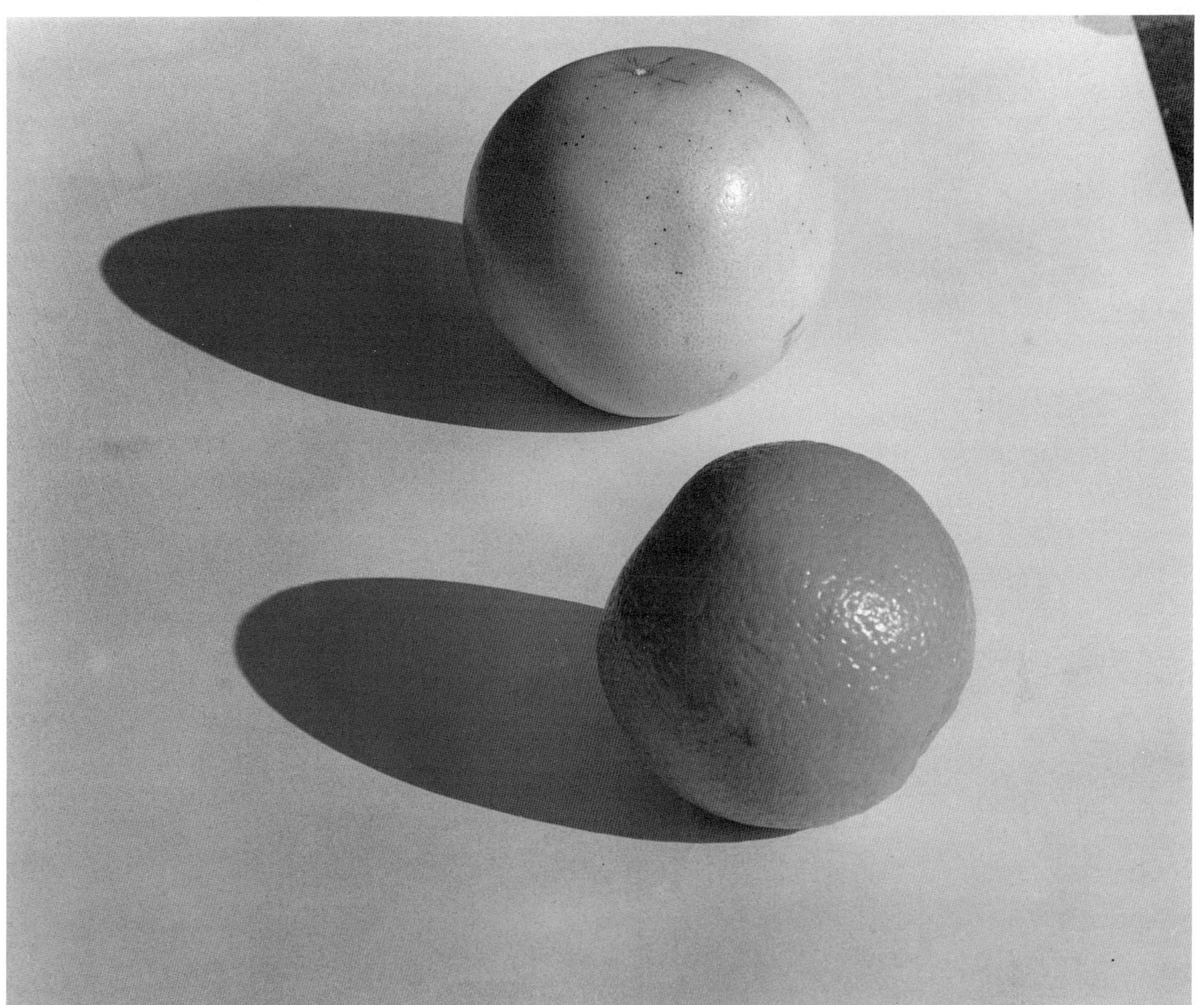

SECOND SETUP. This is really a two-part project. But do both parts at the same time of day, a clear, cloudless early morning or late afternoon. Now place an orange *and* a grapefruit on that large sheet of white paper, again sufficiently below eye level so that you can see the shadow of each fruit very clearly. Place the orange in front of the grapefruit, and keep them far enough apart so that they don't overlap and their shadows don't merge into a single shape. You want to see two separate shapes for the fruit and two separate shapes for their shadows. You'll probably find it necessary to keep the whole setup well below eye level, while you stand above the setup and look down. If the setup is too close to eye level, the shapes of the orange and grapefruit are likely to overlap—which would obscure the project's objective.

EXTRA PROJECTS

Now try two variations of this setup. First, switch the fruits around, with the grapefruit in front and the orange in back. Does this reversal of their positions produce a change in their colors? Paint a first statement and see. Next, try an even more radical change. Replace the sheet of white paper with a black sheet. Can you still see the shadows the fruits cast? What color are they? Don't try making any predictions. Just paint that first statement carefully and you'll find out.

First Statement, Kevin Kennedy.

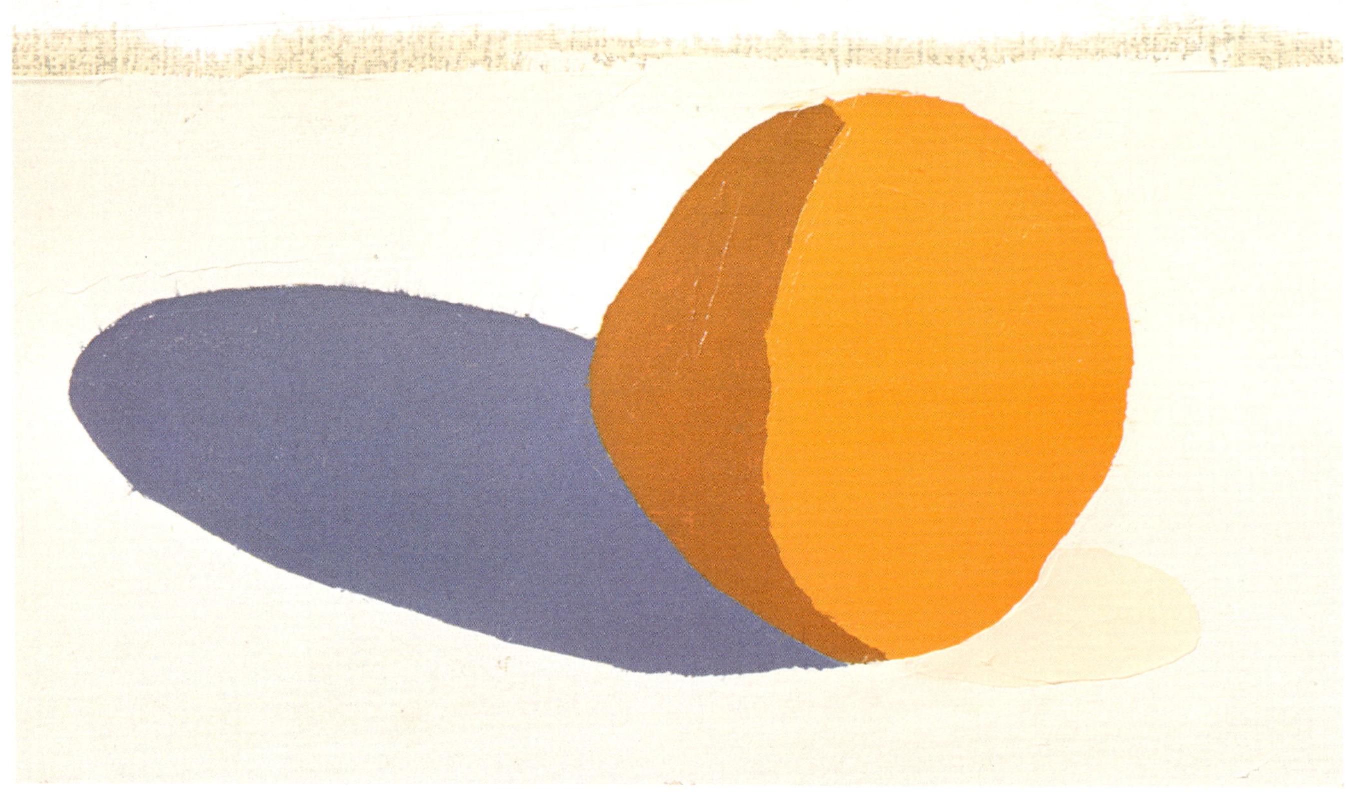

FIRST STATEMENT. Working on a horizontal, half sheet of canvas paper, and using your 2:3 viewfinder, paint a first statement in just five color spots. This five-color-spot statement should fill the lower half of your paper. (For now, leave the upper half blank.) What matters are those five color spots:

1 for the light side of the orange
1 for its dark side
1 for the sheet of paper beneath the orange
1 for the shadow of the orange on the paper
1 one for the reflection of the orange on the paper.

OBSERVATIONS. The primary purpose of this project is to teach you more about cast shadows and reflections—how they behave outdoors compared to how they behave indoors. You've already learned the folly of defining shadow as an absence of light. Certainly, you no longer expect to see shadows as dark and lacking in hue. But perhaps you're still inclined to accept the dictionary definition of shadow as "an area of *comparative* darkness." If you look carefully through your spot screen and paint these five color spots faithfully, you will now see how surprisingly light and "colorful" a shadow can be, especially outdoors. Remember Leonardo's definition of a shadow as "an area illuminated by lesser light." Here, the sun is obviously the greater light, illuminating the light side of the orange and the light area of the paper. But what is the "lesser light" that illuminates the shadow cast by the orange? You can answer that by looking at the hue of the shadow. The "lesser light" is the sky. Another important color spot—that you can see in your outdoor setup and in the color plate—is the reflection that the orange casts on the paper.

FIRST STATEMENT, SECOND SETUP. You'll probably need a full sheet of canvas paper to give you enough room to paint this more spacious composition. Use your 3:4 viewfinder. All I want you to do is paint another first statement, this time with nine color spots. But you cannot simply repeat the color mixtures of the earlier picture of the orange alone, merely introducing new mixtures for the grapefruit. The day is different and so is its light. Use your spot screen to look at each color area as if you've never seen it before (which is true), and mix each color spot faithfully, disregarding whatever you might remember from the previous statement. Yes, most of the colors are apt to be similar if you're working at the same time of day on the same rooftop with the same object. But take nothing for granted. You can be quite wrong. Start this new statement from scratch. Here are the nine color spots.

1 for the light side of the grapefruit
1 for its dark side
1 for the shadow the grapefruit casts on the paper
1 for the grapefruit's reflection on the paper
1 for the light side of the orange
1 for its dark side
1 for the shadow that the orange casts on the paper
1 for the orange's reflection on the paper
1 for the paper beneath the two fruits

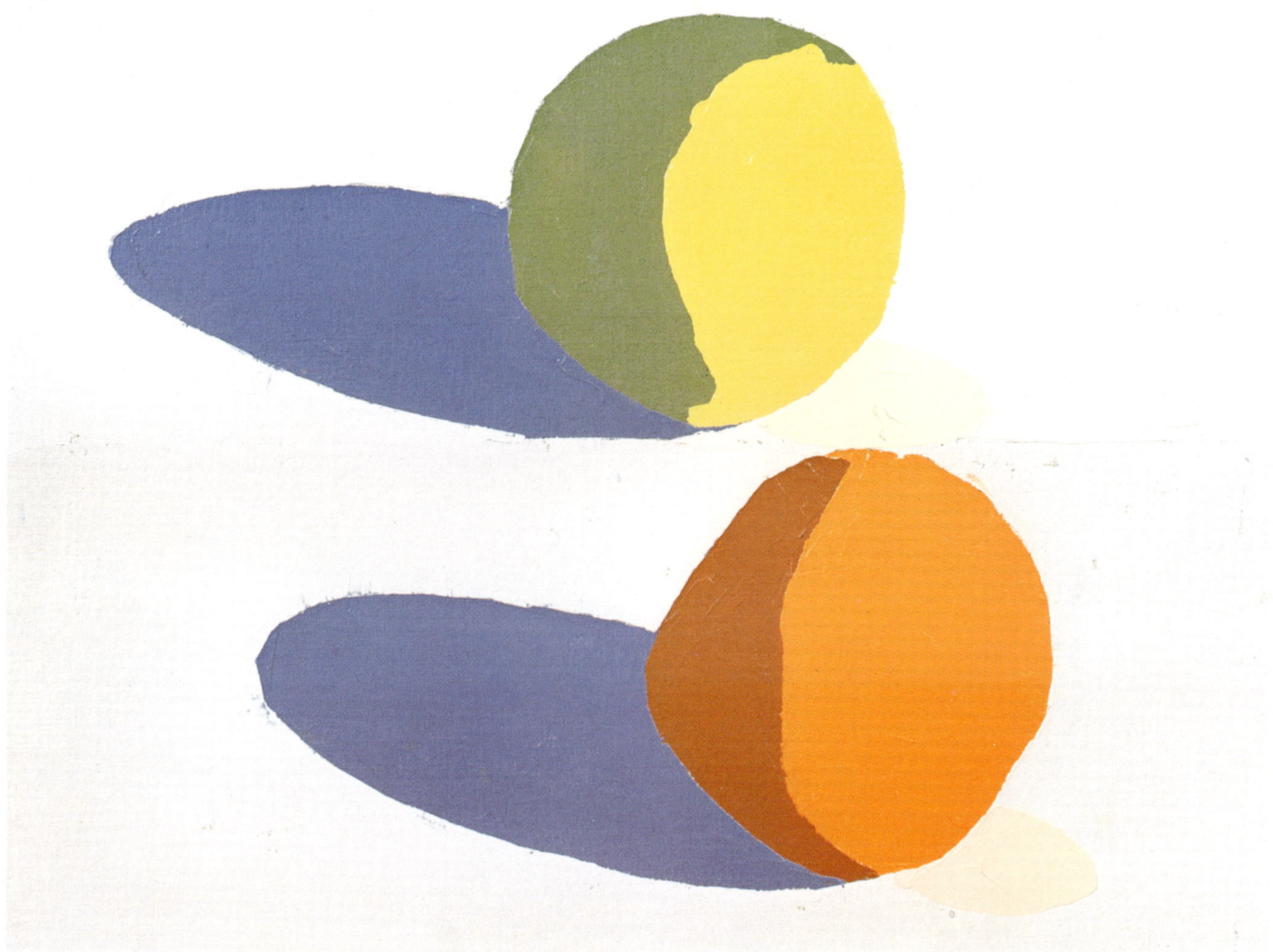

First Statement, Second Setup, Kevin Kennedy.

OBSERVATIONS. Now you're painting two objects in sunlight, each casting its own shadow. The hues of the orange and grapefruit are obviously different, yet the hues of their shadows are similar but not quite the same. When you painted that first statement of the orange outdoors, you discovered that the cast shadow was illuminated by the blue of the sky. Now in this second "first statement", this "lesser light" illuminates *both* cast shadows. The shade sides of the two fruits are different hues, but their cast shadows are similar—though not exactly the same. And both fruits cast their own unique reflections on the paper.

BLACK AND WHITE IN LIGHT AND SHADE

SETUP. Up to this point, each object you've painted has been one solid color. Now you're going to move on to an object whose surfaces display two colors. Make or find a white cardboard box that measures about 3″ × 5″ × 7″ (75 × 125 × 175 mm). Cereals, foods, detergents, and household goods often come in such boxes, although they may not be pure white and they may be the wrong size. It's not hard to cut down such a box and paste white paper over it. Then cut some strips of black paper that will be somewhat smaller than the sides of the box and paste these strips—or panels—onto the white box, leaving white borders, as you see here. Make sure that you leave plenty of white. Now line the left wall of the setup box with yellow paper, the right wall with blue, and the floor with red. With the setup box in

SETUP BOX POSITION 3

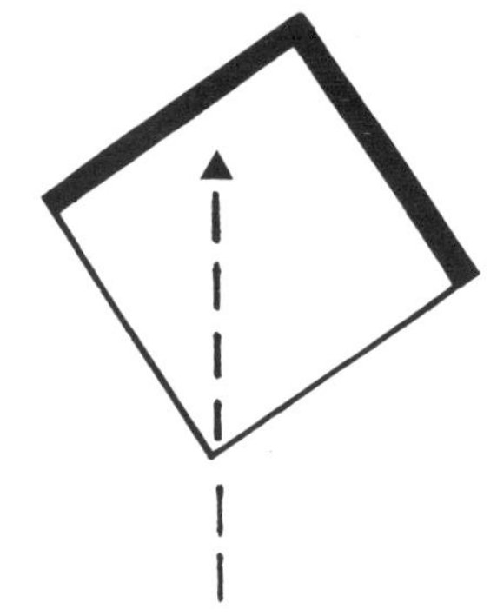

The corner of the setup box is to the right of your line of vision. You can see more of the left wall than the right.

Position 3, pose the paneled box so that its back faces the corner where the two walls of the setup box meet. Your setup lamp should be at the left and quite low, casting a tall shadow on the right wall of the setup box, but no shadow on the left wall. The shadow on the right wall should be almost as tall as the paneled box. The lamp should also be close enough to cast a strong light on the face of the paneled box, but keep direct light off the top and right side of it.

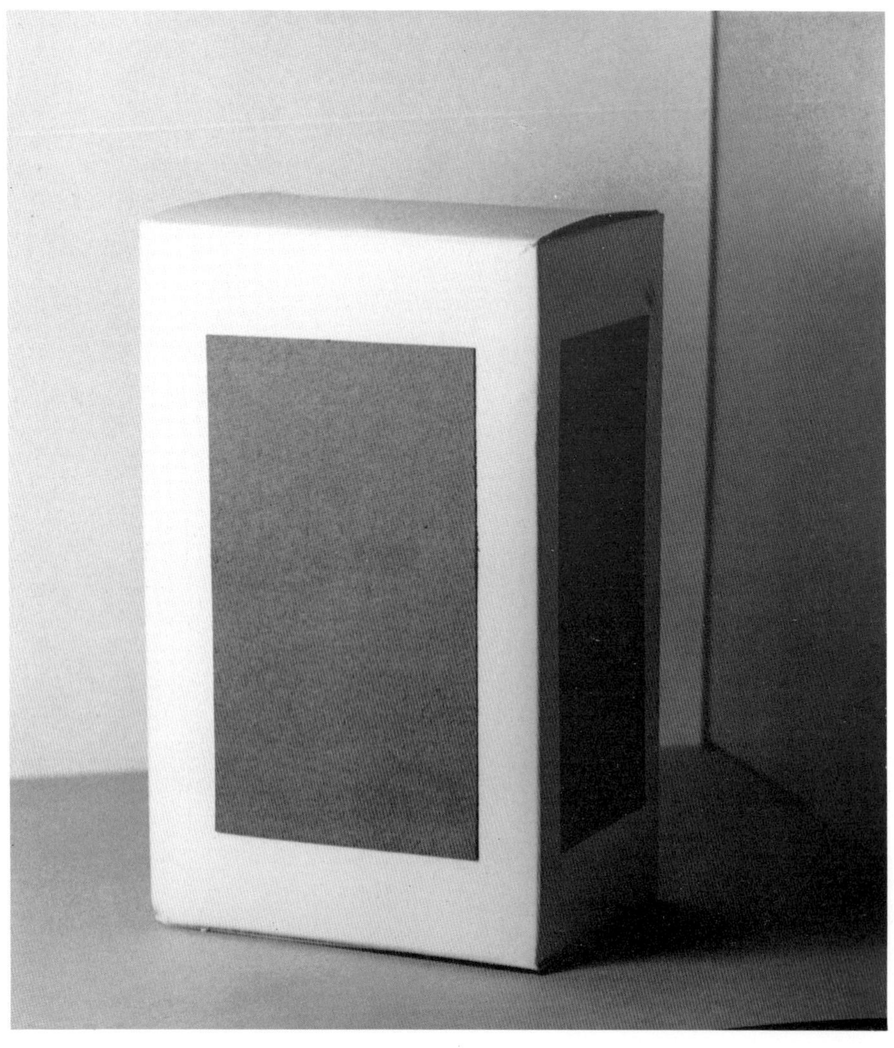

FIRST STATEMENT. Work on a full sheet of canvas paper, held vertically. For this composition, use your 3:4 viewfinder to frame your subject. It should take ten color spots to complete the first statement:

- 1 for the left wall of the setup box
- 1 for the right wall
- 1 for the floor
- 2 for the left face of the paneled box
- 2 for its right face
- 1 for its top
- 1 for the shadow on the floor
- 1 for the shadow on the right wall.

OBSERVATIONS. The point of this project is to call your attention to the unpredictability of the dark and light color spots that compose the box. The "white" top of the box is actually darker than the "black" strip of paper that's pasted on the lighted face of the box. In fact, the "white" top of the box turns out to be almost as dark as the black strip that's pasted on the right side of the box. The black strips pasted on the face and side of the box are the same color outside the setup, but they're certainly not that color under different degrees of light. In short, white can be darker than black, and black can be lighter than white.

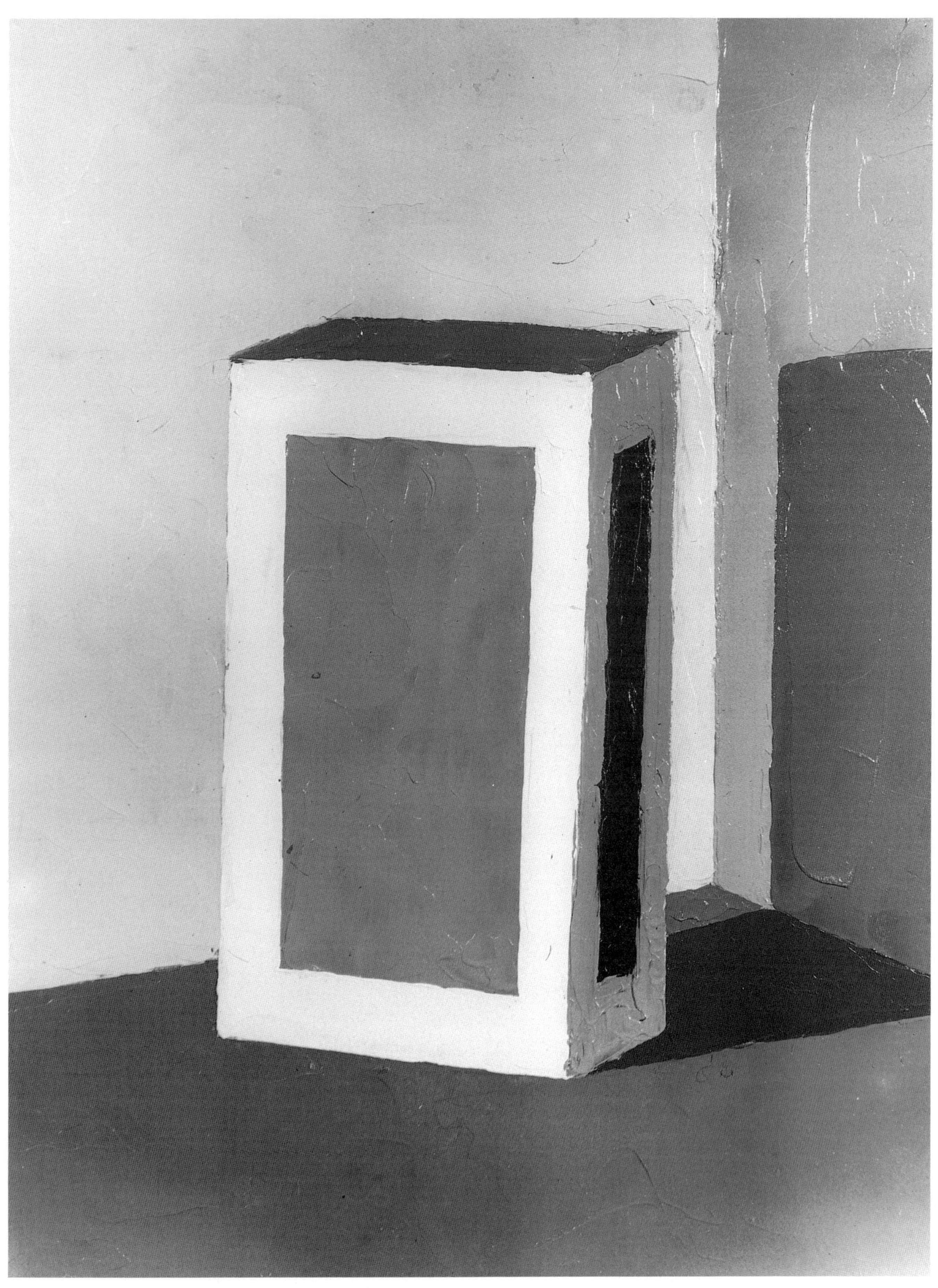

First Statement, Alfred Tyrol.

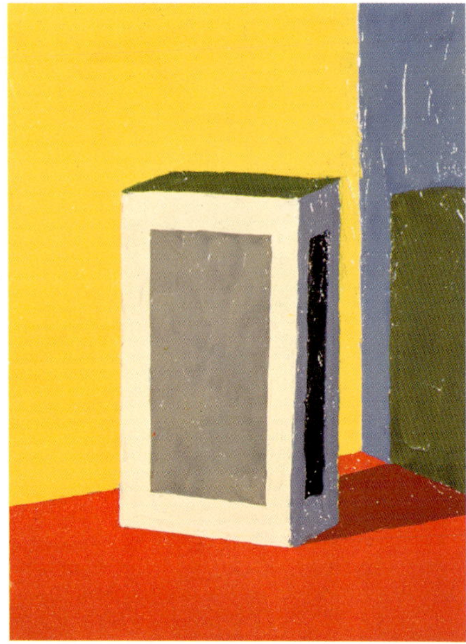

Second Statement, Alfred Tyrol.

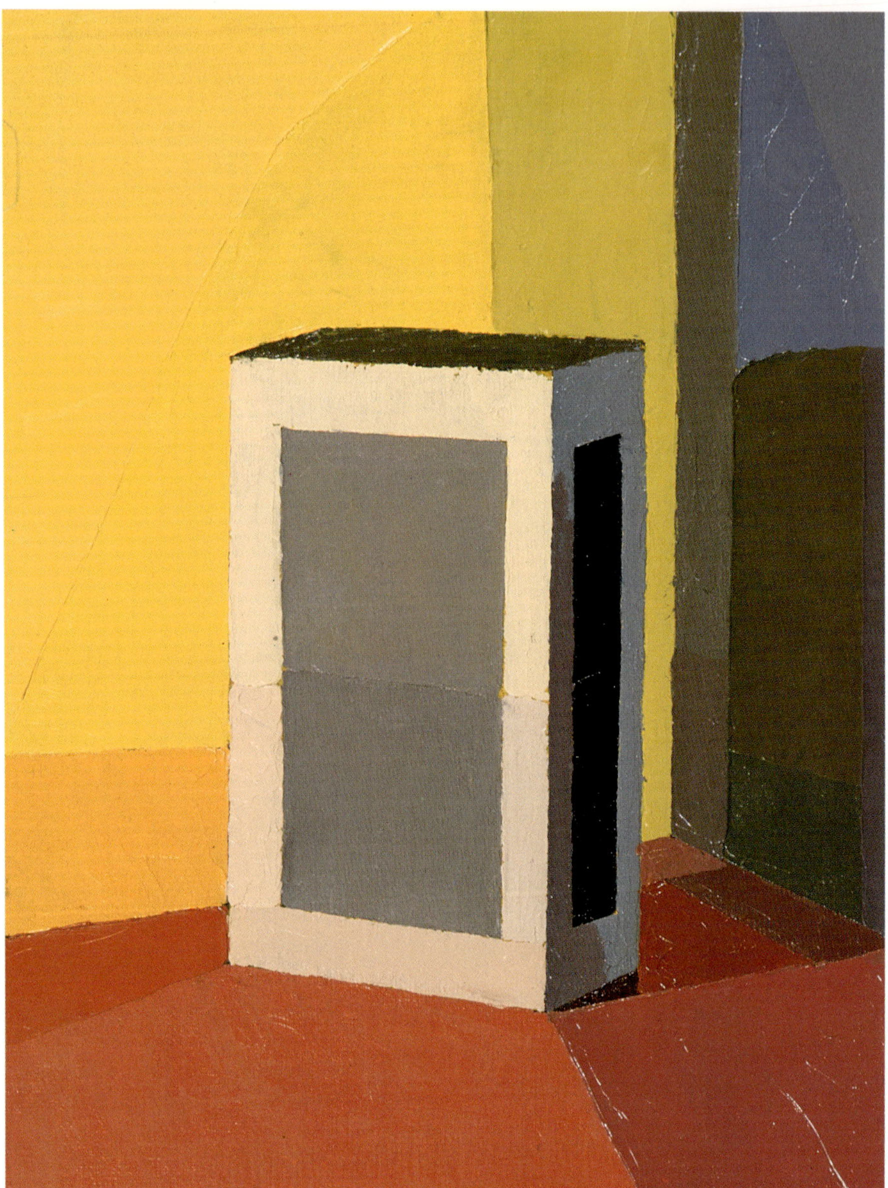

SECOND STATEMENT. Now go back and look for the subtle color changes within your first big color spots. Working on one color spot at a time, scrape out and repaint the study—or simply overpaint it if the first statement has dried. You'll now produce a second statement that should contain somewhere between two dozen and three dozen color spots, yet will still be a highly simplified version of the subject. Don't look this early for every subtle shift in color, but for the big changes, like the shifts from dark to light on the face of the paneled box. Just represent those shifts by dividing the face into a few big, rectangular color spots. Look for those same shifts throughout the subject and represent these color variations with big, flat shapes. Look for the following color spots:

- 4 for the left wall of the setup box
- 4 for its right wall
- 4 for its floor
- 4–6 for the left face of the paneled box
- 4–6 for its right face
- 1–2 for the top
- 2–3 for the shadow on the floor
- 2–3 for the shadow on the right wall

OBSERVATIONS. As you continue to explore this subject, identifying color spots through your spot screen and carefully mixing them on your palette, you are rapidly discovering how much color exists within what people normally call black and white. You see how much the colors of the box depart from the black and white they're supposed to be. Nonetheless, the viewer of your study still *reads* them as black and white.

Third Statement, Alfred Tyrol.

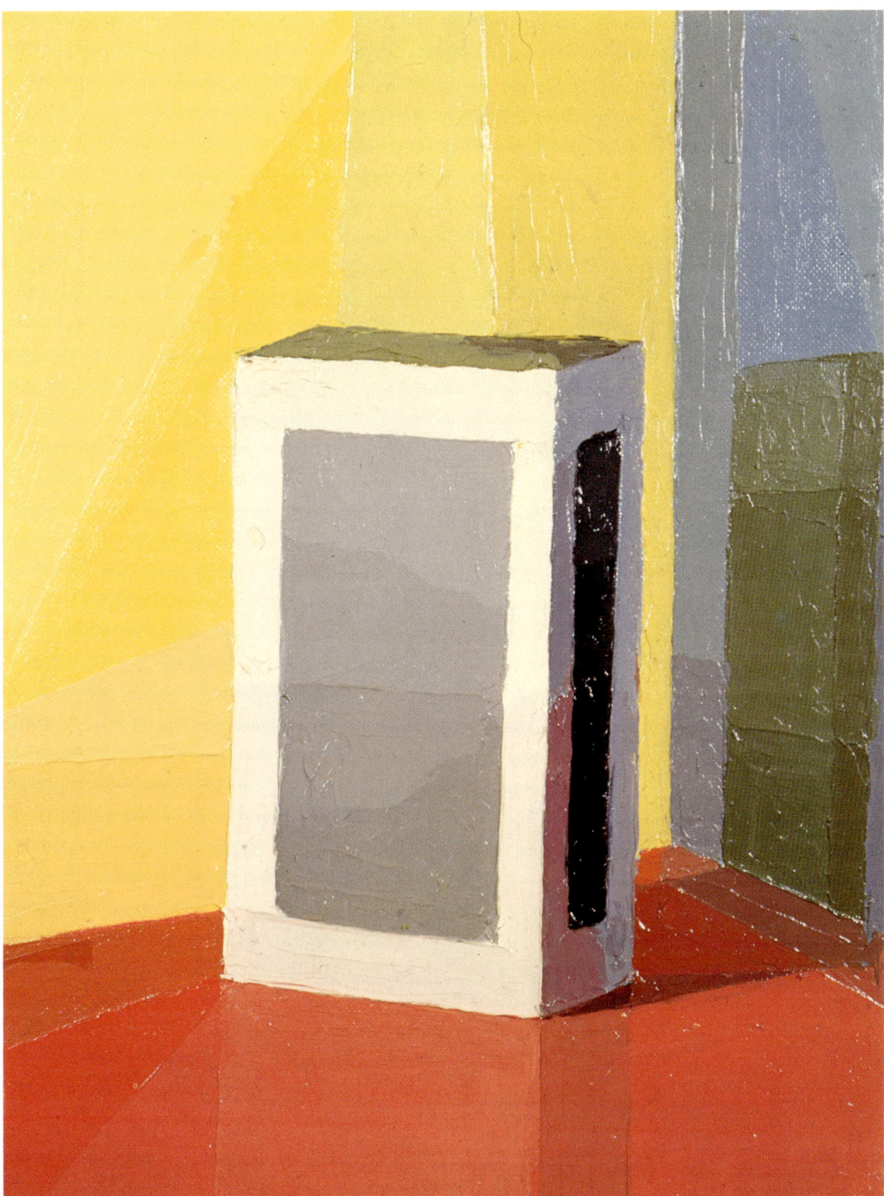

THIRD STATEMENT. When you work on the third statement, remember that this final statement has two distinct functions. First, you're reexamining all the color areas of the second statement and further subdividing the spots into smaller and more subtle spots—discovering new transitional spots within and between the color mixtures that you observed and recorded in the first and second statements. Second, you're reviewing every square inch of your picture to correct the second statement. But even at this final stage, don't strive for complexity for its own sake. Although the color spots will multiply, keep your study as simple as you can, and continue to strive for the fewest and biggest color spots that do the job. Paint only the color spots you really see. Remember these three words as you look through the spot screen at your model: keep your color spots *few, large*, and *simple*.

OBSERVATIONS. In Projects 1 and 2, you painted white and black subjects separately. Each subject was illuminated in its own way. Now you're painting a single subject that's both black and white—and both colors are subjected to the same lighting conditions. Now you'll see how these two colors respond when they're placed side-by-side—that is, how they're literally transformed by their environment—by direct or indirect and reflected light—by greater and lesser light.

EXTRA PROJECT

Having painted a rectangular box, try to find a cylindrical one. Cover it with white paint if it's not white already. Then paint circular stripes around it with 1" (25 mm) bands of contrasting colors, such as red, white, and green; or orange, white and blue. Line the setup box with whatever bright colors you prefer. Light the model from the side, like the paneled box in this project. Paint three statements, and see how the stripes are transformed as they move around the cylinder from light into darkness.

LIGHT AND SHADE ARE COLORS

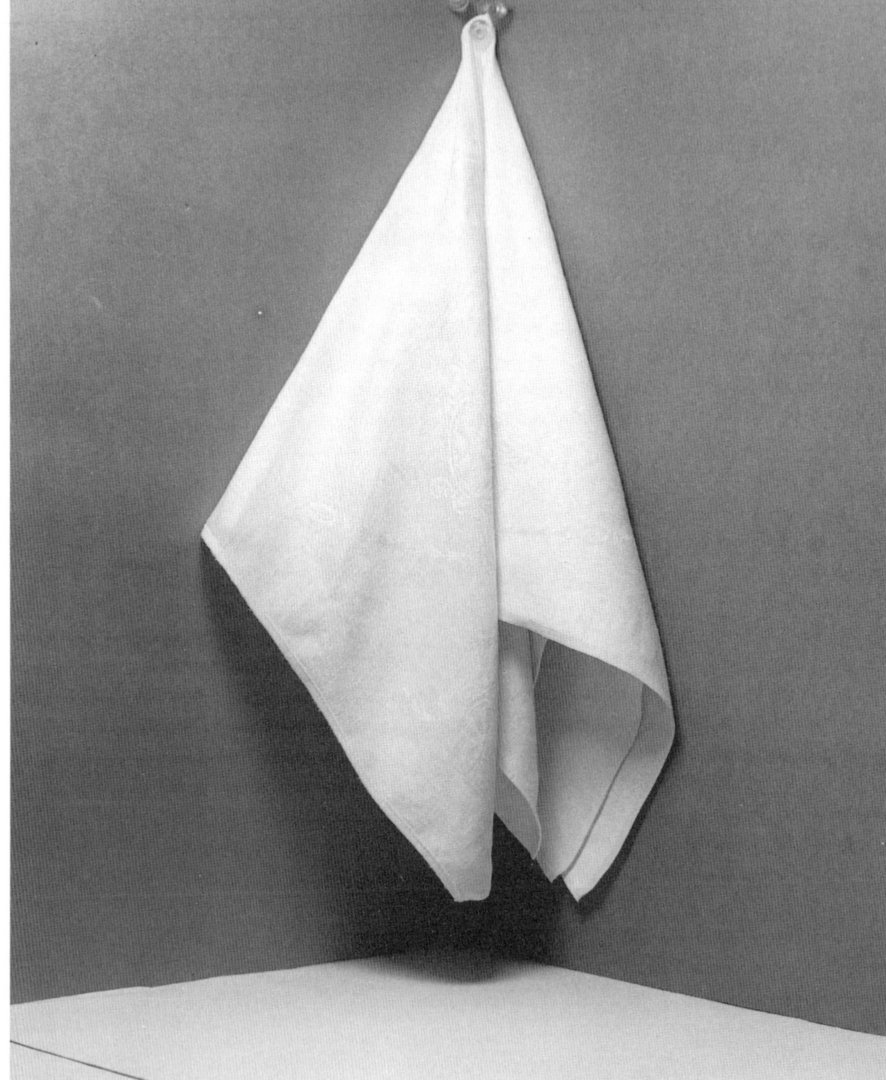

SETUP. Your first project was to paint a first statement of a white object. Now you're going to paint a series of three statements of a more complex white object. Find a heavy, white cloth napkin. Nowadays they're not easily come by, but grandmothers often have them tucked away. (You can also try to beg, borrow, or buy one from a restaurant.) Launder the napkin by hand, iron it, but don't fold or crease it.

Line the left wall of the setup box with red paper, the right wall with blue, and the floor with yellow. With the box in Position 2, pin the center of the napkin at the corner of the setup box where the left and right walls meet—high enough for the four corners of the napkin to fall just short of the setup box floor. Allowing some of the underside of the napkin to show, drape the cloth in a few big folds. Arrange the setup lamp above the napkin, just enough to one side to create areas of light and shade on the folds. The lamp should be close enough for the light to fall directly on the walls and floor of the setup box, to form a strong shadow within the napkin's underside, and to fill the setup box corner with shadow.

SETUP BOX POSITION 2

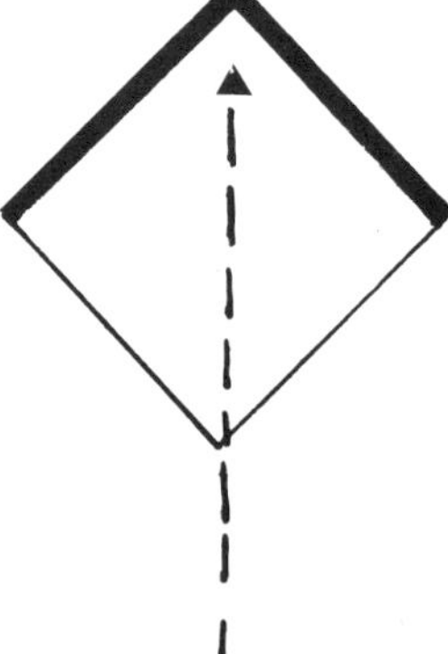

The corner of the setup box is directly in line with your eye; you see both walls equally. The corner of the box should be in the dead center of your picture, although the napkin actually covers the line where the walls meet.

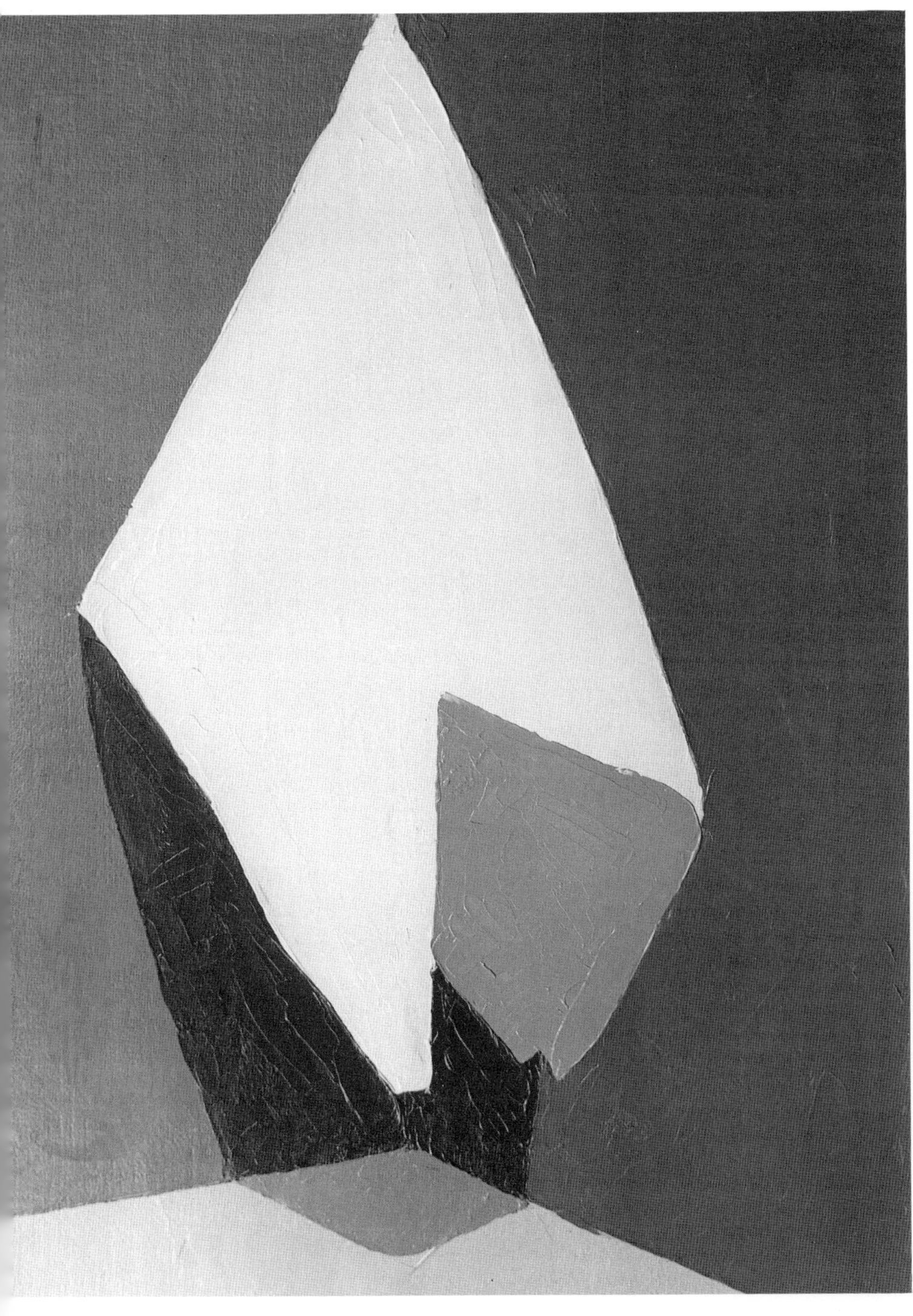

FIRST STATEMENT. This project will need a full sheet of canvas paper, held vertically. Use your 3:4 viewfinder to compose the picture. As you scan the napkin with your spot screen, remember that the purpose of a first statement is to summarize the subject by painting the minimum number of large color spots. So don't get caught up in all the small shapes within the shadow area at the bottom of the folded napkin. Try to visualize that area of shadow as a single spot. Ignore the hints of shadow within the large lighted area of the napkin. Paint that big area as a single light color spot. You should be able to summarize the main color areas in eight color spots:

2 for the walls of the setup box
1 for its floor
1 for the lighted area of the napkin
1 for its dark area
2 for the shadows on the walls
1 for the shadow on the floor

OBSERVATIONS. The first thing that should be evident is that each of the four elements in the setup—the napkin and the three planes of the setup box—divides into two areas: one of light and one of shade. And it's rewarding to compare each element's light part with its shade part. This comparison reveals that light and shade are not simply variations of a single color, but rather two separate colors. So what you cannot do is predict that the shadow on the red wall will be a darker red, the shadow on the blue wall a darker blue, the shadow on the yellow floor a darker yellow, or the shaded area of the napkin a darker white—whatever that might be! Nor is the napkin likely to be white at all! Your spot screen will certainly reveal that it's an off-white of some kind—which is to say a very light version of one hue or another.

First Statement, Alfred Tyrol.

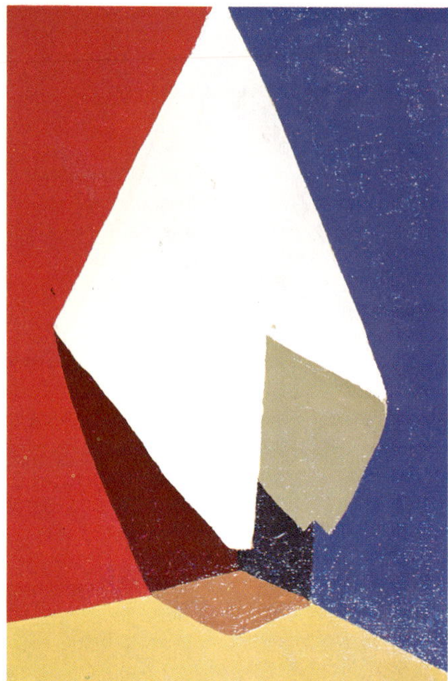

Second Statement, Alfred Tyrol.

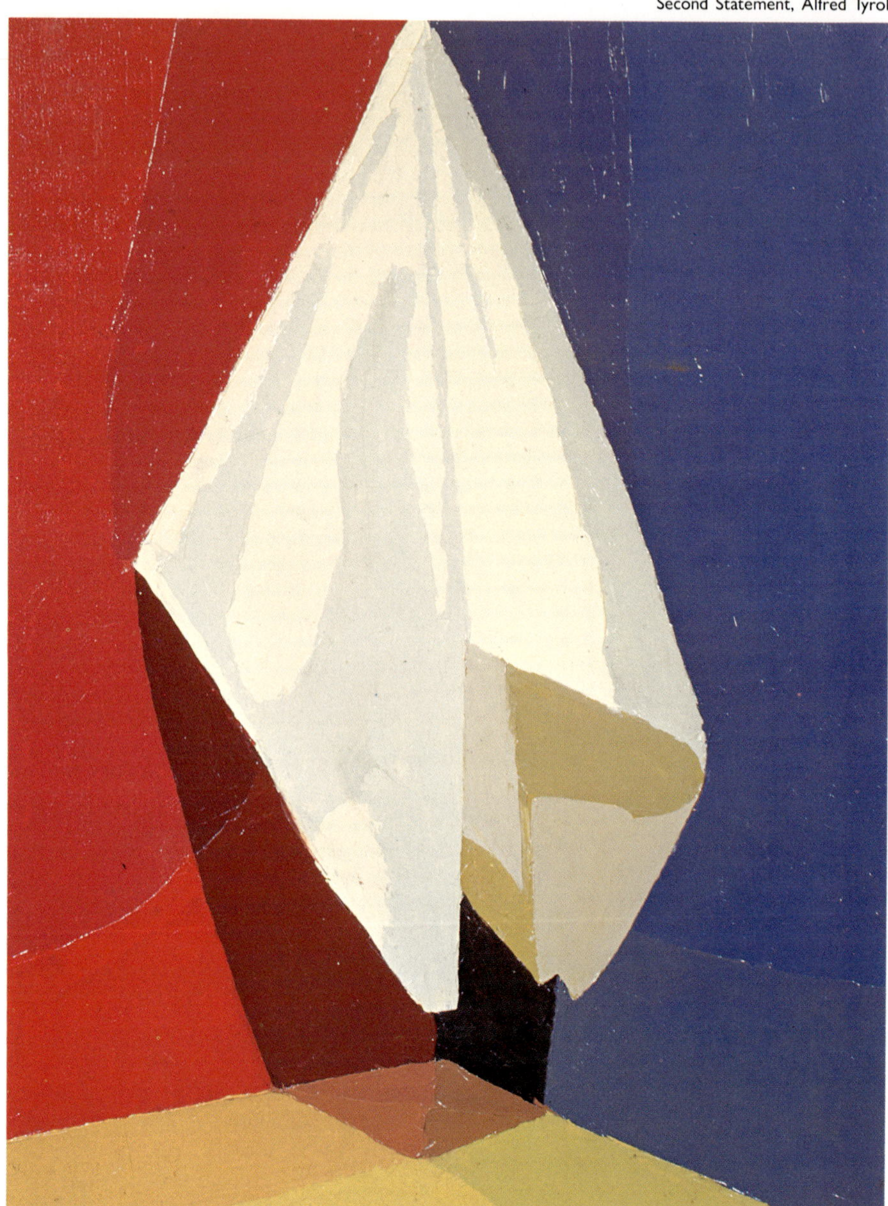

SECOND STATEMENT. Working on this same sheet of canvas paper, move on to a second statement. Now you should begin to look for some of the slightly darker areas within the lighted shapes of the napkin, walls, and floor of the setup box. You also should begin to discover some variations within the small shaded area of the napkin, as well as within the cast shadows on the walls and floor of the box. I won't try to guess how many color spots you're going to find in this second statement, but it's likely to be about two dozen. The color spots in your second statement will probably be organized something like this:

- 3 for the light area of the left wall
- 2 for the napkin's shadow on the left wall
- 3 for the light area of the right wall
- 2 for the napkin's shadow on the right wall
- 3 for the light area of the floor
- 4 for the napkin's shadow on the floor
- 4 for the light area of the napkin
- 4 for the dark underside of the napkin.

OBSERVATIONS. Go back and examine the completed second statement. Try to sort out the logic and those various color spots. For example, examine the walls of the setup box and try to identify which color spots are influenced by the adjacent wall, or by the floor, and both the wall and floor. Other areas are influenced by neither the walls nor the floor but by the direct light. As you go on with the projects in this book, you'll begin to predict which color areas will influence one another. But don't try to predict the specific colors. You *must* do this by observation alone.

Third Statement, Alfred Tyrol.

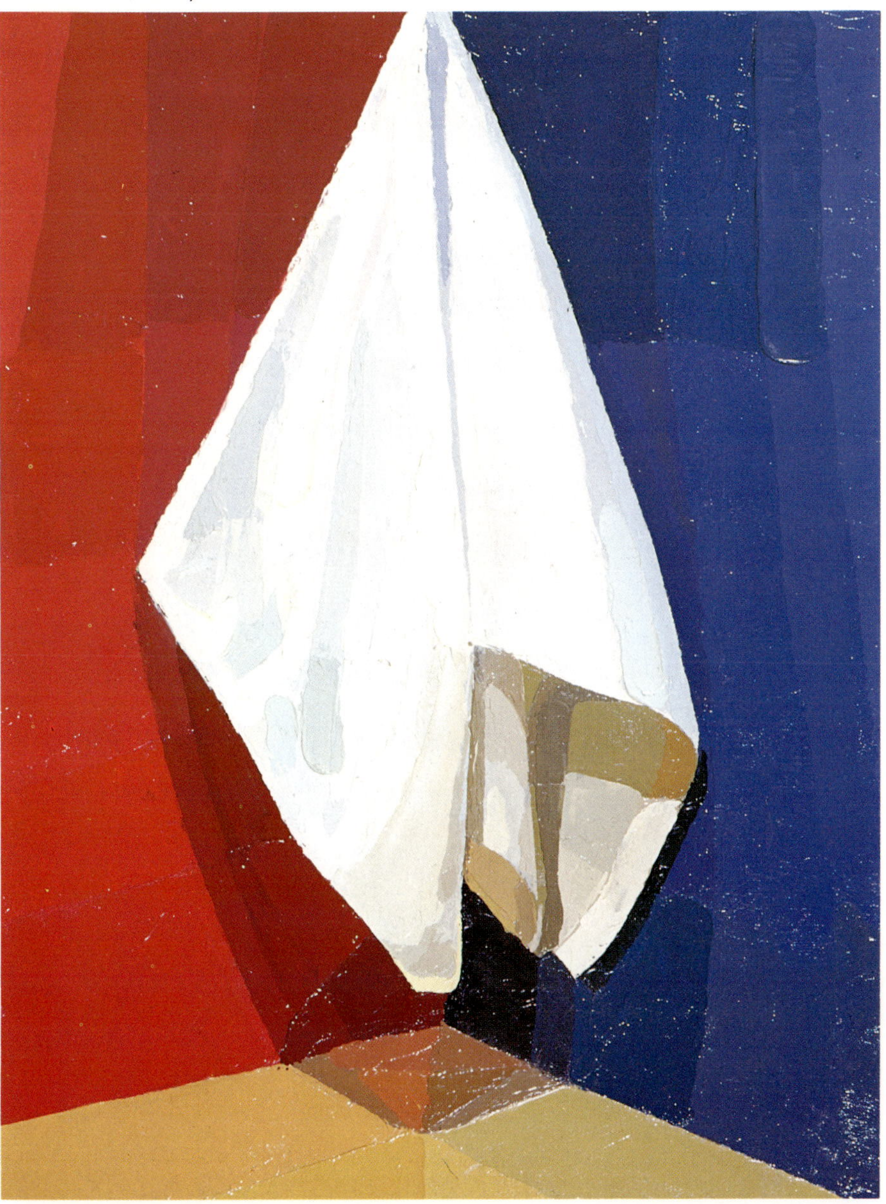

THIRD STATEMENT. There are still more color spots to be discovered on the walls and floor of the setup box—and, of course, on the napkin—and you'll have to decide how far to take your third and final statement of these three planes. It is also fascinating here to explore all the very subtle transitional color spots within the supposedly white napkin. Many of these color spots are so easily buried under the blanketing effect of the color you *know* the napkin to be! You can find them only with the aid of the spot screen. But if you observe and record these very quiet color spots correctly, the napkin will look more three-dimensional at this final stage of the project than it did in your first and second statements.

OBSERVATIONS. Without consciously attempting to render the pattern of light and shade on the napkin, but by simply recording each color spot you've seen, you'll produce a solid and realistic rendering of the soft folds and curving planes of the cloth. You'll also abandon, once and for all, any notion that light and shade are simply lighter and darker versions of a single hue. When in Project 5 you saw light fall on one side of an orange and shade fall on the other—the light side was not just lighter orange or the shade side just darker orange. They were totally different colors.

EXTRA PROJECT

Take down the white napkin and tack up another piece of cloth that's roughly the same size, but a different color. Keep the lighting and the setup box position the same. Paint three statements, revealing how the colors of the setup box influence the new subject, and how its color influences the planes of the box.

SPACE INFLUENCES COLOR

SETUP. Buy half-a-dozen oranges that are evenly colored—with no patches of green or yellow—and as alike as possible. Line the floor and left wall of the setup box with white paper, and then line the right wall with pale gray. You should see only the white wall and white floor, not the gray wall. Your setup light should be at the left, low enough to cast good-sized shadows on the floor of the setup box. As in the photograph, arrange one pair of oranges so that they actually touch, and arrange another pair so that one orange overlaps the other. If some of your oranges do have green or yellow areas, turn them so that those areas face away from you and out of sight. By the way, you might also forget the setup box for this project, and spread your oranges on a white cloth-covered tabletop placed against a white wall. Whether you arrange the oranges in the setup box or on a white tabletop, the important thing is to make sure that they aren't surrounded by anything that can influence their color. You'll soon see why.

SETUP BOX POSITION 5

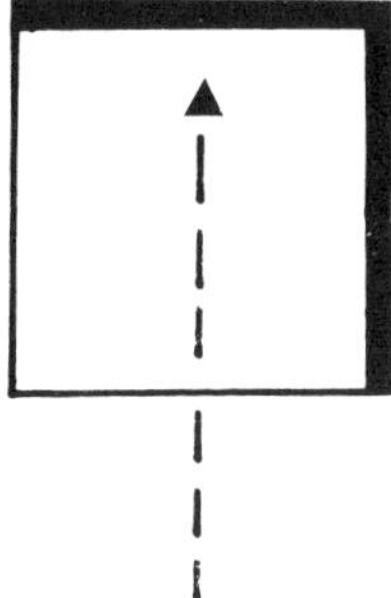

The left wall is perpendicular to your line of vision, while the right wall is parallel to your line of vision. You're looking straight at the left wall and not seeing the right.

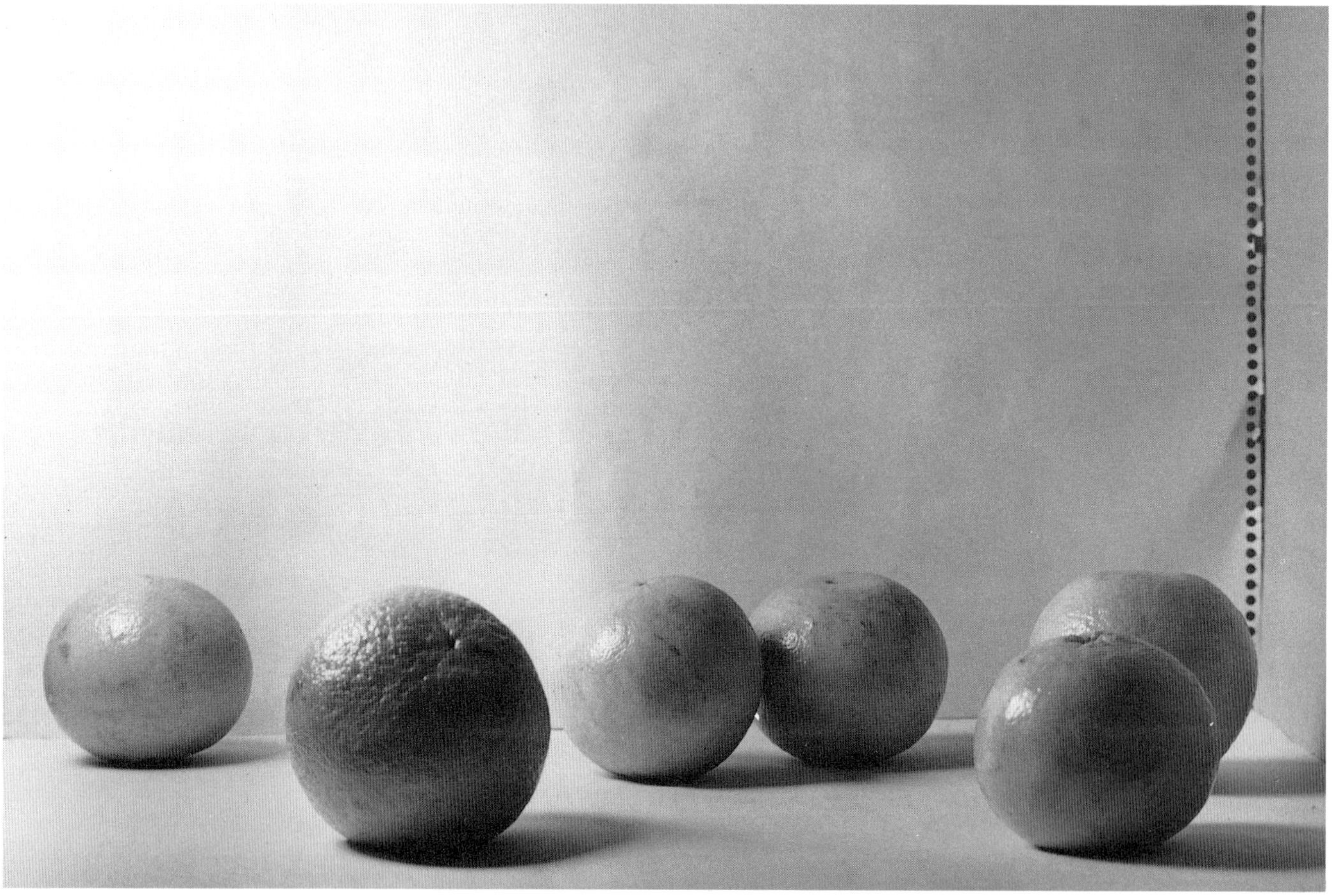

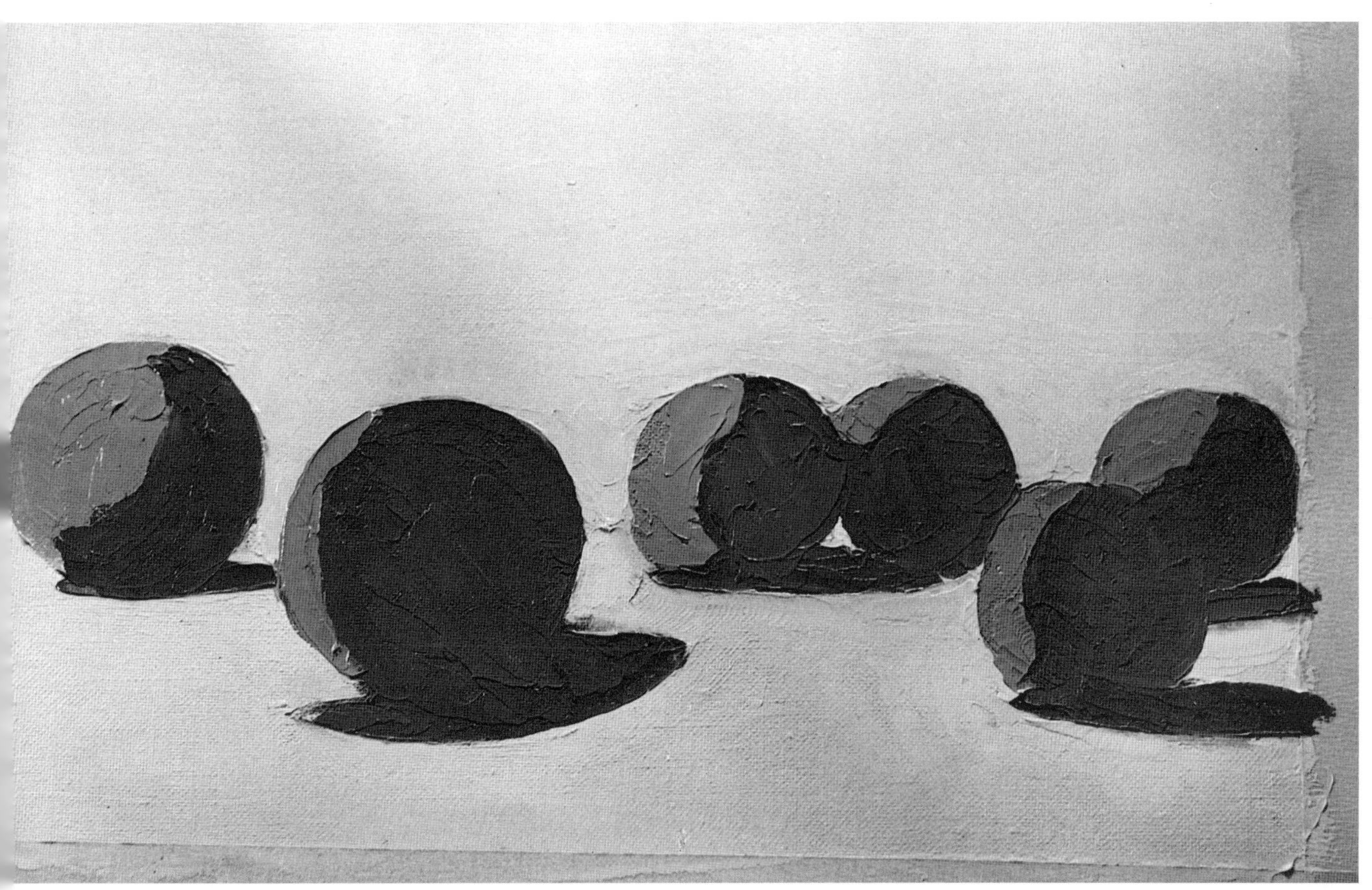

FIRST STATEMENT. This is a fairly spacious composition, so be sure to work on a full sheet of canvas paper. Use your 3:4 viewfinder to compose your picture. You should be able to summarize what you see in just four colors. Use your spot screen to identify the color of the light side of one of the central oranges, and then use this color for the light sides of *all* the oranges. In the same way, use your spot screen to identify the color of the dark side of one of the central oranges, and use that color on the shade sides of all six. Your other two colors will be the color of the horizontal plane on which the oranges rest, and the color of the background wall. That's a total of four colors to be laid down:

1 color for the light sides of the oranges
1 color for their dark sides and cast shadows
1 color for the setup box floor
1 color for the back wall.

OBSERVATIONS. Pick up some of the color you've mixed for the light sides of the oranges. Looking through your spot screen, compare the color on the knife with the light sides of all six oranges. By now you ought not be surprised to discover that all those light sides are different; the color on the knife matches only whichever central orange you looked at when you mixed the color. Now look at the dark color that you mixed to paint the shade sides of the oranges and their cast shadows—and make the same comparisons. The colors of the shade sides and shadows are all different too. This color matches only the dark side of the *one* orange you looked at when you were mixing this dark hue. What accounts for all this variation? It doesn't seem to have much to do with the influence of the white wall and floor. The strongest factor seems to be the distance of the oranges from the light source and from each other. Those closer to the light are apt to be lighter, while those further away are apt to be darker. Another factor seems to be the influence of the oranges on one another.

First Statement, Alfred Tyrol.

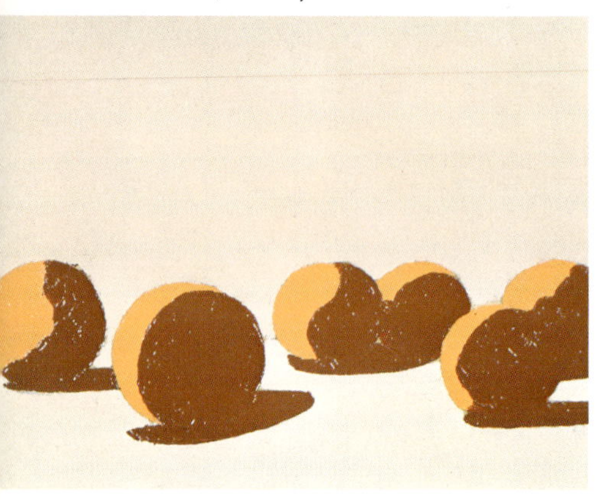

SECOND STATEMENT. When you carry this project forward to its second statement, keep in mind what you've already learned from painting that first statement. The light and dark sides of each orange will show themselves to be different from those of the other five. Identify and mix each of these colors with your spot screen. In the first statement, you used the same color to mix the dark side of each orange and its cast shadow; now look for the difference in color between the dark side of each of the oranges and its shadow on the tabletop or setup box floor. Finally, try to separate the supposedly white floor and wall of the setup box into several big color spots that catch the variations in hue, luminosity, and intensity as each plane moves farther away from the source of direct light. You'll probably need about two dozen color spots for this second statement:

6 for the light sides of the oranges
6 for their dark sides
6 for the cast shadows
6–8 for the floor and wall of the setup box.

Second Statement, Alfred Tyrol. [A color plate of this step is often unavailable because the student worked directly over the second statement to obtain the third statement—Ed.]

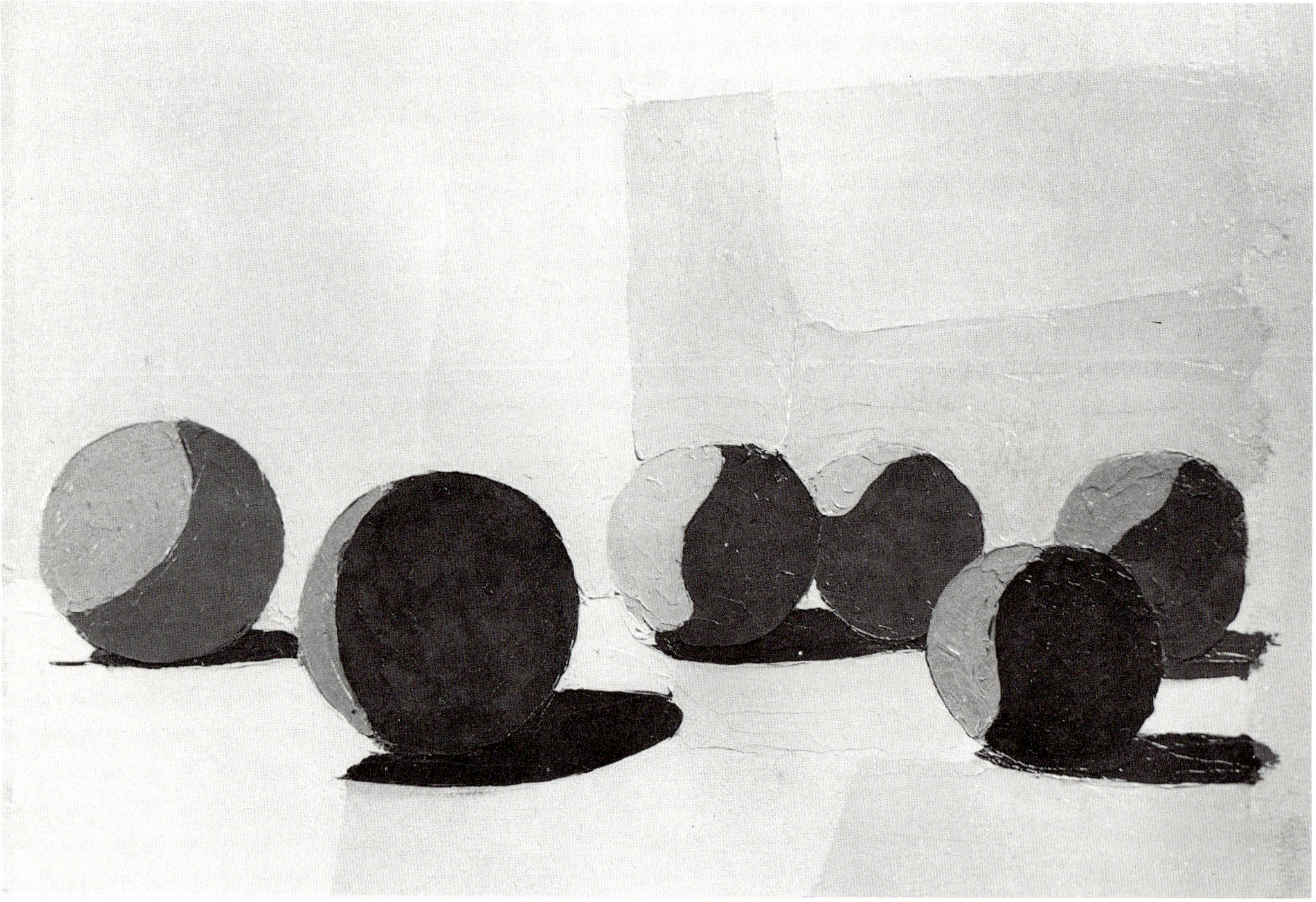

OBSERVATIONS. Simply by looking at each orange as a unique trio of color spots—light side, dark side, and cast shadow—you'll give some individual character to each orange. Each piece of fruit will become clearly different from all the others. Now it should be obvious to you that even a slight change in the location of any object produces significant changes in hue, luminosity, and intensity—changes that are equally important in the light side, dark side, and cast shadow of that object. So you cannot just mix three batches of color and apply them mechanically to all the oranges (or apples or pears—or trees or houses—or people) that stand before you.

THIRD STATEMENT. But you still have not done full justice to the richness and complexity of these six models. Your second statement is still little more than an elaborate first statement. So now you must go on to paint a third statement, paying equal attention to the color variations within the lighted sides of the six oranges, the transitional colors that fall between the light and dark sides, and the "lesser lights" reflected in the dark sides and the cast shadows. There can be no predetermined limit to the number of color spots required by such a third statement, but the student who painted this picture has found as many as a dozen color spots in each of several of the oranges. And there are still more color spots to be found in the wall and floor of the setup box, revealing the subtle gradation of the light.

Third Statement, Alfred Tyrol, Collection of Horace Lilholt.

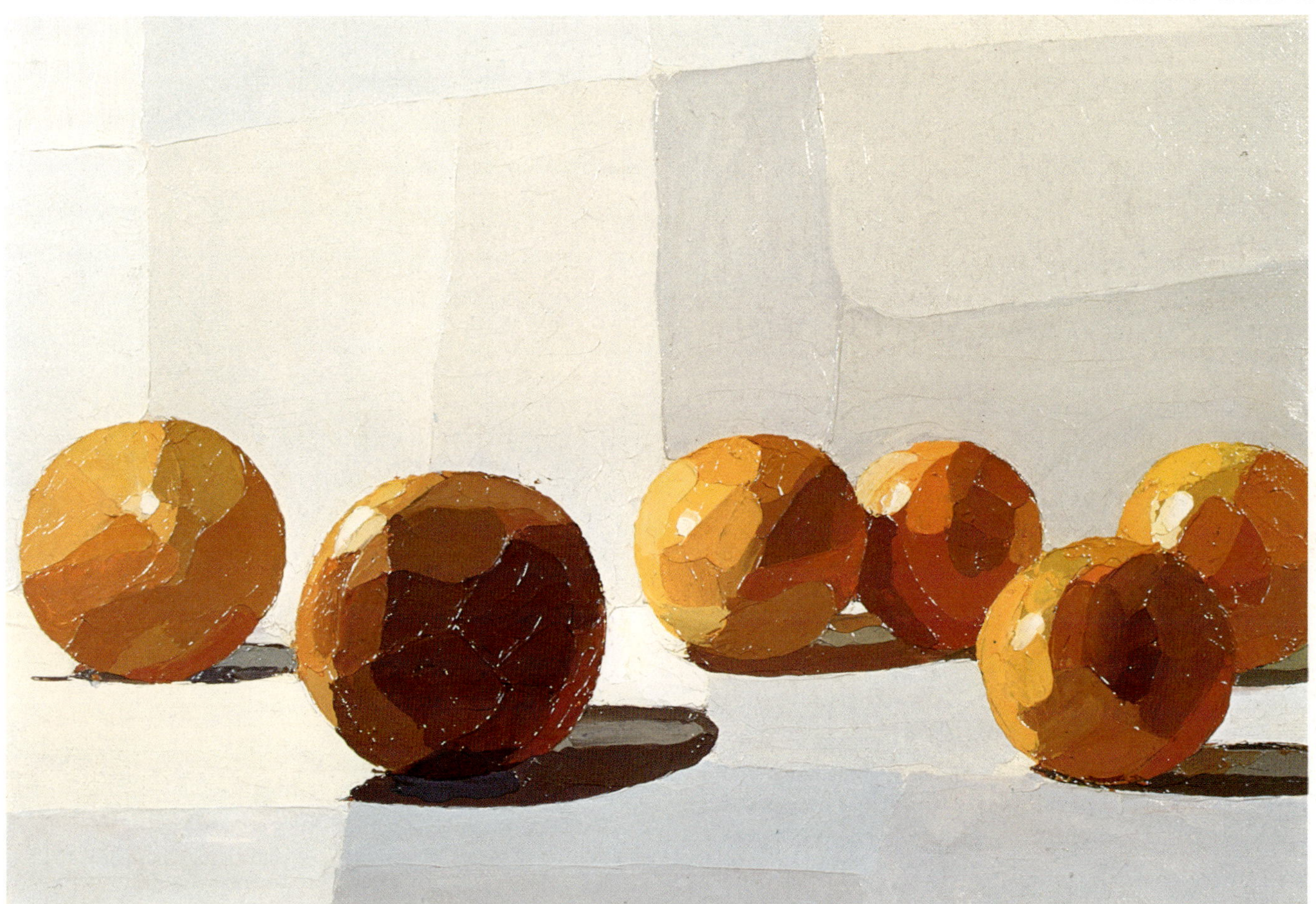

OBSERVATIONS. When I first spoke about the function of the third statement, I mentioned *transitional* colors. These are the color spots that fall between the bold, purposely oversimplified color spots that you identify in the first and second statements. As you paint these transitional color spots, you no longer see too strong a contrast between the light and dark sides of the oranges. Instead, you see a logical progression of hue, intensity, and luminosity as your eye moves around each form. It's this progression of colors that creates the illusion of three-dimensionality that you begin to see at this stage. In painting this final statement, save the highlights for last. Don't be tempted to paint them pure white, however bright they may look. Like everything else, even each highlight has its own color. Look at each highlight separately and with extreme care, and match its color.

EXTRA PROJECT

Pick up the oranges and cover the floor and left wall of the setup box with blue paper, leaving the gray paper on the right wall. Or cover the tabletop with blue. Then replace the oranges in their same positions, keeping the lamp where it was, and start again, painting your first, second, and third statements. Now observe how the new background color influences the oranges.

METAL IS NO MYSTERY

SETUP. Students often think that metal is especially hard to paint because "metallic" color is supposed to be different, somehow, from all other colors. This project should rid you of that notion. The model is an aluminum saucepan—clean, but not new, so it doesn't have a glassy shine. Line the setup box with red paper on the left wall, blue paper on the right, and yellow on the floor. Then pose the saucepan in profile, with its handle pointing toward your right, and the body of the pan concealing the corner of the setup box. Make sure that the setup is sufficiently below eye level so that you can see down into the pan. The setup lamp should be above and somewhat to the left, so that the cast shadow of the saucepan's handle extends slightly further to the right than the handle itself. But that cast shadow should remain entirely on the yellow floor of the box.

SETUP BOX POSITION I

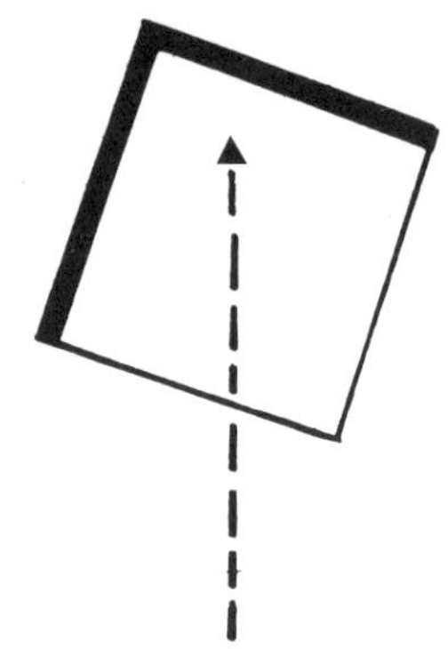

The corner of the setup box, where the walls meet, is to the left of your line of vision. You see more of the right wall than the left. You should see a fair amount of the floor.

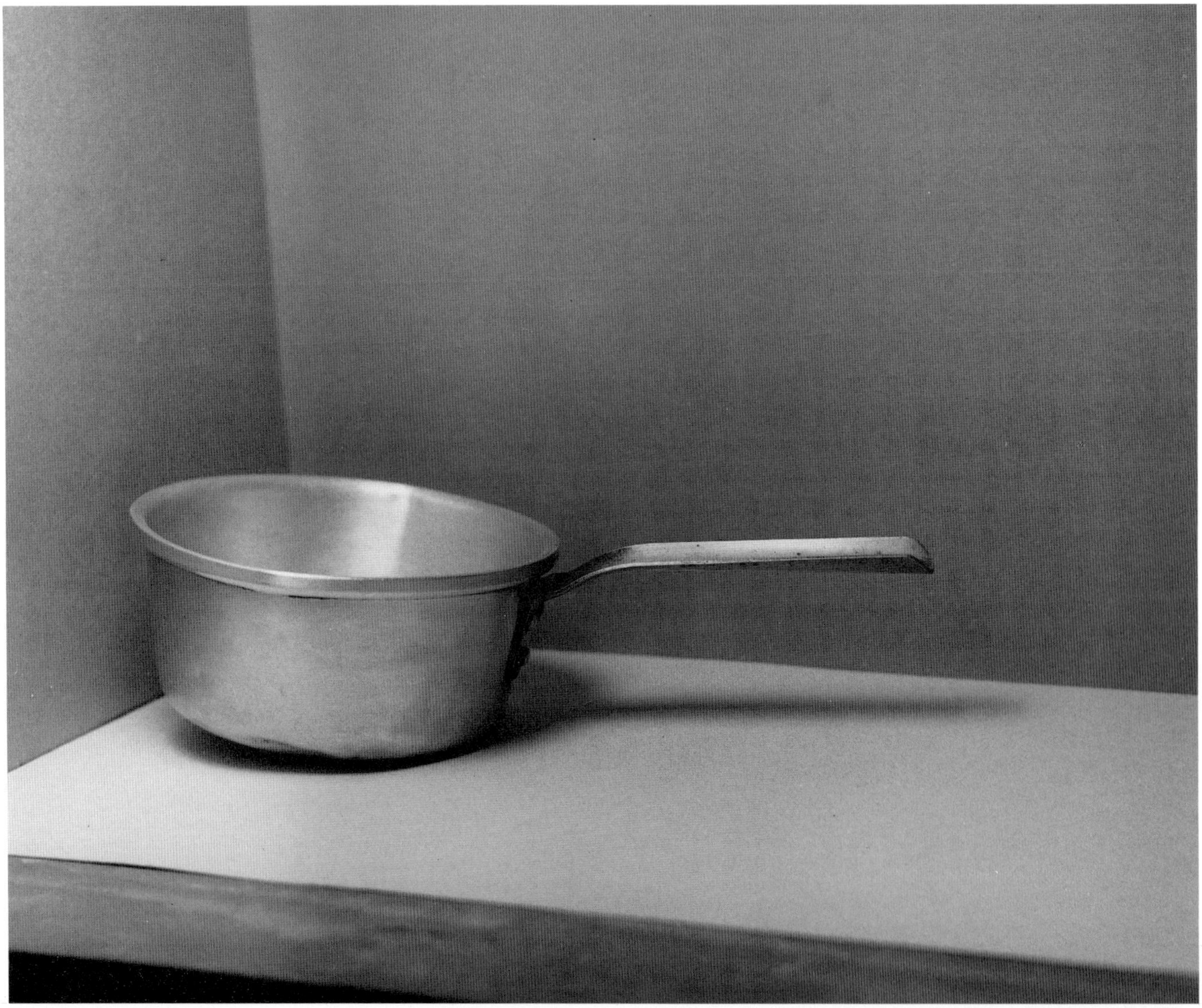

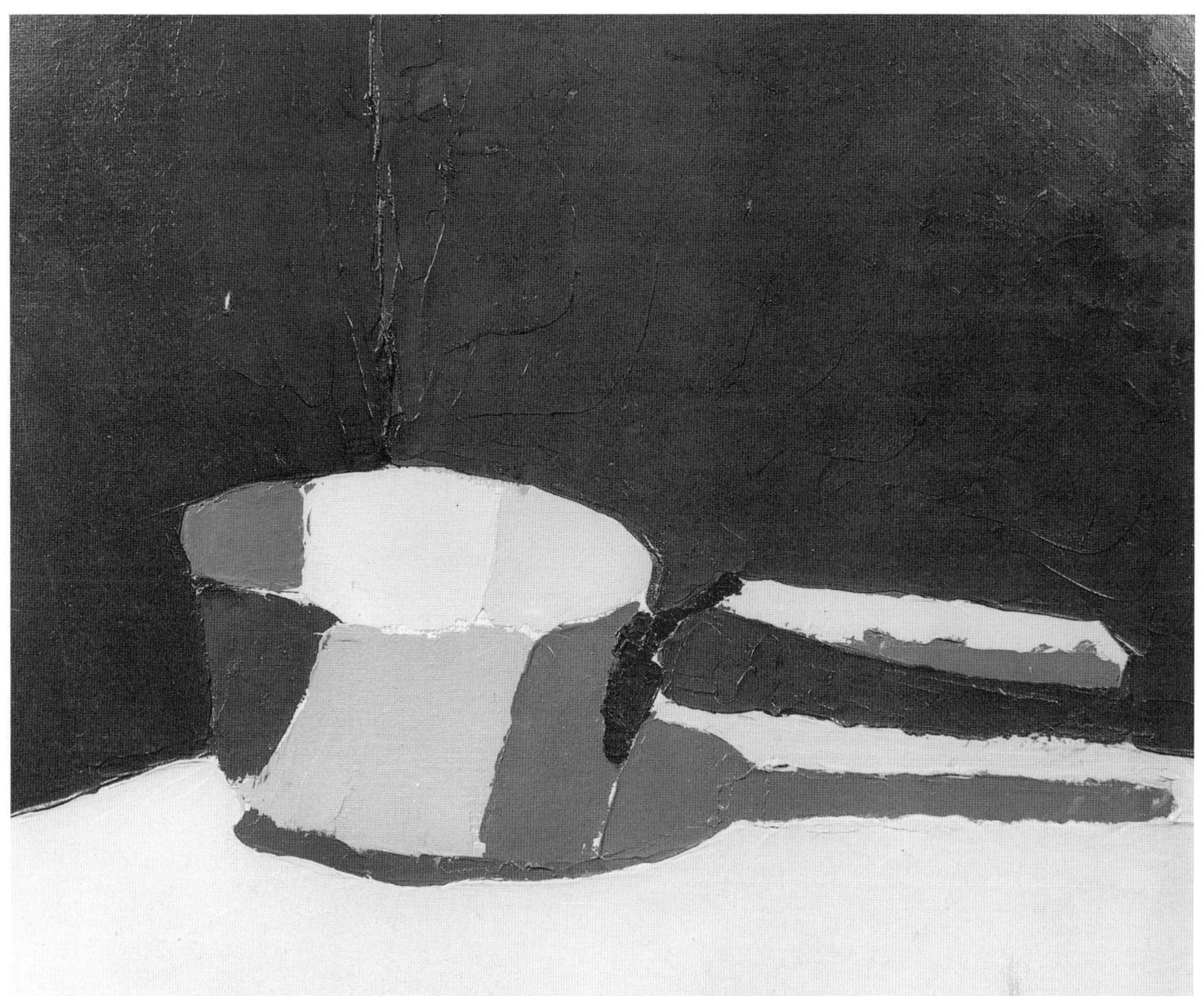

FIRST STATEMENT. This is your first model made of metal. But don't let this bit of knowledge intimidate you. Metal is much easier to paint than you think. Forget that it's shiny and forget the word "metallic" and just look at the saucepan in the setup box the way you'd look at any other object—made of any other material—and try to see the big color spots, as if you were looking at an orange. The first statement illustrated here was painted in fourteen color spots. That's slightly more elaborate than a typical first statement, but the student felt that he needed those extra color spots to capture the reflections in the pan:

- 3 for the walls and floor of the setup box
- 3 for the inside of the pan
- 3 for the outside
- 3 for the handle
- 2 for the cast shadow on the floor.

OBSERVATIONS. Those nine color spots on the pan may not add up to metal just yet, but they do add up to a saucepan, even in this highly simplified statement. If those nine color spots are correct, you already have a strong sense of the form of the pan. The difference between the two color spots of the cast shadow is impossible to see in this black-and-white photograph, but it will be more evident in the color illustration. You're now beginning to get the point that metal is made of color spots, just like any other material.

First Statement, anonymous student.

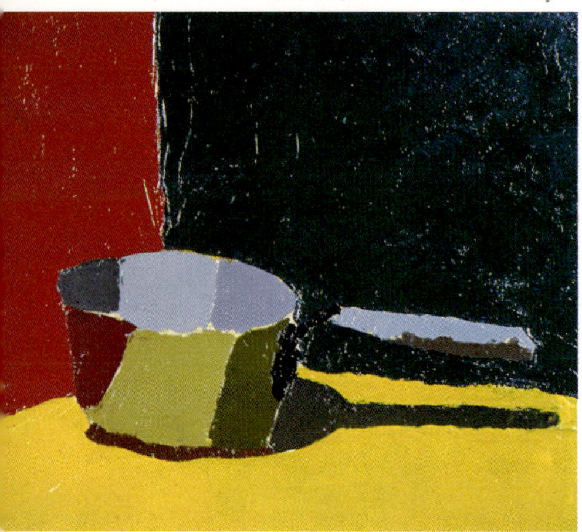

SECOND STATEMENT. You're certainly reaching the stage where you no longer need to have the number and disposition of the color spots spelled out for every second statement. The principle, of course, is that the second statement will usually contain three or four times as many color spots as the first statement. This arithmetic isn't arbitrary, but is based on the experience you've had with the projects you've done so far. You'll find that this particular second statement requires a lot more color spots than the second statements in the preceding projects.

Second Statement, Richard Gleason.

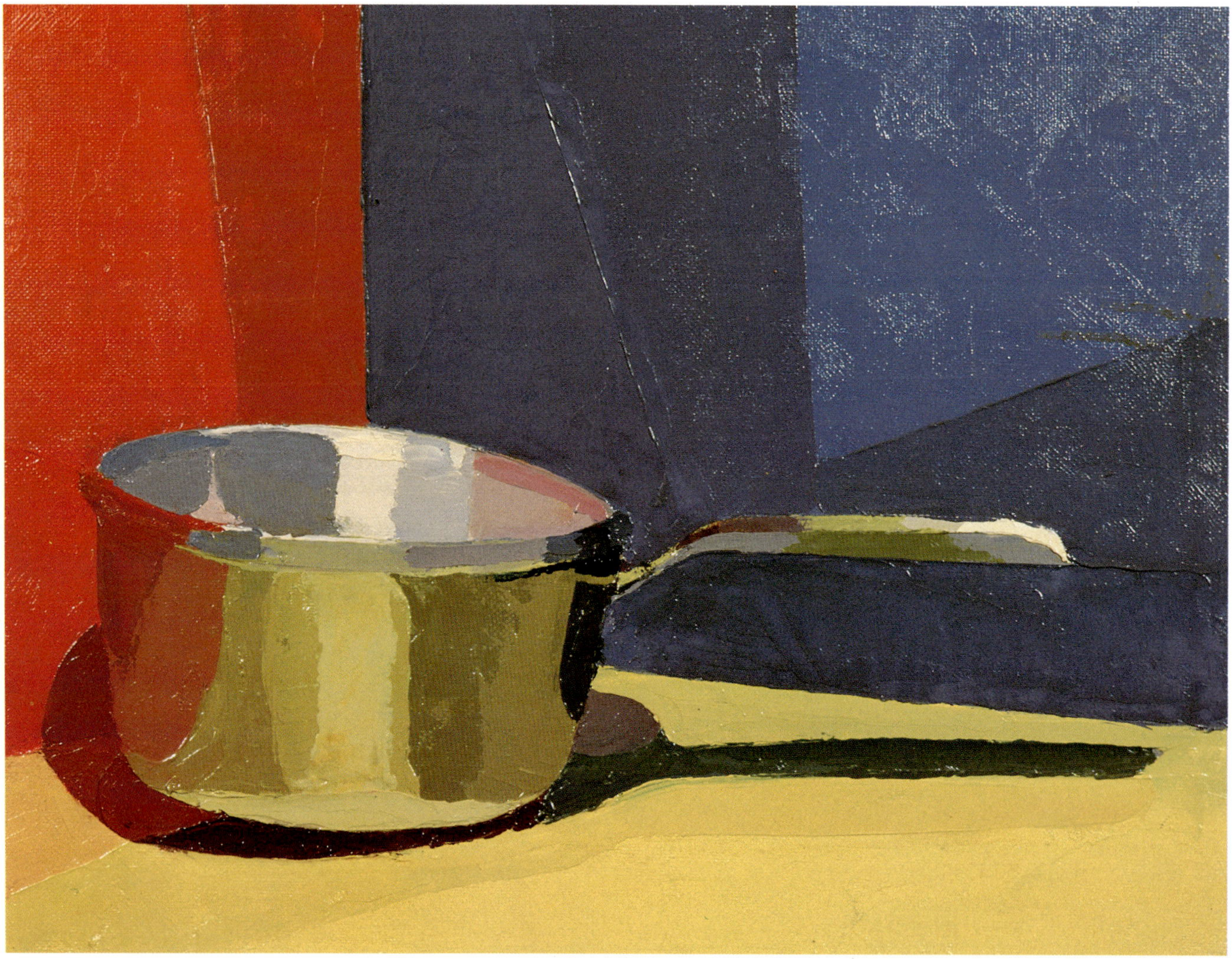

OBSERVATIONS. By the time you've painted this elaborate second statement, you'll certainly know that there's no point in searching for some special sort of silvery gray when you have to paint an object made of silver, pewter, tin, steel, or aluminum. Nor will you wonder what shade of orange comes closest to the color of copper, or what shade of yellow looks most like brass or gold. And you certainly won't even look for silver or gold paints. I hope that the mystery of painting metal has vanished forever. You know that if you simply look at your model in its setting, identify the oil color spots—on the model and its setting—and lay them down in their proper places, the look of metal will magically appear.

Third Statement, Don Stern. [Notice what has happened when three different people paint the same setup—you get three different personal points of view. That is why it's so important to paint your own setups—not copy the sample paintings shown here!]

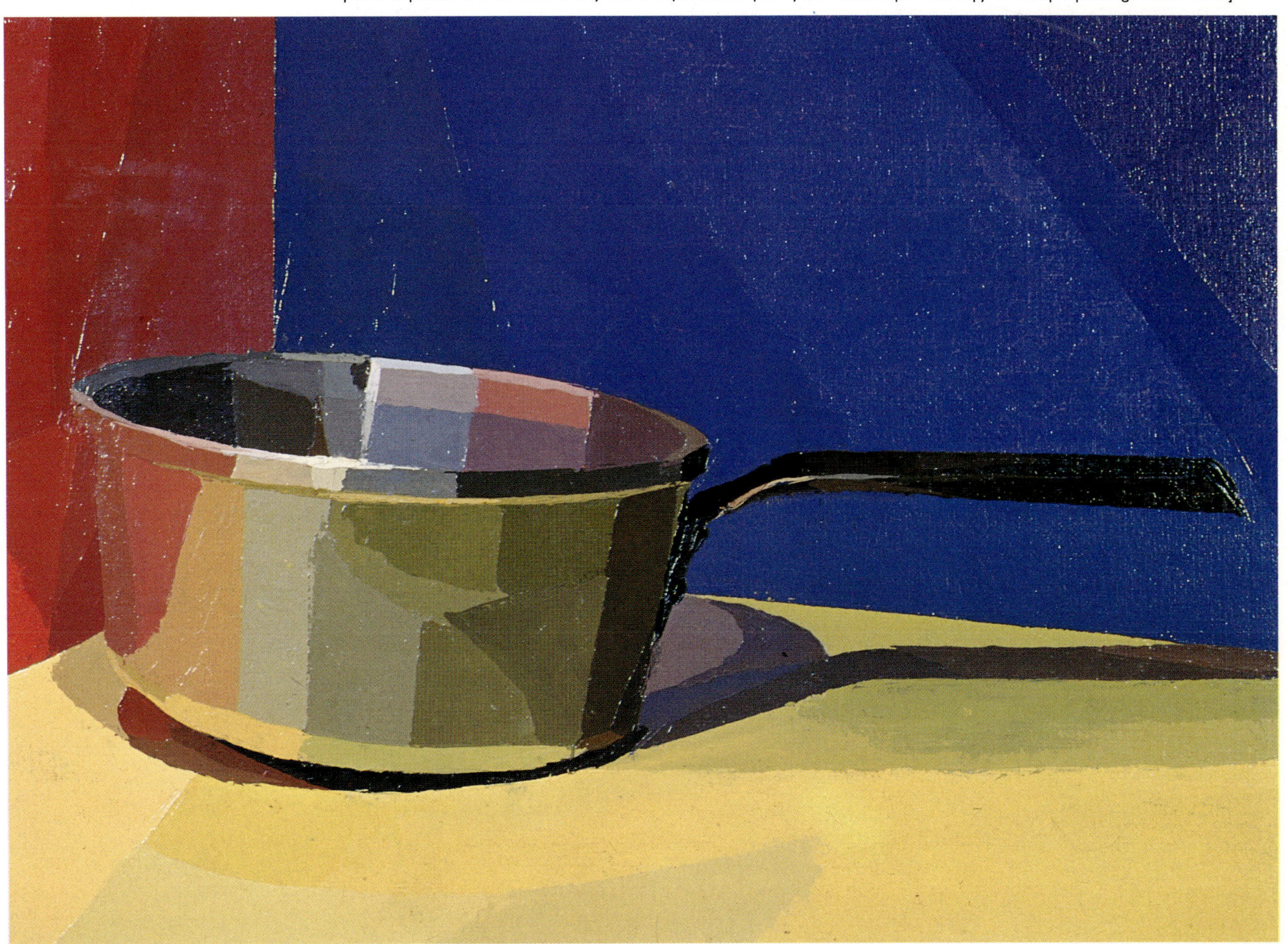

THIRD STATEMENT. Your second statement probably looks so convincing and "metallic" that you may wonder whether there's any point in painting a third statement. You feel you could really stop here. But it's good experience to force yourself to look even more closely at the endlessly fascinating reflected color in the surface of the saucepan. You *will* find more color spots. But don't *more* than double the number of color spots that appeared in your second statement. Just look for areas where you can make corrections and connections—where you can find more of those transitional colors that make the pot look even more solid and three-dimensional. Be sure not to neglect the walls and floor of the setup box, paying special attention to the saucepan's effect on *them*. The metal saucepan isn't the only reflecting surface in the picture.

OBSERVATIONS. Studying your finished third statement, you'll certainly be aware that very little of the saucepan is anything like the silvery gray that aluminum is "supposed" to be. It's almost impossible to point to any one particular color spot and say "that's the color of aluminum." Like every object you've painted in the ten preceding projects, the aluminum saucepan is a reflecting surface that takes much of its color from its surroundings. But on the shiny surface of any piece of metal, the impact of these reflected colors is even more evident. Metal, like water, often seems to have no distinct color of its own, but takes and throws back the colors of its setting. However, if you record all those reflected colors faithfully, the aluminum saucepan does turn out to look like aluminum. It's a paradox—and it works.

EXTRA PROJECT

Now that metal is no longer a mystery, and painting it no longer seems like a miracle, try a brass or copper object, preferably something simple, like a bowl or pot. Line the setup box with the same colors—or similar ones—and use the same lighting. Remember the lesson you've learned in this project. Forget the theoretical color of brass or copper (or pewter or gold) and just record those color spots as you see them.

WHAT COLOR IS WOOD?

SETUP. Wood, unlike metal, suggests no mystery. But that doesn't mean that it's easy to paint. For this project, your model is a plain wooden bowl. A much-used salad bowl is ideal, but a chopping bowl will do. Old salad bowls, having absorbed considerable oil, take on a rich coloration and develop surfaces sleek enough to pick up and reflect light and color. A chopping bowl is apt to be dry and dull, but will become just as interesting as an old salad bowl if you give it a liberal coat of vegetable oil, let it soak in and then wipe off the excess. Line the left wall of the setup box with light blue or light green, the floor with a darker yellow-green, and the right wall with gray—since you won't be painting the right wall, there's no need for it to influence the rest of the setup. With the setup box in Position 5, pose the bowl in the center of the floor. The whole setup should be well below eye level, so that you can see somewhat more of the inside of the bowl than the outside. Set the lamp above the bowl and slightly to the left, producing a big shadow on the floor.

SETUP BOX POSITION 5

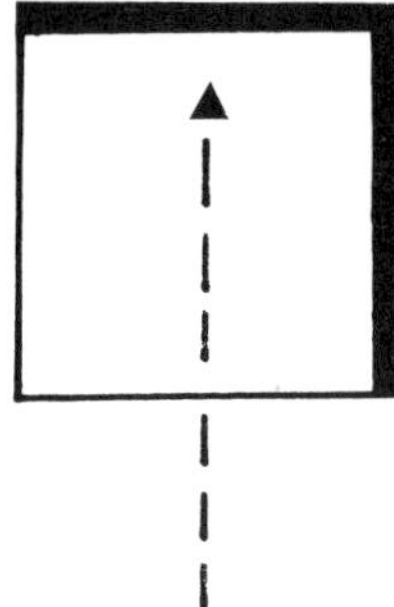

The left wall is perpendicular to your line of vision, while the right wall is parallel to your line of vision—so all you see are the left wall and the floor of the setup box. In effect, the left wall becomes a back wall.

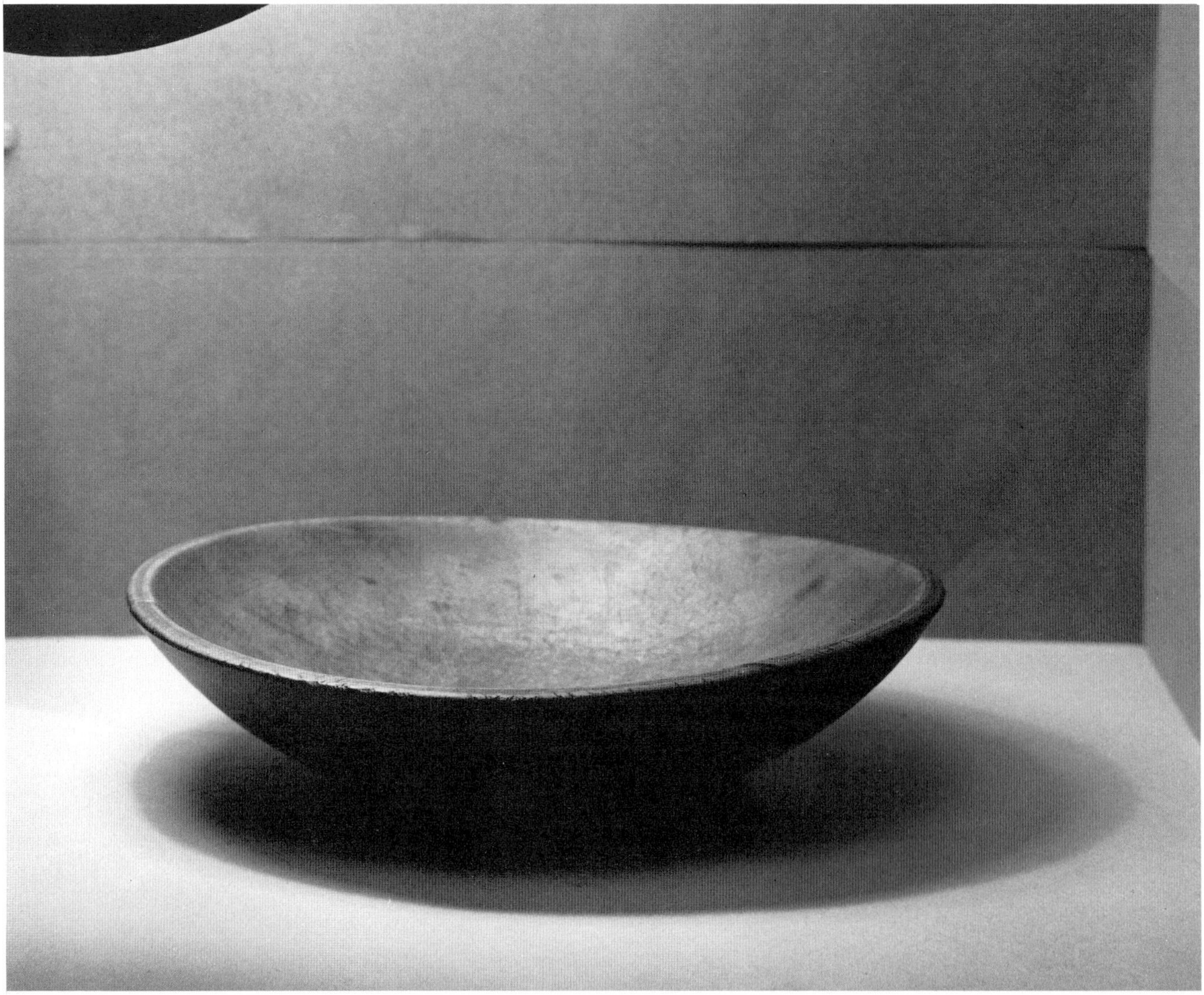

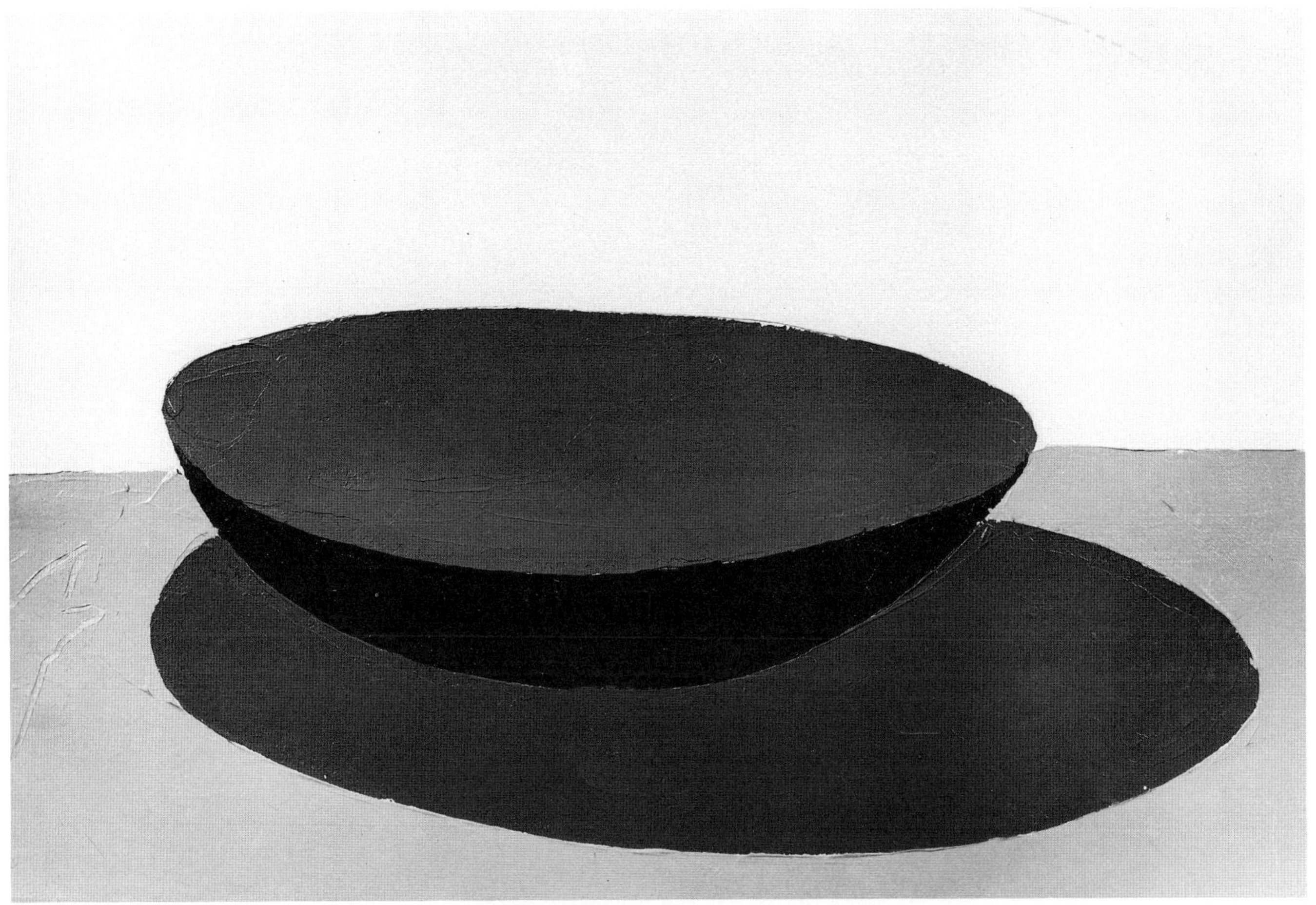

FIRST STATEMENT. In one sense, this is the simplest possible first statement because it involves so few color spots. You should be able to summarize the entire setup in just five color spots. But the older a wooden salad bowl, the more subtle its form is likely to be. You must get the curves of each color spot exactly right for viewers to read this first statement as a salad bowl. Really concentrate on the shapes and proportions of each color spot as you paint the following five:

1 for the wall of the setup box
1 for its floor
1 for the inside of the bowl
1 for its outside
1 for the shadow cast by the bowl.

OBSERVATIONS. The slightly eccentric elliptical form of a wooden salad bowl will force you to look very intently at the shape of each color spot. Despite the simplicity of the subject, you may—because of their shapes—find these color spots harder to paint than the simple geometry of cylinders, cubes, and spheres, which have dominated the projects so far. This project will also force you to face up to the real meaning of that forbidden word "brown." After you've learned how to paint something as *seemingly* difficult as metal, you may think that wood's a cinch. After all, everyone knows the color of wood: it's just "brown." But when you mix the two big color spots of the bowl in this first statement, you find that the concept "brown" won't do. You must be more precise. As you mix those two colors for the inside and outside of the bowl, it will become obvious that each mixture is a very dull version of some specific warm color. Is the inside of the bowl a dull yellow-orange, a dull orange, a dull red-orange? Is the outside a dull red-orange, a dull red, a dull red-violet? Whatever verbal description you arrive at, it won't be just "brown."

First Statement, Richard Gleason.

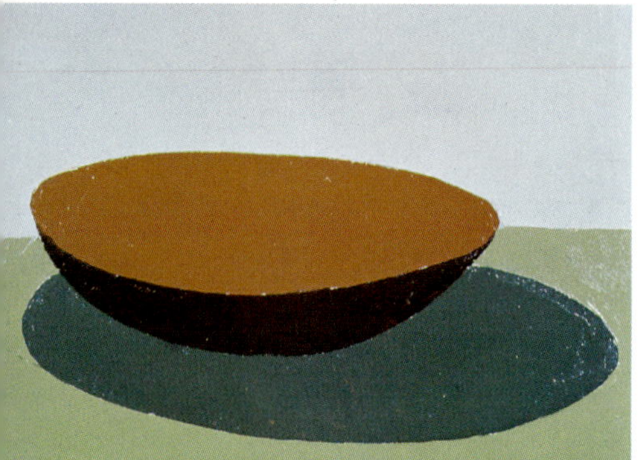

Second Statement, Richard Gleason.

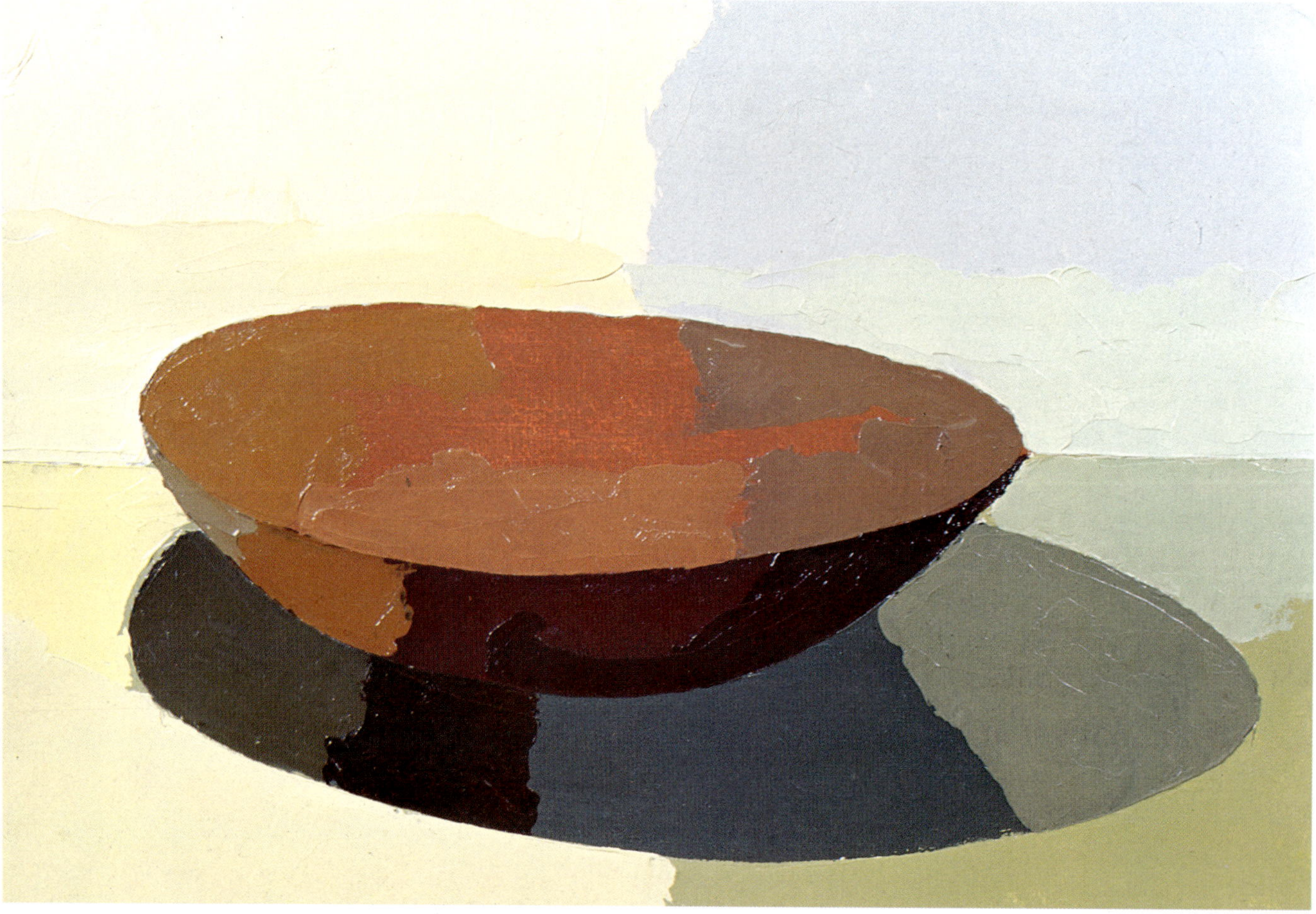

SECOND STATEMENT. Re-examining the bowl and its surroundings for your second statement, you should be able to find roughly four color spots in each of its five major areas. By now, you've gone through this process a dozen times, and you know that looking for this quartet of color spots isn't some abstract rule—the four spots are really there, reflecting the influences of all the colors on one another. So your second statement ought to show:

4 for the back wall of the setup box
4 for the floor
4 for the inside of the bowl
4 for the outside
4 for the shadow cast by the bowl.

OBSERVATIONS. Because you know that the bowl is a single material from edge to edge—just plain wood—you may be tempted to make those eight color spots mere variations of a single hue. But don't yield to that temptation. They're not just variations of "wood color," differing only in luminosity. They differ also in hue and intensity. So you can't just mix up a big batch of one dull warm color and then modify it slightly to arrive at those eight different color spots. You *must* observe, mix, and lay down each color spot as something unique. Nor should you be deceived by the simplicity of the other big color areas: the back and floor of the setup box, and the shadow beneath the bowl. The color spots within these big shapes aren't mere variations in luminosity either, but must also be seen as unique color mixtures. If you pay proper attention to the uniqueness of each color spot, this second statement will communicate something quite complex: the concave inner surface of the bowl, and the convex outer surface, each responding to the color of its surroundings in its own way.

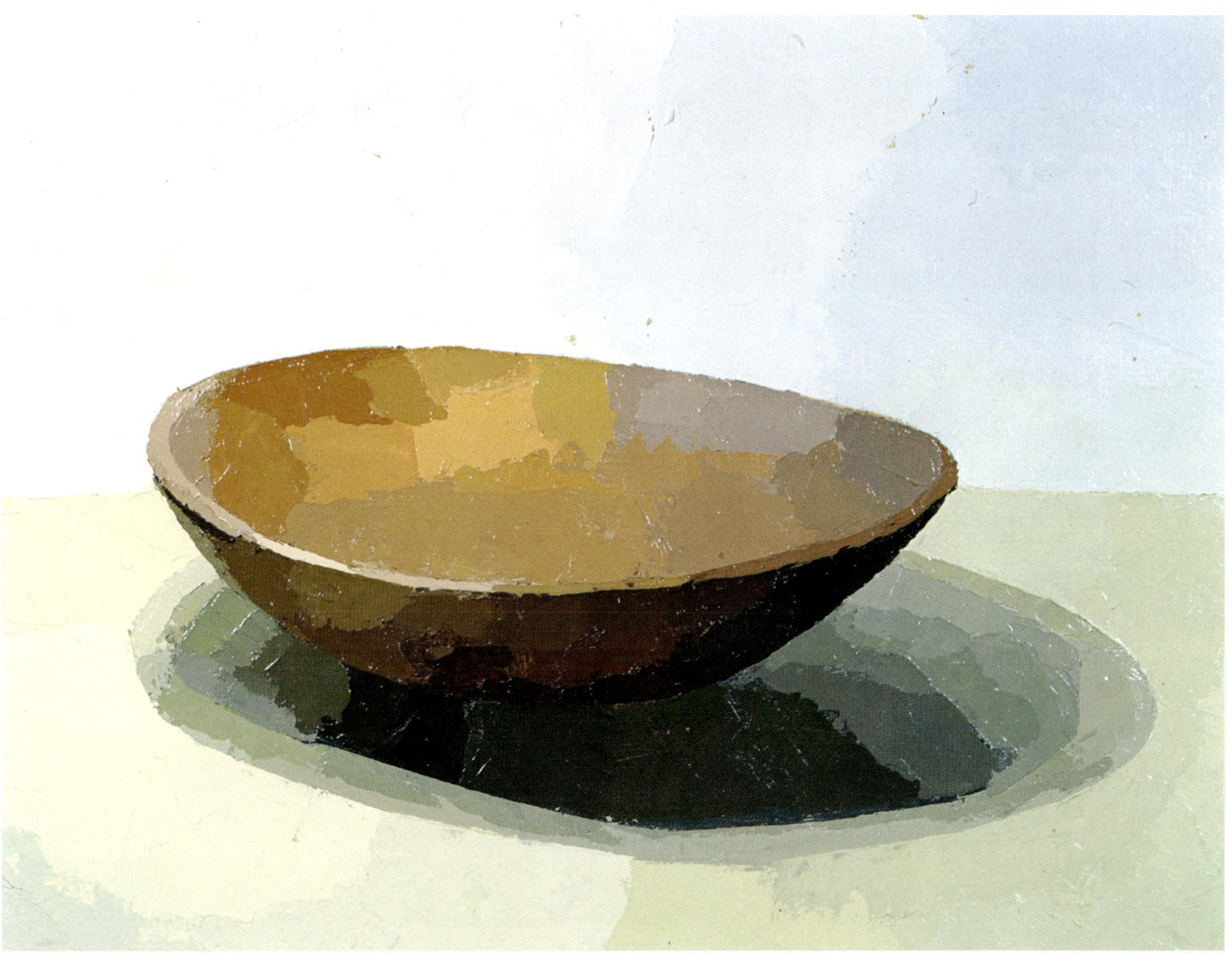
Third Statement, Richard Gleason.

THIRD STATEMENT. Go on to a third and final statement, employing only as many color spots as you need to produce a convincing and complete image of the bowl and its setting. In your first and second statements, you paid no attention to the rim of the bowl, but now look more carefully at the color spots on the rim, which will make your bowl far more realistic and three-dimensional. Also pay particular attention to the complexity of the shadow cast by the bowl on the floor of the setup box.

OBSERVATIONS. When you finish that third statement and look at your study, you're going to see that the bowl displays a surprisingly wide range of colors—warm and cool, light and dark, bright and dull, and most (if not all) of the six basic colors of the spectrum. Although few of these colors, taken separately, could be called "wood color," *together* they read as wood. The ellipse of spots that constitute the rim of the bowl, for all of its many colors, doesn't look like some festive garland, but reads simply as the edge of an ordinary wooden bowl reflecting various influences of light and color. Perhaps most fascinating of all is the shadow cast by the bowl, also revealing a wide range of hues, luminosities, and intensities, yet maintaining its integrity as a shadow on a level surface. As in previous projects, this "model" and its shadow are strongly influenced by the colors of the environment. In those earlier projects, it was often easy to attribute one group of color spots to one plane of the setup box, another group to another plane, and so on—the influences seemed direct and specific. In this project, they tend to be more indirect and less specific. As you paint, you should not be trying to analyze which plane influences which color spot. Look only at the "model" and concentrate on the color spots themselves.

EXTRA PROJECT

Now cover the back wall of the setup box with white paper, leaving everything else the same. This simple change will alter the whole setup so radically that you will have a new and rewarding series of variations on the color problems of the original exercise. Paint all three statements.

SURFACES AREN'T SCARY

SETUP. Beginning painters are often intimidated by surfaces and textures. So it's worthwhile to paint two models of about the same size, shape, and color, but differing mainly in surface qualities—hard versus soft, shiny versus matte, and so on. Find an ordinary, solid-colored ceramic mug—the kind that roadside diners and cheap restaurants use to serve coffee. Then find a well-proportioned pear, of a solid color without too many variations, and close in size and color to the mug. Place the setup box in Position 5. Line the invisible right wall with gray paper, and the floor with white. If your two models are green, line the left wall—which now serves as the background—with violet or orange paper; if your models are brown, line the left wall with green; and if they're yellow, line it with violet or blue. Set the mug and pear in the center of the setup box, side by side, about 1″ (25 mm) apart, and aligned with the front edge of the setup box floor. The light of the setup lamp should come from above and from the left, so part of the mug's shadow falls on the left side of the pear, while the pear's shadow falls only on the floor.

SETUP BOX POSITION 5

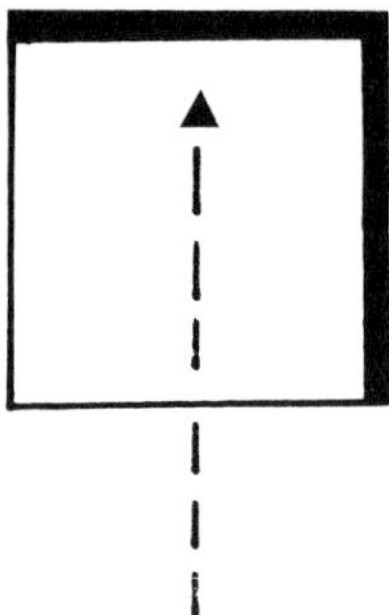

The left wall is perpendicular to your line of vision, while the right wall is parallel to your line of vision—and out of sight. In effect, you see only the left wall, which becomes the back wall.

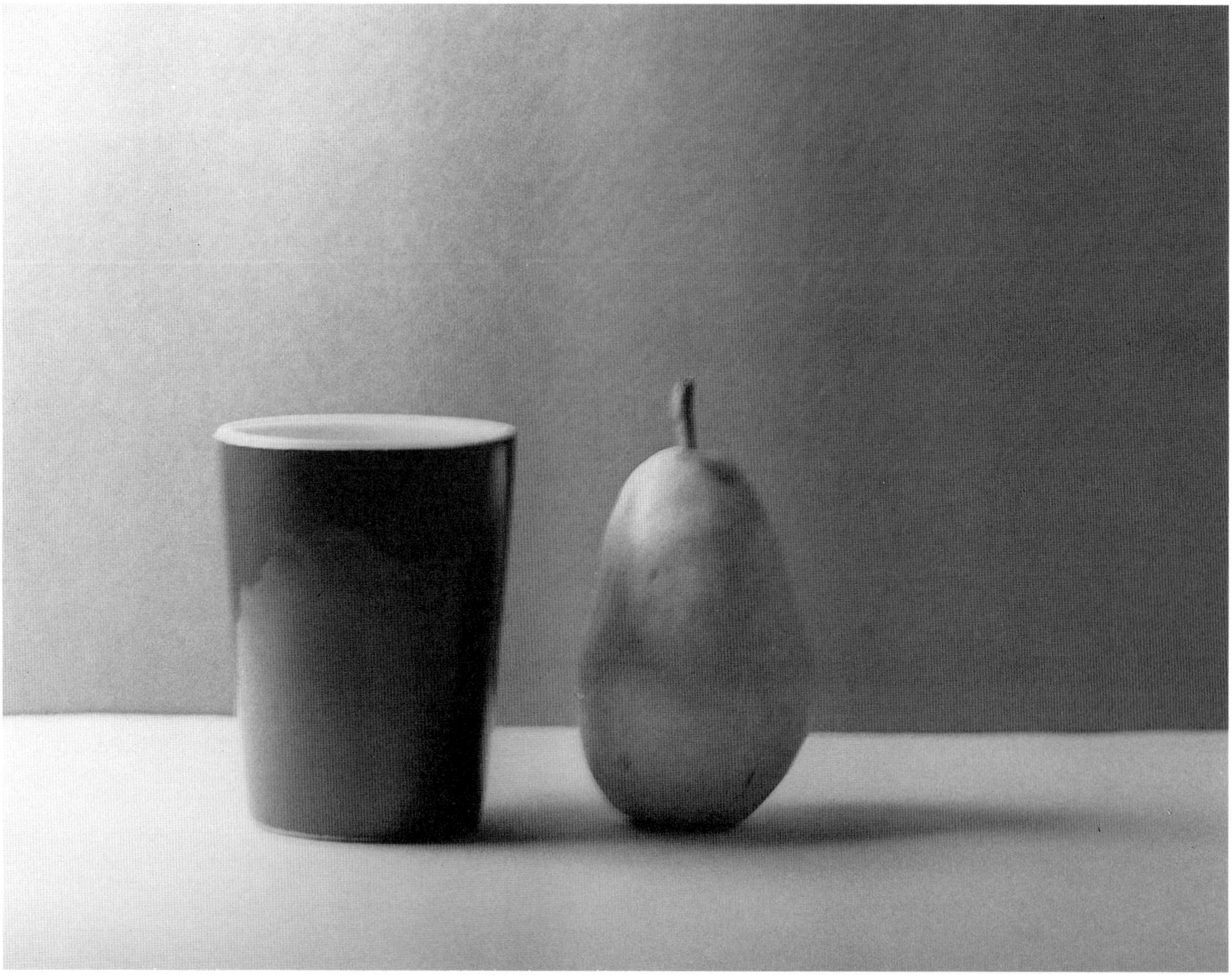

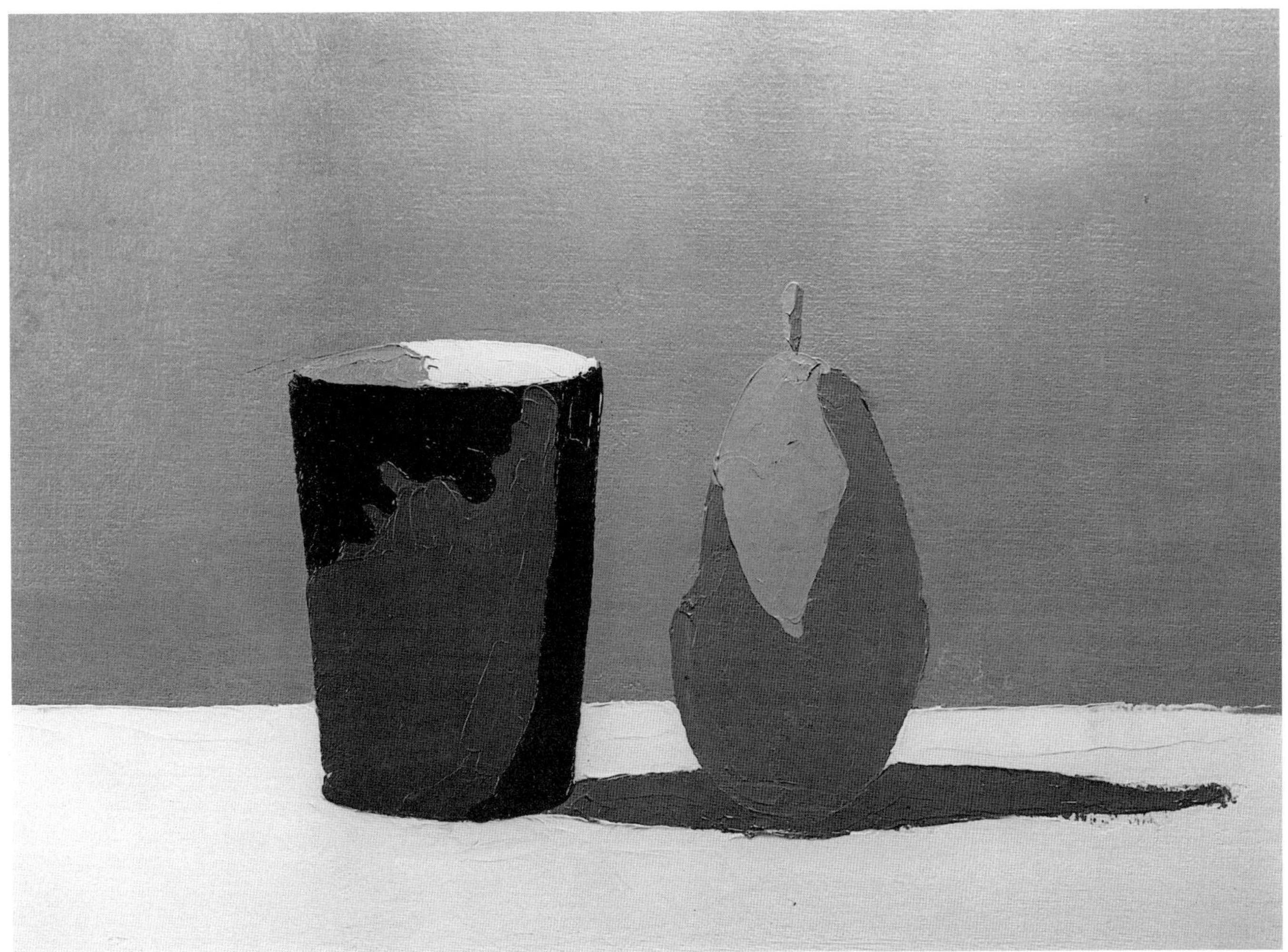

FIRST STATEMENT. This initial statement will be somewhat more complicated than the first statement you painted in the previous project, since you have two objects to paint, and one of them, the pear, is not a simple geometric solid. Work on a full sheet of canvas paper, held horizontally, and use your 3:4 viewfinder to compose your picture. The student who painted the first statement illustrated here needed a dozen color spots. I think that should be about the right number for your first statement:

1 for the back wall of the setup box
1 for the floor
2 for the inside of the mug
3 for its outside
4 for the body and stem of the pear
1 for the cast shadow on the floor.

OBSERVATIONS. Studying the pattern of light and dark on the two forms, you'll see that their lights and darks don't follow a predictable arrangement. You can't just assume that all the lights will be on one side and all the darks on the other. That may work out in an architectural rendering of a classical column, but it doesn't work out like that in the real world, which is full of unpredictable effects of light and color. So it's essential that you study the location and shape of each color spot on the mug and pear, even if the darks don't seem to fall where they're "supposed" to fall—like the ragged color spot under the lip of the mug, or the shadow of the mug falling on the left side of the pear. Where light and dark meet on both these forms, don't be tempted to blend them and create a soft edge, even if you see it in the actual model. Discipline yourself to work with flat, distinct color spots that have clearly-defined edges. The blending takes care of itself—in the viewer's eyes. Notice that the mug is turned so that you can't see its handle. At some point, you may like to paint a variation of this project with the mug turned so that you *can* see its handle. But follow this arrangement now.

First Statement, Alfred Tyrol.

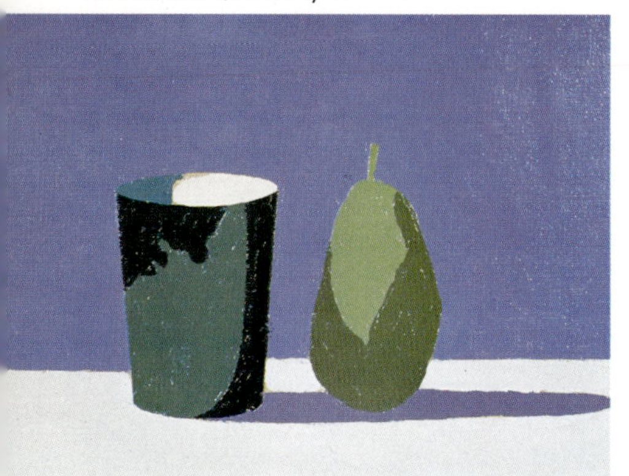

SECOND STATEMENT. As you begin to find additional color spots in your second statement—roughly three or four times as many color spots as you painted in your first statement—both "models" grow rounder and more solid. It's unnecessary to blend lights and darks together to produce the effect that artists call "modeling." This tends to happen by itself as the color spots multiply. Your second statement will probably work out to have something like the following arrangement of color spots:

- 4 for the back wall of the setup box
- 4 for the floor
- 4 for the inside of the mug
- 8 for the outside
- 8–10 for the body and stem of the pear
- 4 for the shadow on the floor.

Second Statement, Alfred Tyrol. [Again, a color plate of this step is unavailable—an unfortunate, infrequent occurrence.]

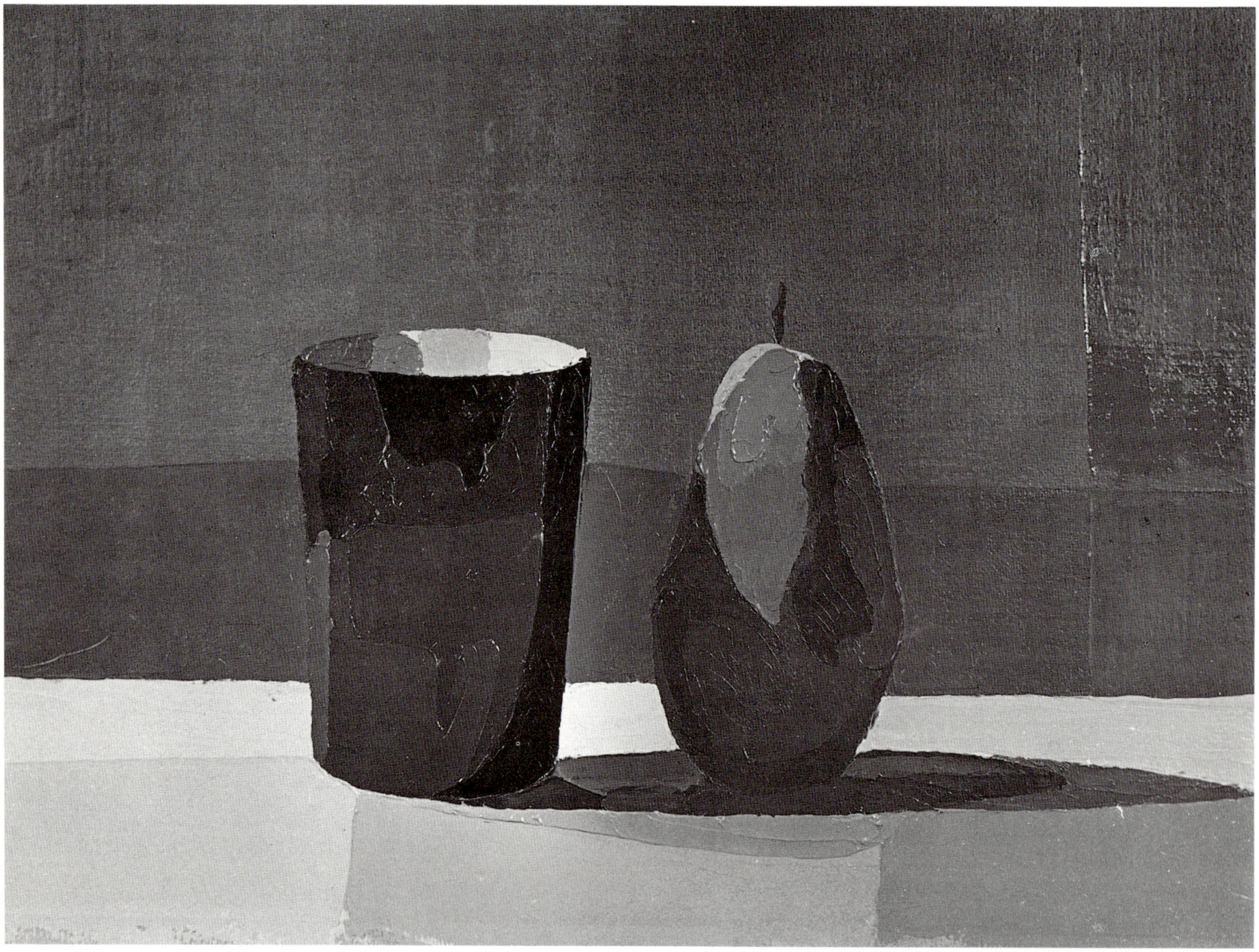

OBSERVATIONS. At the beginning of this project, I said that surfaces and textures often intimidate beginning painters. They think there's some special way to paint a shiny surface like that of the glazed ceramic mug, and still another special way to paint a matte surface like that of the pear. But as you paint these two objects, placing each color spot where it belongs and paying as much attention to both the *exact shape* and the *exact color* of each spot, you'll probably forget the whole question of surfaces and textures. You'll stop thinking "the mug is supposed to be shiny" and "the pear is supposed to be matte." You'll learn that there's no special secret to painting either one of these surfaces, and you'll see that the mug soon begins to look like a mug and the pear begins to look like a pear *anyway*.

Third Statement, Alfred Tyrol.

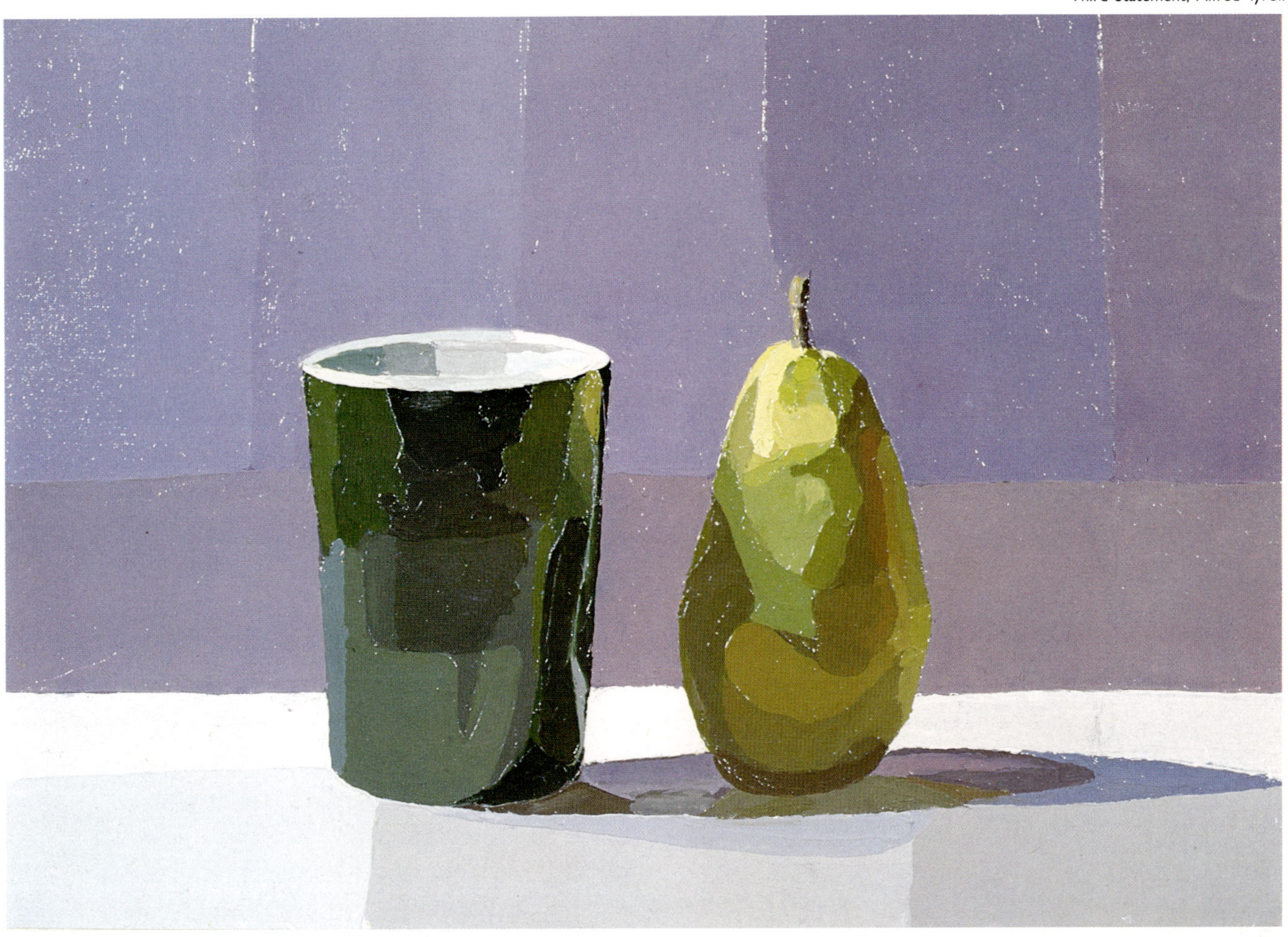

THIRD STATEMENT. You should be able to find many more color spots when you paint your third, and final, statement. But it's important to be selective. You can't make any arbitrary rule that the third statement ought to have two or three or four times as many color spots as the second statement. It's a matter of judgment. This student has painted just enough new color spots to correct the second statement, to add transitional tones, and to bring out such details as the rim of the mug. And he has had the good judgment to stop before he went too far.

OBSERVATIONS. This third statement reinforces the basic lesson of Project 13, namely that surface texture happens by itself if you just paint the right color spots in the right places—and don't think about surface and texture at all! For reasons that I can't really explain, the color spots on the mug make the surface look shiny, glazed, and lustrous, while the color spots on the pear add up to a matte and opaque surface. This is more evident in the color reproduction.

EXTRA PROJECT

Look for other pairs of objects—one shiny and one matte—that have similar colors and will give you variations of this project. Try a matte, unglazed flowerpot and a highly polished apple, for instance. Or try a potato and some shiny metal container from the kitchen. Keep the lighting the same and then paint three statements of the setup.

EVEN TWINS DON'T LOOK ALIKE

SETUP. In Project 13, you found out what happened when two dissimilar objects were placed side by side. Now you're going to discover what happens when two similar objects are set apart, with a totally different kind of object placed between them. Buy two green apples of the same type, as alike as possible in size, shape, and color. And find a clean, preferably new, terracotta flowerpot, somewhat larger than the apples. Line the left wall of the setup box with gray, the right wall with bright blue, and the floor with white. Turning the setup box to Position 4, set the flowerpot in the center of the floor and then place the apples on either side of the pot so that all three stand in a row, without touching. The setup lamp should be at the right and low enough for the right apple to cast its shadow on the right side of the flowerpot, and for the left apple to stand *entirely* in the shadow cast by the flower pot.

SETUP BOX POSITION 4

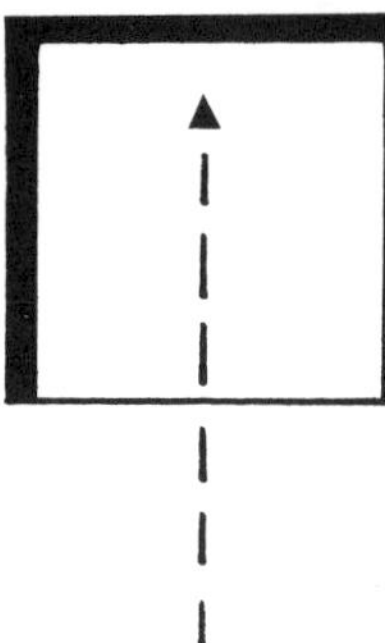

The right wall of the setup box is perpendicular to your line of vision, cutting straight across it, while the left wall is parallel to your line of vision and on your left, out of sight. You see only the right wall, which now becomes the back wall. The setup should be well below your eye level, so you can see plenty of floor.

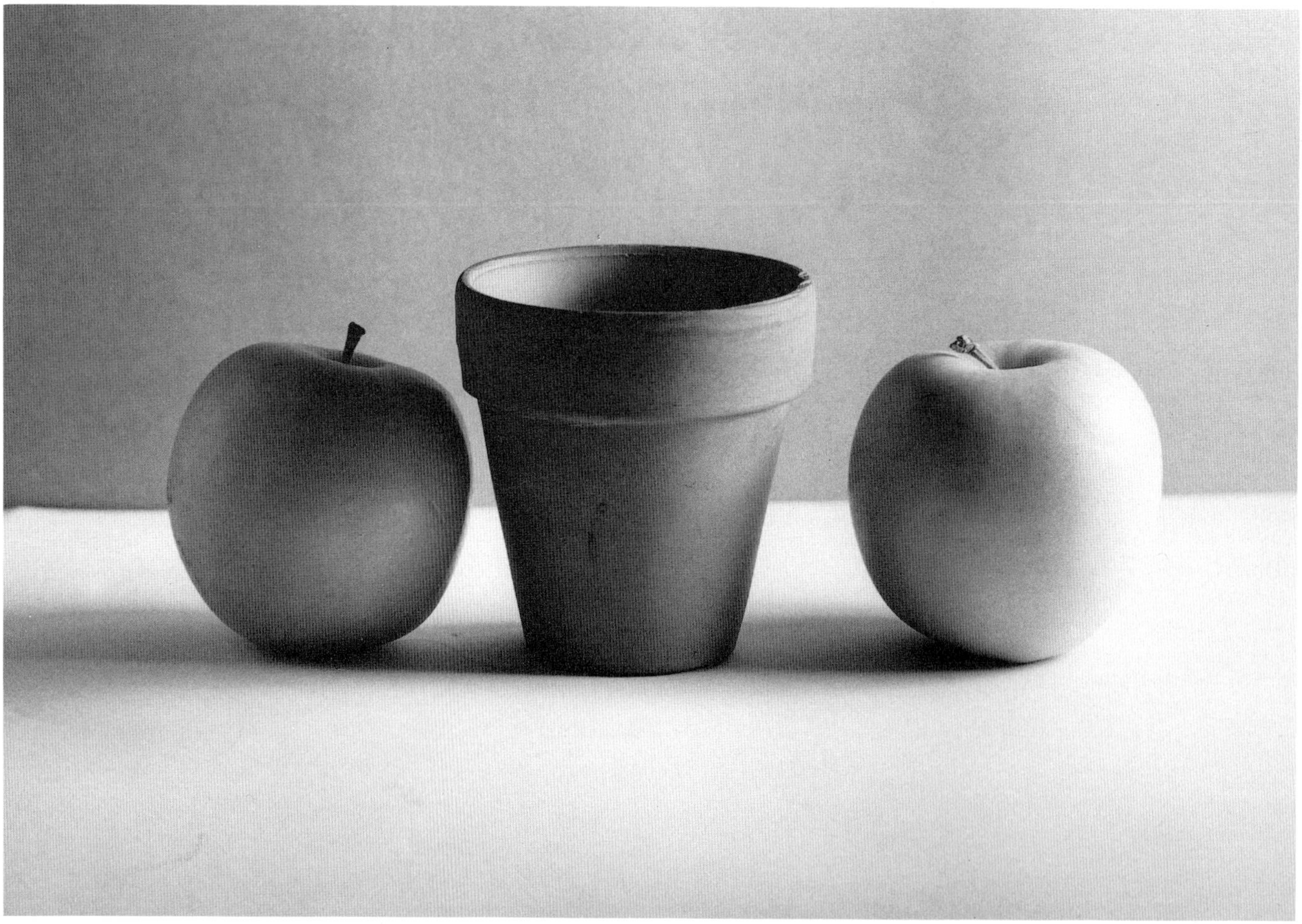

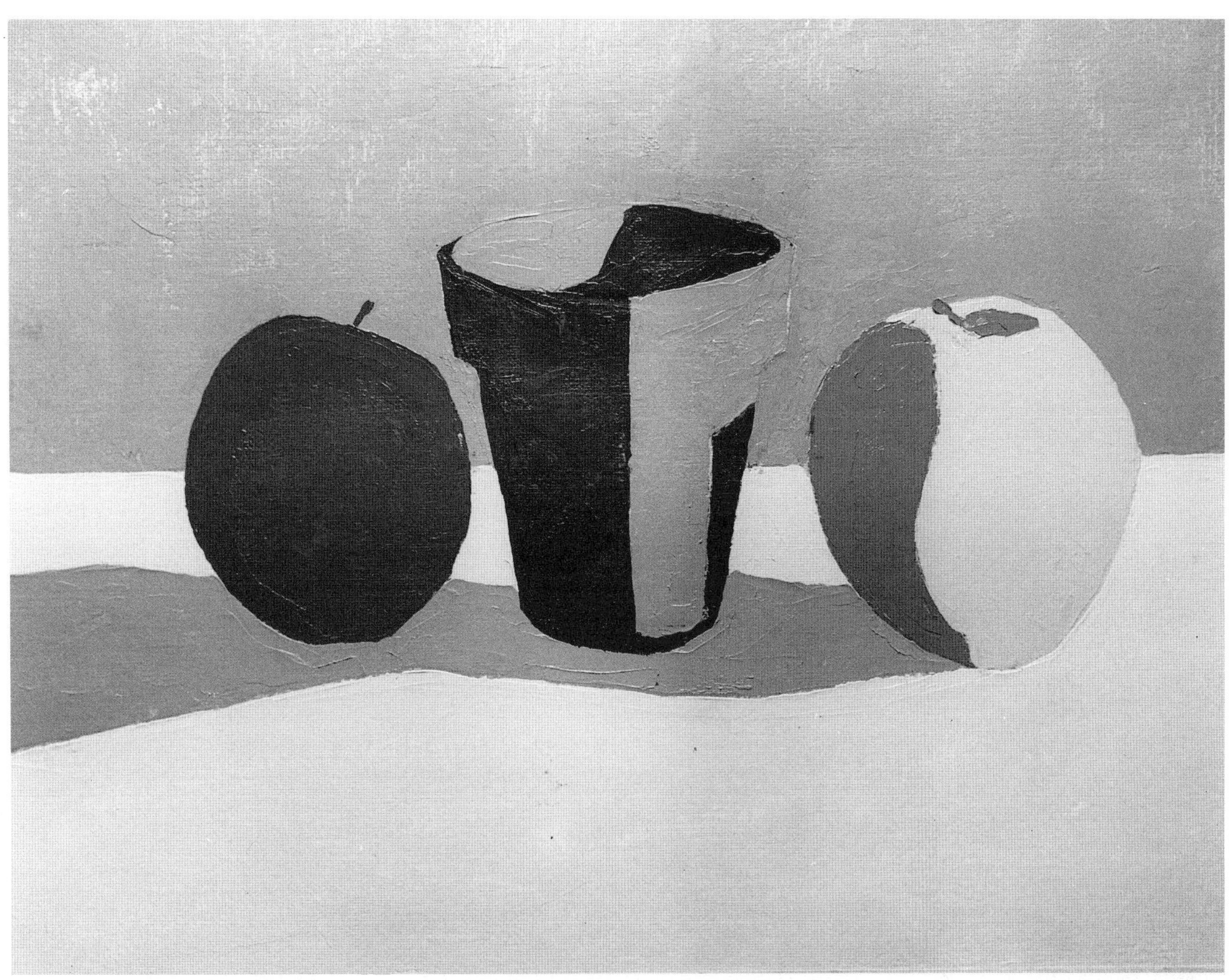

FIRST STATEMENT. Clearly, the purpose of this project is to challenge you to paint two similar objects—the green apples—in totally different lighting situations. One apple is strongly lit, while the other is in shade. Work on a full sheet of canvas paper, held horizontally, and use your 3:4 viewfinder to compose your picture. The student who painted this first statement was able to do it in eight colors. (Note that I said colors, not color spots.) Here's how those colors are distributed in the study illustrated above:

1 color for the setup box wall
1 color for the floor
1 color for the left apple
2 colors for the flower pot
2 colors for the right apple
1 color for the cast shadow on the floor.

OBSERVATIONS. Although I've said many times that you must look at each color spot separately, it's also true that the function of the first statement is to summarize the subject in the fewest possible colors. So it's no crime to create a single color for the four color spots of the floor, using that same color for each spot. (You did this earlier, when you painted the six oranges.) In the same way, a single color appears on the two shaded parts of the right apple, and the two lighted parts of the flowerpot. When you're working on a first statement and trying to keep things as simple as possible, it makes sense to use the same color on several spots that appear on the same surface. However, as soon as you begin work on a *second* statement, you must begin to look for the differences between these color spots—and remember that it's unlikely that you can use any color for more than one spot.

First Statement, Kevin Kennedy.

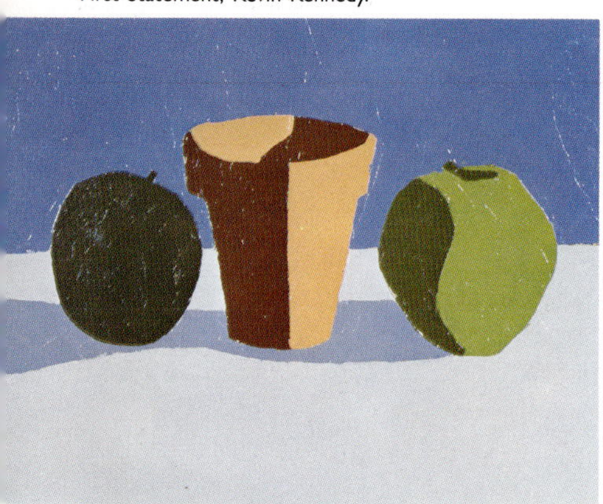

SECOND STATEMENT. Now study the two apples, the flowerpot, and the planes of the setup box to find the transitional colors—particularly those colors that fall between the strong, oversimplified lights and darks of the first statement. You'll certainly find such transitional colors on the apple at the right and the flowerpot, as this student has done. You should also find several lighter color spots within the apple on the left that sits in the shadow of the flowerpot. Your new distribution of color spots should be something like this:

4 for the back wall
4 for the floor
4 for the left apple
6–8 for the right apple
6–8 for the flowerpot
4 for the cast shadow.

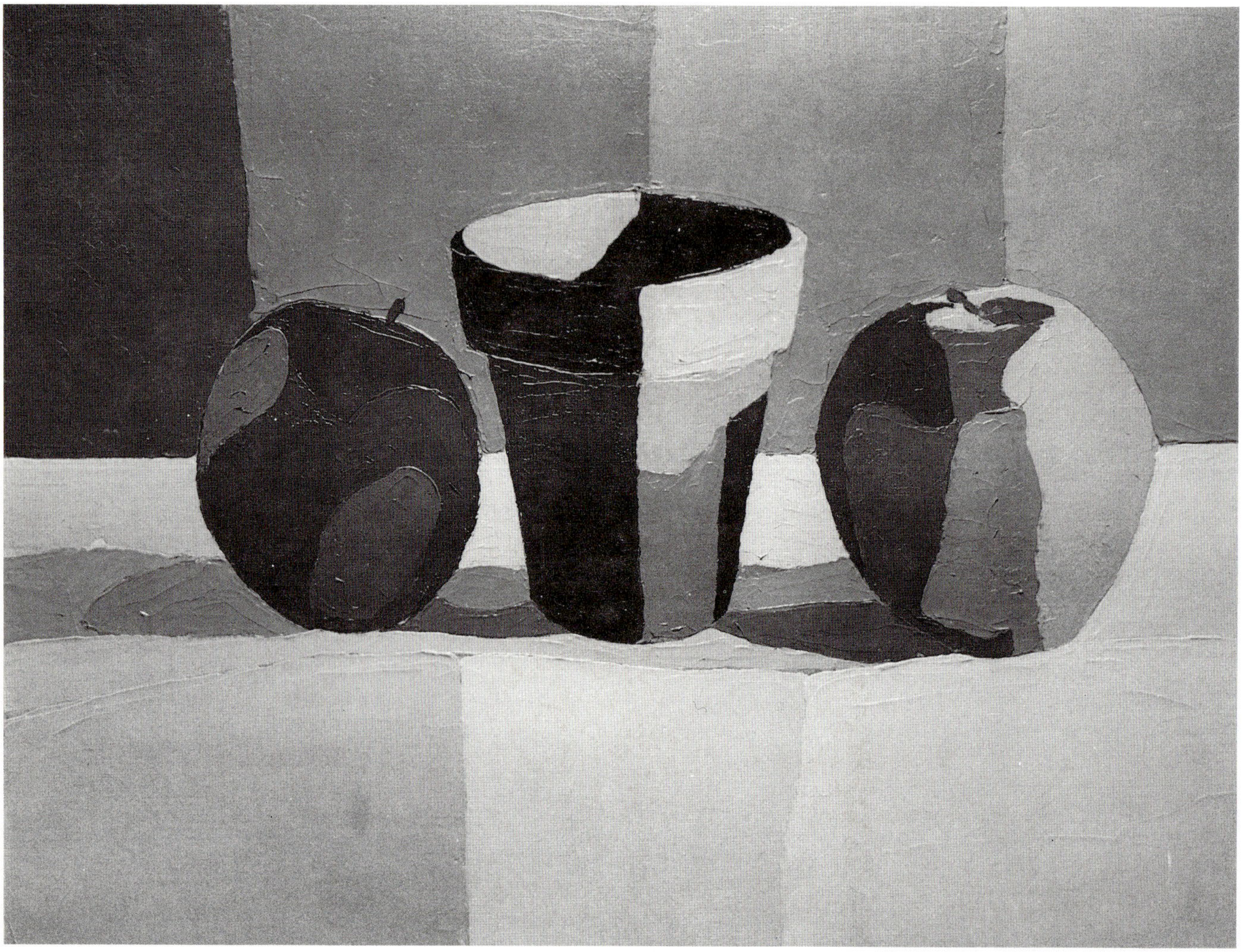

Second Statement, Kevin Kennedy

OBSERVATIONS. Looking at the second statement reproduced here—and looking at your own second statement—you'll see that there's a certain order (I hesitate to call it logic) in the sequence of the various color spots. On the walls and floor of the setup box, there's an orderly gradation from light to dark, with the lightest color spots at the right, nearest the setup lamp. A similar gradation of color spots appears on the apple at the right, where the color spots also follow a light-to-dark sequence, similar to that on the setup box walls and floor. The color spots on the flowerpot also respond to the direction of the light, and to the shadow cast by the apple on the right. Sometimes this order is easy to see, and sometimes it is not, depending upon the subject and the character and fall of the light. But you should not perform this kind of analysis to paint those color spots convincingly. It's just reassuring to look at the finished statement—after the work is done—and discover that your color spots aren't arbitrary or accidental.

Third Statement, Kevin Kennedy.

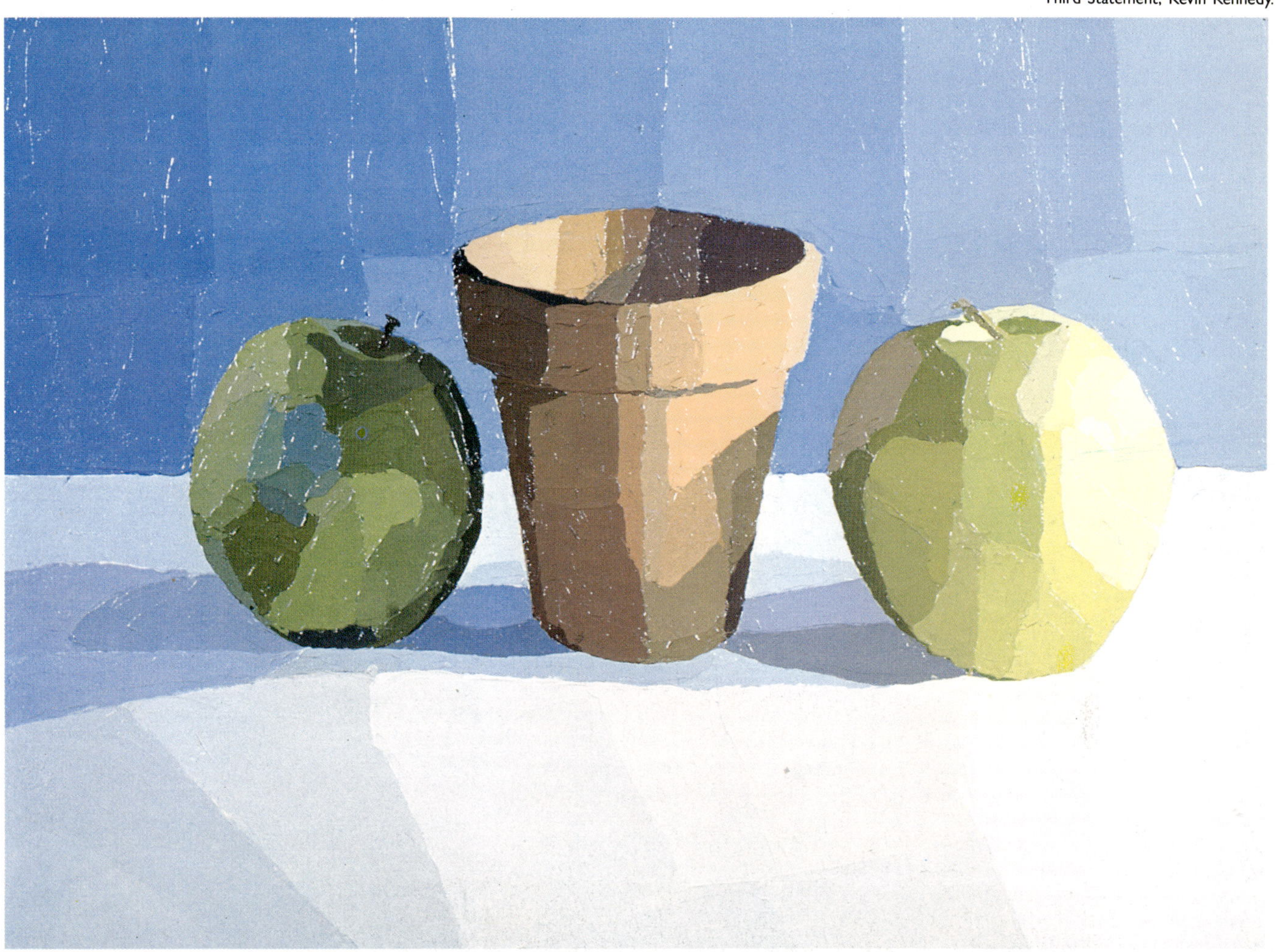

THIRD STATEMENT. Continue to look for the transitions betweeen the color spots in the second statement—the smaller, more subtle spots that give the forms greater solidity. As you identify these subtle color spots, you'll see that they still follow the same order as the bigger, simpler color spots of the second statement. But don't think *too much* about that order or you'll start painting what's "supposed" to happen, what you expect, rather than what you actually see. Don't make any rules for this painting—or for any other. Just put down the color spots you identify with your spot screen. If you lay them down accurately, their order emerges by itself.

OBSERVATIONS. In that third and final statement, you have two apples that start out looking as alike as two peas in a pod—of the same species, and similar in size, shape, and color. But when you actually start to paint them, faithfully recording that one is half in light and the other entirely in shade, their colors prove to be entirely different. There's not a single color spot on one apple that's identical to a single color spot on the other. The pattern of color spots on each apple is totally different, and yet the viewer's eye takes all these differences into account and still recognizes the kinship between the two apples—precisely because you so faithfully painted the visual differences.

EXTRA PROJECT

Look for other nearly identical objects that you can pair up and paint under similar circumstances. A row of three eggs—two white, one brown—would be a good choice—and fun. Be sure to line them up so that their light and shaded sides are similar to the arrangement on the apples and flowerpot that you've just painted.

SLICING BREAD INTO MANY COLORS

SETUP. Your next model is a loaf of white bread. The best choice, of course, would be a handsome, wholesome, homemade loaf—one fresh from the oven of a local bakery. Obviously, packaged bread, already sliced, can't hold a pose. Line the floor of the setup box with white paper and the right wall with a cool color—blue, green, blue-green, blue-violet, or violet. Line the left wall with gray; since you won't be painting this wall, you don't want its color to influence the setup. Turn the box to Position 4, so the right wall becomes the back wall. From the middle of the loaf, cut a slice 1″ (25 mm) thick, and lay it obliquely on the floor of the setup box, flanked by the two bigger chunks of the loaf, also turned obliquely. You should be able to see the tops and sides of the big chunks, as well as their cut faces. Arrange the setup lamp to the left and toward the front of the setup box, so that the cut face of one big chunk is in light, while the other cut face is in shade. The big chunks should cast shadows behind them, while the small slice should cast a small shadow onto the cut face of the right chunk.

SETUP BOX POSITION 4

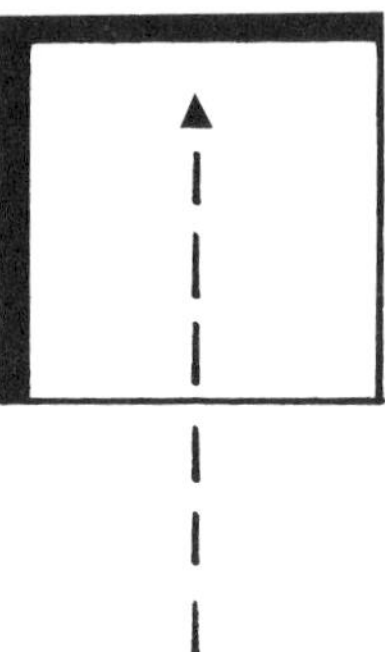

The right wall is perpendicular to your line of vision—cutting straight across it—while the left wall is parallel to your line of vision and to your left, out of sight. In effect, you see only the right wall, which becomes the back wall. The box is well below eye level, so you see plenty of floor.

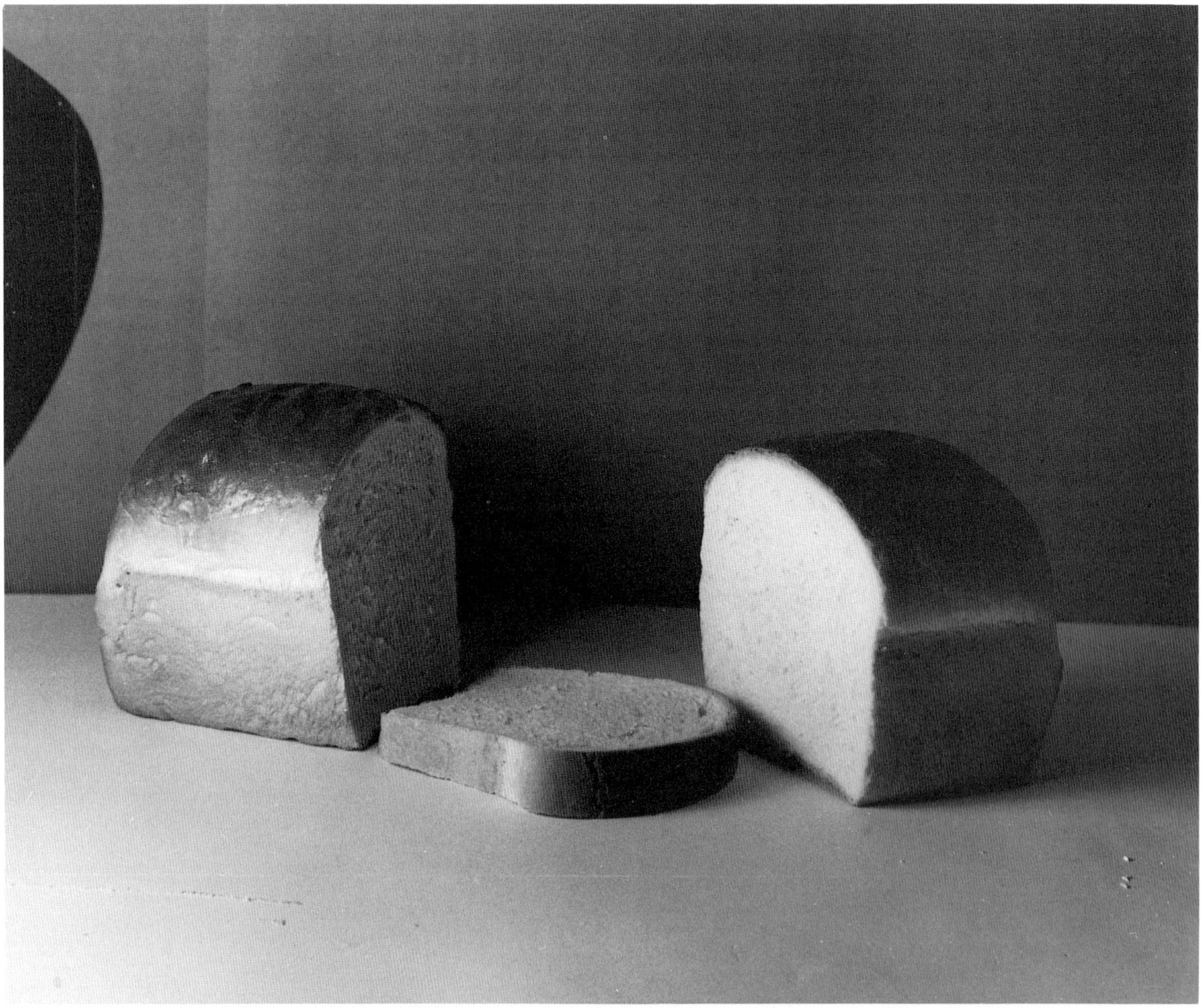

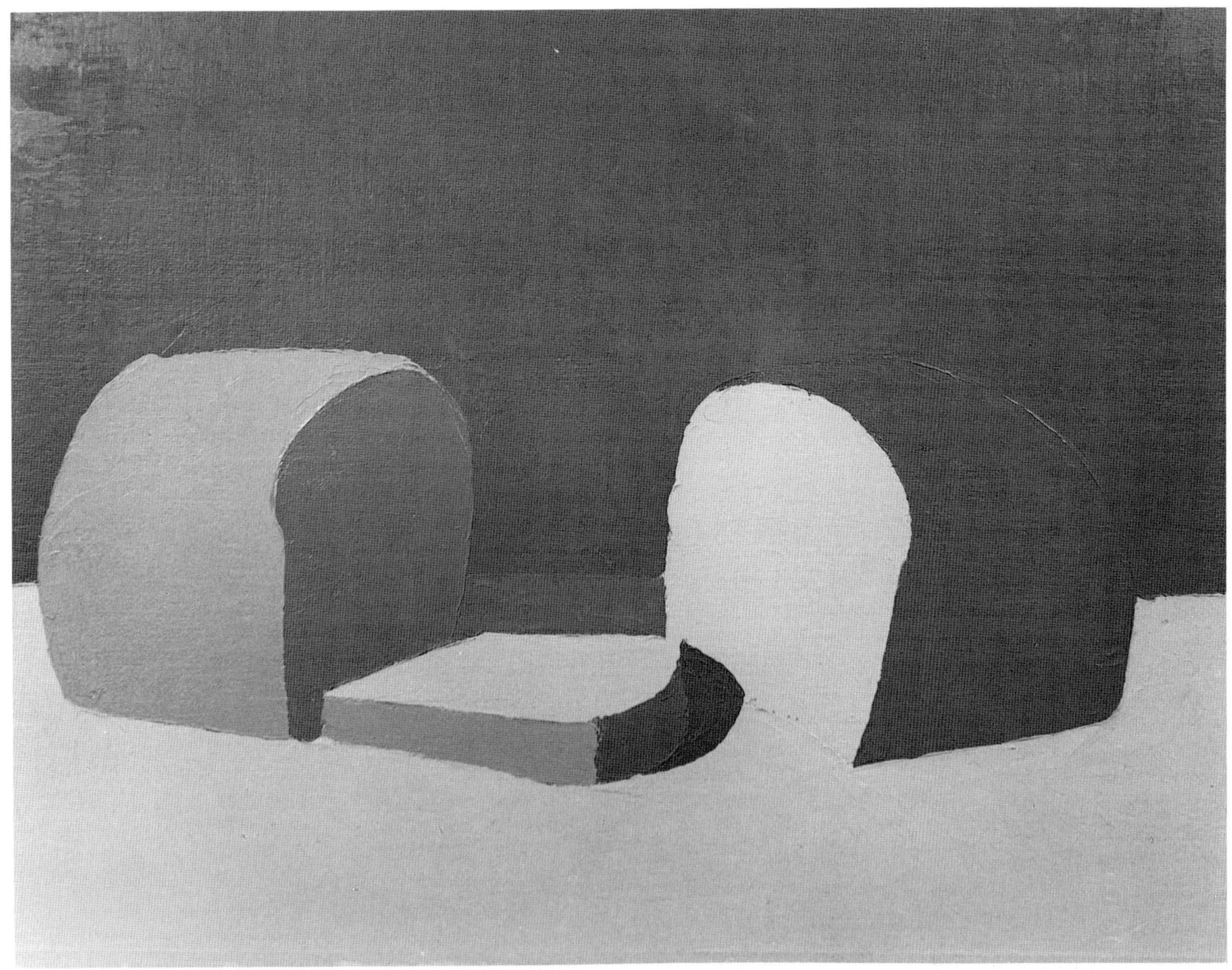

FIRST STATEMENT. This project requires a full sheet of canvas paper held horizontally. Use your 3:4 viewfinder to compose the study. You're going to need to mix something like eight colors, although some of these mixtures will appear in more than one color spot. Here are the colors:

1 color for the back wall of the setup box
1 for the floor
1 for the lighted crust of the left chunk and the lighted crust of the slice
1 for the shaded crust of the right chunk and the shaded crust of the slice
1 for the lighted, cut face of the right chunk and the lighted top of the slice
1 for the shaded cut face of the left chunk
1 for the shadows on the floor
1 for the shadow that the slice casts on the right chunk.

OBSERVATIONS. In Project 14, you painted two almost identical objects—two green apples—that were of the same object-color throughout but were transformed by light and shadow. Now you're taking this problem further. You're painting three pieces of the same object. That is, you're taking a loaf of bread and cutting it so that you can see both the pale inside and darker outside of the loaf. And you have placed these three pieces in a rather complex relationship, so that some areas are in light, others are in shade, and still others are partly cast into shadow. In this first statement, you can see some radical transformations. For example, the two chunks of bread turn out to be totally different colors, even though they're halves of the same loaf.

First Statement, Alfred Tyrol.

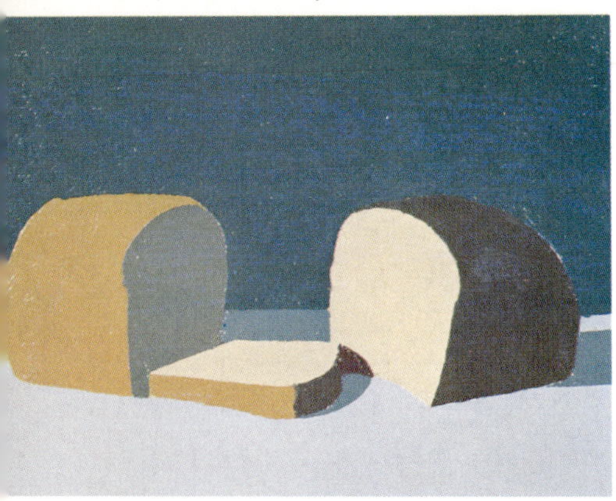

SECOND STATEMENT. The shapes of the two chunks, as well as of the slice of bread lying on the floor of the setup box, are so simple that your second statement may not be much more complicated than the first. In the example reproduced here, the student has simply doubled the original number of color spots in the three pieces of bread, and quadrupled the number of color spots in the back wall and floor. As you begin your own second statement, try to organize your color spots something like this:

- 4 for the back wall of the setup box
- 4 for the floor
- 4 for the chunk of bread on the left
- 4 for the chunk of bread on the right
- 5–6 for the slice of bread
- 4 for the shadows cast by the bread.

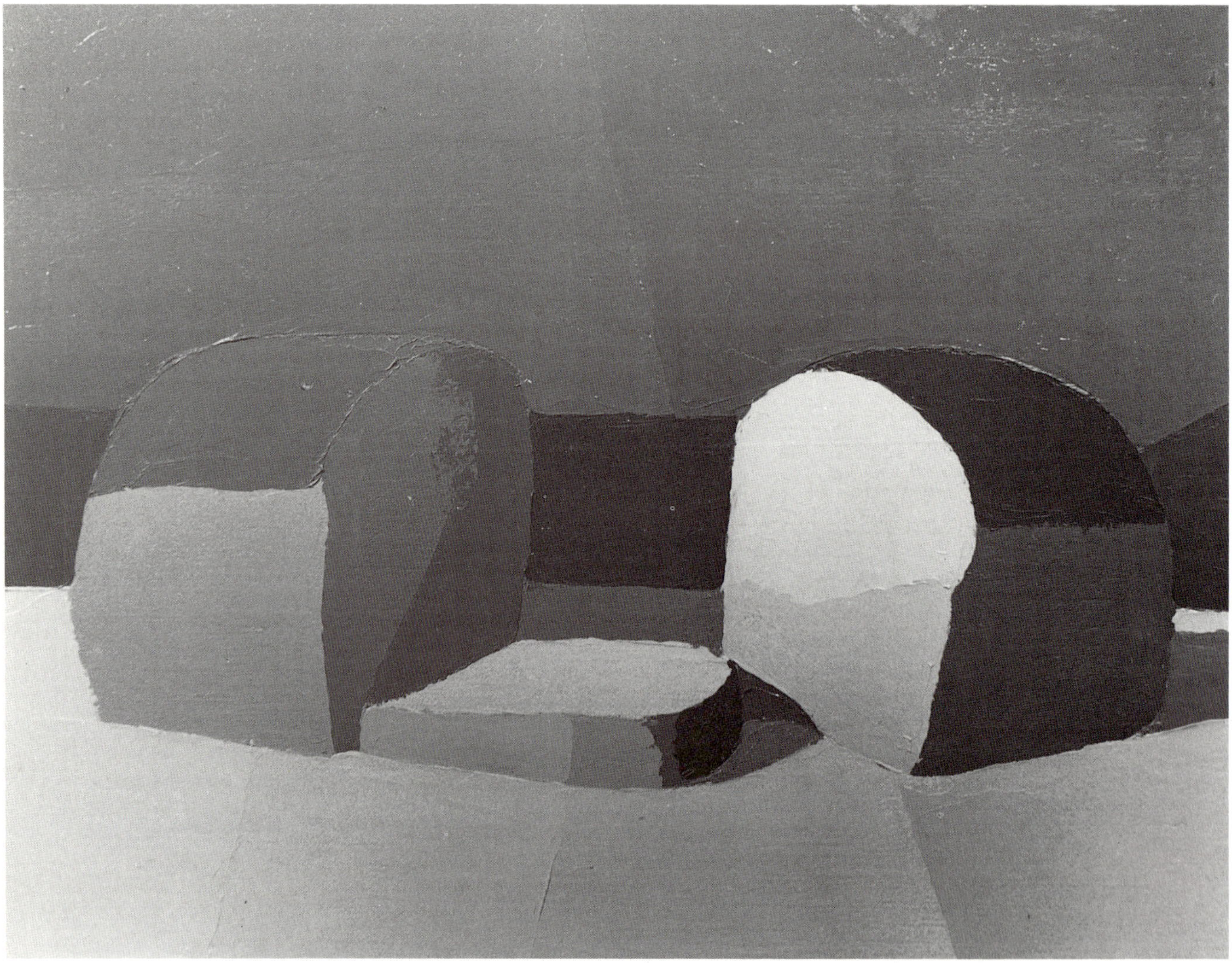

Second Statement, Alfred Tyrol.

OBSERVATIONS. Having painted a dozen second statements by now, you can see that some require only a limited number of color spots, while others demand a far more elaborate pattern of color spots to do the job. It's a matter of judgment. When you paint the second statement, you should still strive for much of the simplicity of the first statement, revealing new color spots without disrupting the basic color pattern of the first statement. Equally important, you must try to carry forward all areas of the second statement at the same rate of progress. That is, just try to find a few new color spots within each major area and stop there. Don't develop one area of a painting at the expense of its other areas. Don't get carried away and subdivide one area into a dozen small color spots, while you find only two or three new color spots in the adjacent area.

Third Statement, Alfred Tyrol. Collection of William Fotaides.

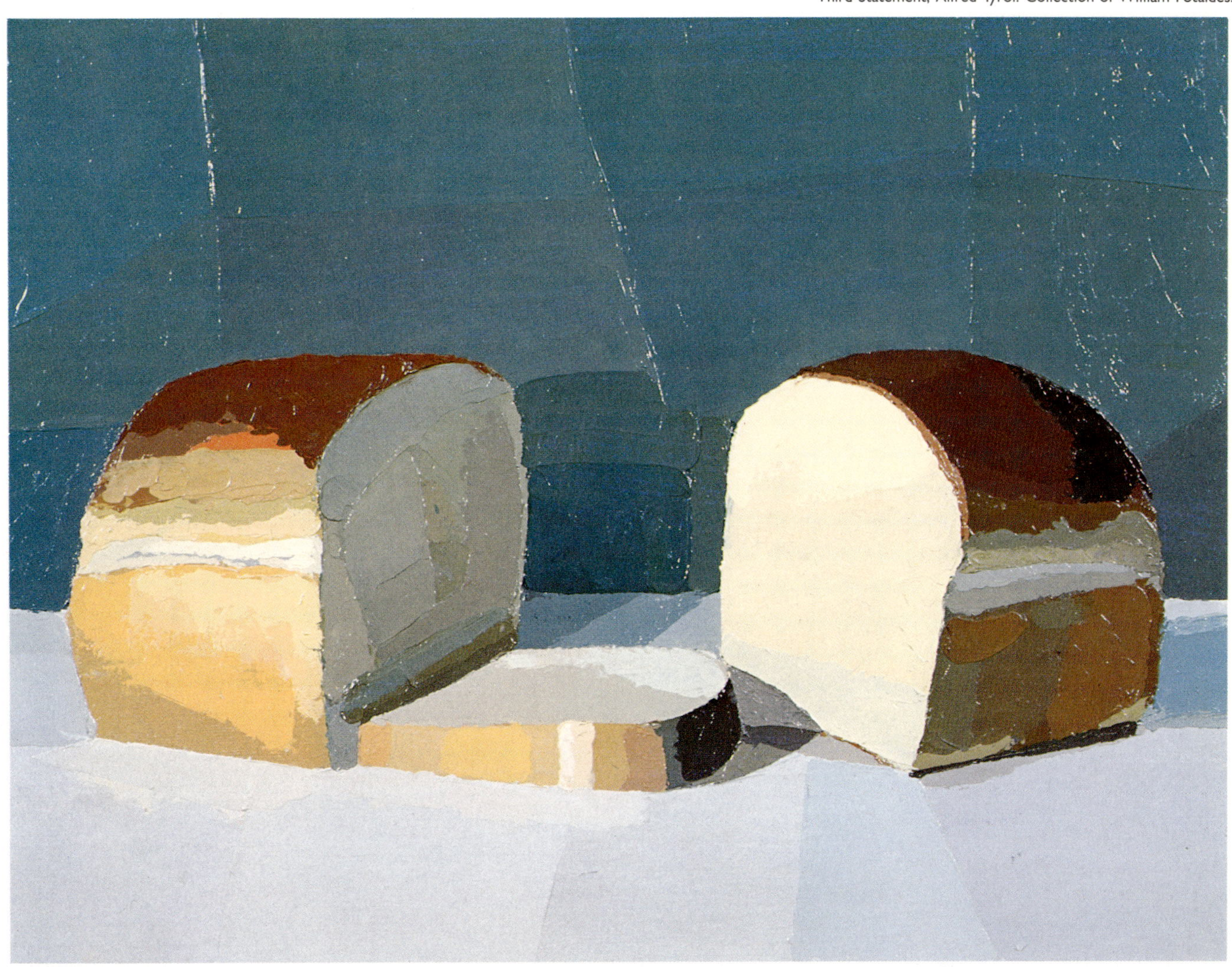

THIRD STATEMENT. Now you can really let yourself go. Explore the setup for as many color spots as you think you need to communicate the full richness of the loaf in its environment. But, even at this stage, be selective. Don't multiply color spots for the sheer fun of it. In the third statement reproduced here, the student has discovered many more new color spots on the left chunk of bread than on the right, but he's still painted the slice of bread very simply—because he feels that just these few more color spots are enough to communicate the character of his subject. The floor of the setup box is also painted more simply than the back wall. Economy is a virtue in art.

OBSERVATIONS. The basic lesson here extends what you learned by painting Project 14. The two identical chunks of bread—cut from the same loaf—become totally different from each other when they're placed at different angles in relation to the light. The most obvious difference is between the two cut faces of the chunks—one in light and the other in shade. There are just as strong differences between the side planes of the two chunks, and more subtle differences between their top planes. The slice of bread, lying on its side, reveals its own unique pattern of color spots. Yet we still read all three pieces of bread as parts of a single loaf.

EXTRA PROJECT

Try the same setup with a loaf of a different color, perhaps whole wheat or some other kind of dark, whole-grain bread. Or, if you think you can handle it, try a loaf that has a more complex form, such as a twisted loaf or a braided bread.

A NEW ANGLE ON COLOR

SETUP. Select a bright blue sheet of paper from the stack of colored paper you've been using to line the walls and floor of your setup box. Cut the sheet to 12″ × 16″ (31 × 41 cm) if it's not already that size. Fold the sheet in half, so that the two halves now measure 8″ × 12″ (roughly 20 × 31 cm). Then fold one of the halves again, so that you get two sections that measure 4″ × 12″ (about 10 × 31 cm). Look at the photograph to see the direction of the folds. The center fold should form a peak, while the smaller fold turns back on itself. The whole thing should look like an irregular, reversed letter Z. Now line the left wall of the setup box with light green paper, the right wall with orange, and the floor with yellow. Turn the setup box to Position 1. Then place the folded sheet obliquely on the floor of the setup box so that the left back corner of the sheet touches the green wall, and the right back corner touches the orange wall. Locate the lamp above and to the right, but low enough so that the light falls on the inclined plane of the folded paper, but not on its other planes, which remain in shade.

SETUP BOX POSITION 1

The corner—where the walls meet—is to the left of your line of vision. You see more of the right wall than the left. The setup is well below eye level, so you can see plenty of floor.

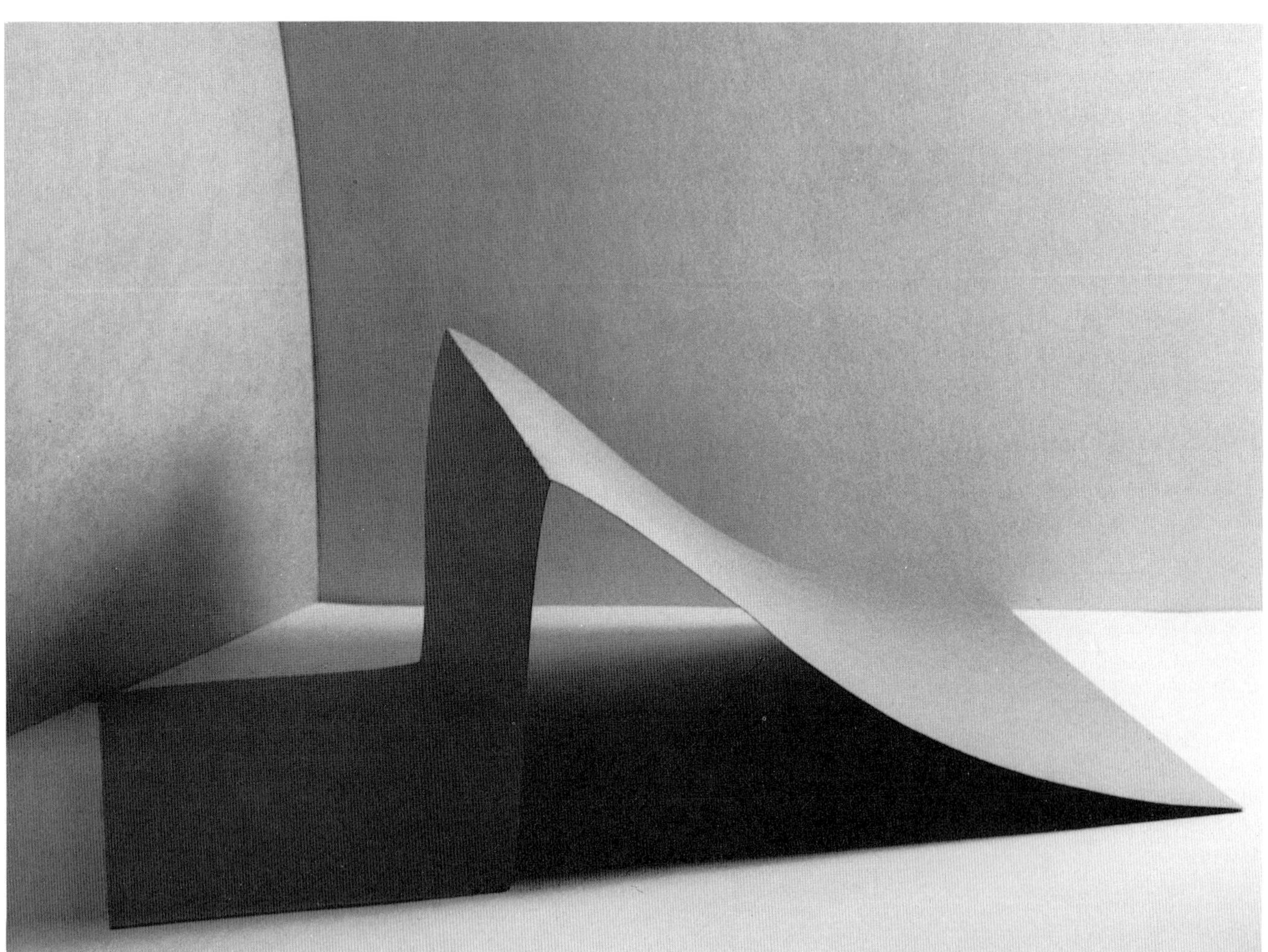

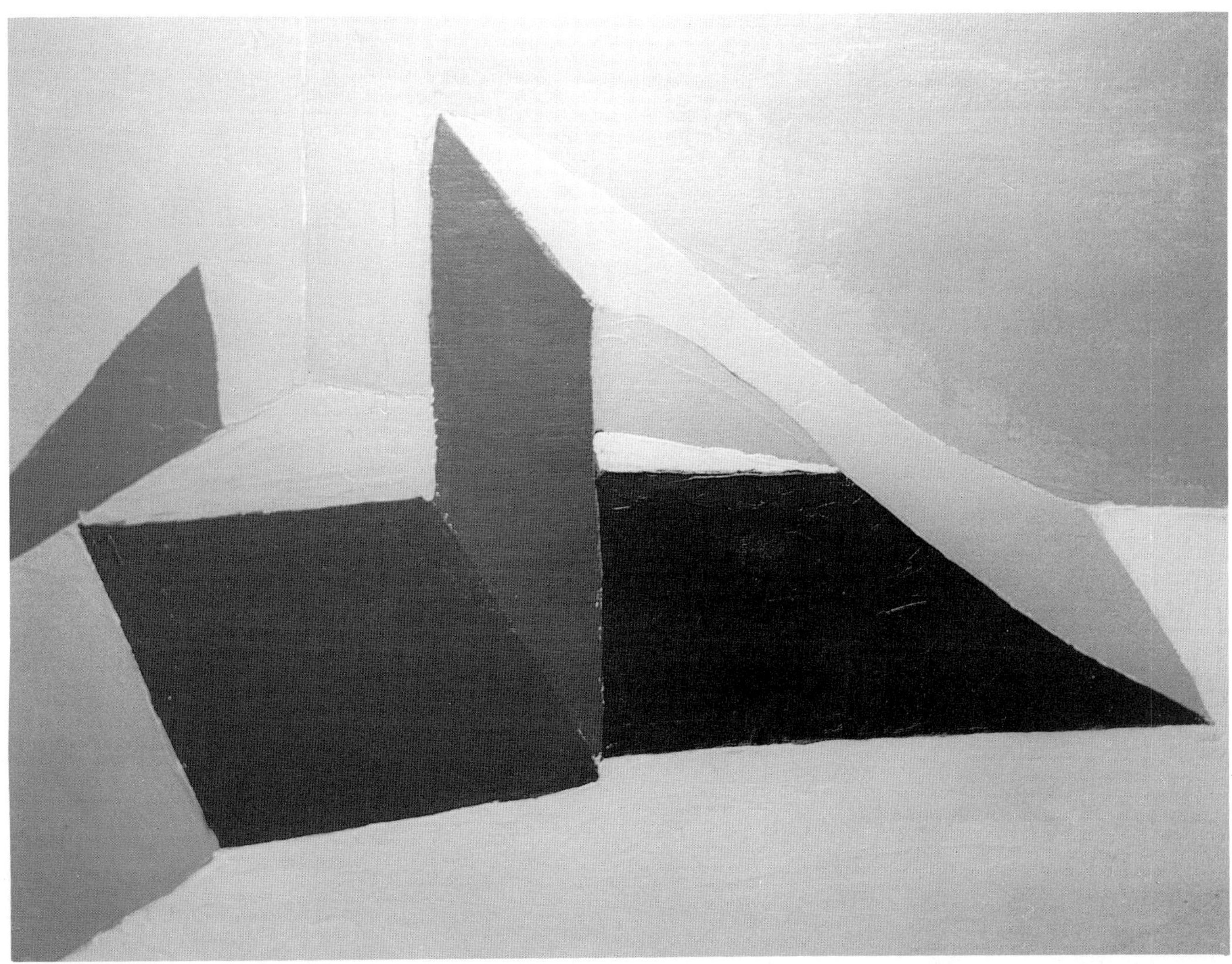

FIRST STATEMENT. Work on a full sheet of canvas paper, held horizontally, and use your 3:4 viewfinder to frame the composition. The folded paper, the walls and floor of the setup box, and the cast shadows will form quite an intriguing geometric design. Your first statement should summarize each flat plane of the paper and of the setup box as a single, angular color spot. You'll need several color spots for the cast shadows. The most difficult thing in this project could be getting the shapes and directions of the cast shadows right. As you can see, the student who painted this first statement had problems with those shadows, but he finally corrected them, as you'll see in the color plate on page 88. Here's how the color spots should work out:

- 2 for the walls of the setup box
- 3 (all one color) for the floor
- 3 for the planes of the folded paper
- 4 for the cast shadow on the floor and left wall.

OBSERVATIONS. What becomes apparent as soon as you paint the three color spots of the folded paper is another of Leonardo's observations: "Opaque bodies seldom show their natural color." As you have doubtless come to appreciate, object color often turns out to be relatively unimportant. Only the diagonal plane of the folded paper bears any resemblance to the blue sheet that you cut, folded, and placed in the setup box. The way an object of uniform color responds to its surroundings will continue to astound you. No matter how many years you've been painting, the surprises keep coming.

First Statement, Kevin Kennedy.

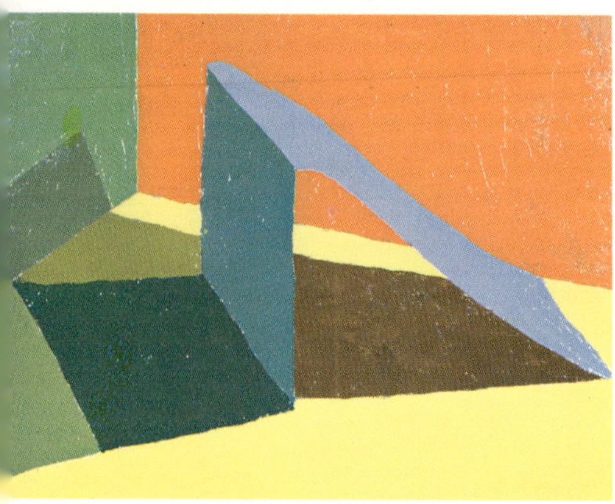

SECOND STATEMENT. Review the whole setup once again with your spot screen and look for the subdivisions within the planes of the paper, searching for the color spots that show the response of each plane to the direct light and to the indirect light that comes from the surrounding planes. Each plane of the folded paper will probably subdivide into two or three color spots. If you haven't succeeded in getting the shape and direction of the cast shadows right in your first statement, try to correct these problems now. Your second statement will probably work out to somewhere between two dozen and three dozen color spots:

4–5 for the right wall of the setup box
4–5 for its left wall
4–5 for its lighted floor
5–6 for the cast shadows
8–10 for the planes of the folded paper.

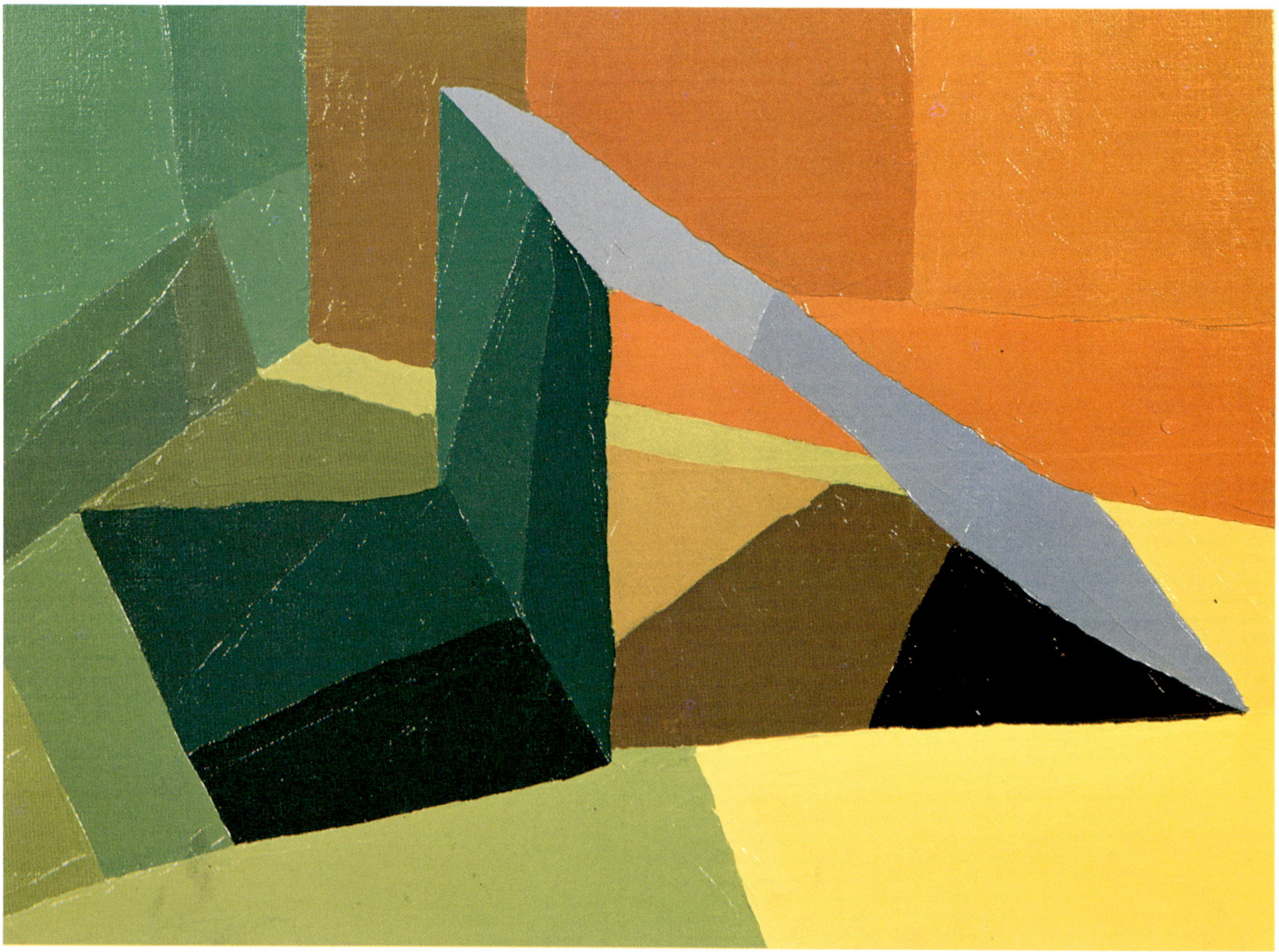

Second Statement, Kevin Kennedy.

OBSERVATIONS. By the time you finish painting this second statement, you'll see that the object color (or local color) has virtually disappeared without a trace. The interactions of the various color planes have their own logic, which you may want to analyze *after* you paint the individual color spots. This kind of analysis tends to be easier when you're painting a subject that consists entirely of flat planes, rather than a round or irregular object like an apple or a loaf of bread. For example, you can probably make a fairly accurate guess about the sources of the five color spots that appear in this student's rendering of the left wall of the setup box, which is influenced not only by the adjacent planes, but by the cast shadow.

Third Statement, Kevin Kennedy.

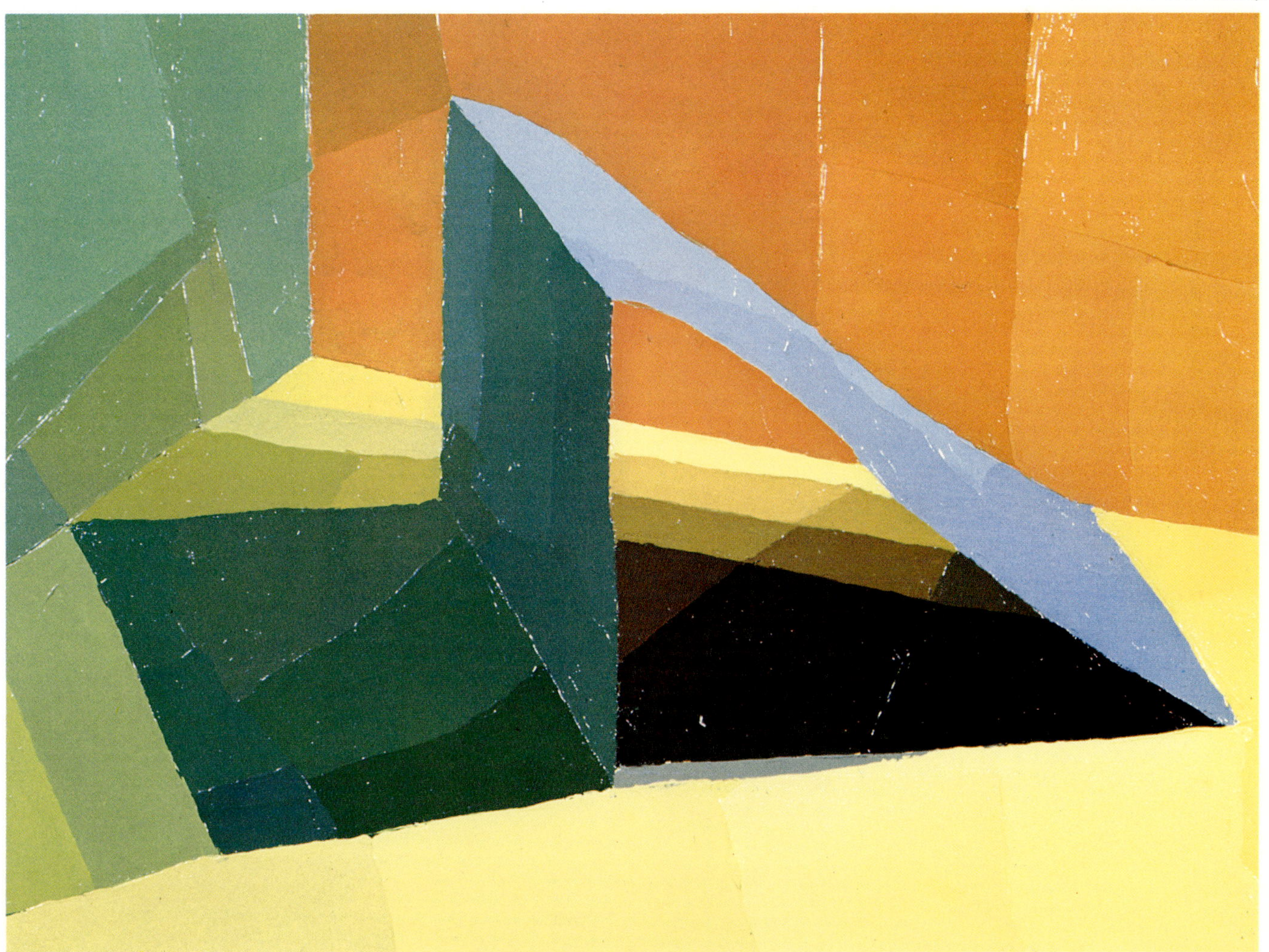

THIRD STATEMENT. Because of the simple form of the folded paper, you won't need vastly more color spots to complete your third statement. This student has finished his study of the folded paper with fairly big, angular color spots that clearly follow the rule that you must *always* use as few color spots as necessary—and then stop. This final statement is also developed evenly throughout: that is, there's no one plane where you see a great many more color spots than you see in any other plane.

OBSERVATIONS. This is a particularly dramatic example of the way environmental influences take over and subdue the object color. It's also time to start thinking about how the meaning of these projects relates to future painting problems when you "graduate" from this highly controlled series of still-life exercises. Thus, painting a single sheet of folded paper will tell you a lot about how to paint the folds in the fabrics that people wear, and even about the geological "folds" in the landscape. It's not a very far leap from painting a piece of folded paper to painting the jagged, diagonal planes of a mountain range. The same basic principles apply.

EXTRA PROJECT

Try exactly the same setup with any colors that suit you. A folded sheet of orange paper can be a dramatic change of pace. A folded sheet of white paper can give you a fascinating lesson in the effects of reflected color on object color. For an even more dramatic experiment, choose any sheet of colored paper and then paint a contrasting stripe of color lengthwise, from one end to the other.

SEEING THROUGH TRANSLUCENCY

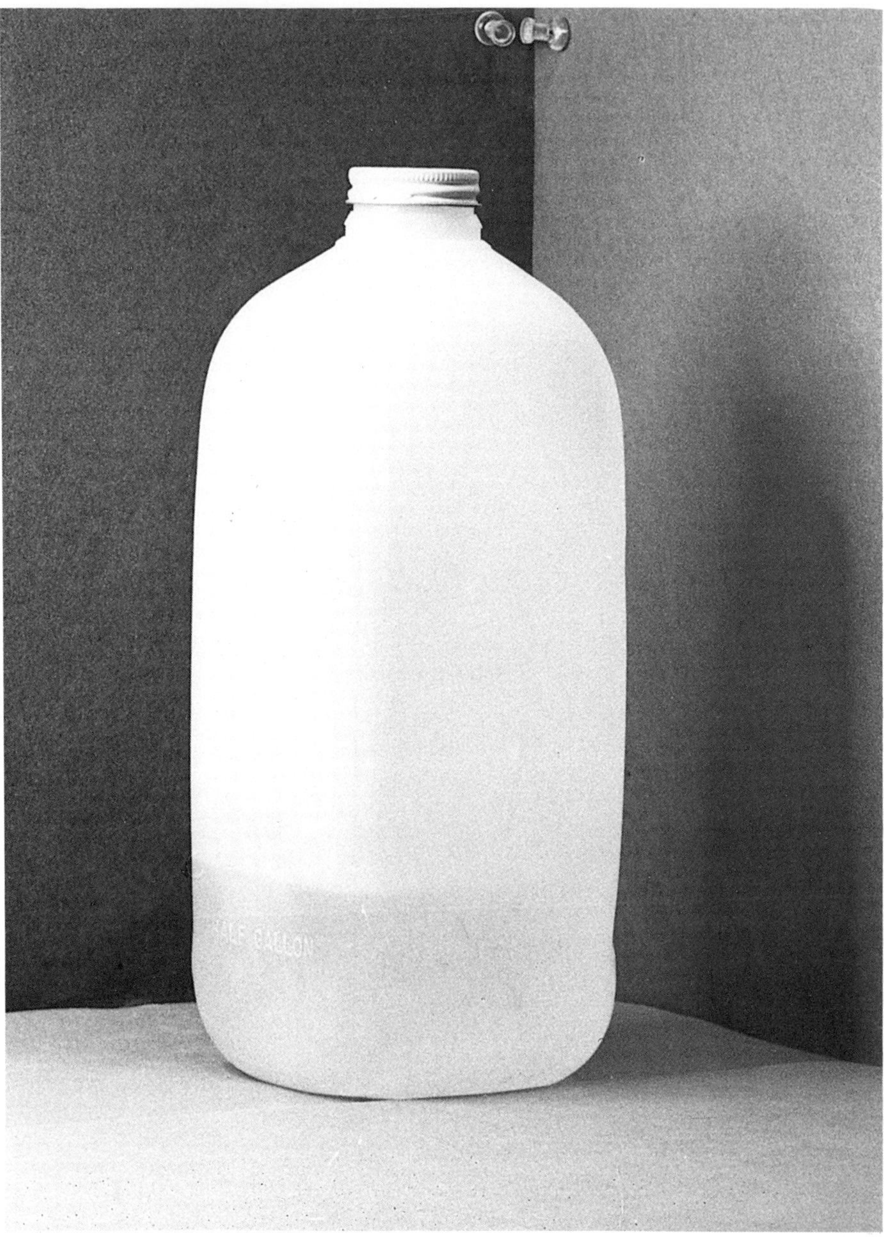

SETUP. Till now, you've painted objects that were entirely opaque, reflecting all the light they receive, and transmitting none. Now it's time to tackle translucency. Procure a big jug of colorless, cloudy plastic—the kind that's often used to package half a gallon (or 2 liters) of cider. (Be sure to drink the cider; we want an empty jug!) Soak off the paper label, rinse out the jug, pour in about a pint (or half a liter) of water, and then recap the jug. Turn the setup box on end to suit this upright subject. Line the left wall of the setup box with green paper, the right wall with blue, and the floor with red. With the upended box in Position 2, pose the jug so that it overlaps the corner of the setup box, where the two walls meet. The handle of the jug should be in back and out of sight. Ideally, the shape of the jug should be slightly angular, so that one of its corners will point toward you. Your eye level ought to be at about the midpoint of the jug. The setup lamp should be in front of the setup box and to the left, so that the jug casts a sizable shadow on the floor and right wall of the box.

SETUP BOX POSITION 2

The corner of the setup box, where the walls meet, is in line with your eye. You see both the right and left walls equally.

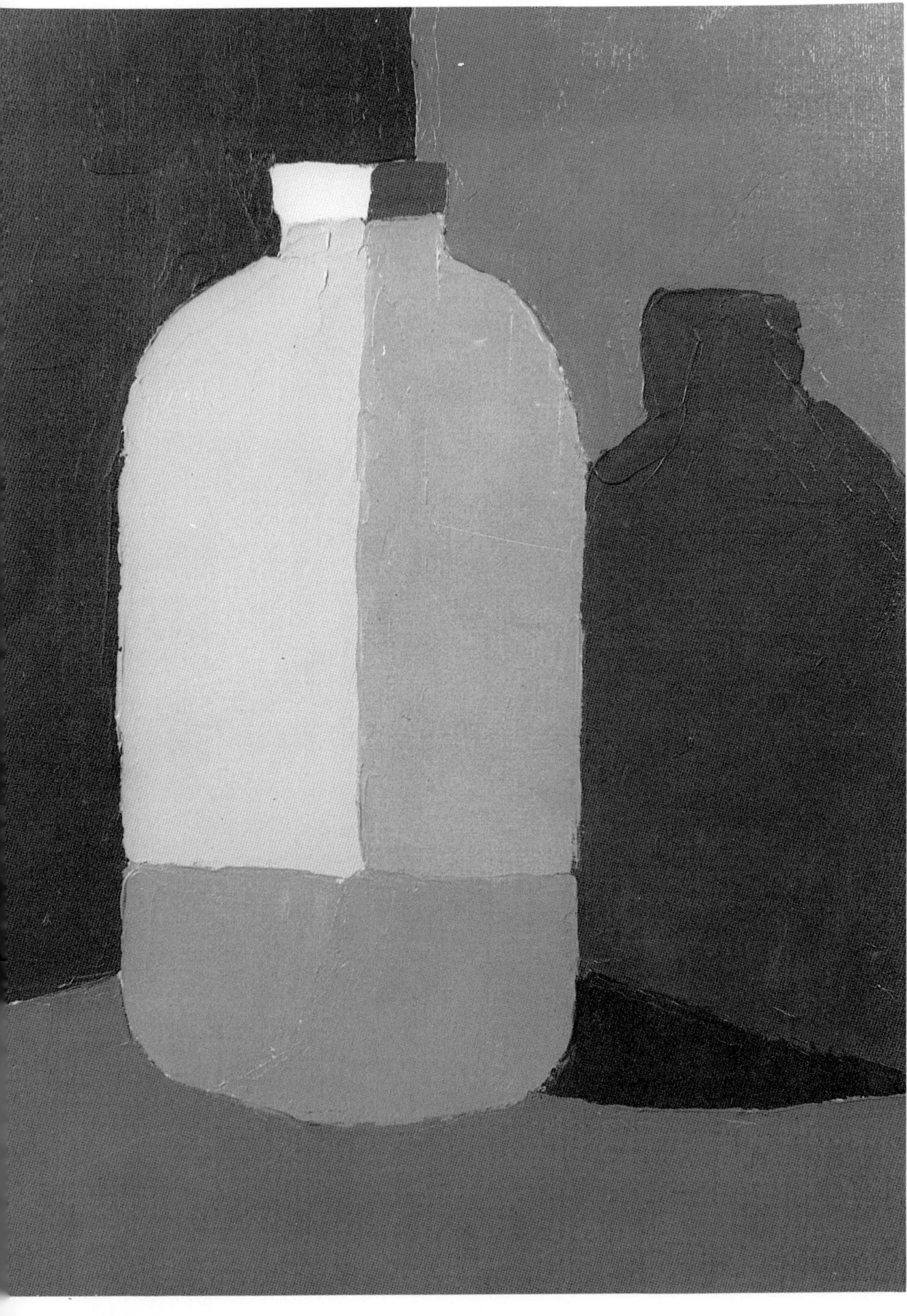

FIRST STATEMENT. Work on a full sheet of canvas paper, held vertically, and use your 3:4 viewfinder. Since this is the first time you're going to paint an object that's not opaque, you may be a bit anxious. But I want you to forget about translucency and just go ahead and paint the big color spots of the jug as you would paint any opaque object. Look for these eleven color spots:

- 2 for the walls of the setup box
- 1 for its floor
- 2 for the cap of the jug
- 2 for the empty upper part of the jug
- 2 for the water-filled lower part
- 2 for the cast shadow on the floor and wall.

OBSERVATIONS. If you observe and mix all those color spots with reasonable accuracy, the colors of the jug will begin to convey some of that mysterious, opalescent quality that you *thought* would be so difficult. You may find it hard to see two distinct color spots in the lower section of the jug—the part that's filled with water. If that is so, and all you see there is a single color spot, then paint only that single color spot. I don't expect you to follow my instructions uncritically, inventing color spots just because I ask you to look for them. Paint only the color spots you find; your observations don't have to agree exactly with my suggestions, or with the student work reproduced along with the projects. In the first statement shown here, notice that the shadow on the right wall is lower than the actual jug. That's not a mistake—the shadow is lower because the setup light is higher than the jug.

First Statement, Richard Gleason.

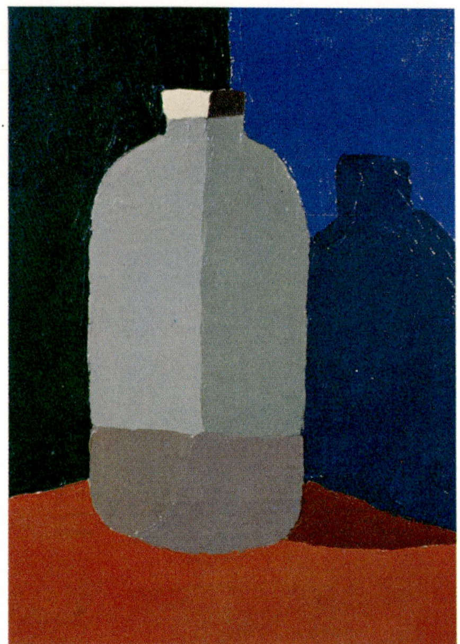

Second Statement, Richard Gleason.

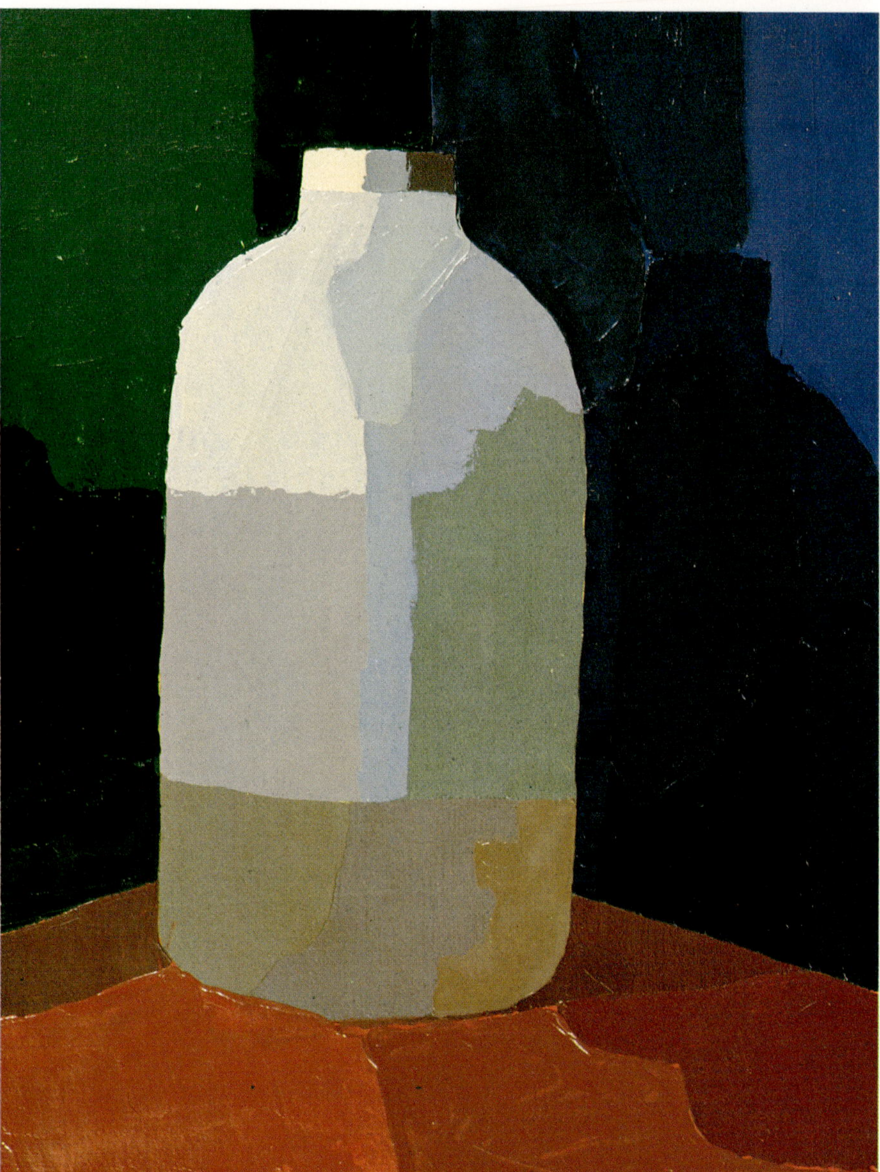

SECOND STATEMENT. You've gone through the process of creating a second statement at least fourteen times by now, so I'm sure you're beginning to anticipate my instructions. That is, you're beginning to make those decisions that I've been making for you until now. So now I won't tell you exactly how many color spots to look for in your second statement. You know the general rule that—when you get to the second statement—each big color spot of the first statement will probably subdivide into three or four smaller color spots. (Naturally, it doesn't *always* work out that way, since some surfaces are simpler than others.) So now look again at the jug and its surroundings, and find your own color spots for your second statement. The original eleven color spots of the first statement will probably develop into somewhere between thirty and forty color spots. The precise number is up to you.

OBSERVATIONS. Think back, for a moment, over all the projects you've done so far, and try to summarize a few things. Every setup really consists of three elements: the planes of the setup box; the object (or objects) within the box; and the shadow (or shadows) cast by whatever you posed in the setup box. So, a typical first statement is likely to start out with three big color spots for the planes of the setup box; one or more big color spots for the "model" in the box; and one or more color spots for the cast shadow. Add them all up, and you'll see that a typical first statement rarely has more than a dozen color spots, and often as few as half-a-dozen. Now, assuming that, when you get to the second statement, you subdivide each of these big color spots into three or four, a typical second statement is apt to run somewhere between twenty and forty color spots, and perhaps a few more if the subject is fairly complicated.

Third Statement, Richard Gleason.

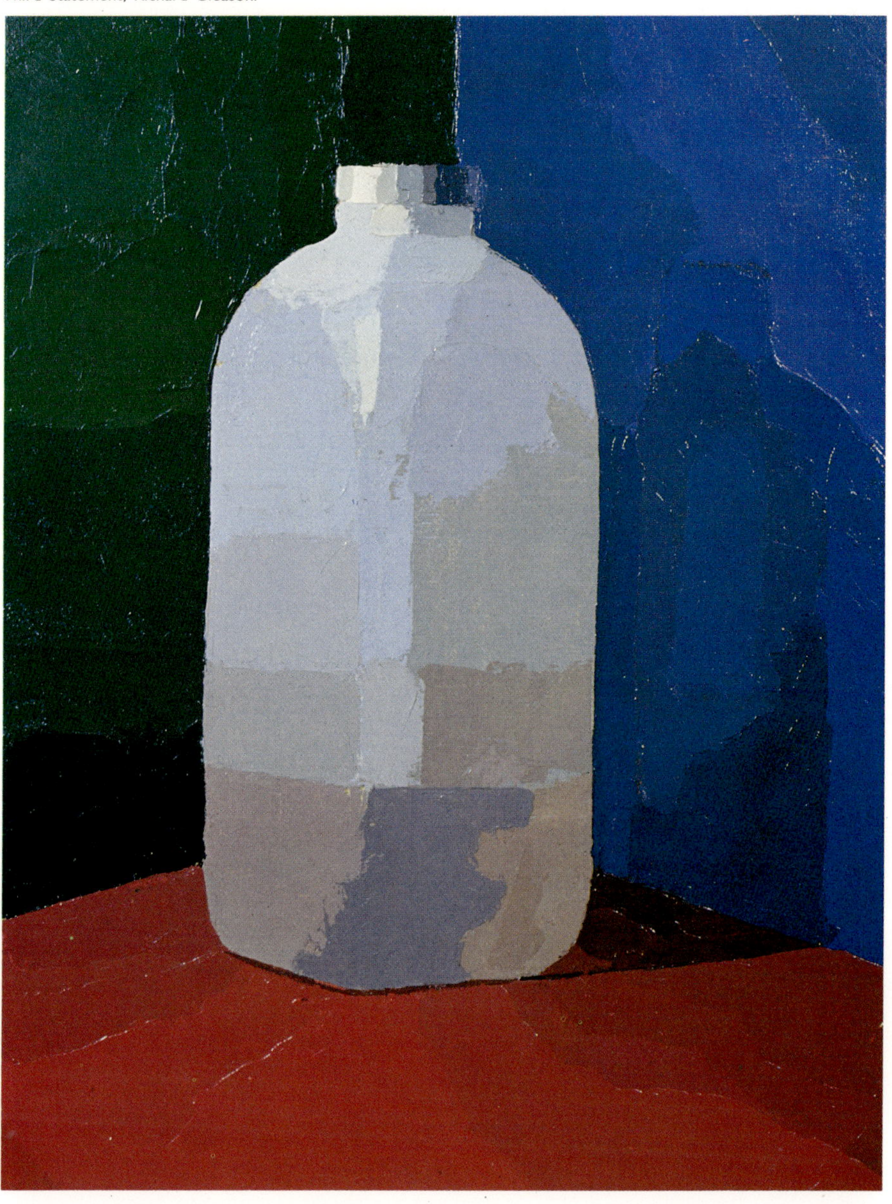

THIRD STATEMENT. A second statement, like the one you've just done, sometimes looks slightly disjointed. Some color spots may seem to jump out at you, while others may look just wrong or somehow out of place. The contrasts between color spots also may be too strong, suggesting the need for transitional color spots inserted between them. A second statement rarely looks as complete and decisive as either a first or a third statement. That's why you go on to paint a third statement—to make corrections and insert transitions. First go over the entire second statement to determine what's awry. Use your spot screen to double-check the hue, luminosity, and intensity of every color spot that looks dubious. Also check their size, shape, and position relative to those spots that look right. Then make these corrections as you repaint the entire surface. Now start looking for connections—what I call *transitions*. Scrutinize the setup again with your spot screen. Look especially hard at the areas *between* the color spots you've painted in your second statement. Search for contrasts that seem too harsh, and add in-between colors to make the statement look more realistic. One note of caution about these transitions: never make an in-between color spot by blending two adjacent color spots or mixing their colors to make a third. A transitional color spot must be newly seen and freshly mixed. It is a *new* color spot.

OBSERVATIONS. Your third statement reinforces what you already saw in the first statement, namely that a translucent object is no harder to paint than an opaque one—if only you forget about its translucency. There's no problem unless you *create* the problem by imagining something especially difficult about translucent color. Having learned this lesson, you'll then be prepared to paint other supposedly difficult, translucent subjects, such as milk glass, clouds, snow, the shimmering reflections in an icy pond, a frosty window, pearls, or an infant's skin.

EXTRA PROJECT

Pour out the water from the jug and replace it with some colorful liquid, such as cold tea or leftover cider—or another fruit juice. Line the setup box with different colors, which should now be a matter of personal taste. Keep the lighting the same. And proceed to paint three more statements.

A BAGFUL OF COLOR

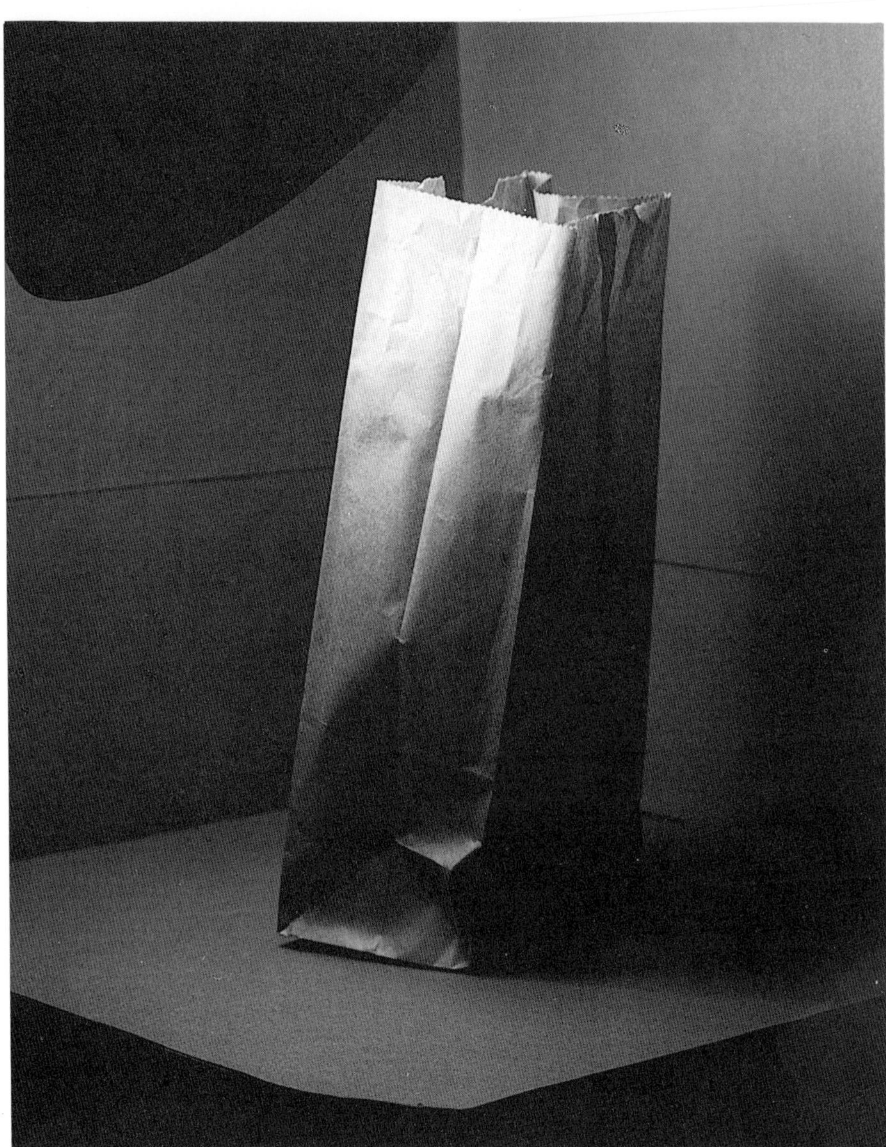

SETUP. A paper bag, unlike a plastic jug, is theoretically opaque. But, if the light is right, parts of the bag can become translucent. The resulting play of opacity and translucency can be a visual delight. For this project, your "model" is an ordinary brown paper bag, slightly battered from use, so it exhibits interesting creases and folds. You turned the setup box on end when you painted the vertical composition of the plastic jug—and you may want to do this again for this tall "model," too. Line the left wall of the setup box with green paper, the right wall with red, and the floor with blue. Turn the up-ended box to Position 2. Drop some weighty object, like a thick paperback book, into the bottom of the paper bag to help it stand upright. Then put the bag in the center of the setup box. Your lamp should be toward the front and at the left, so that some light shines through the bag to create a translucent effect, also casting a sizable shadow on the floor and right wall. The bag should be placed just low enough to let you see a bit of the inside.

SETUP BOX POSITION 2

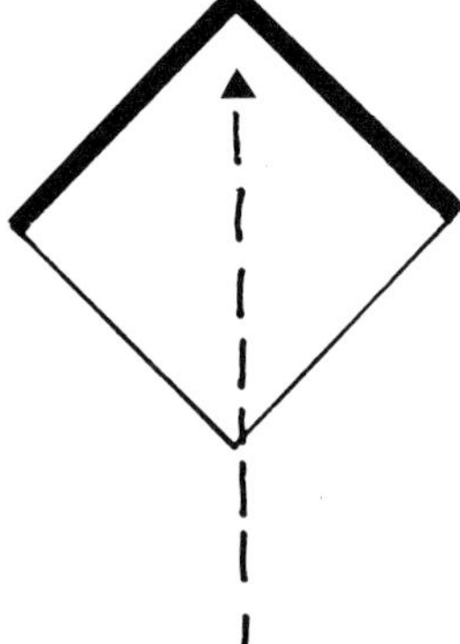

The corner of the box, where the two walls meet, is directly in line with your eye, so that you see both walls equally. The box is just low enough so that you see a fair amount of floor.

FIRST STATEMENT. Now hold your full sheet of canvas paper vertically. Use your 3:4 viewfinder to frame your composition with the bag in the center of the viewfinder window. In painting this first statement, your goal is simply to establish the solidity of the object, without worrying too much about whether it looks like a paper bag yet. The bag is a fairly blocky object, so concentrate on the planes of your model, as well as the planes of the surrounding setup box. Also pay attention to the shapes of the shadows. In the statement illustrated here, the student summarized what he saw in just ten color spots:

3 for the lighted walls and floor of the setup box
1 for the shaded area on the left wall
4 for the lights and darks on the bag
2 for the shadow on the floor and wall

OBSERVATIONS. Once you've laid them down on your canvas paper, these ten color spots may strike you as little more than a pretty pattern of shapes and colors. But don't be impatient if the bag still doesn't look like a bag, and might just as well be a rock. The main thing is that the bag looks solid if you've put the right color spots in the right places. And it does look as if it occupies space, as any solid object should. Notice that this first statement captures not only the cast shadow that runs across the floor and up the right wall, but also a big patch of dark on the left wall. The upright bag isn't a simple arrangement of two planes, front and side. The folds of the bag actually break the front into two planes and the side into two more planes—which become four big color spots.

First Statement, Richard Gleason.

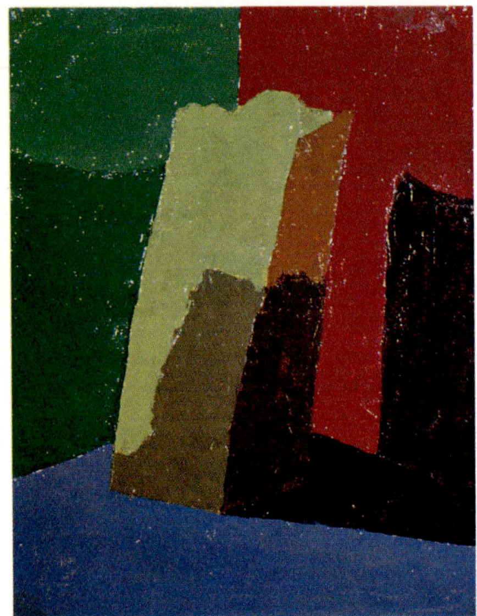

Second Statement, Richard Gleason.

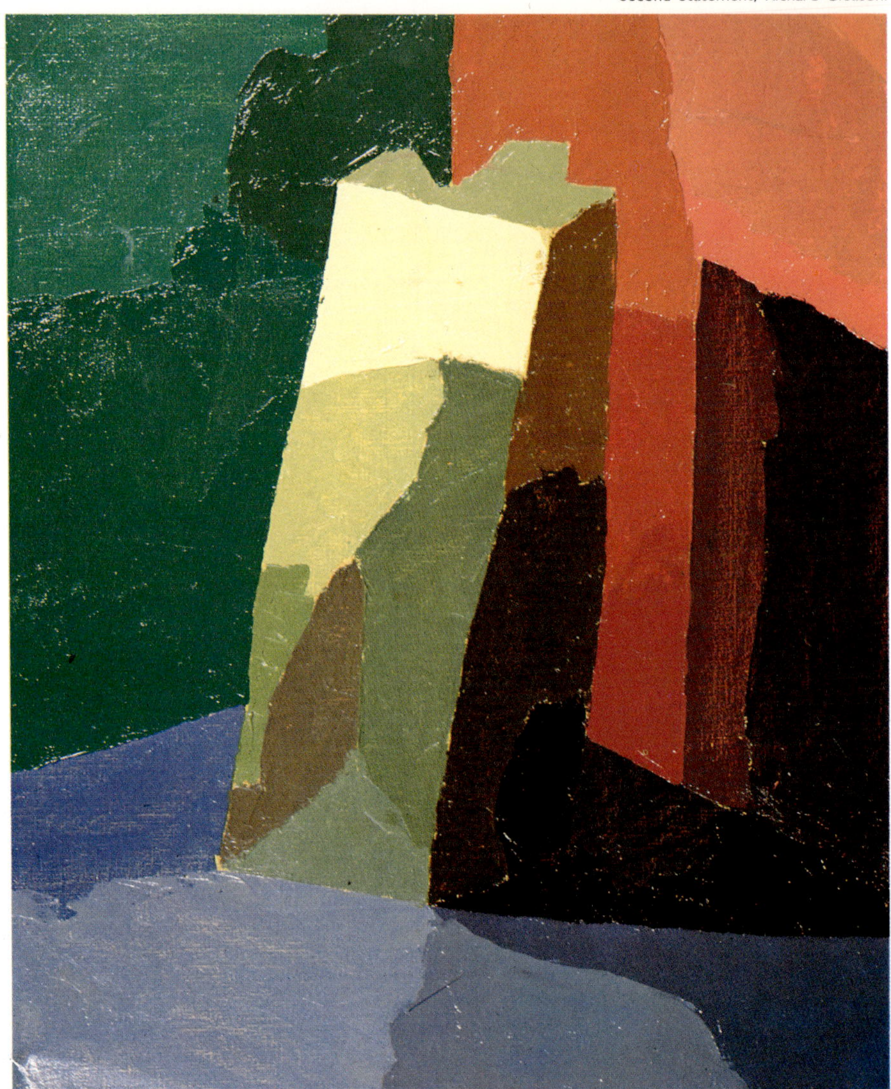

SECOND STATEMENT. Now study the irregular folds and creases in the paper bag to find additional color spots. But don't consciously say to yourself: "The bag folds here, so this must be another color spot." Forget that what you're painting is a paper bag and just look for those color spots as areas with rather irregular perimeters that must be recorded as accurately as you can. If you make the right decision about the hue, luminosity, intensity, size, shape, and position of each color spot, then all the color spots, taken as a whole, will eventually register as a series of folds.

OBSERVATIONS. As you multiply the color spots—going back over the ten big color spots of the first statement—you're certainly learning the lesson that this supposedly "brown" paper bag can't be painted accurately with any color even vaguely resembling "brown." When you go through the process of naming, mixing, and matching each color spot, you can see why "brown" is a forbidden word: every one of those mixtures turns out to be a subdued version of some very specific hue. The bag doesn't look like a bag just yet, but it's getting there. In the meantime, simply by painting each color spot as a flat area with its own unique character, you're making the bag look more solid, and you're creating a distinct sense of the space within the setup box.

Third Statement, Richard Gleason.

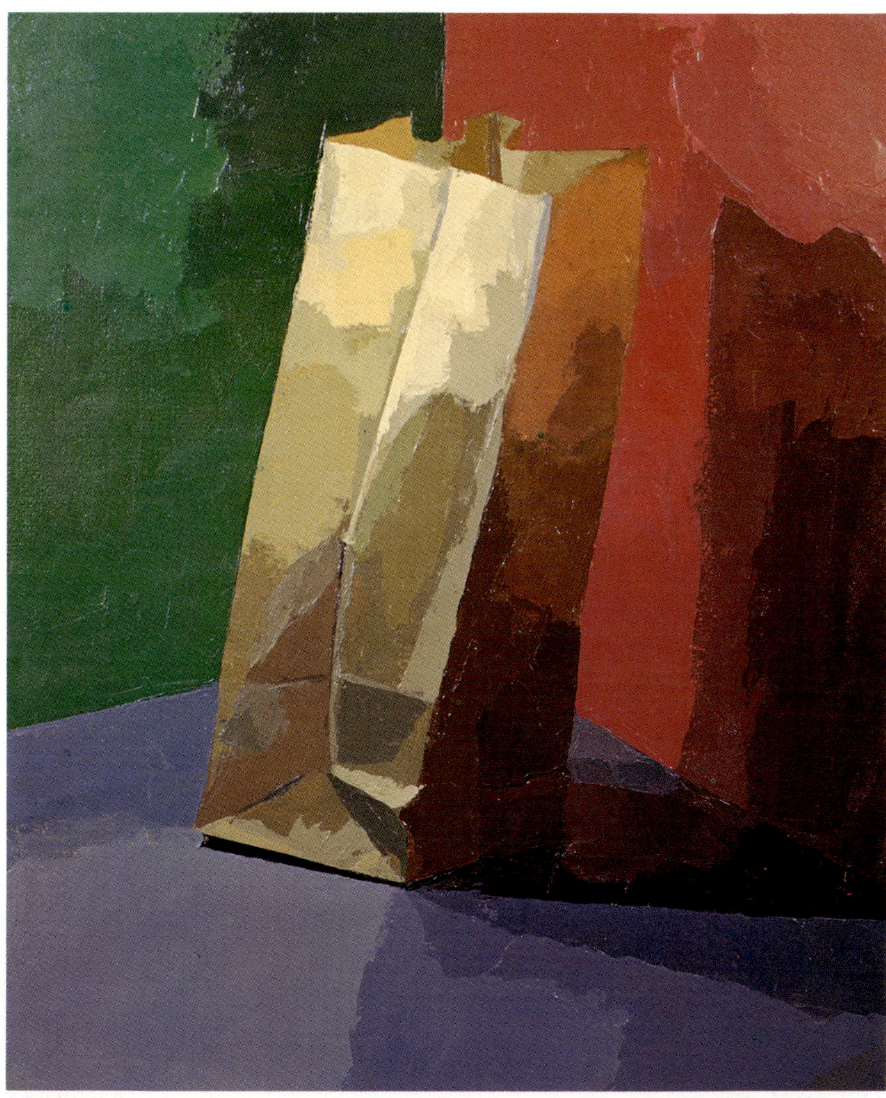

THIRD STATEMENT. At this stage, the bag really comes to look like a bag. But you must keep resisting the temptation to say to yourself: "Now I'm going to make the bag look more realistic by putting in all those nice creases and folds." As you add each new color spot, creating transitions and making corrections, focus your attention on that color spot alone. For example, as you get down to the complicated shapes at the bottom of the bag, just paint them as the ragged rectangles and polygons you see—and all by themselves, almost, they become folds of paper. In the same way, as you put together the luminous color spots at the top of the bag, don't remind yourself that you're trying to capture the translucent effect of the light shining through the paper; let the color spots do that job for you.

OBSERVATIONS. This certainly is growing into a more complex subject than you might have expected when you started to paint it. Now look at the finished third statement and ask yourself some questions. Does the bag look solid enough, and does the surrounding space of the setup box look convincing? Do the bag and the setup box in your painting seem to fit with each other, and work together as well as their originals do in the actual setup? Does your bag boast as interesting a play of translucency and opacity as you see in the actual bag? Finally, has all of this been done with sufficiently smooth transitions and a minimum of false notes—that is, do the color spots seem to hold their place in the picture rather than leap out or fall back? If you can answer *yes* to all these questions, congratulations. If not, go back and try again.

EXTRA PROJECT

Now do the same project with an all-white paper bag, posed and lit in the same way. Change the colors on the walls and floor of the setup box to suit your taste. Carry the project through the usual three statements. When you finish painting the white bag, paint a single stripe of bright color around its middle and then start again.

A LOOK AT TRANSPARENCY

SETUP. You've probably been wondering when you're going to paint something not translucent but *transparent*—and here it is. Your "model" for this project is a glass dish of a *single, unmodulated color*. Structurally, the dish should be as simple as possible. A dessert dish or a salad plate will do. You won't be painting the left wall of the setup box, so line it with gray paper so it exerts the least possible influence on the rest of the setup. If your dish is a primary hue—red, blue, or yellow—line the right wall and the floor of the box with the other two primaries. If your dish is a secondary hue—green, orange, or violet—line the right wall and floor with the other two secondaries. With the setup box in Position 4, locate the dish in the center of the box, and place the entire setup just below your eye level so that the top of the dish looks like a long, narrow ellipse. Place your setup lamp directly above the dish so that the cast shadow is substantial and clearly visible from where you work.

SETUP BOX POSITION 4

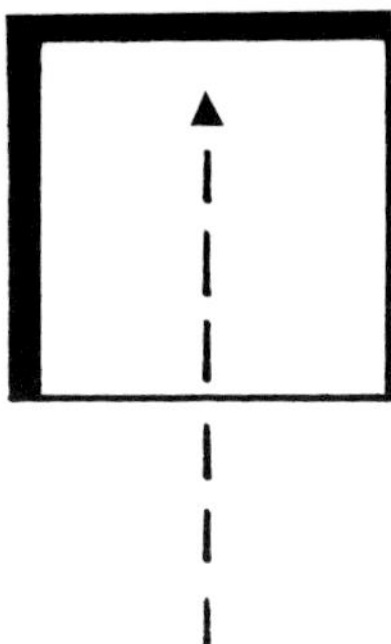

The right wall is perpendicular to your line of vision—cutting straight across it—and the left wall is parallel to your line of vision, off to the left and out of sight. In effect, you see only the right wall, which becomes the back wall.

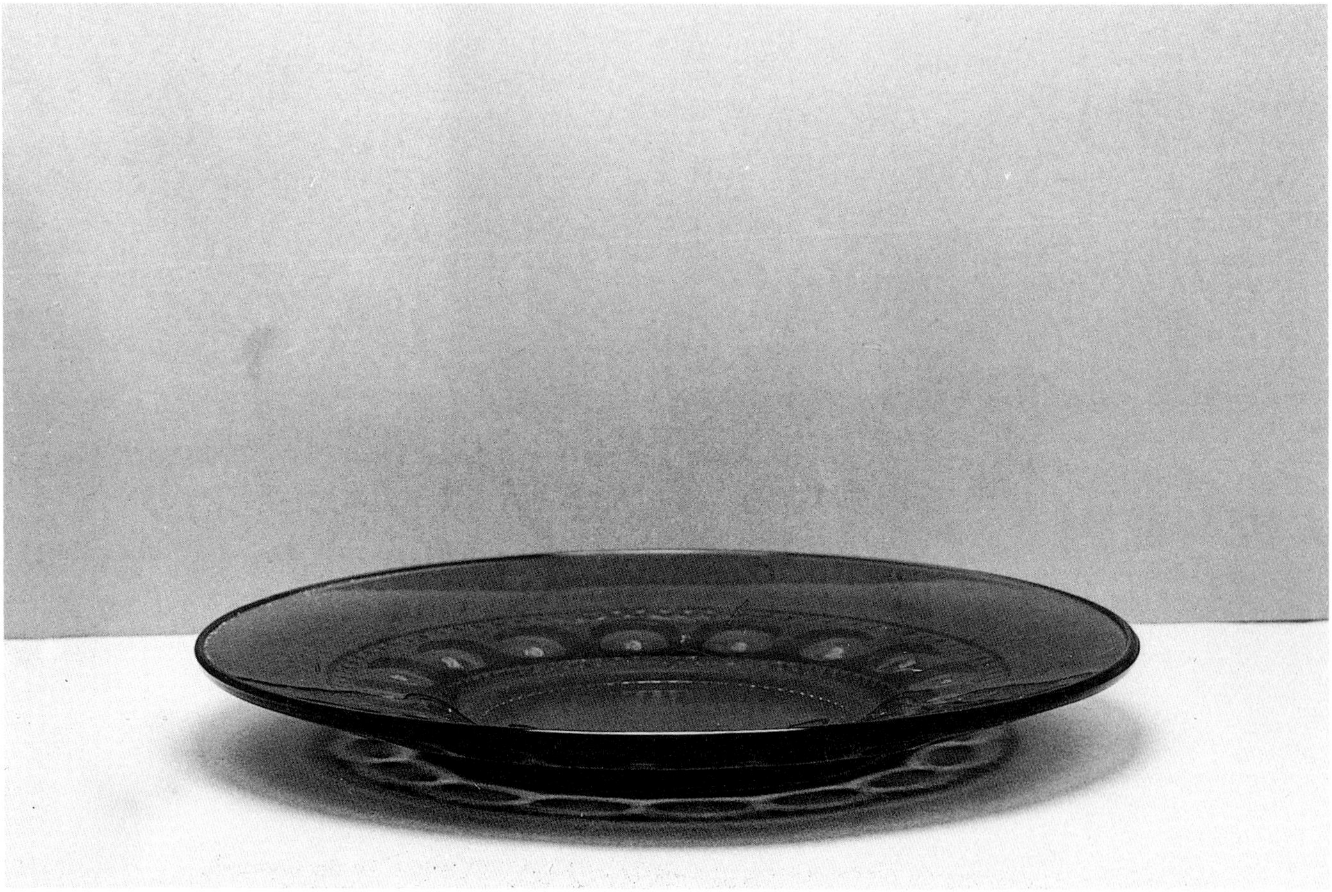

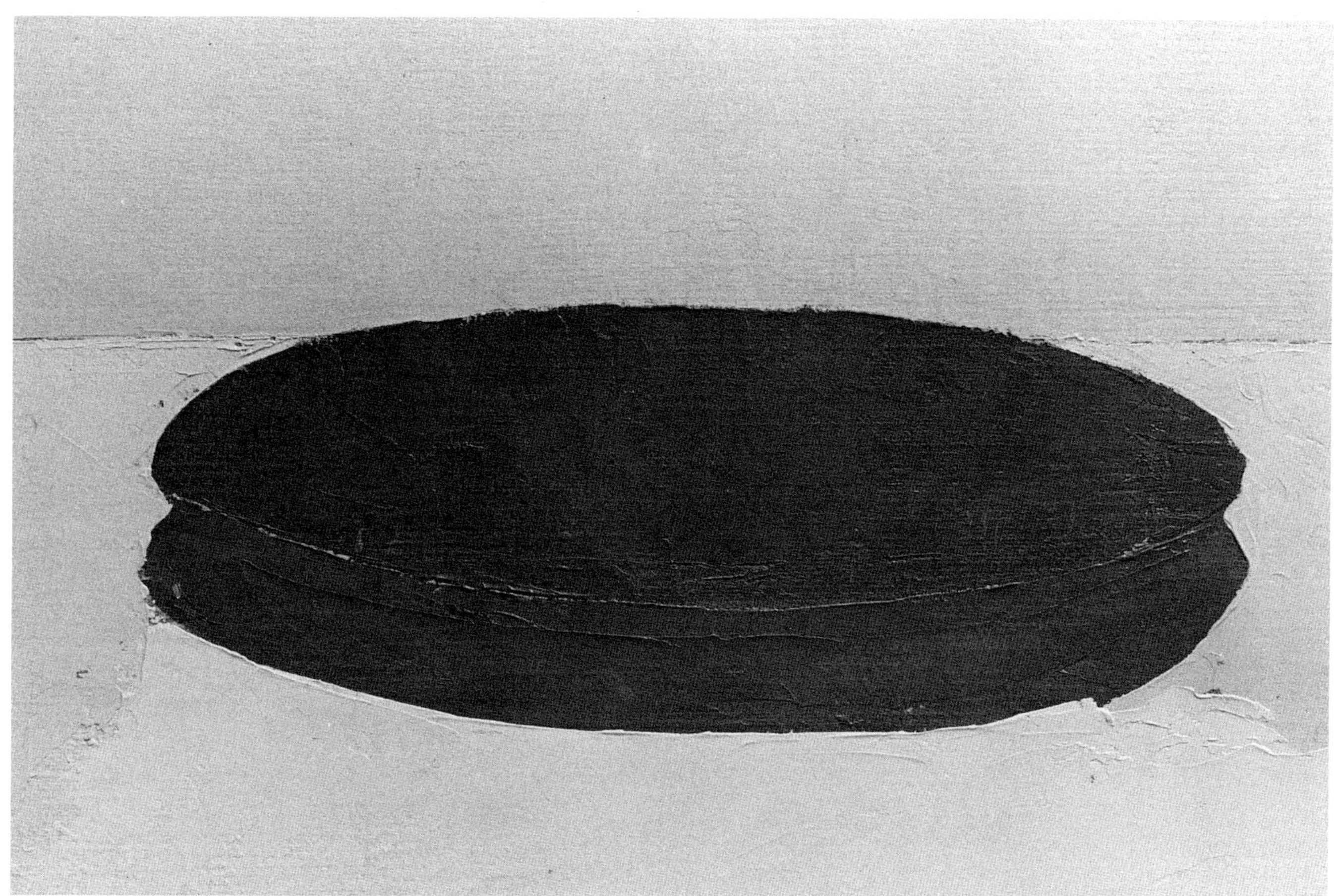

FIRST STATEMENT. When you painted the supposedly difficult aluminum saucepan in Project 11, you succeeded because you set aside your preconceptions about the special nature of metal. Instead of asking for the "secret" of painting silvery metal, you went to work on it in the same way that you've painted everything else—identifying, mixing, and matching the right color spots until the saucepan turned out to look metallic simply because the right color spots were in the right places. And that's the way you're going to paint the supposedly difficult subject of colored glass. Start out with an extremely simple first statement in just four color spots:

1 for the back wall of the setup box
1 for the floor
1 for the top surface of the dish
1 for its underside *and* cast shadow.

OBSERVATIONS. The crucial color spot in this first statement is the top surface of the dish—which calls for minimal thinking and maximal *looking*. Again, if you abandon what you *think* you know about the color of the dish, you'll come up with a couple of discoveries. First, no matter how strong the color of the actual dish may be—the color of glassware is usually very intense—you'll find that this is *not* the dominant factor in the color you see on the surface of the dish. Second, despite the transparency of the glass, you'll find that you can't see the floor color transmitted through it—at least not from where you're working. In short, the color of the top surface—once the dish is placed in the setup box—is totally unpredictable. To paint it, you're forced to abandon all logical analysis and simply paint the colors you see. Of course, in the first statement it won't look like a glass dish yet. But don't worry. Just go on to the second statement. (By the way, you may notice that the first statement reproduced here has an extra color spot at the right of the dish; the student went a bit beyond the essential four color spots—and that's fine.)

First Statement, Don Stern.

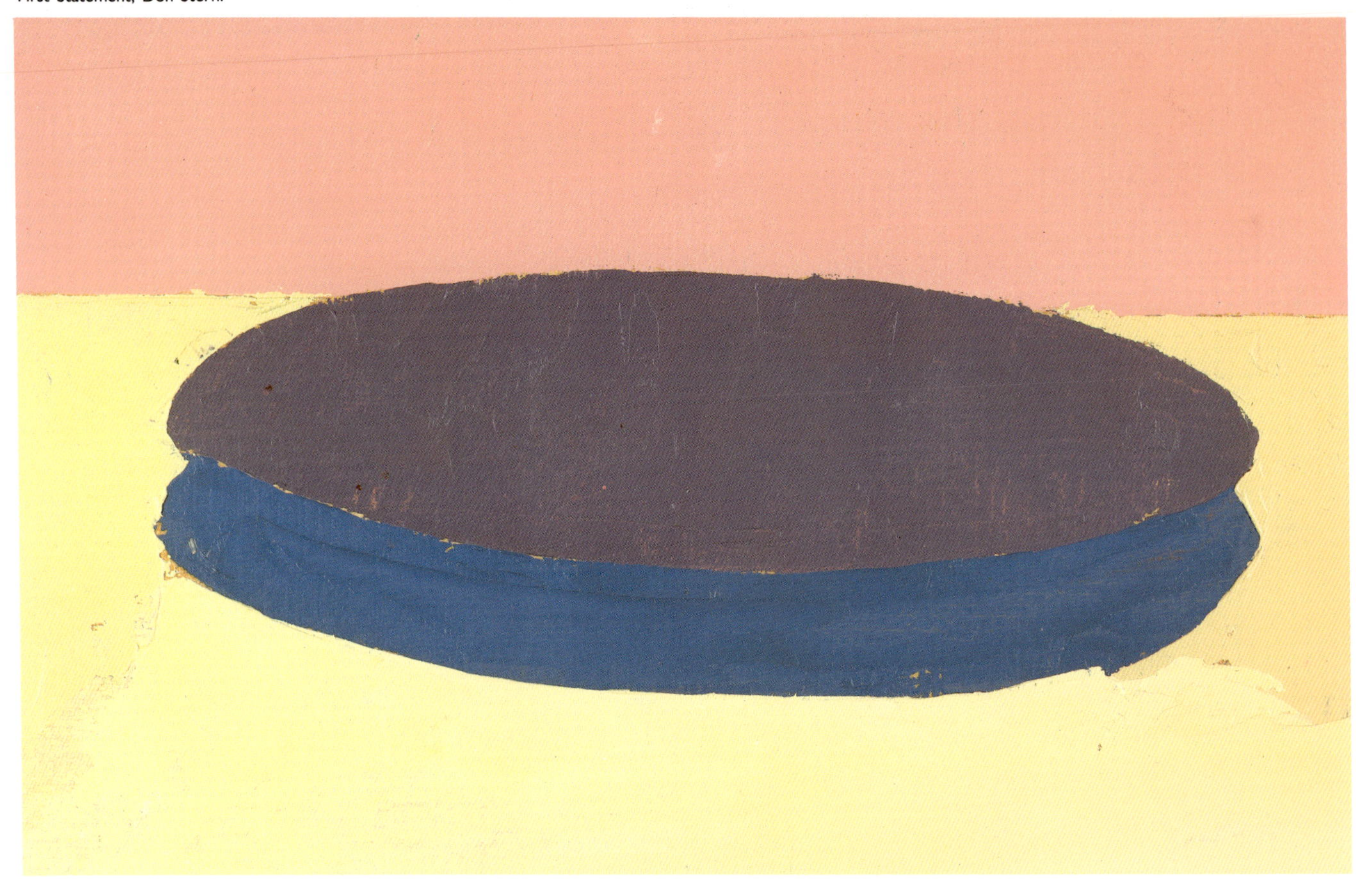

FIRST STATEMENT. This summary in five color spots (by Don Stern) serves simply to cover the canvas paper and lay out the essentials. It can't even begin to be a likeness of the colored glass dish, but it does establish one very important point. It's not the top of the dish, but its cast shadow that tells us that we're looking at a blue dish. We can also see that the back wall of the setup box has strongly influenced the color of the top of the dish.

Second Statement, Don Stern.

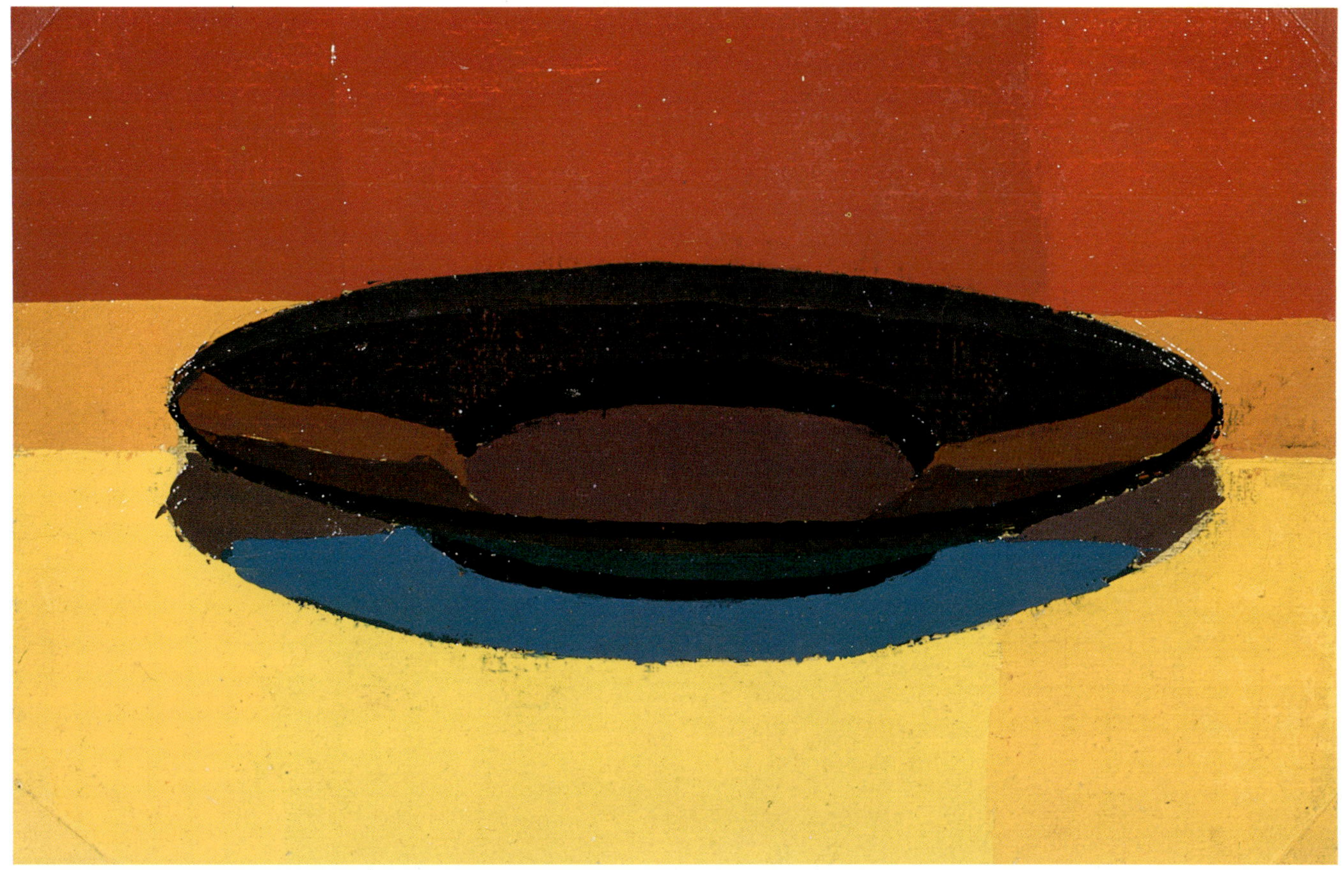

SECOND STATEMENT. To transform those four big color spots into a brilliant, transparent glass dish, you're only going to need a second statement—not a third. The job is far simpler than you expect. I won't tell you how many color spots you'll need in this second statement, but try to be economical. Paint only one color spot for each area of pronounced color difference. Proceed just far enough to make your study look like the setup, but no further. You can omit highlights, as the student has done in the second statement shown here—even without highlights, you can capture a strong likeness of the glass dish. Now the crucial color spot is the cast shadow. It's hardly influenced—if at all—by the back wall or the floor. After you've painted it, you may try to figure out where its color comes from, but it may be a waste of time.

OBSERVATIONS. The colors of the second statement defy all prediction, which is exactly the point. This project forces you to overcome the assumption that the top surface has to be the *object color* (or *local color*) of the dish. It just doesn't work out that way in this setup. You're also forced to abandon any hope that the cast shadow will be some variant of the color of the floor of the setup box. And if you guessed that the cast shadow was going to be a mixture of the blue plate and the yellow floor—a green shadow—that guess has also turned out to be wrong. More than any project you've painted so far, this one forces you to abandon all logic, all memory, all rational assumptions, and just paint with your eyes. Above all, you must stop thinking "glass" and "blue"!

EXTRA PROJECT

This particular project is such a fascinating challenge that you might want to try *two* extra projects. First, paint the same dish with different colors on the wall and floor. Second, keep the surroundings the same and replace your first dish with another of a different hue. Be ready for some surprises. Nothing will behave as you expect.

A GLASS OF WATER ISN'T COLORLESS

SETUP. Having confronted and solved the problem of painting a colored, transparent object in Project 19, you're now ready to face a model that's colorless—at least *theoretically*. Get a plain tumbler of clear, colorless glass. Wash and rinse it till it sparkles. Then half-fill it with clear water. While the water settles, ridding itself of bubbles, line the left wall of your setup box with green paper, the right wall with red, and the floor with blue. Turning the setup box to Position 2, put the glass of water in the corner so that it overlaps the meeting point of the walls and floor. Arrange the lamp above your model and slightly in front.

SETUP BOX POSITION 2

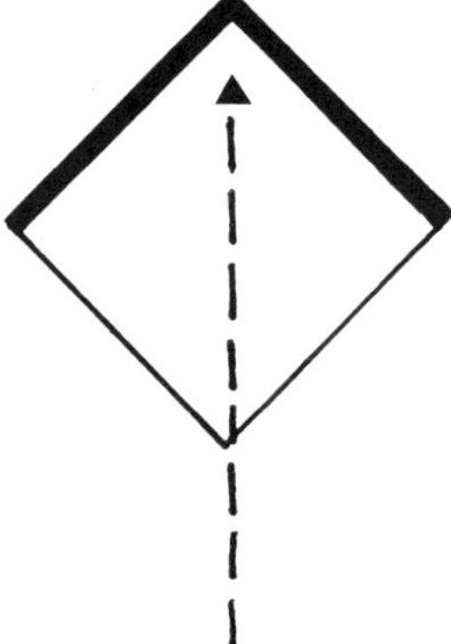

The corner of the box is directly in line with your eye. You're staring straight at the line where the walls meet. You see both walls equally and you also see a fair amount of floor because the setup is well below eye level.

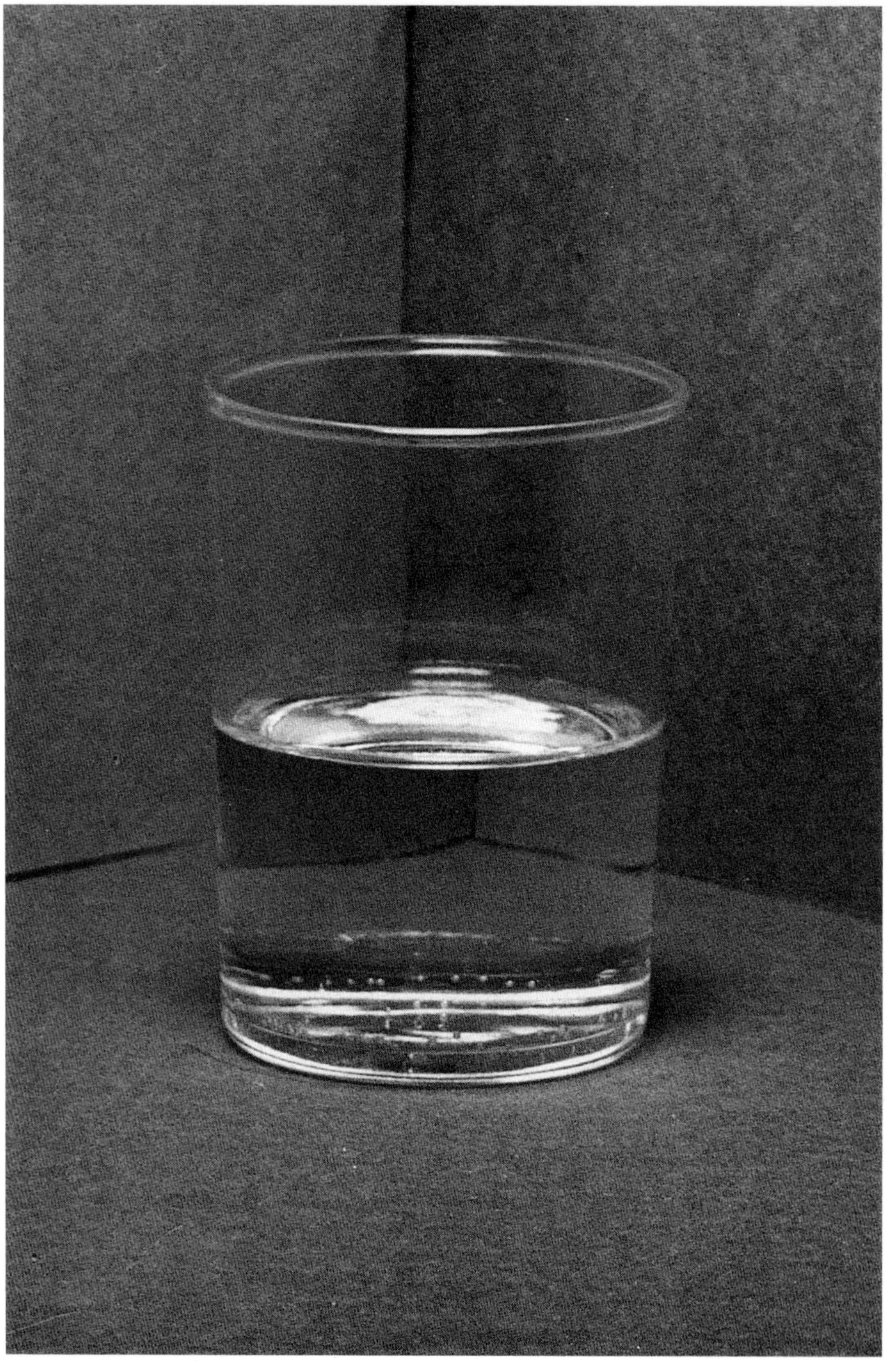

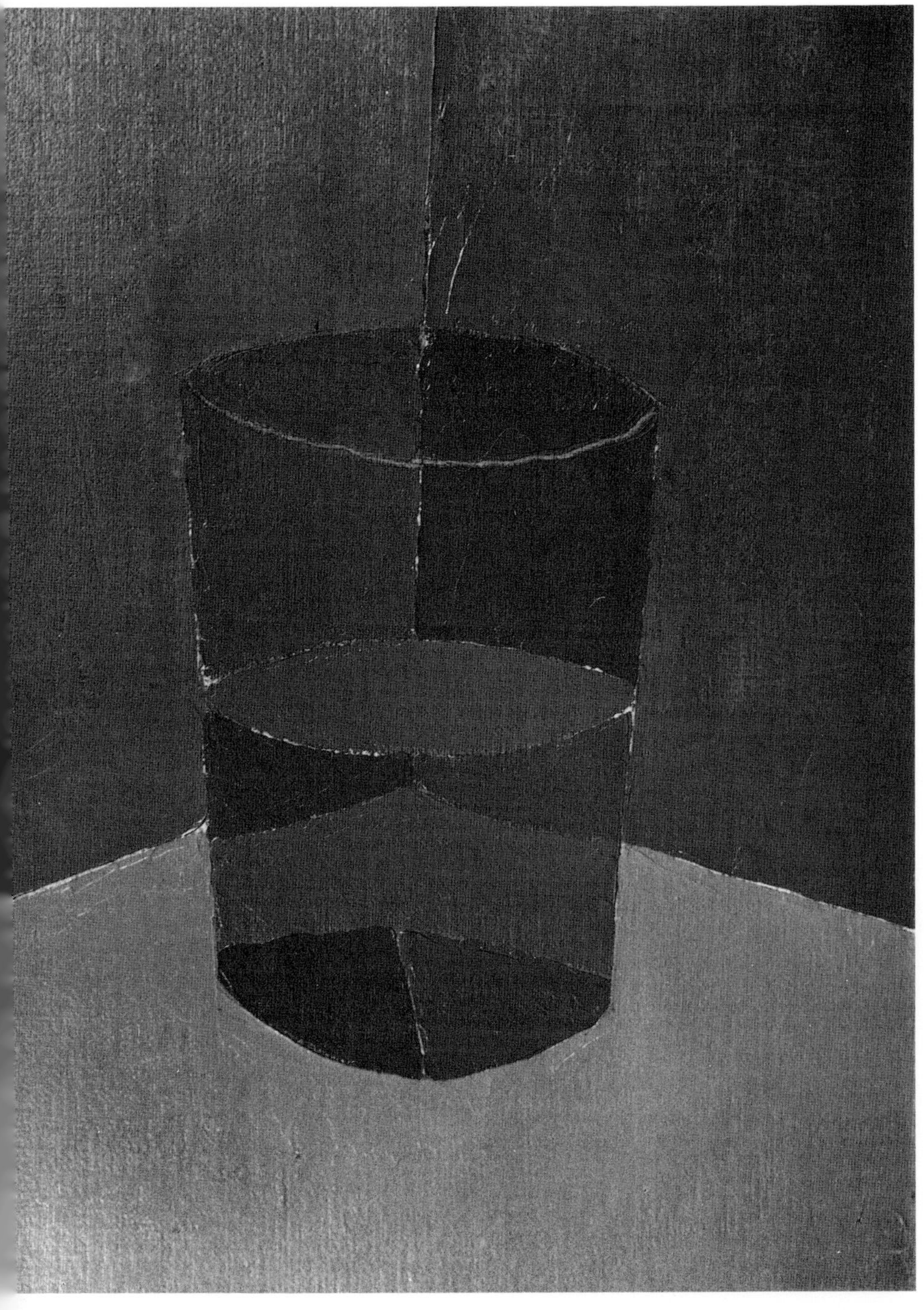

FIRST STATEMENT. Here, some students panic. Glass *and* water? That's double trouble! Both the container and its contents are colorless, clear, and shiny. A clear glass tumbler, alone and empty, would be tough enough. But filled—or still worse, half-filled! And with *water*? But don't lose your head. This ultimate example of colorlessness is no ordeal. Just forget that you're painting a transparent subject, and a supposedly colorless one, and look at the whole setup simply as yet another pattern of color spots. You should be able to paint your first statement in about thirteen color spots—somewhat more than usual—but you'll see why:

2 for the walls of the setup box
1 for the floor
4 for the walls seen through the top half of the glass
1 for the surface of the water
2 for the walls seen through the water
1 for the floor seen through the water
2 for the base of the glass.

OBSERVATIONS. You've already painted a translucent object (the plastic jug); a shiny object (an aluminum saucepan); and a transparent object (a colored glass dish). With that experience behind you, you won't find this glass of water as difficult as you may think. All you're doing is looking through the empty glass and the clear water to see how the walls and floor of the setup box come through. The environment of the model actually divides up in a neat and symmetrical pattern. The empty half of the glass and the water-filled half each reveals that environment in its own way. The color influences on the model are, when you come down to it, absolutely obvious—except for the base of the glass, which doesn't show the floor of the setup box (as you might have expected), but reflects the two walls.

First Statement, Kevin Kennedy.

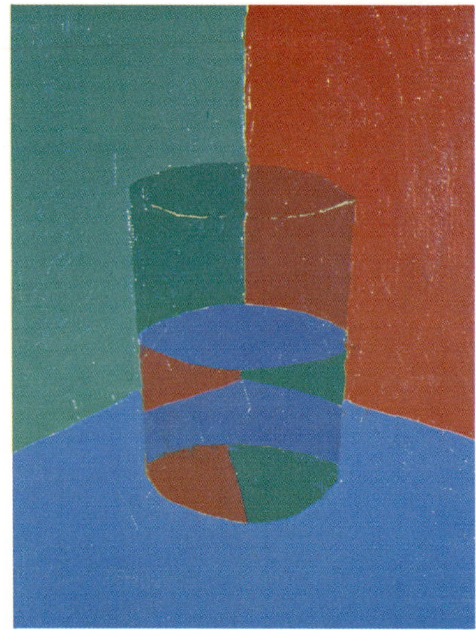

Second Statement, Kevin Kennedy.

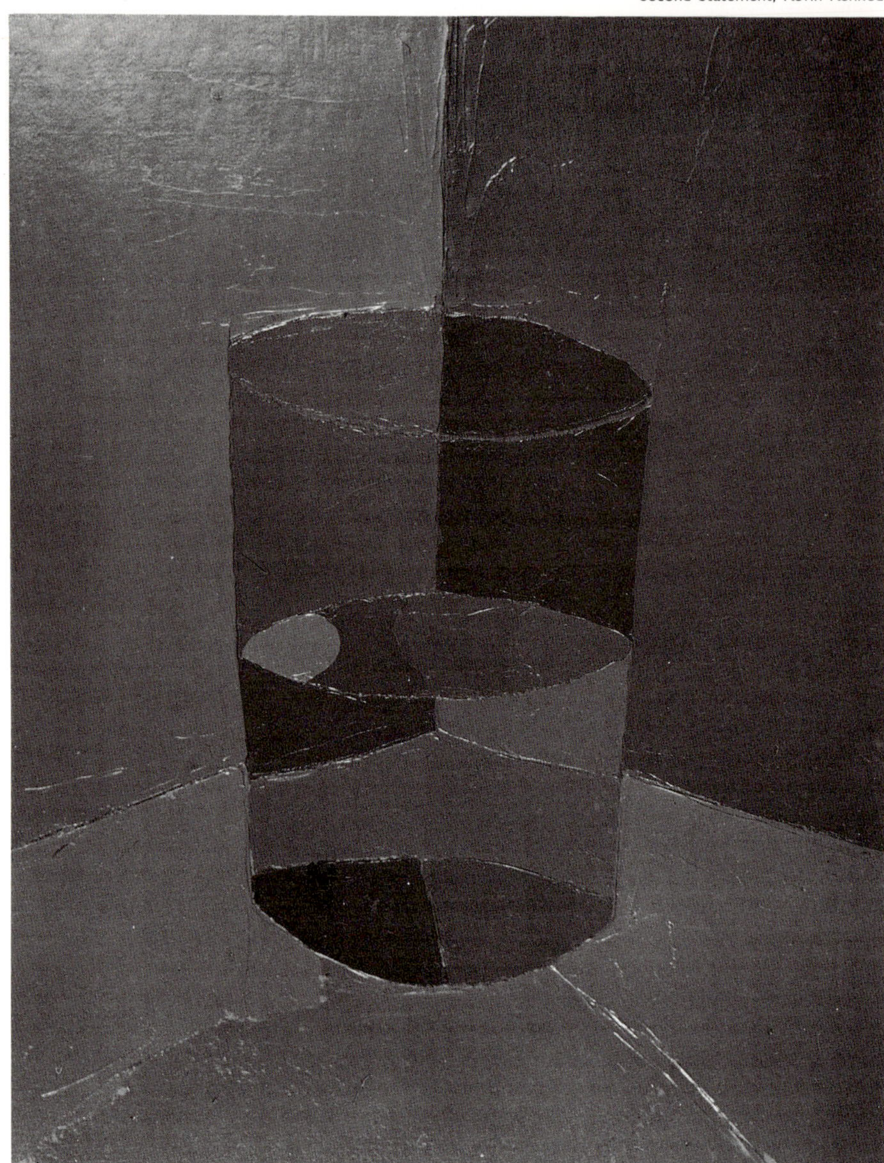

SECOND STATEMENT. The student's second statement is only slightly more complex than his first statement. He breaks up the elliptical surface of the water into four color spots and he divides the floor into four color spots (which may be difficult to see in this black-and-white photograph). He also uses the second statement as an opportunity to make subtle, but important corrections in the first. For example, he repaints the walls of the setup box, making delicate changes in their luminosity, and he makes similar adjustments in the color spots of the glass.

OBSERVATIONS. The lesson, of course, is that there's leeway for personal judgment about what really constitutes a second statement—for that matter *any* statement. This student has made the decision that his second statement won't benefit by creating too many new color spots, and so has carried it just far enough to create a satisfying study. He also knows that correcting color spots can be every bit as important as multiplying them.

Third Statement, Kevin Kennedy.

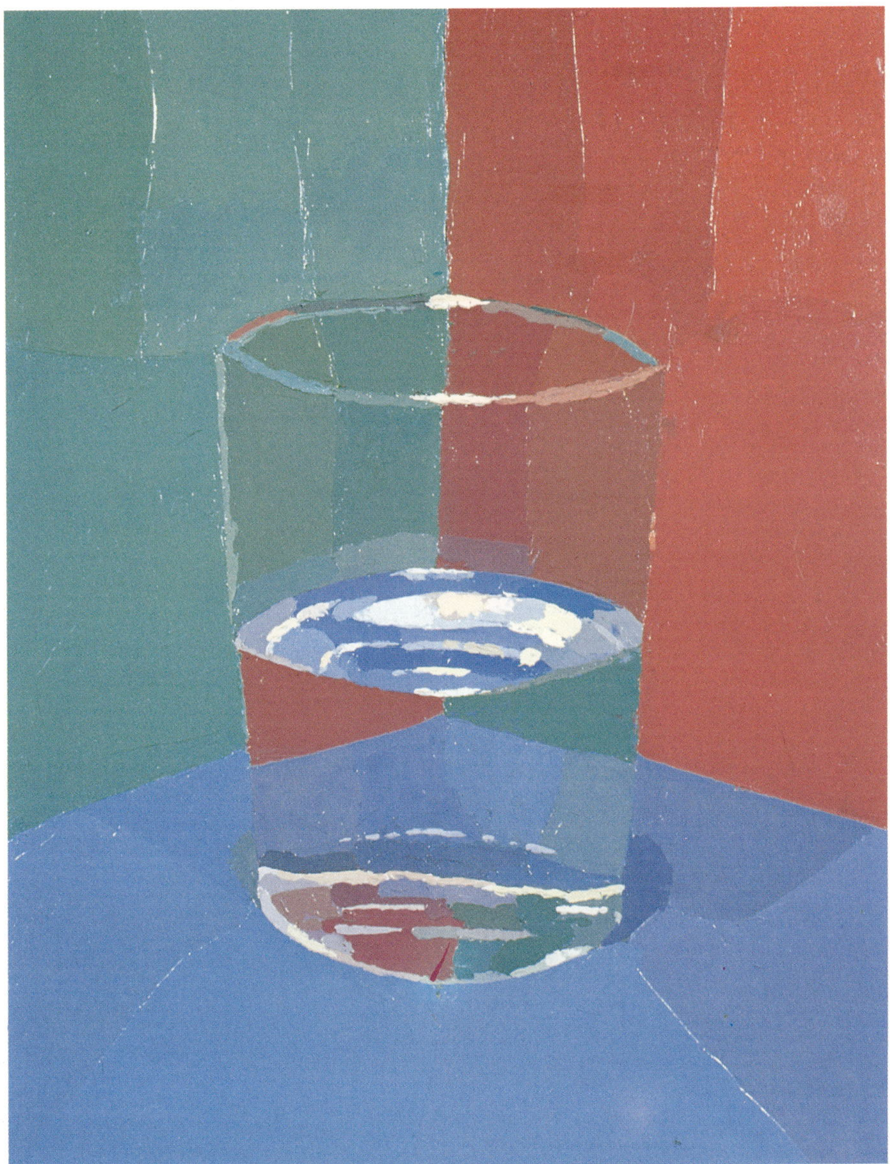

THIRD STATEMENT. Both these statements seem to be such complete and satisfying designs that it may appear difficult to go beyond them to a third statement. But neither of these two statements fully considers the interlocking influences of the walls and floor of the setup box on one another—and how these additional color spots in the walls and floor show up through the glass. Nor do these first two statements record the small color spots that appear on the rim of the glass, on the surface of the water, and on the base of the glass, many of which come under the heading of highlights. Now go back and record these phenomena, as well as the cast shadow that was omitted in the earlier statements.

OBSERVATIONS. The fascination of painting a supposedly colorless object is that such material—whether it's glass, water, or ice—takes its colors almost entirely from its surroundings. For this reason, a half-filled glass of clear water could be any color, depending upon in what color setting you place the "model." And for this same reason, a body of water or a sheet of ice outdoors can be any color (or colors) that it picks up from the nearby landscape. So Project 20 is more than just an exercise in painting a glass of water, but holds the key to painting some of the most common elements in the landscape. No, the glint and glitter that you add to your third and final statement isn't the color of glass *or* water. Those new color spots are reflections of the light source, plus some additional color spots picked up from the surrounding walls and floor of the setup box. Light, after all, is also part of the environment.

EXTRA PROJECT

To add an extra complication to Project 20, pour the clear water out of the clear glass, and then half-fill the glass with some colored but also transparent liquid, such as freshly steeped tea, rosé wine, or cranberry juice. (Nothing too dark like black coffee or red wine.) You can leave the walls and floor of the setup box intact, or you can try a new color arrangement. All the colors are up to you.

THE COLOR OF GREENERY

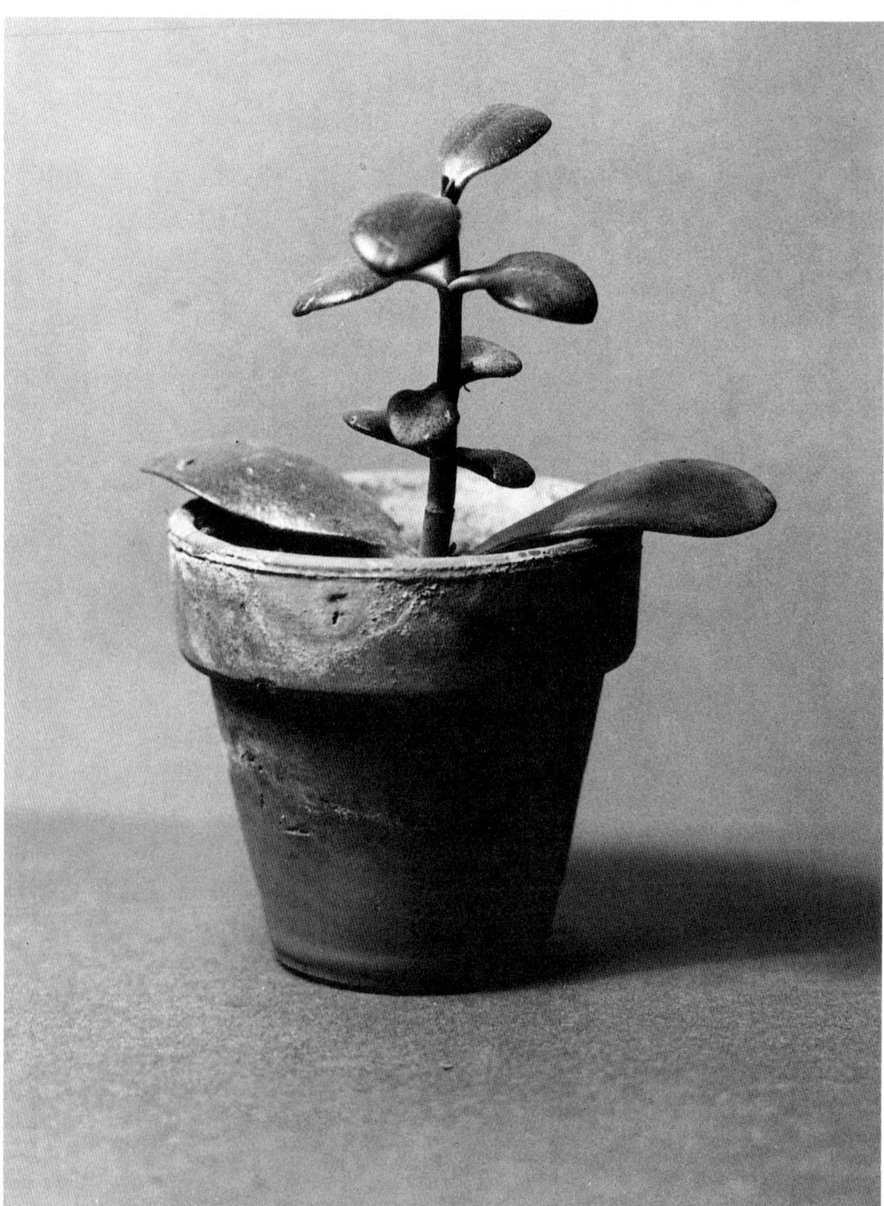

SETUP. Certainly one of the most common household objects is the humble houseplant in its plain terracotta pot. If you don't have one, buy a small, green houseplant with a few large leaves, simply shaped and all solid green. Steer clear of the variegated or patterned leaves that may look lovely on your windowsill, but will confuse the purpose of this project. Be sure that the plant is growing in a terracotta flowerpot (for the well-being of both the plant and your painting). If it's in a plastic container, repot it. Line the setup box with red paper on the left wall, dull green on the floor, and gray on the right wall—which you won't see. Turn the box to Position 5, so that the left wall becomes the background plane and the right wall is out of view. Arrange the plant in the middle of the setup-box floor. Keep the setup box close to eye level so that you don't see the soil, but you do see a little of the inside back wall of the pot. Arrange your setup lamp at the left so it casts a shadow on the floor, but not on the back wall. Some of the leaves should cast shadows on some of the others, as you can see in the photograph.

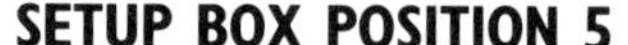

SETUP BOX POSITION 5

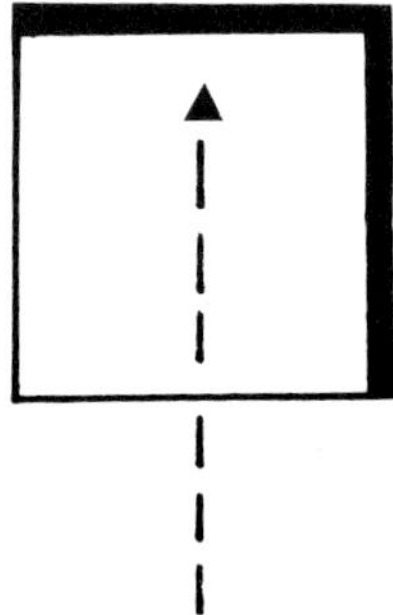

The left wall is perpendicular to your line of vision, and becomes the background plane of the setup. The right wall is parallel to your line of vision and is therefore out of sight. You see only the left wall and the floor of the setup box.

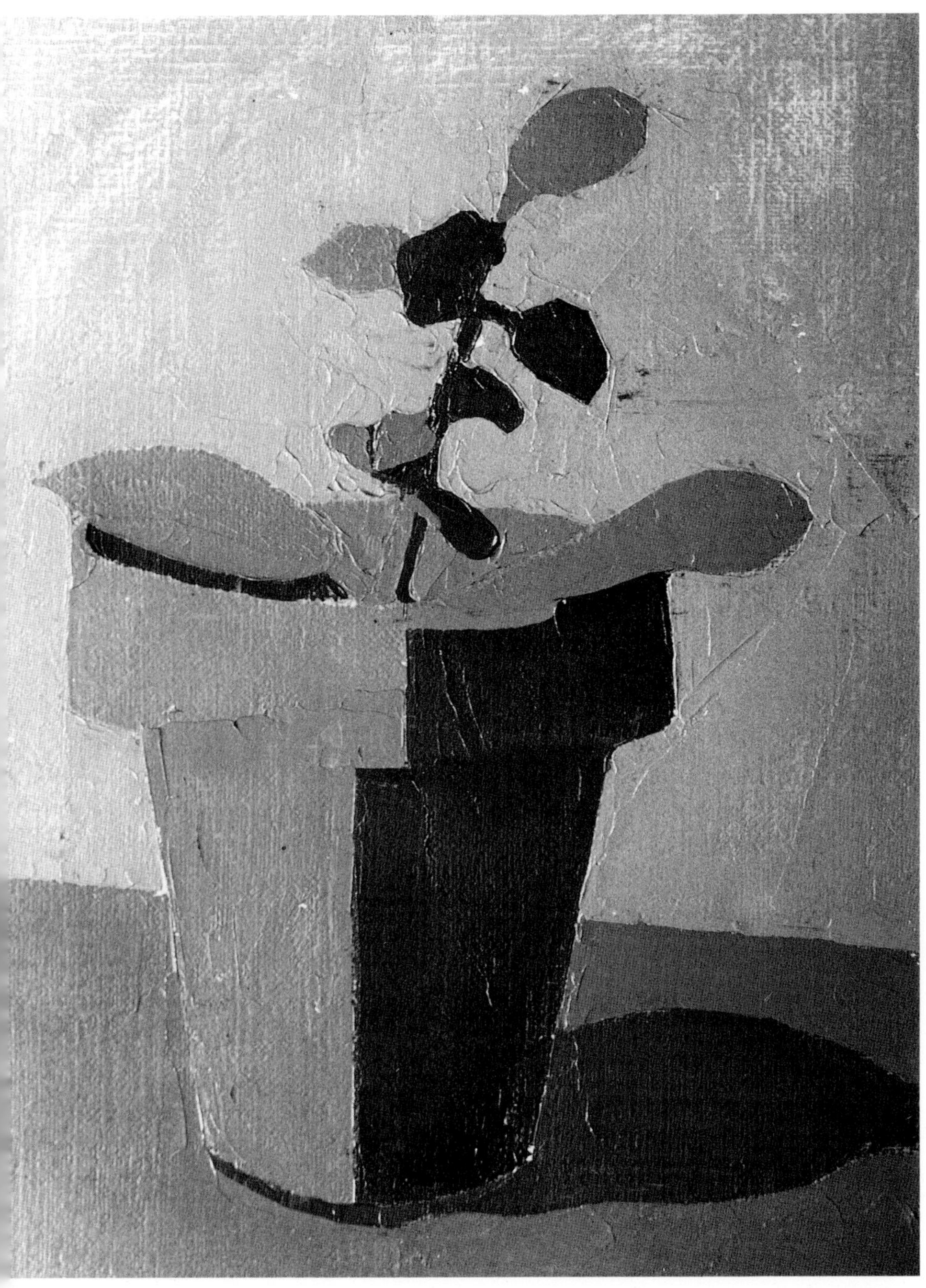

FIRST STATEMENT. Work on a half-sheet of canvas paper, held vertically. Use your 2:3 viewfinder to frame your composition—coming in quite close to the pot and not leaving too much space around it. In the example reproduced here, the student decided to look at the model from a slight angle, rather than head-on, so the line where the wall and floor meet isn't absolutely horizontal, but slightly diagonal. Either way is fine; it's a matter of personal taste. In this simple first statement, it's also permissible to use the same color for more than one color spot. Thus, you may use one color for all the foliage shapes in light, and a second color for all the foliage shapes in shade. (This won't work, of course, when you get to the second statement.) At this early stage, of course, you're not matching every color area you see, so much as trying to find a few colors that typify the general colors of the setup. You should be able to summarize the setup in seven colors, distributed as follows:

1 for the back wall of the setup box
1 for the floor
1 for the foliage in light
1 for the foliage in shade
1 for the parts of the flowerpot in light
1 for the parts in shade
1 for the shadow on the floor.

OBSERVATIONS. All the projects that you've painted so far have involved big, solid, even simple geometric shapes in which it was easy to see large color spots. Now, as you paint the smaller, more delicate shapes of the house plant, you'll find that the method works just as well for intricate, irregular shapes, like the plant's stem and leaves. The color spots are smaller and their complex shapes demand very careful observations, but you can still paint a convincing first statement if you divide the plant into simple color spots that represent no more than specific areas in light and shade. By now, the pot should be easy. All you have to identify are its light and shade sides, and paint them in two big color spots. Despite the complexity of the shapes of the plant, the finished first statement communicates instantly. You already have a handsome "poster" of a house plant in a pot—so handsome that it's tempting to stop here. But don't. Go on.

First Statement, Kevin Kennedy.

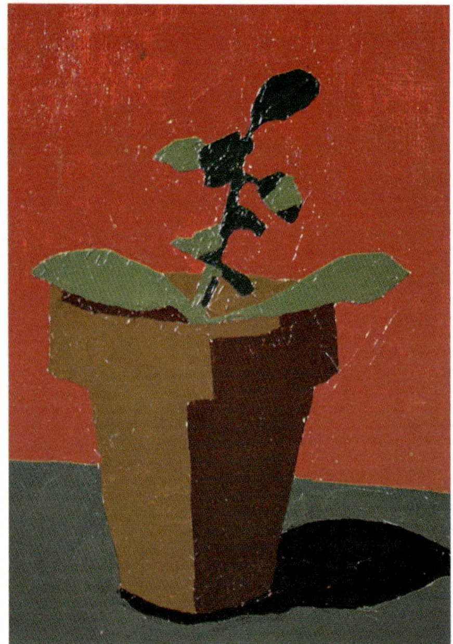

Second Statement, Kevin Kennedy.

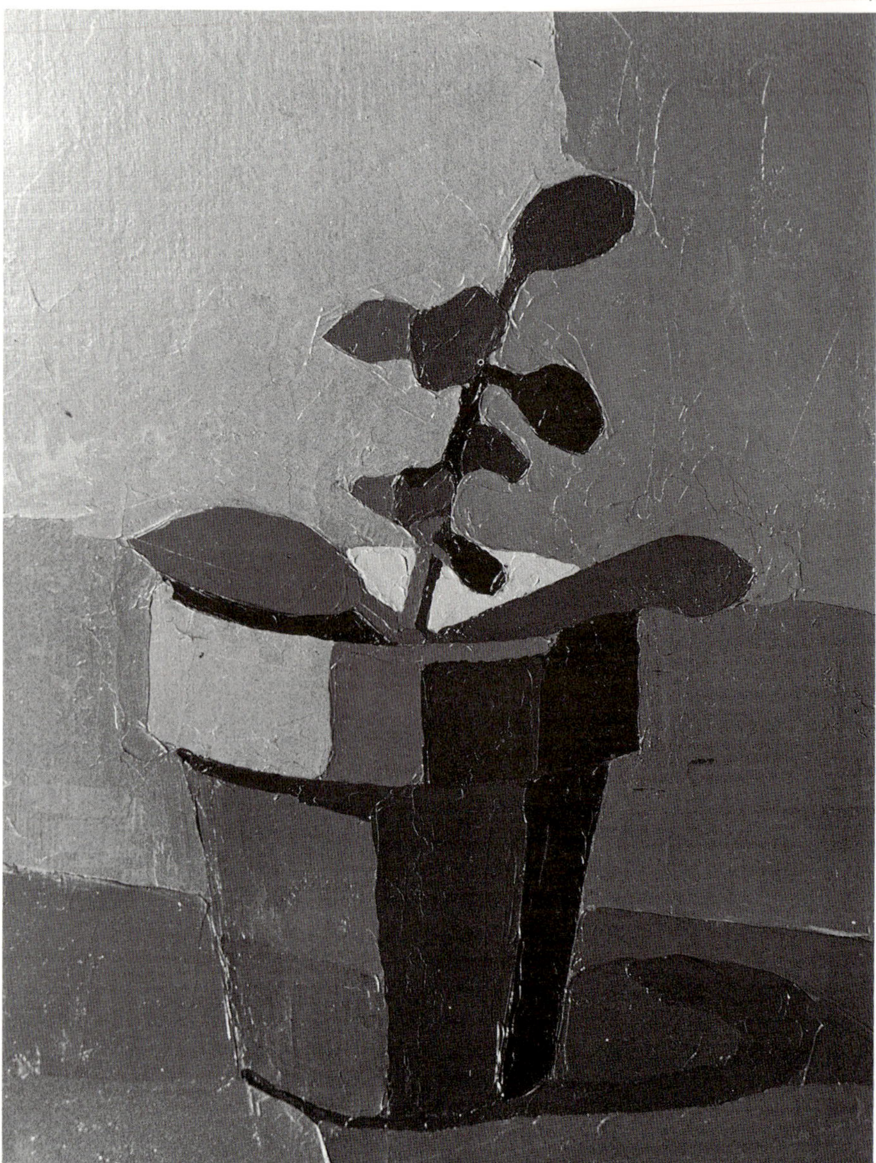

SECOND STATEMENT. As you scan the setup through your spot screen, do your best to find three or four color spots for each of the big color areas in the first statement. It should be quite easy to find four color spots for the collar of the flowerpot and another four for the lower part of the pot. You'll need at least two color spots for the light and shade inside the pot. However, the foliage is more complex. No two leaves are exactly the same. So don't be tempted to mix three or four colors on your palette, and then use each color in several places. You must discipline yourself to look at each leaf separately and create the colors just for that leaf. Nor do the color spots of the stems necessarily match those of the leaves; so look at each section of the stem separately, and treat it as a separate color spot, no matter how small. Finally, don't neglect the job of discovering new color spots in the wall and floor of the setup box. I can't tell you exactly how many color spots you'll need for this second statement, but it's probably going to be somewhere between two dozen and three dozen.

OBSERVATIONS. What you're doing in this project, of course, is bringing all your accumulated experience to bear on a cluster of small, irregular shapes that jut out in different, unpredictable directions, catching varying degrees of light. Looking at the flowerpot, you can see that it displays some kind of orderly progression of color spots from light to dark, with the lightest spots facing the light source, and the darkest spots farthest away from the light source. Once you've painted the color spots on the pot, their being there is easily accounted for. But the leaves of the houseplant don't allow you any simple, obvious accounting. They stick out in all directions, receiving various amounts of light, responding in their own ways to the colors of the environment, overlapping and casting shadows on one another. Some turn toward the light and some turn away—and have subtly different object-colors to begin with. So, each leaf forces you to look at it and paint it as the unique phenomenon it is, whose color you can't possibly predict. In this sense, the houseplant is a microcosm of the living forms of the landscape—trees, shrubs, grasses, weeds—and the lessons you learn from painting this simple plant will help immeasurably when you start to paint outdoors.

Third Statement, Kevin Kennedy. Collection of Elaine Comparone.

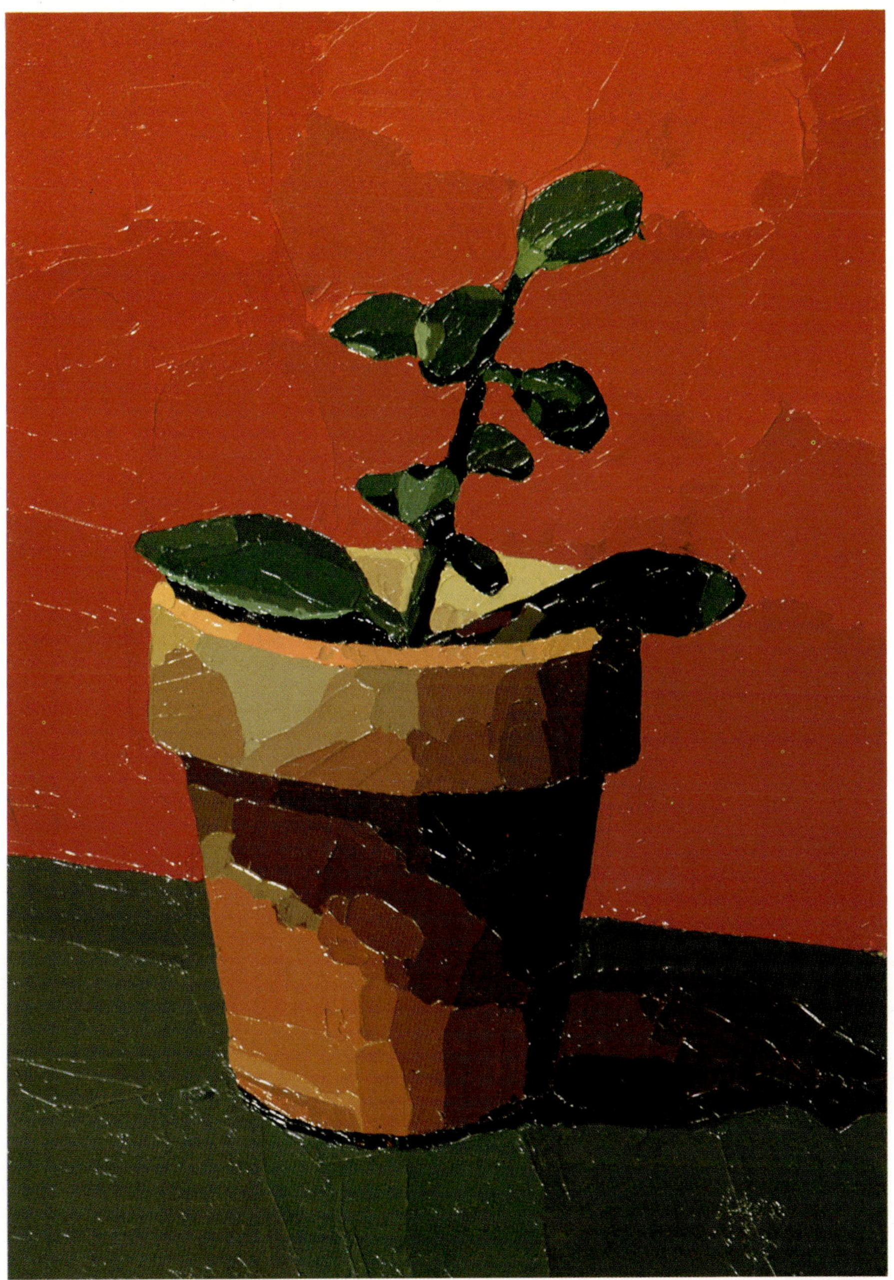

THIRD STATEMENT. In your first statement, you found two "typical" colors for the foliage: one for the foliage in light, and another for the foliage in shade. Then, when you went to work on your second statement, you looked at each leaf separately and saw a unique color spot for that leaf. Now, moving on to your third and final statement, your assignment is to look even more closely at each leaf and stem and find multiple color spots within each. You're looking for such tiny color spots that the ¼″ (6 mm) hole in your spot screen may seem too big. So you may want to take an ordinary nail and punch a smaller hole at the other end of the spot screen. Small as they may be, each leafy shape has its own special pattern of color spots that respond to the light and to the color influences of the environment. Although it's hard-to-impossible to predict how, there's no question that each leaf is influenced by the planes of the setup box, the terracotta pot, and by many of the other leaves. So you'll probably need at least three or four color spots to paint each leaf. And you'll need many more color spots to record all the delicate, transitional tones on the flowerpot and the planes of the setup box. This student needed over one hundred color spots to paint the third statement illustrated here. (And you may finally admit defeat on this one point of trying to predict color and give it up—in favor of looking and seeing.)

OBSERVATIONS. Perhaps the most important lesson of Project 21 is that every form in nature—no matter how small—has its own unique reaction to light and environmental color. Thus, the smallest leaf or stem will reveal its own complex pattern of color spots if you look closely through your spot screen and really paint the colors that you see. With this lesson in mind, you'll never go outdoors to paint landscapes and simply try to create one standard green mixture for deciduous trees, another standard mixture for evergreens, and so on. The range of possible greens is vast. Equally important, these supposedly green growing things aren't solid green any more than the houseplant that you've just painted. Any hue may turn up among those color spots, depending upon light, atmosphere, and environmental influences. That's why landscape painting is so infinitely fascinating.

EXTRA PROJECT

To prove this point about the variety of color spots that may turn up in a theoretically green plant, experiment with different colors on the wall of your setup box, while you retain the same houseplant in the same position and lighting. What colors appear in the leaves when the wall of the setup box is yellow and the floor is orange? What happens when the unseen right wall is no longer lined with gray, but with a third brilliant color, perhaps violet or blue? And, perhaps, paint the plant again in one of these new combinations of setup colors.

UNSTILL LIFE

SETUP. Painting a few simple flowers will bring this series of projects to an upbeat end. The best model for this project is any flower that has a few large petals, rather than a lot of little ones. For this reason, anemones make better models than, say, daisies. I don't insist on anemones, but they're great if you can get them. If not, ask the florist to recommend something else that has a few big, colorful petals, such as tulips or daffodils. Buy two very fresh anemones (or something comparable) of two different colors, and stick them into the narrow neck of a liquor or wine bottle filled with fresh, cold water. Line the setup box with blue paper on both walls, and gray on the floor—which will be out of the picture. Place the box in Position 3, with the lip of the bottle at eye level. Set your lamp directly above the blossoms, but high enough to protect them from its heat.

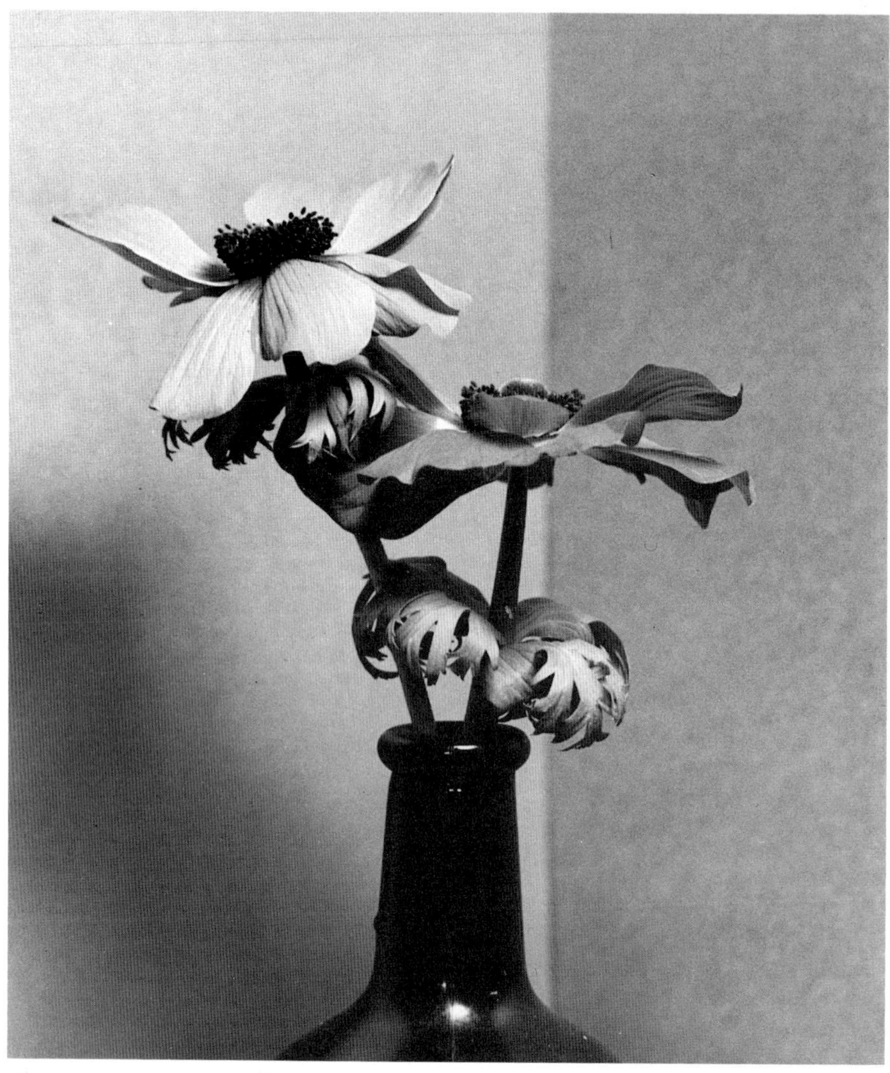

SETUP BOX POSITION 3

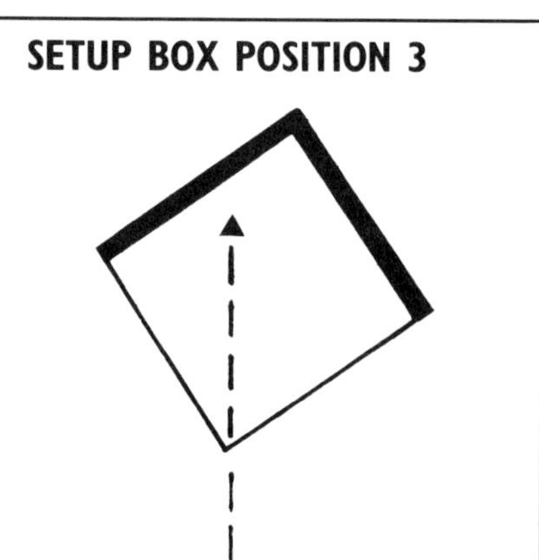

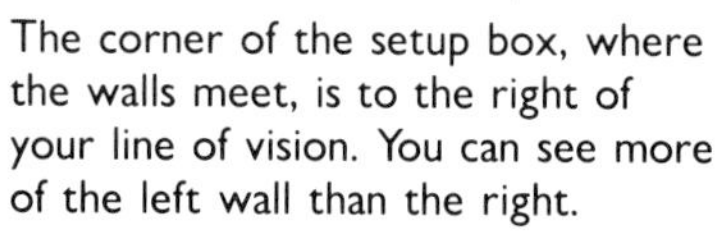

The corner of the setup box, where the walls meet, is to the right of your line of vision. You can see more of the left wall than the right.

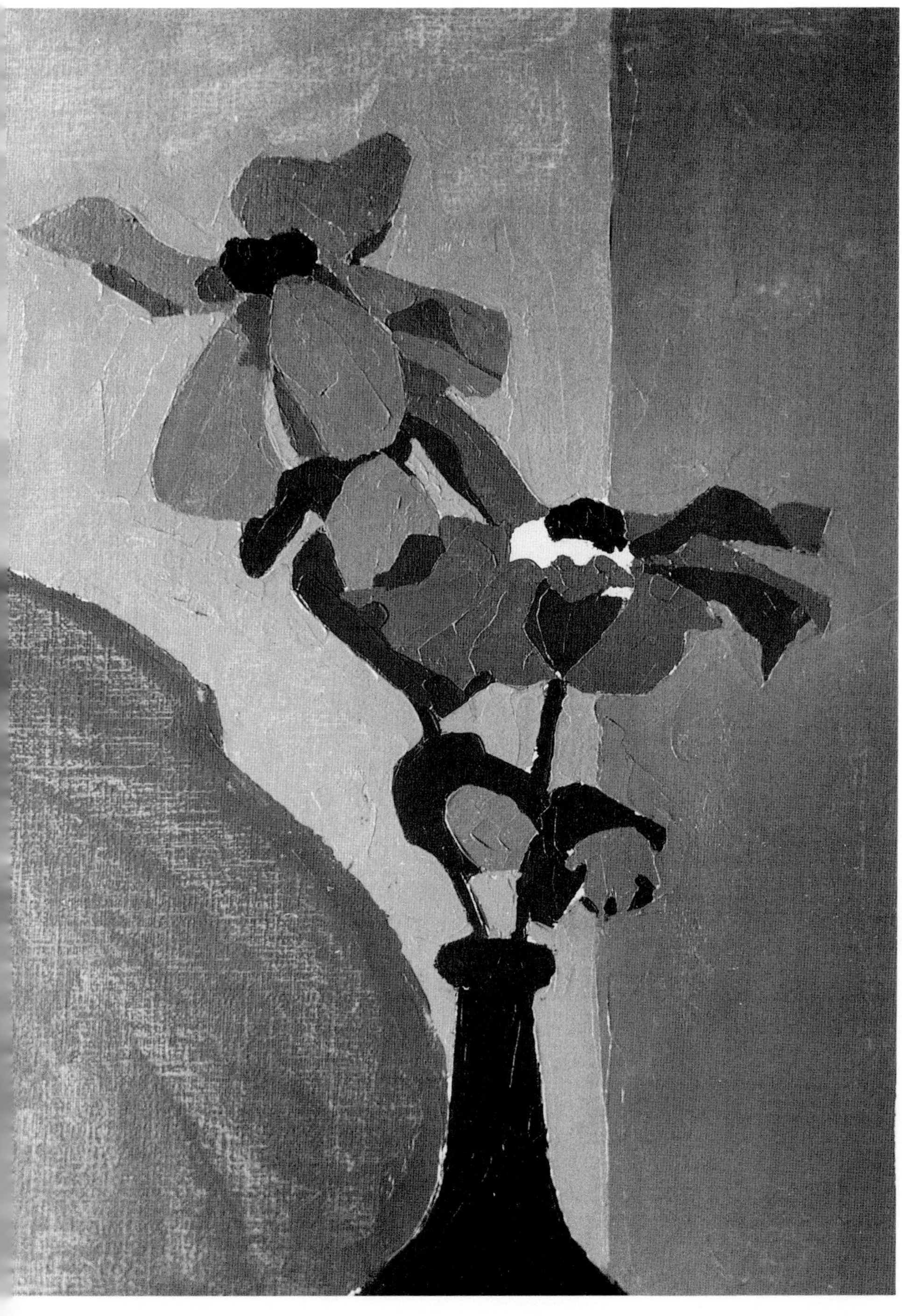

FIRST STATEMENT. You're going to need a full sheet of canvas paper, held vertically, even though you're not going to paint the entire bottle. Use your 3:4 viewfinder to frame just the flowers and the "neck and shoulders" of the bottle. I want you to paint a fairly ambitious first statement of the flowers, although you can keep the walls of the setup box quite simple. I think you'll need about a dozen color mixtures—distributed as I'll explain below—and you *must* work fast!

2 colors for the light and shade on the first blossom
1 for the center of the first blossom
2 for the light and shade on the second blossom
1 for the center of the second blossom
2 for the light and shade on the leaves and stem
2 for the light and shade on the bottle
2 for the walls of the setup box
1 for the shadow on the left wall.

OBSERVATIONS. Soon after you get started on your first statement, you'll hear yourself uttering the ancient lament of art students: "The model moved!" Flowers, even when they're cut, are *alive*. They continue to respond to light and temperature. Although these flowers are not really your first live models—the houseplant and the fruits were alive too—their very obvious responsiveness will introduce you to the chief characteristic of live models: mobility. That's why you've got to work fast. It's good practice, too, because when you "graduate" from these twenty-two projects, you'll probably want to start painting people and landscapes. You'll be painting a living, changing world that demands quick looking and rapid painting.

First Statement, Kevin Kennedy.

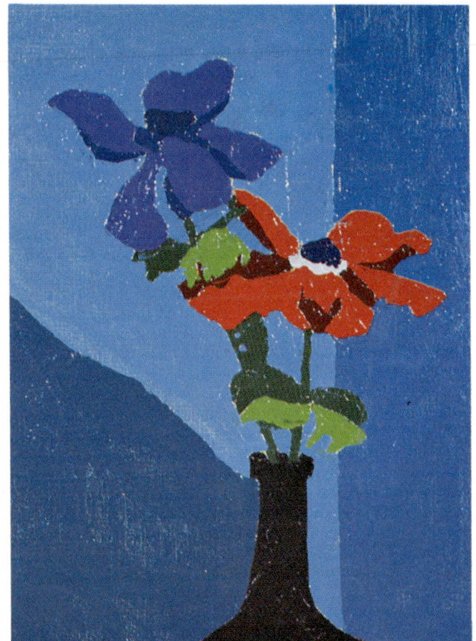

Second Statement, Kevin Kennedy.

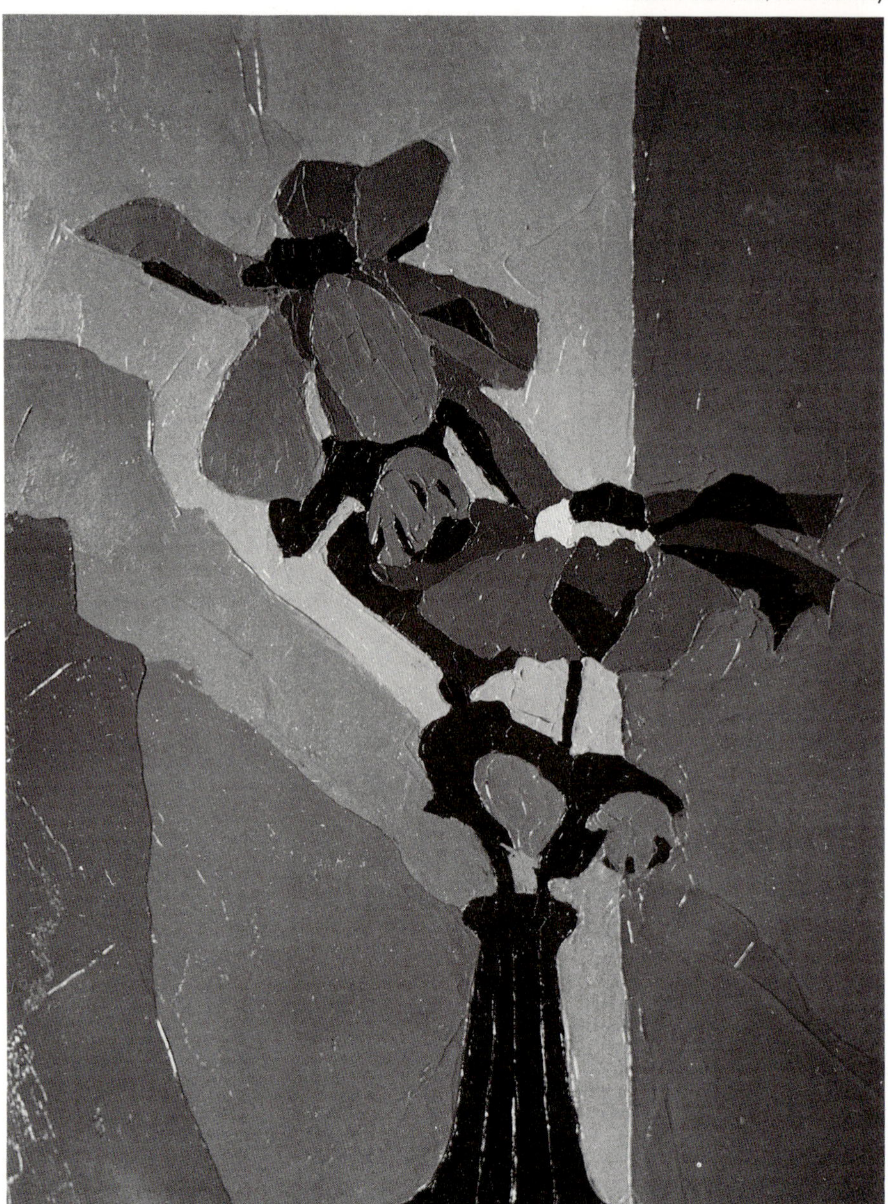

SECOND STATEMENT. If possible, you should move right into your second statement as soon as you've finished the first. In fact, the ideal way to paint Project 22 is to set aside the whole day and paint all three statements nonstop. If you don't have time for this painting marathon, take a break at the end of your first or second statement and put the flowers in a cool place. The refrigerator is fine because it will keep the flowers fresh. But be cautioned: the petals will change position with any change in lighting conditions. So, if you do take a break between statements, be prepared for some important changes in your "model," and don't be surprised if your next statement looks different from the one before. Nor is that necessarily bad. The change will force you to take a fresh look at your subject.

OBSERVATIONS. Scanning each petal with your spot screen, you'll see once again that the "typical" summary colors of the simplified first statement are no longer enough for the second. Each petal of each flower is, in fact, a separate color spot with its own unique hue, luminosity, and intensity. Fortunately, you're working with a few big petals, which are a lot easier to study and paint than many tiny petals like those of a daisy. In painting this second statement, it's not important to have a great many more color spots among the flowers than you painted in the first statement. What *is* important is that each of these color spots should now be identified, mixed, and laid down with the knife as something separate and different from all the others. Naturally, you'll also discover the usual variety of color spots that appear within the *formerly* simple planes of the setup box and within the cast shadow on the left-hand wall.

Third Statement, Kevin Kennedy.

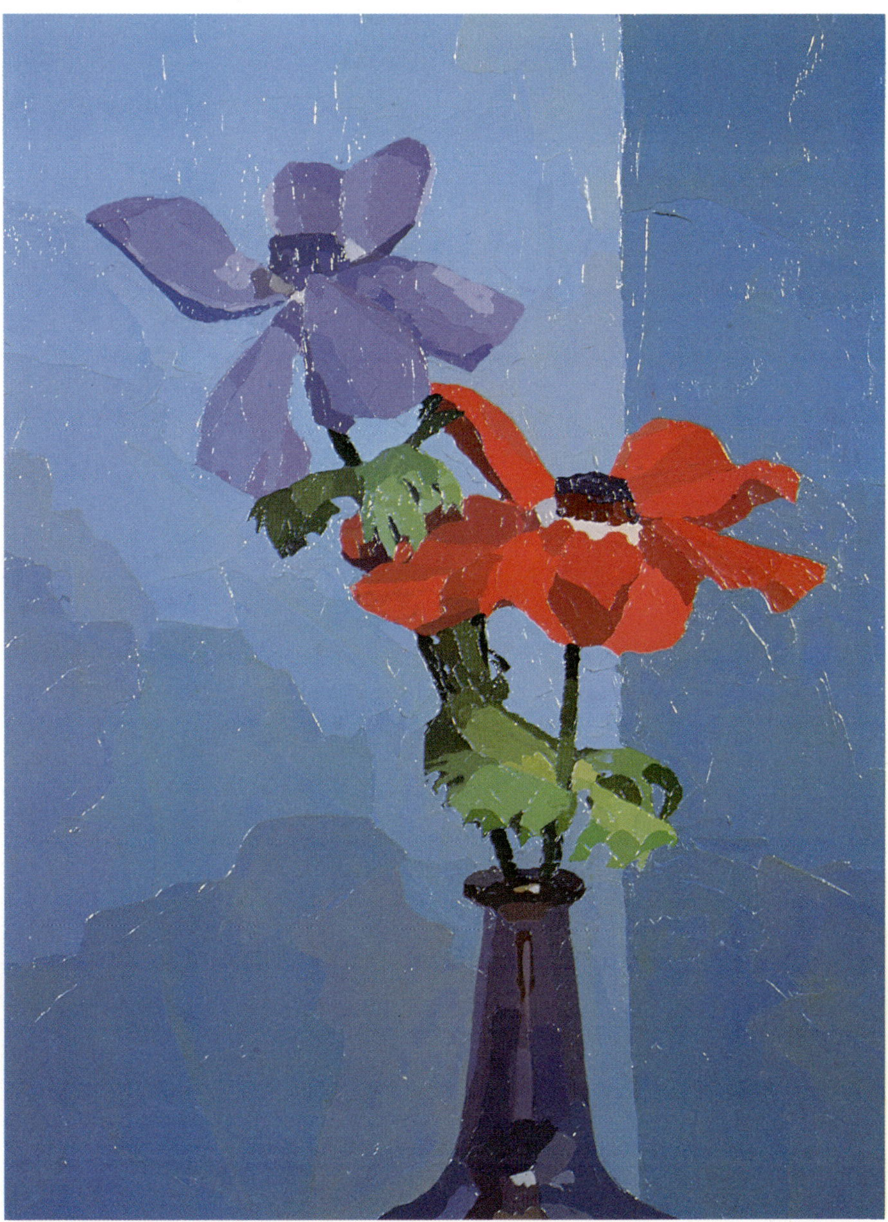

OBSERVATIONS. The lesson of this final project isn't merely technical; it's emotional, too. There's a special excitement in painting a live model. I think you'll feel energized by the challenge of painting something that's living, changing, and responding to light and air, just as you do. The pressure of time is invigorating. That's why it's so exciting to go outdoors and paint landscapes that change before your eyes as the sun moves, the wind blows, and the hours pass. The student who painted this third statement has shown great respect for economy in his number of color spots. But when I hold this painting of two flowers in my hand and find that I can't even count the number of color spots—perhaps there are a couple of hundred—I realize that what carried him so far wasn't merely the desire to be accurate, but the love that he felt for his subject.

THIRD STATEMENT. Rush on to your third statement and keep working as rapidly as you can. If the positions of the flowers have changed since you painted the second statement—perhaps because you had to take another break and put the flowers in the refrigerator again—don't try to push the blossoms back into their original positions. It won't work and you are likely to damage them. Just accept the changes as inevitable, and keep painting. If they continue to move as you paint—and they probably *will*—don't keep correcting and repainting. Lay down each color spot and move on to the next. In the second statement, you were still concentrating on the light and shade areas of each petal, and each section of the stems and leaves. So the second statement didn't have many more color spots than the first. But now, as you paint your third statement, you've got to focus your attention on all the small color spots within each petal, recording not only the simple areas of light and shade, but all the delicate color changes that take place in response to the light and the environment. As you work on the bottle, remember what you learned in Project 19 about painting colored, transparent objects. One more factor becomes more important in this final project than in any of the others you've painted: the negative spaces—that is, the gaps between the flowers, where the left wall of the setup box shines through. Each negative space is just as important as the nearby petals, and they all demand the same degree of attention. If the negative spaces don't look right, the positive spaces that make up the flowers won't look right either.

EXTRA PROJECT

Here you have the whole world of flowers to choose from. Work with any flowers you enjoy—and the seasons and florists permit. Change the walls of the setup box to suit your taste. It's still best to work first with simple forms like tulips, daffodils, and roses, but if you think that you can really take on something as complex as a daisy—go ahead.

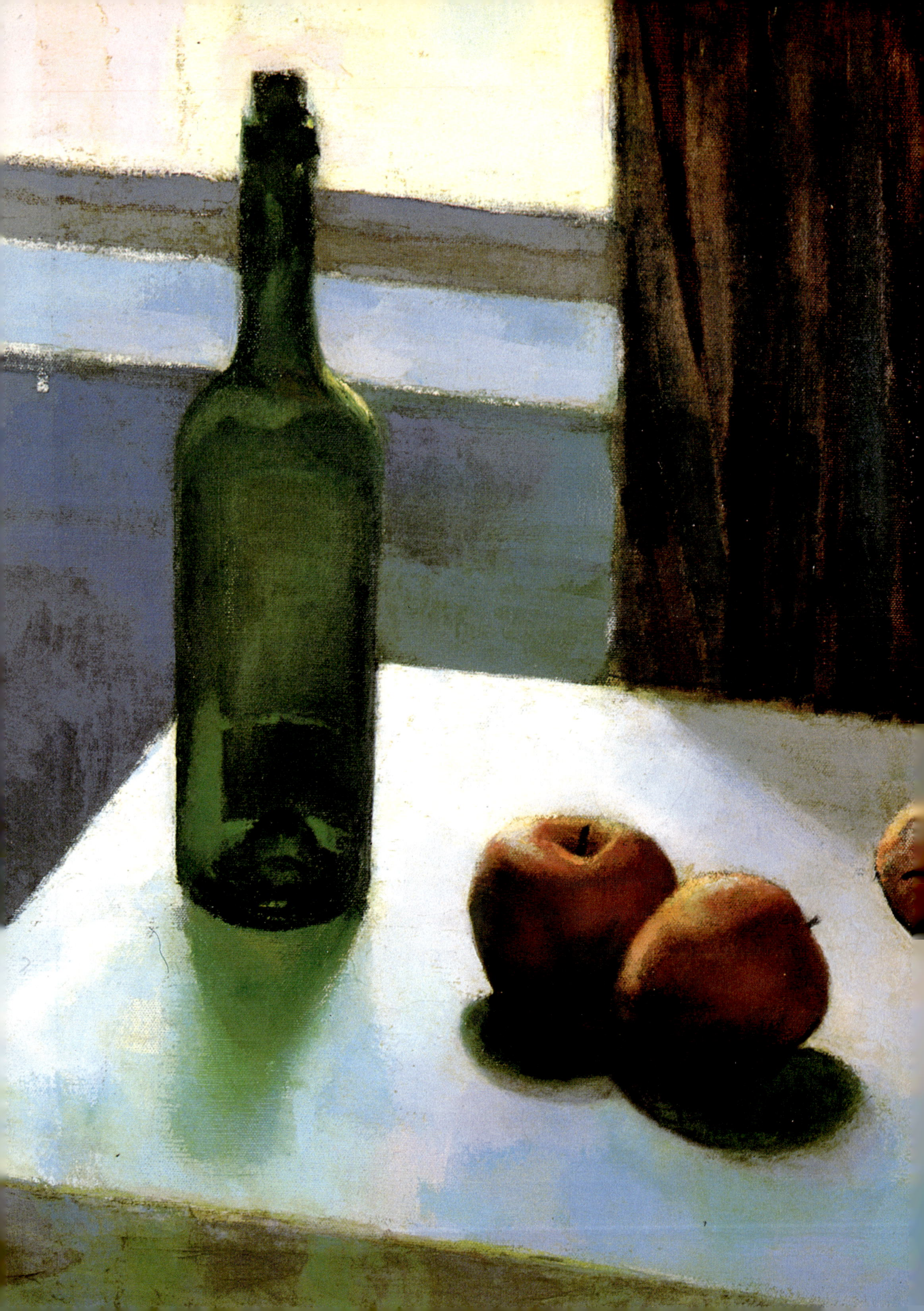

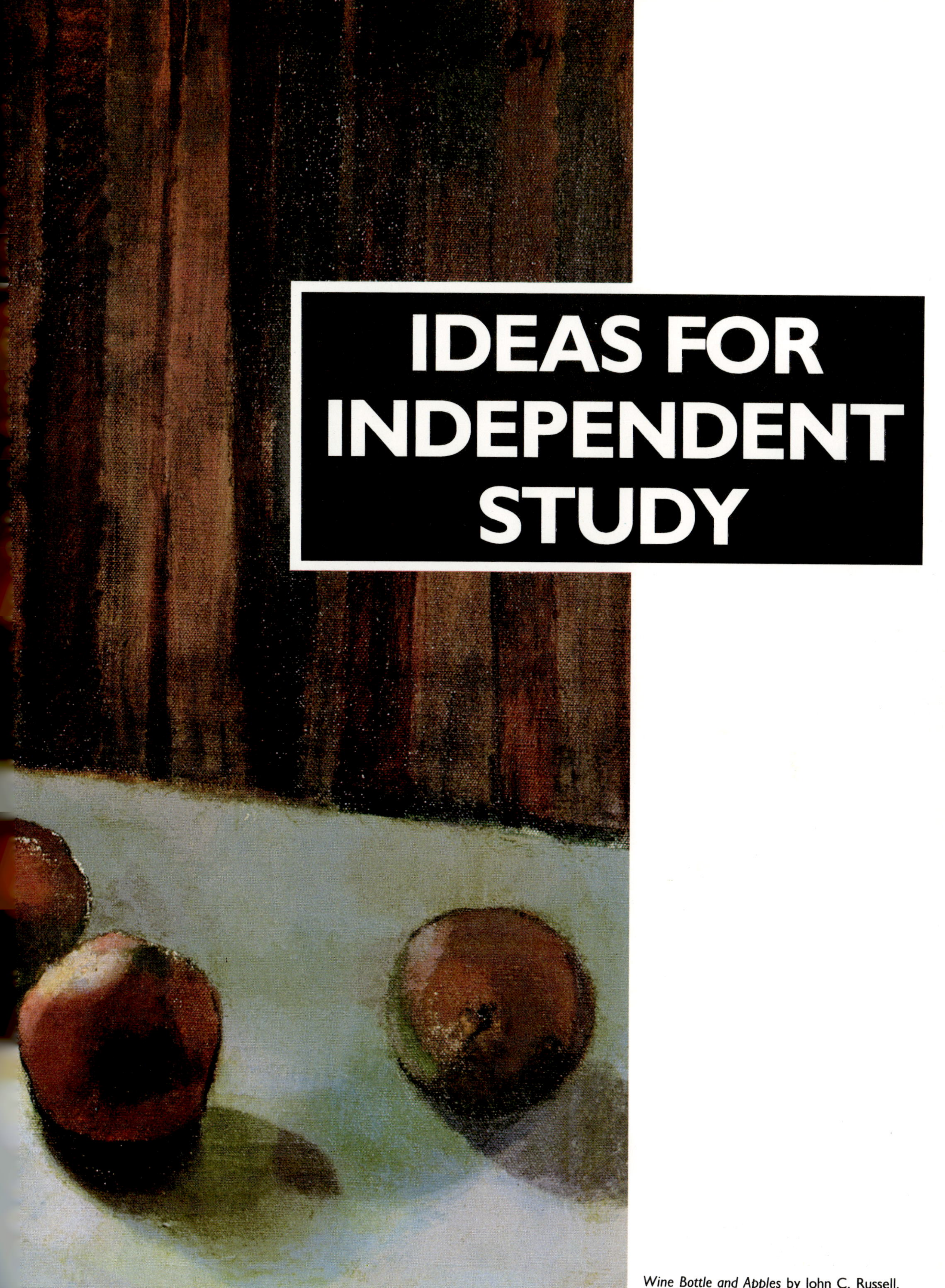

IDEAS FOR INDEPENDENT STUDY

Wine Bottle and Apples by John C. Russell.

PAINT FLOWERS

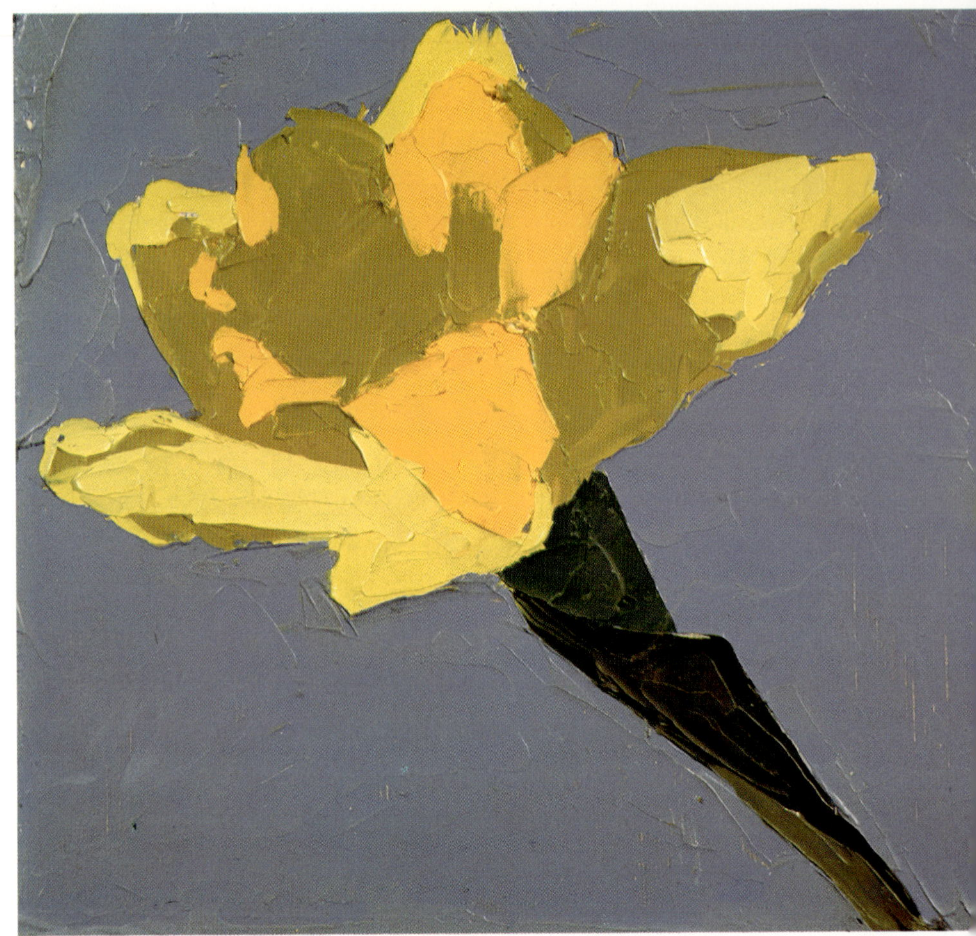

First Statement, Daffodil. A single flower is complex enough to be a study in itself. Painting a closeup—like this study of a daffodil by Jarvis Wilcox—challenges you to look carefully at the exact hue, luminosity, intensity, shape, size, and position of every color spot within the petals. This first statement consists of just seven color spots: three for the multiple colors within the blossom, three for the stem, and one for the background.

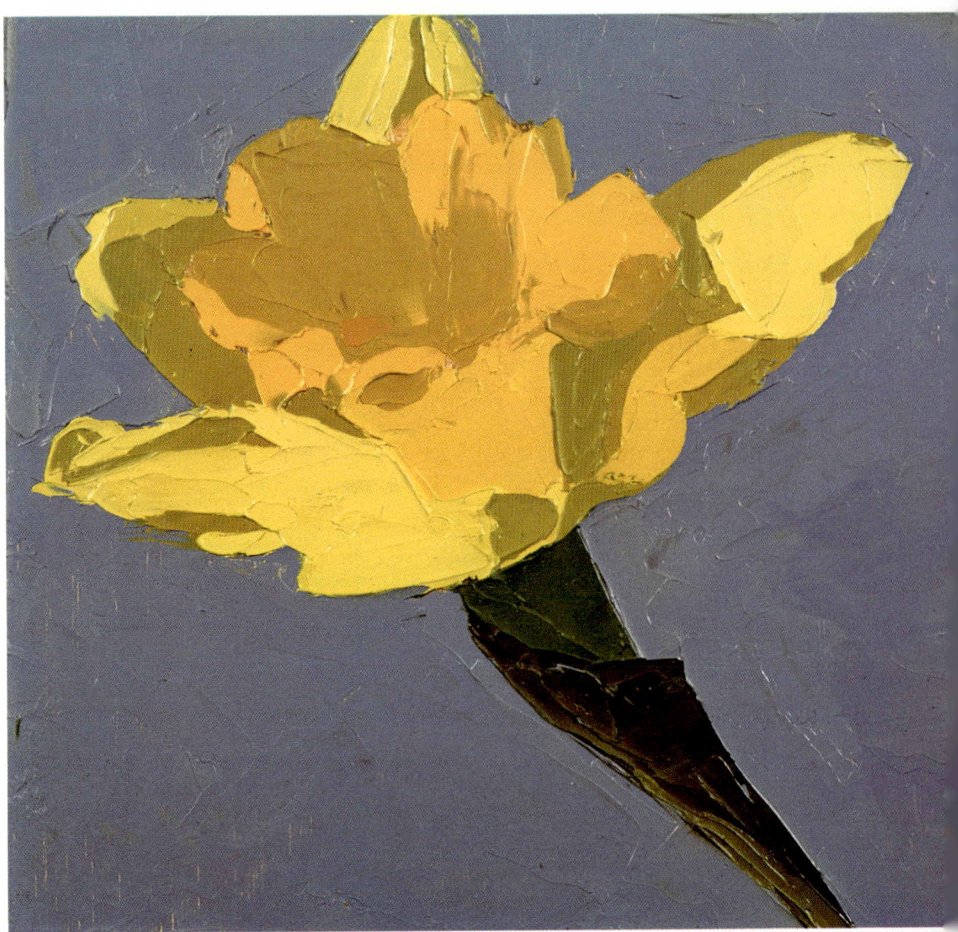

Second Statement, Daffodil. As the student moves on to his second statement, he refines the shapes and colors of the spots. The blossom grows more realistic, but it's still painted very simply.

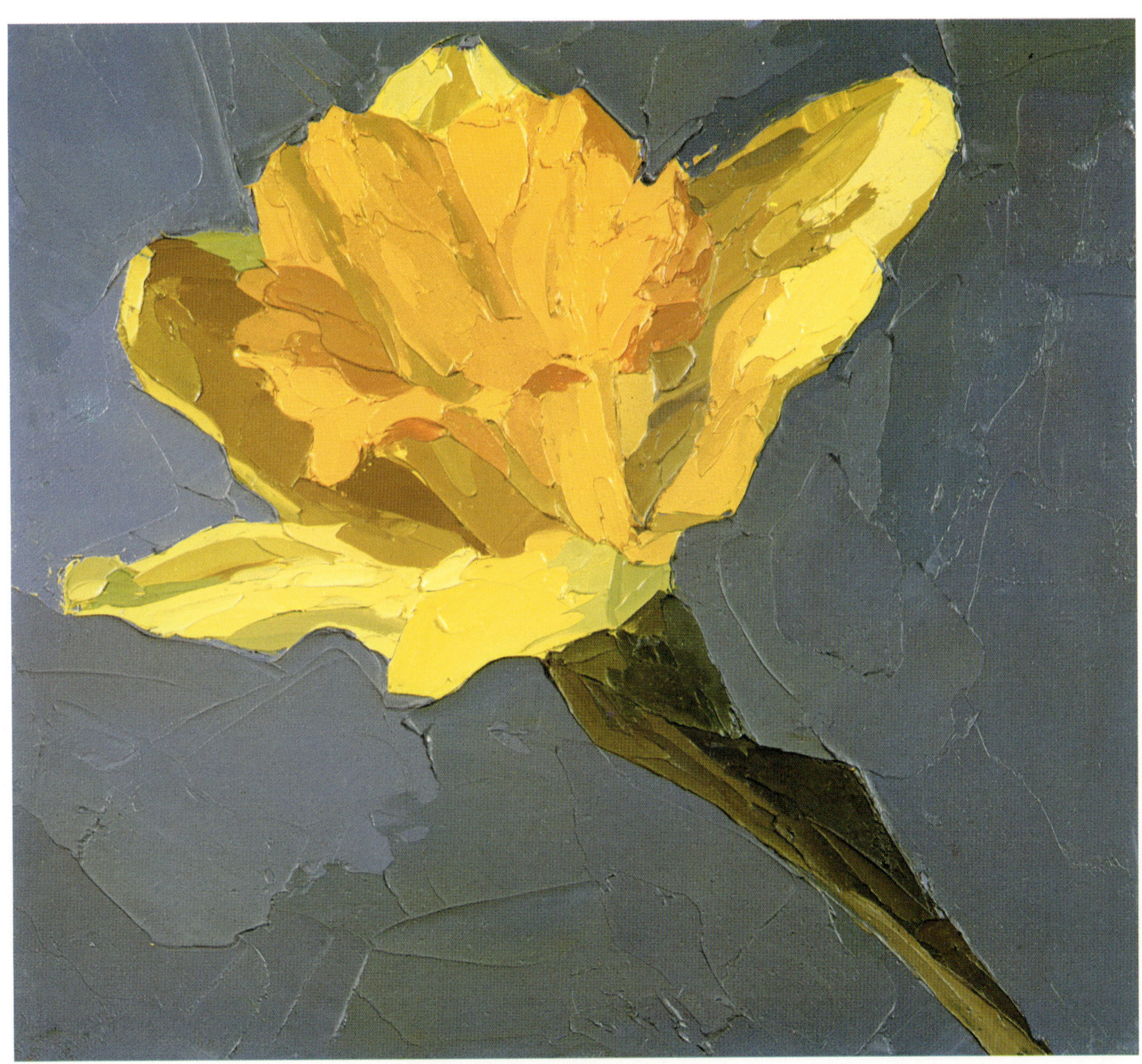

Third Statement, Daffodil. The full detail of the blossom emerges in this third and final statement. As usual, the third statement reveals the greatest variety of color. And this is where the student permits himself to focus on details, represented by the tiny color spots he has deftly placed with the tip of his palette knife. The background also displays a greater range of subtle color spots, suggesting that the flower is silhouetted against the sky rather than the wall of the setup box. It's good experience to pose your subject against the sky because the rapidly changing light forces you to make quick, firm, decisions about the background color spots—an experience that will stand you in good stead when you begin painting outdoors.

PAINT A BOUQUET

Daffodils in a Can. This study of daffodils placed in an ordinary tin can brings together two very different models. The student, Jarvis Wilcox, has painted living flowers that gradually move and change as he works, forcing him to make rapid decisions. He has also captured the complex color spots in the reflecting surface of silvery metal. (The finished study is in the collection of Mr. and Mrs. John Kvernland.)

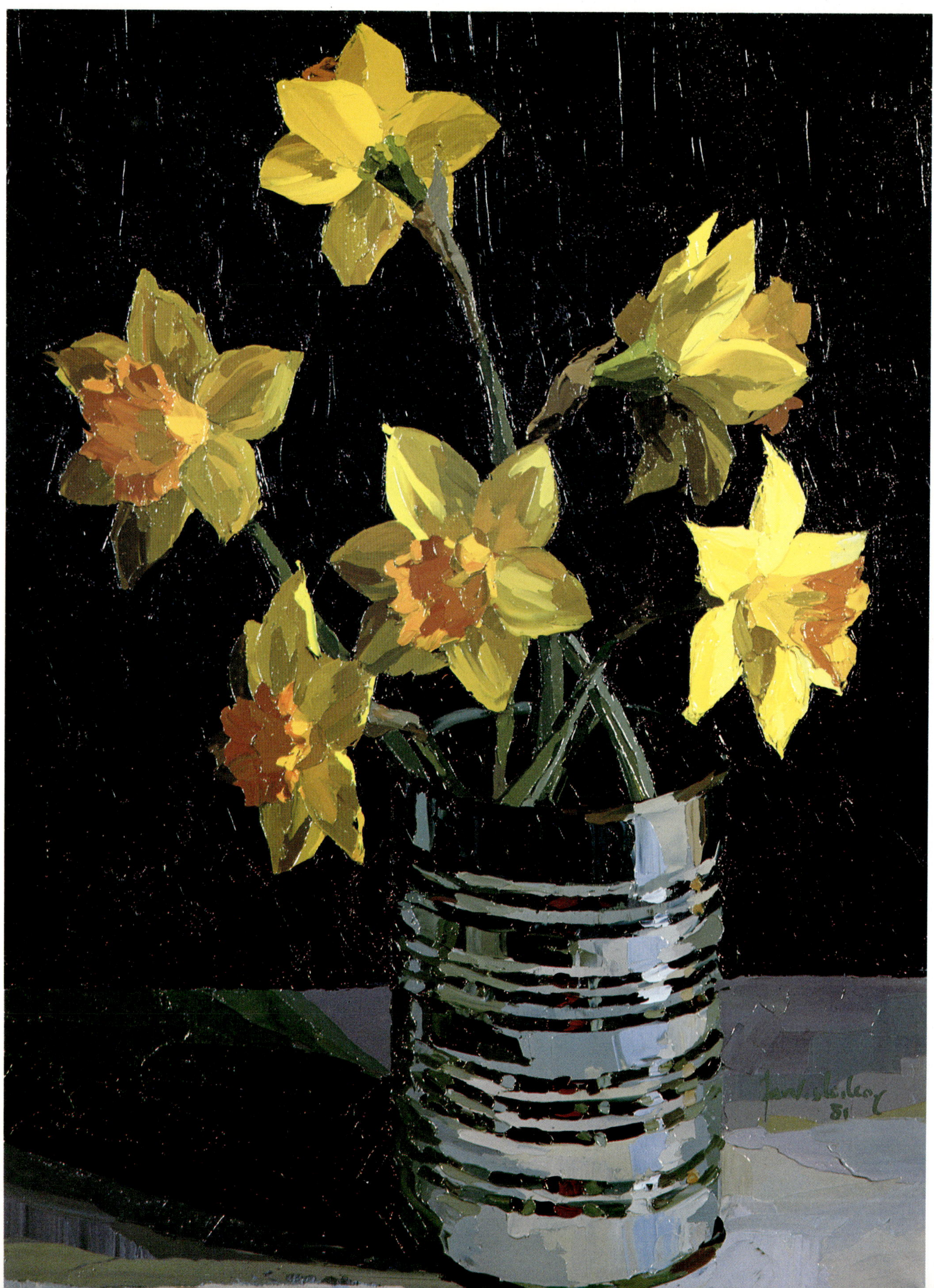

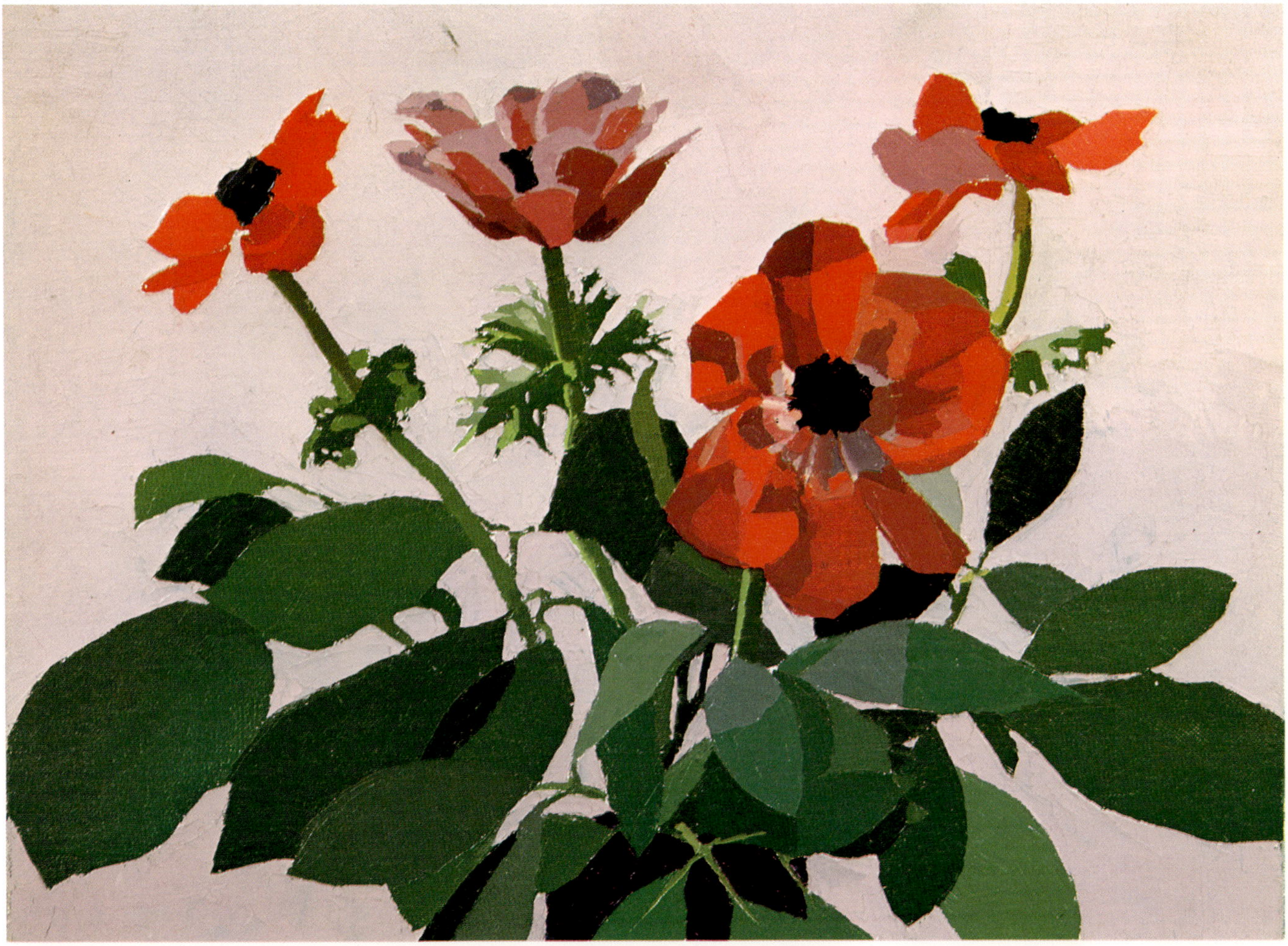

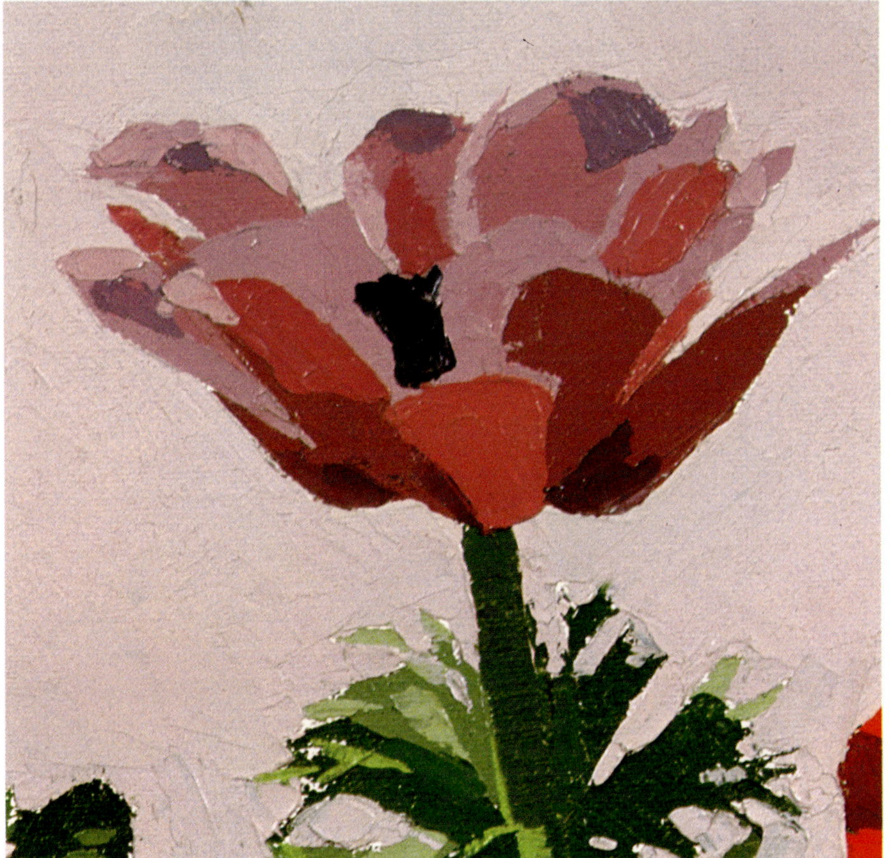

Group of Anemones. When you've developed your skills so that you can work very quickly—identifying, mixing, and laying down each color spot without hesitation—then you'll be ready to tackle a really complicated, live subject such as this bunch of anemones. Don Stern has focused his attention entirely on the blossoms and greenery, eliminating the bowl and table. Each area is observed precisely. This painter knows that a successful pictorial design depends not only on recording the positive areas—the petals, leaves, and stems—but also on capturing the negative spaces, the areas where the background color emerges between the plant forms. Never say to yourself: "Oh, that's just the background." Every inch of a painting is important.

Anemones (detail). Is this a first or second statement? Each leaf is so simple that the greenery seems hardly more than an elaborate first statement. Only the blossoms have been carried further to a stage that seems more like a second statement. Although I've advised you against getting carried away and concentrating a lot of color spots in one area, there are times when it makes sense to break the rules. Here the big central blossom is the focal point, with the greatest variety and number of color spots, while the surrounding shapes are painted more simply.

PAINT FISH

First Statement, Striped Bass. As I've said before, it's good experience to paint a model that rushes you—that teaches you the danger of dawdling. A fish is ideal for that purpose. Buy one in the morning and plan to cook it that same day. Knowing that you've got to eat the fish, you'll race to paint it before it becomes inedible. The elegant simplicity of this first statement, in fact, is in part the result of Don Stern's haste.

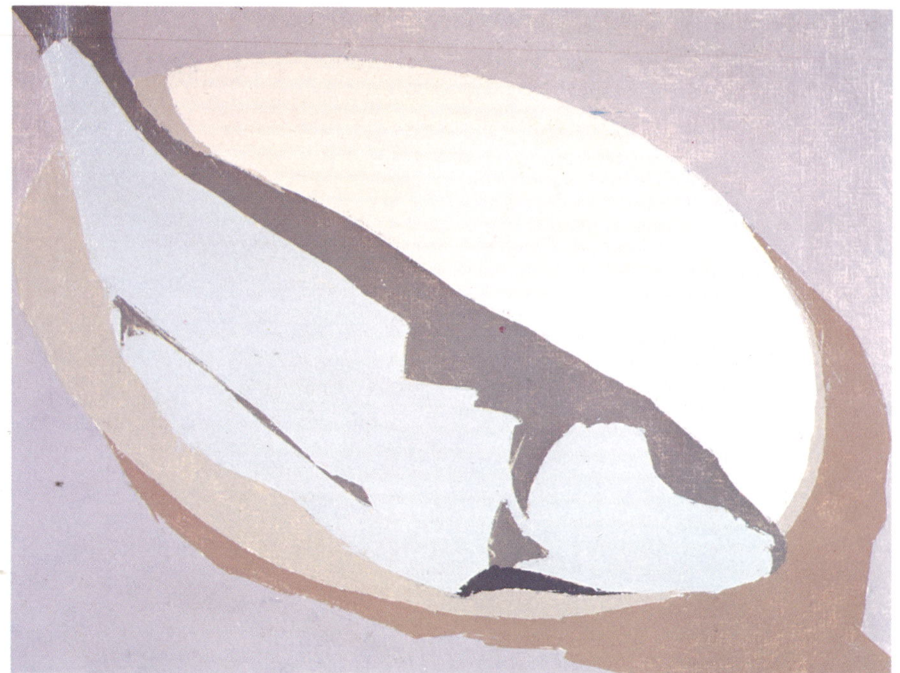

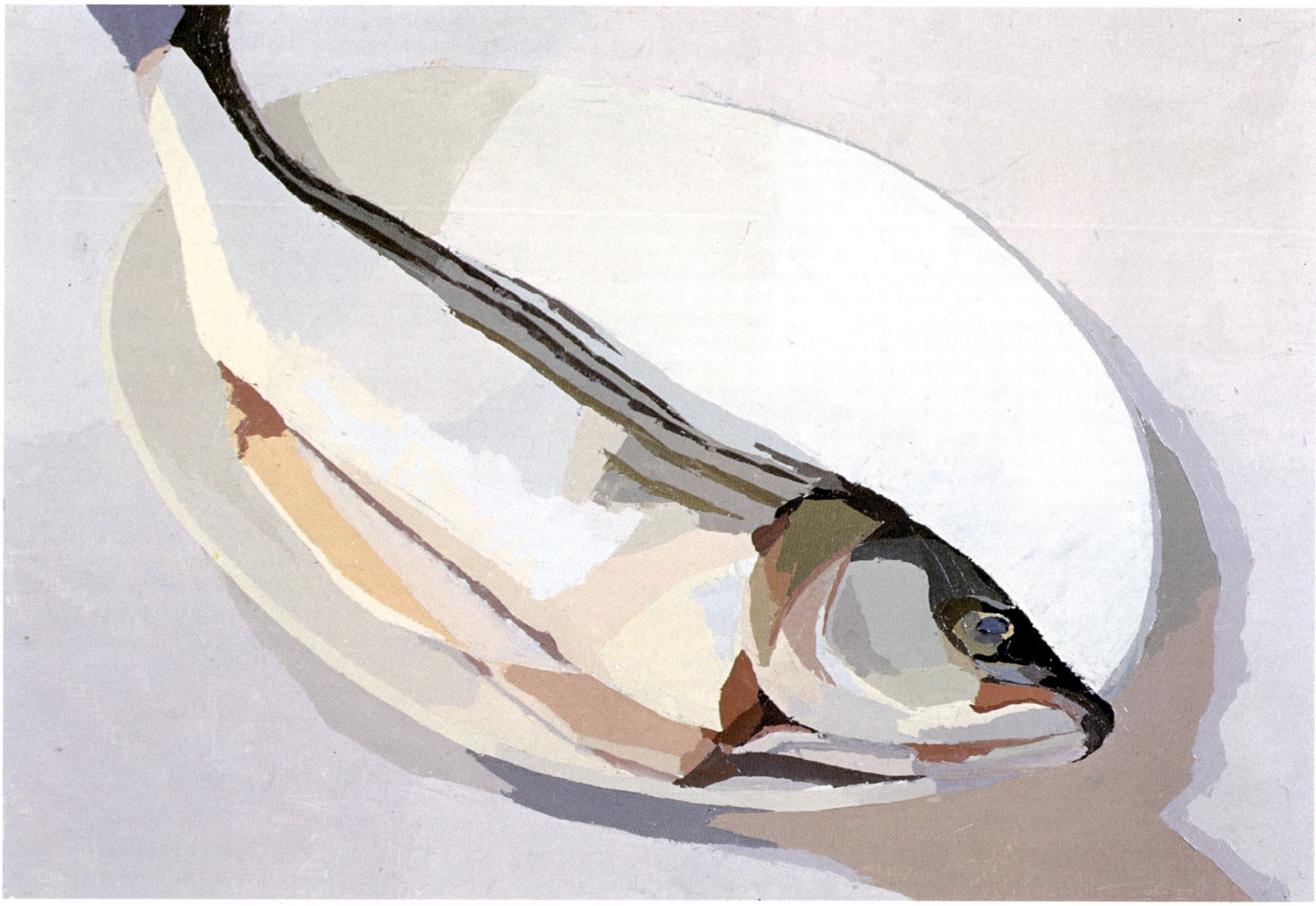

Second Statement, Striped Bass. The shiny surface of a fish provides beautiful colors to paint. But don't be put off by its shine and translucency. A fish is no more difficult to paint than a translucent plastic jug, metal saucepan, or glass plate. Just look for the big color spots and don't get lost in details like fish scales. You'll probably find that a second statement is all you'll have time to do—and perhaps says all you'll want to say. (The painting is in the collection of William Fotaides.)

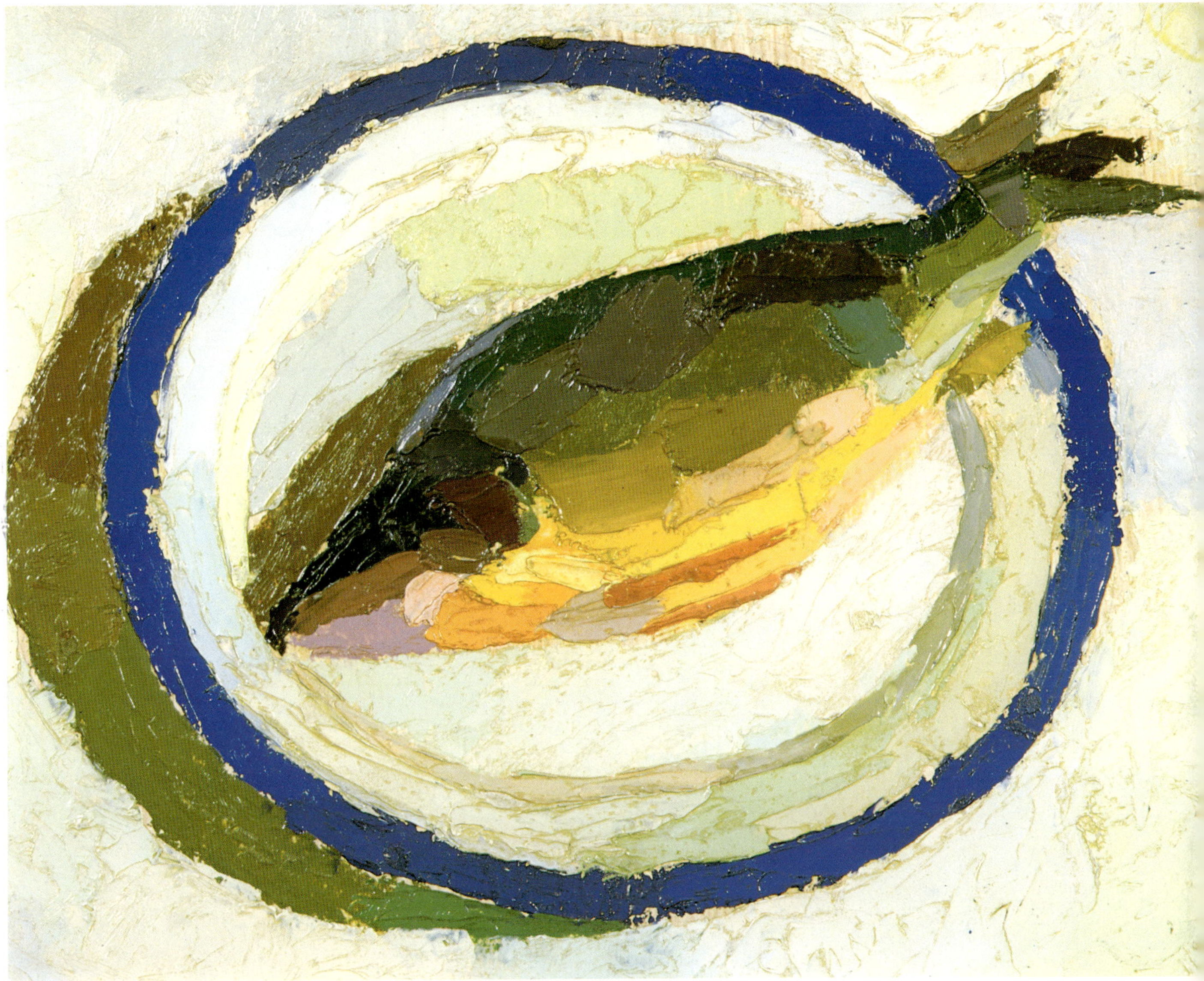

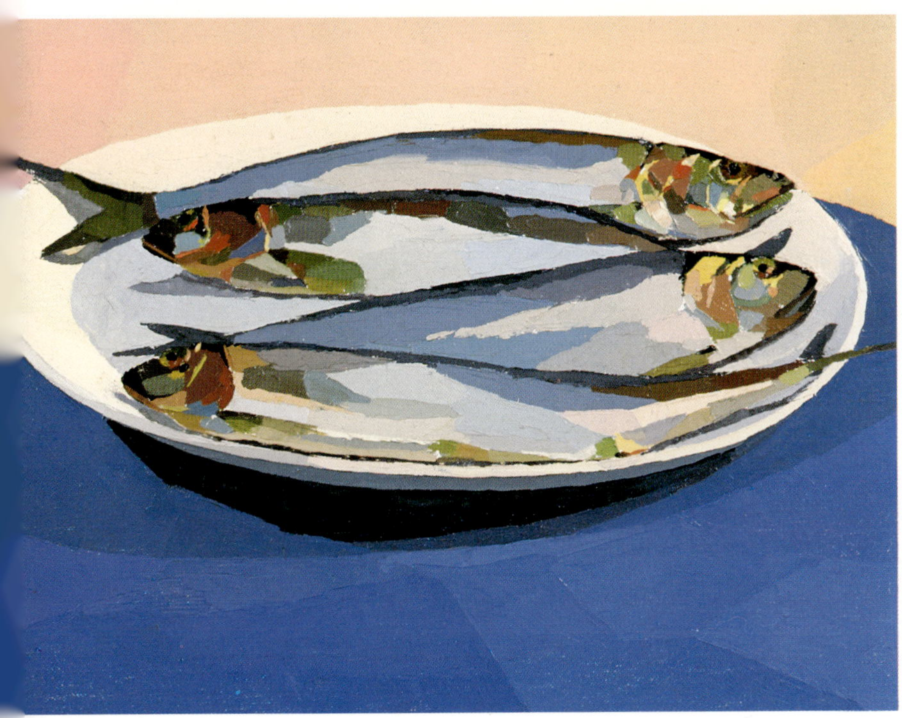

Rainbow Trout. In this study, the body of the fish is painted with large, simple, and bold color spots—as are the dish and its shadow. The painter, Alexander J. Yow, has paid no attention to details, focusing his attention primarily on color variations such as the difference between the tail and its shadow; the subtle color changes in the dark rim of the dish; and the succession of color spots in the dish's shadow. Simply by placing the right color spots in the right locations, he has captured the almost unearthly glow of the fish's body, making it clear why it is called *rainbow* trout.

Four Sardines. Certainly four fish can be harder to paint than one—not that whatever problem they present is multiplied four times, but rather that you have to paint four times as fast before they spoil! You will have to work quickly and decisively, identifying each color spot and mixing it swiftly, and placing it on the painting surface with a few economical strokes. The brilliant surface of the fish was a delight for Don Stern to paint.

PAINT BREAD AND FRUIT

First Statement, Sliced Bread. If you visit a bakery, you'll find that bread comes in a variety of shapes, sizes, surfaces, and colors. This student, Jarvis Wilcox, has found a particularly interesting irregularly shaped loaf and has cut it into chunks and arranged them on a plate. His first statement was laid down in a few large color spots. He pays particular attention to the planes in light and shade. His first statement has been painted with such accuracy that we recognize the subject instantly.

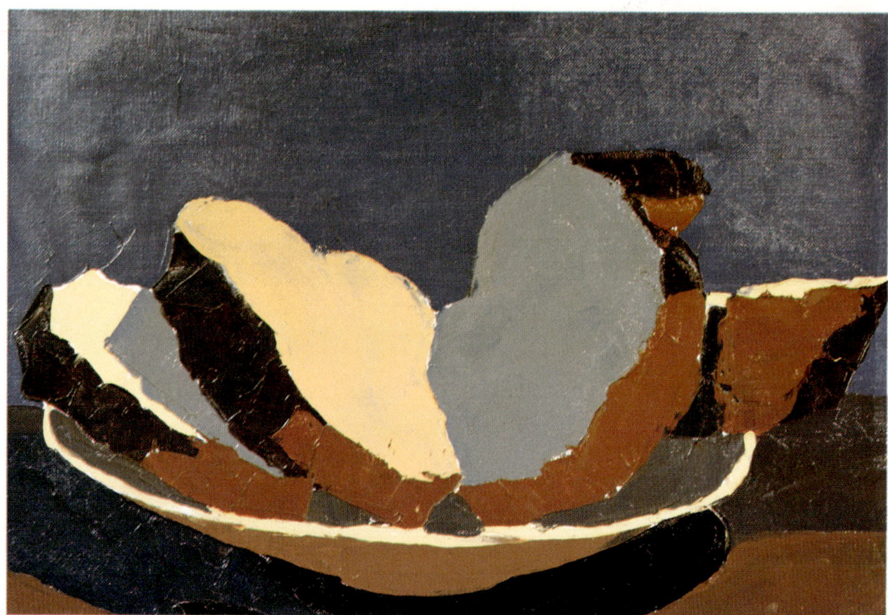

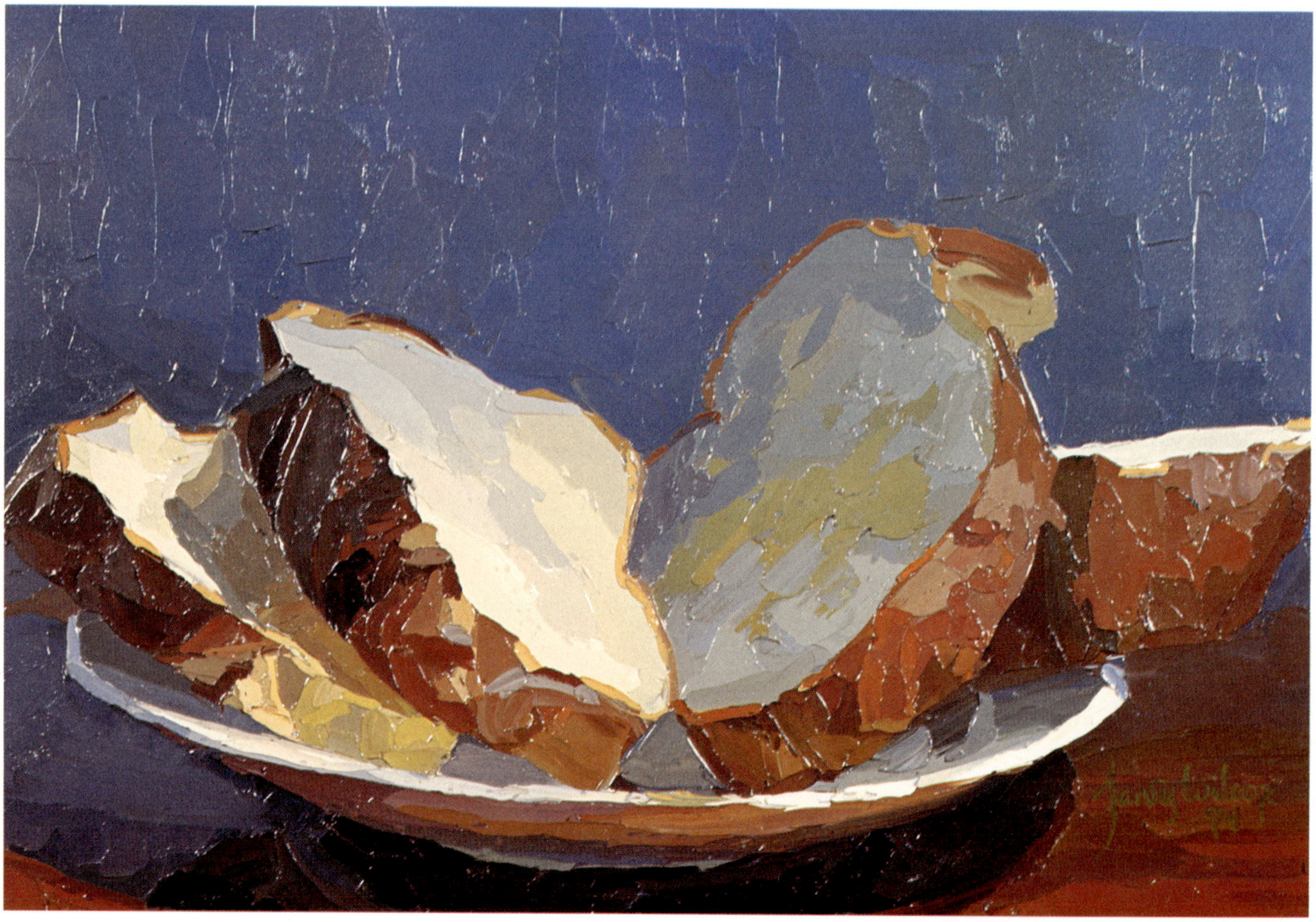

Third Statement, Sliced Bread. It often happens that a painter becomes so caught up in the beauty of the subject—and the challenge of painting it—that he is carried far beyond the demands of just a study and, almost unconsciously, creates a work of art. That's what happened here in this stunning third statement. I find this painting so rich and full of feeling that I often show it in my art appreciation classes. (The painting is in the collection of Erik Falkensteen.)

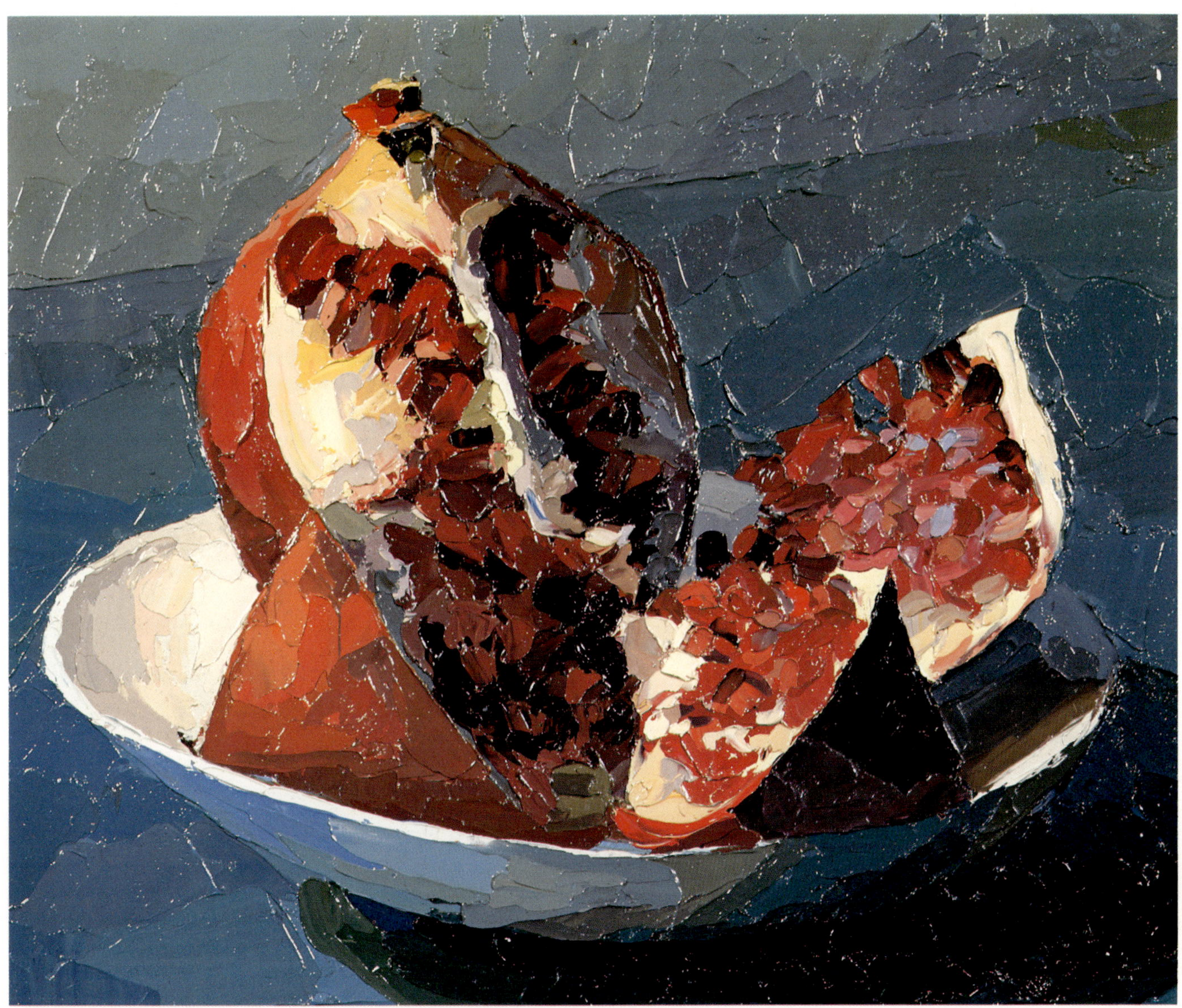

Quartered Pomegranate. Here is another example of that happily frequent phenomenon—the painting that starts out as a study and ends up as a completely satisfying work of art. It is amazing how the student, Jarvis Wilcox, was able to capture the essence of this Mediterranean fruit on so small a canvas. (It measures 12″ × 16″—31 × 41 cm—the size of most of the studies in this book!) Note the artistic economy shown in painting each seed a different color spot applied with a single knife stroke. This dish, with its sectioned fruit, has reminded some viewers of an open jewel box filled with rubies or, perhaps more pertinent, garnets. (The word *garnet* derives directly from the word *pomegranate.*)

PAINT KITCHEN OBJECTS

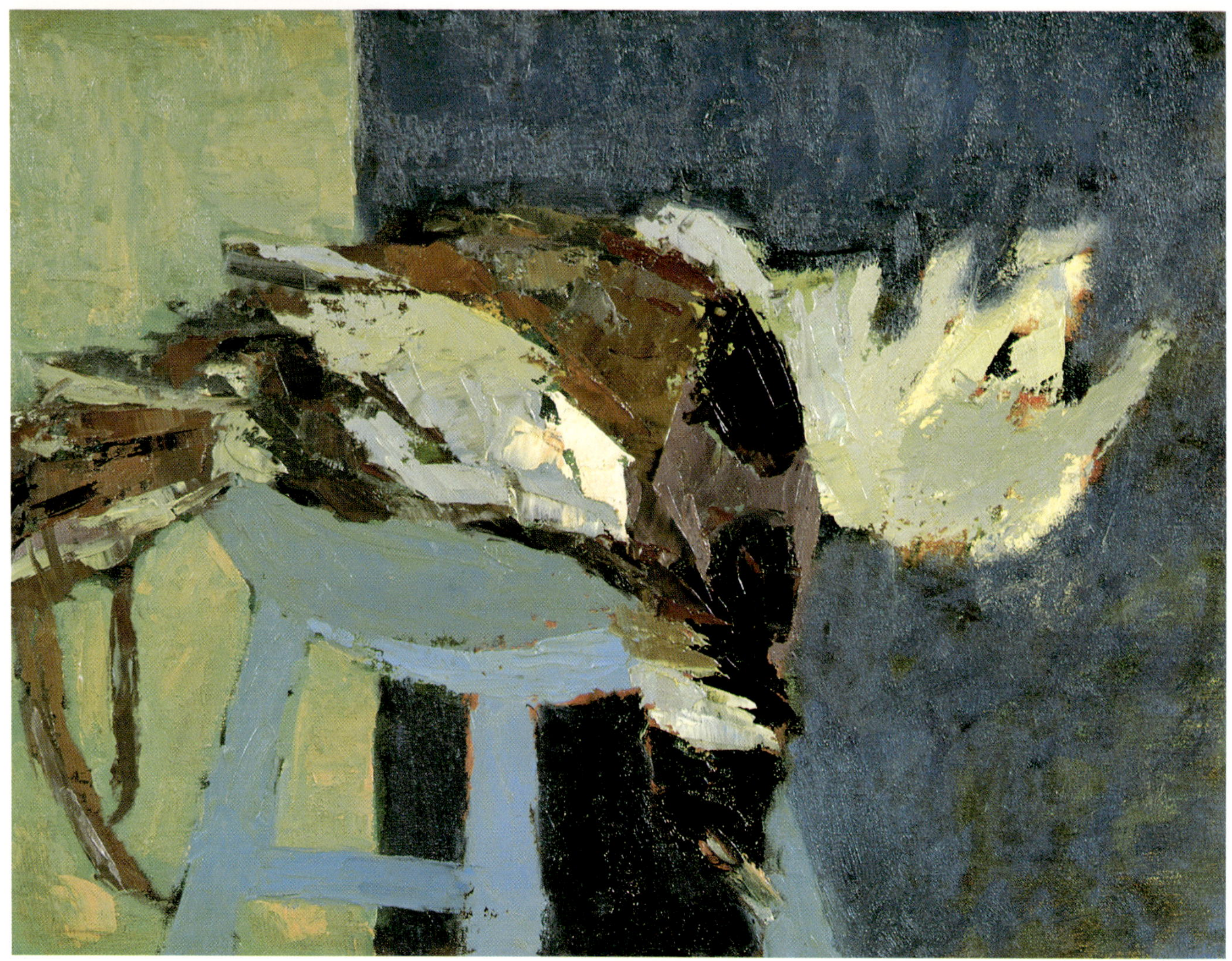

Pheasant. Dead birds—so-called "game birds"—have been a subject for still life painting since the seventeenth century. They are so much the stock-in-trade of still life, that this may explain many people's strenuous declarations, "I just don't like still life!" Yet I find that I don't turn away from Geneviève Baucheron's *Pheasant.* Instead of dwelling on the geometric pattern of the plumage, she has built up the volume of the pheasant's forms—and only incidentally the feel of its feathers—through a careful choice of color spots.

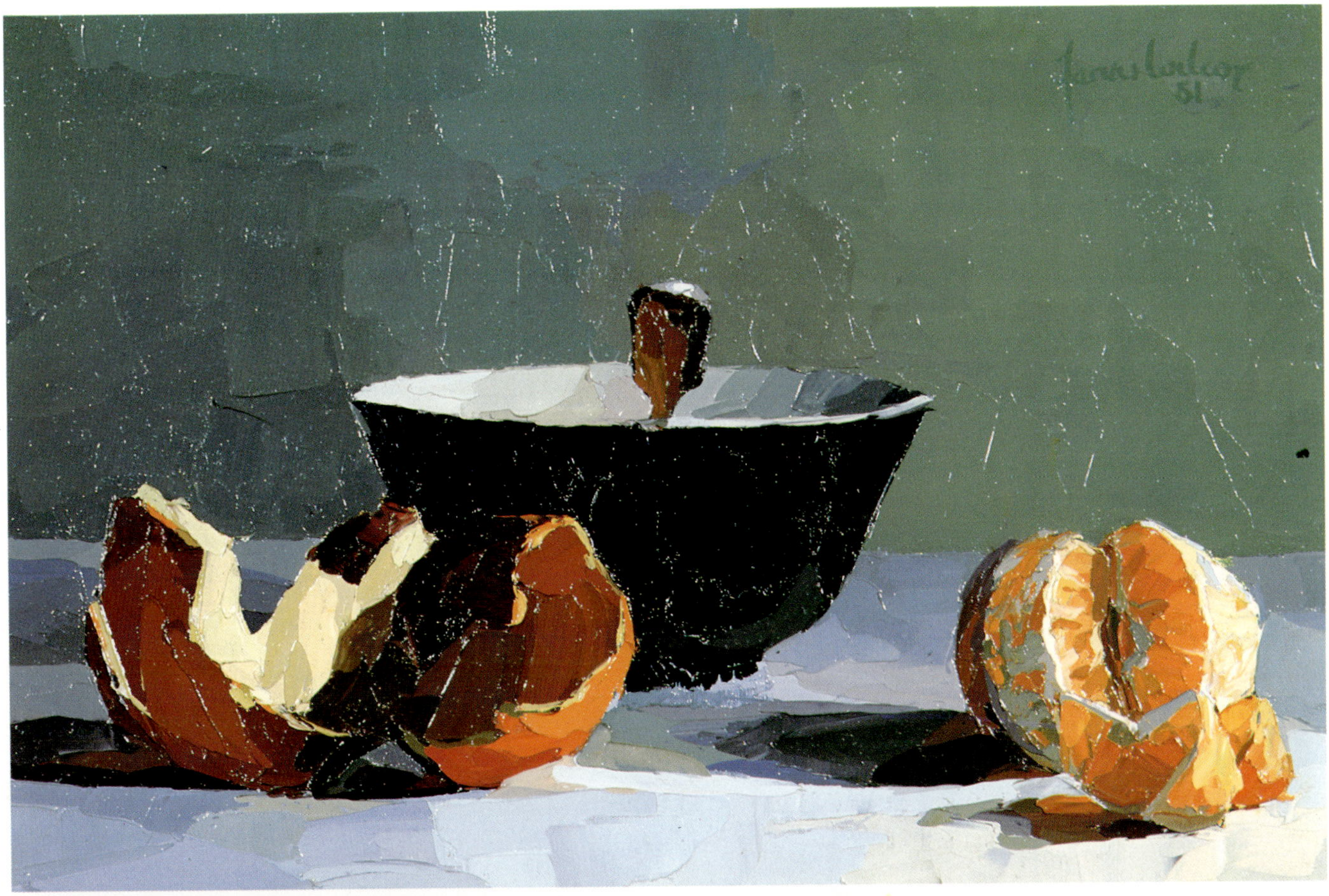

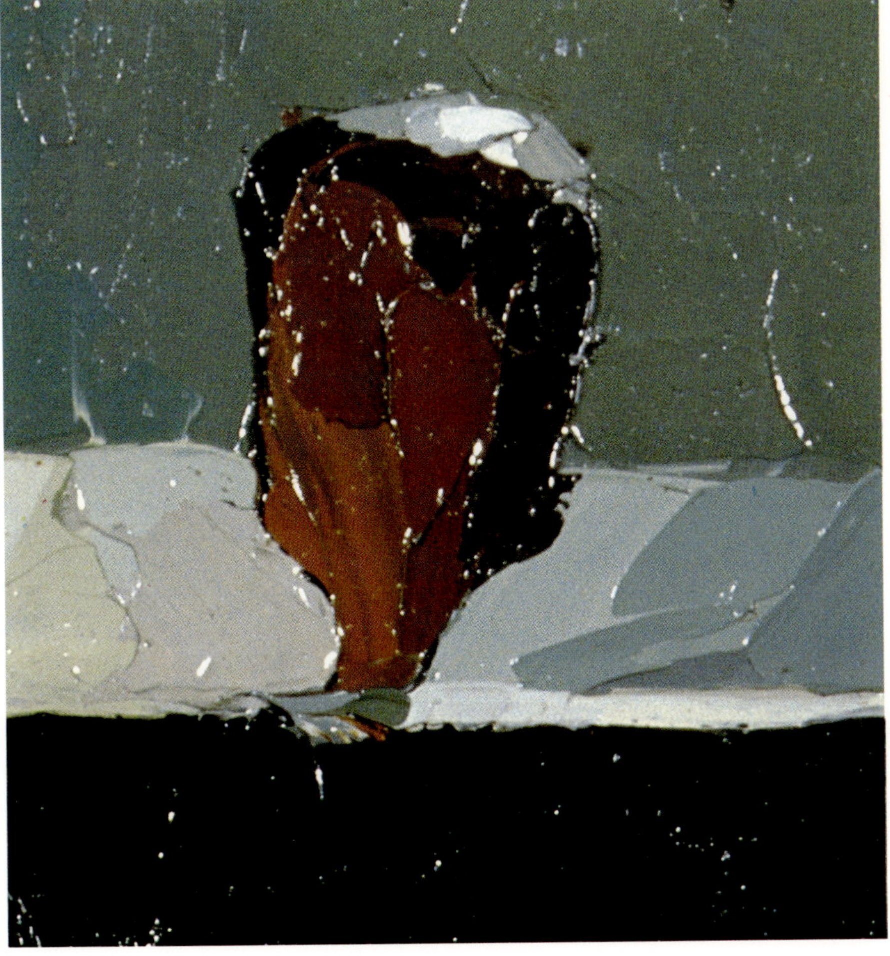

Bowl, Spoon, and Tangerine. Some of the most startling still lifes grow out of the most mundane of models. Here a peeled and partly segmented tangerine, a Japanese rice bowl, and a spoon, all on a bare white tabletop, have evoked an unusual, almost eerie mood. Although there is nothing unusual in the objects themselves or their rather classical, symmetrical arrangement, several contrasts create interest: the dry rind against the luscious, juicy fruit; the hard and solid opacity of the peel against the softer translucency of the tangerine; and the almost flat blackness of the bowl against the aggressive forward thrust of the spoon. Notice how the colors and shapes of the objects, when accurately observed, describe surface qualities and space. For lessons on painting opacity and transparency, review Project 18, the paper bag. (The painting is by Jarvis Wilcox.)

Closeup of Spoon Handle. This extremely close view of the spoon handle serves to disclose the simplicity of the painter's approach. He saw the handle as possessing three distinct areas—a highlight, an area in shade, and light reflected into the shade. This closeup also shows the spoon handle's different colors: the highlight is painted in three spots of very light and dull violet; the area in shade is three spots of a dark and dull red-violet; and the light in the shade area, reflected up from the fruit rind, is painted in three different spots of dulled orange.

EXPRESS A POINT OF VIEW

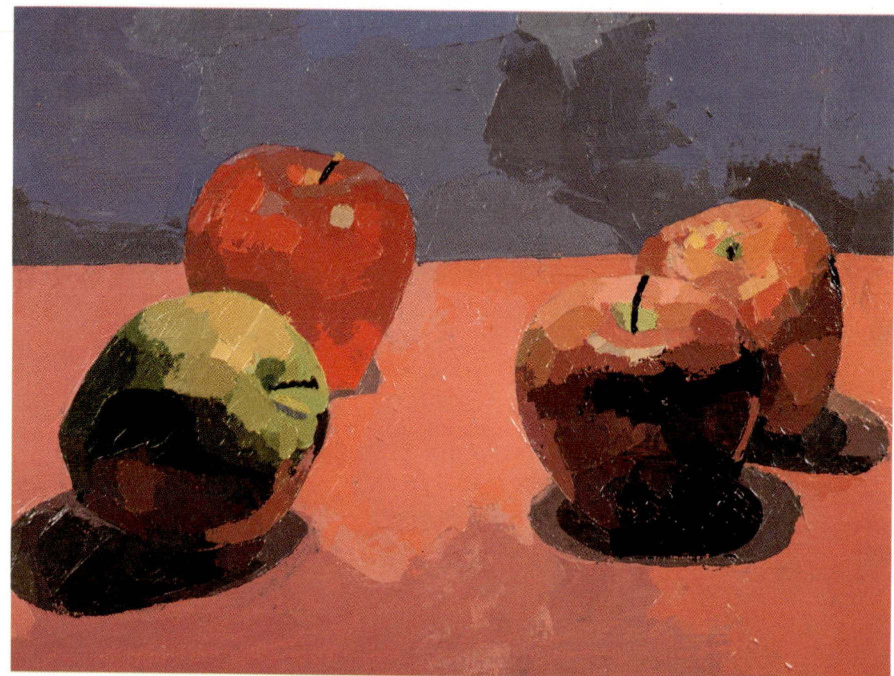

Four Apples, One Student's Version. I include these two studies of the same setup to make an interesting point. Even working within the strict limitations of the system in this book, each student reveals a distinct personality in everything he paints. This balanced, relaxed study of the four apples is the work of a Californian. There's lots of space between and around the apples. Each knife stroke is squarish and placed on the canvas paper with a firm, measured movement of the hand. The student, Richard Gleason, has used his viewfinder to frame a composition that's quiet, stable, and spacious.

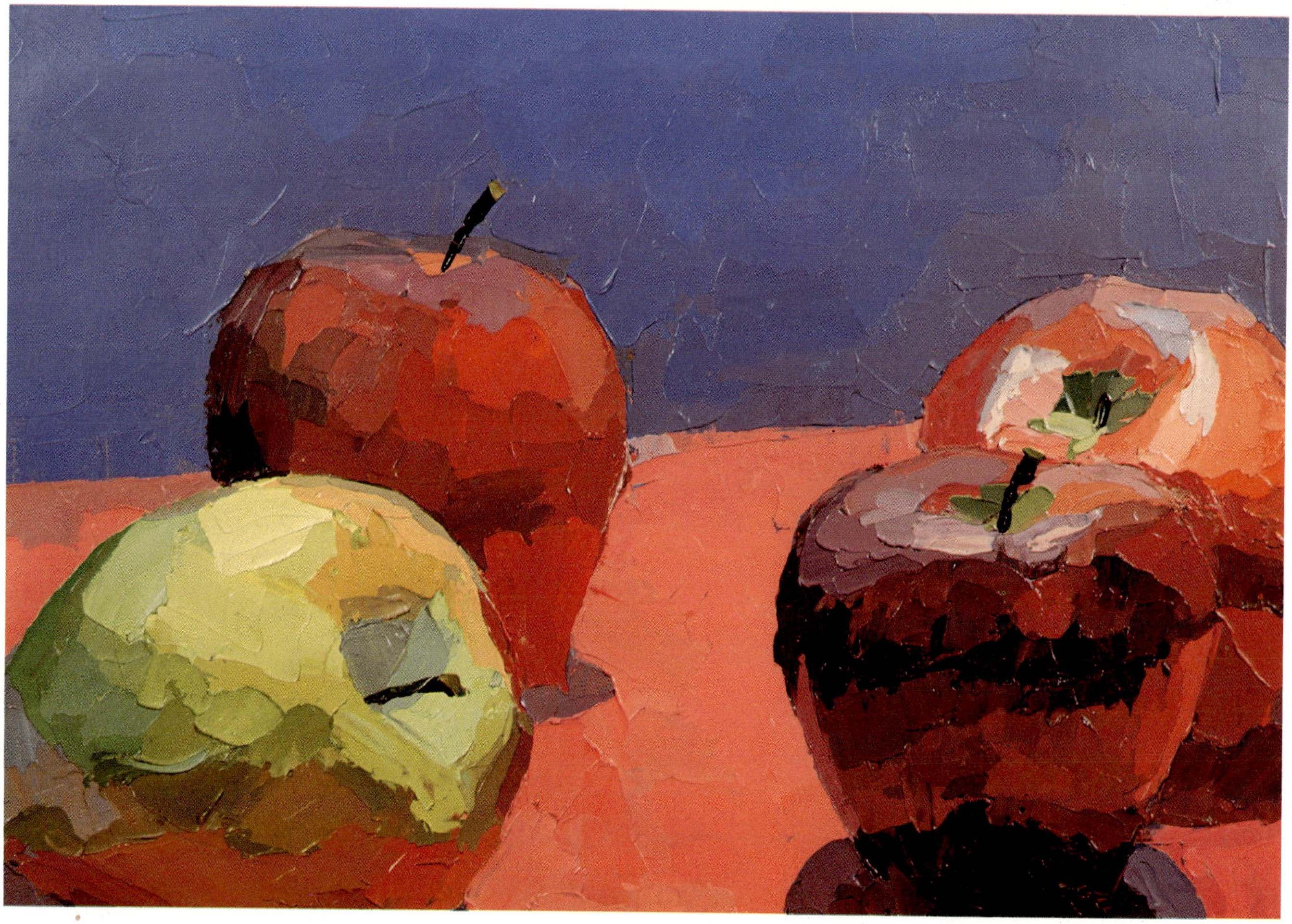

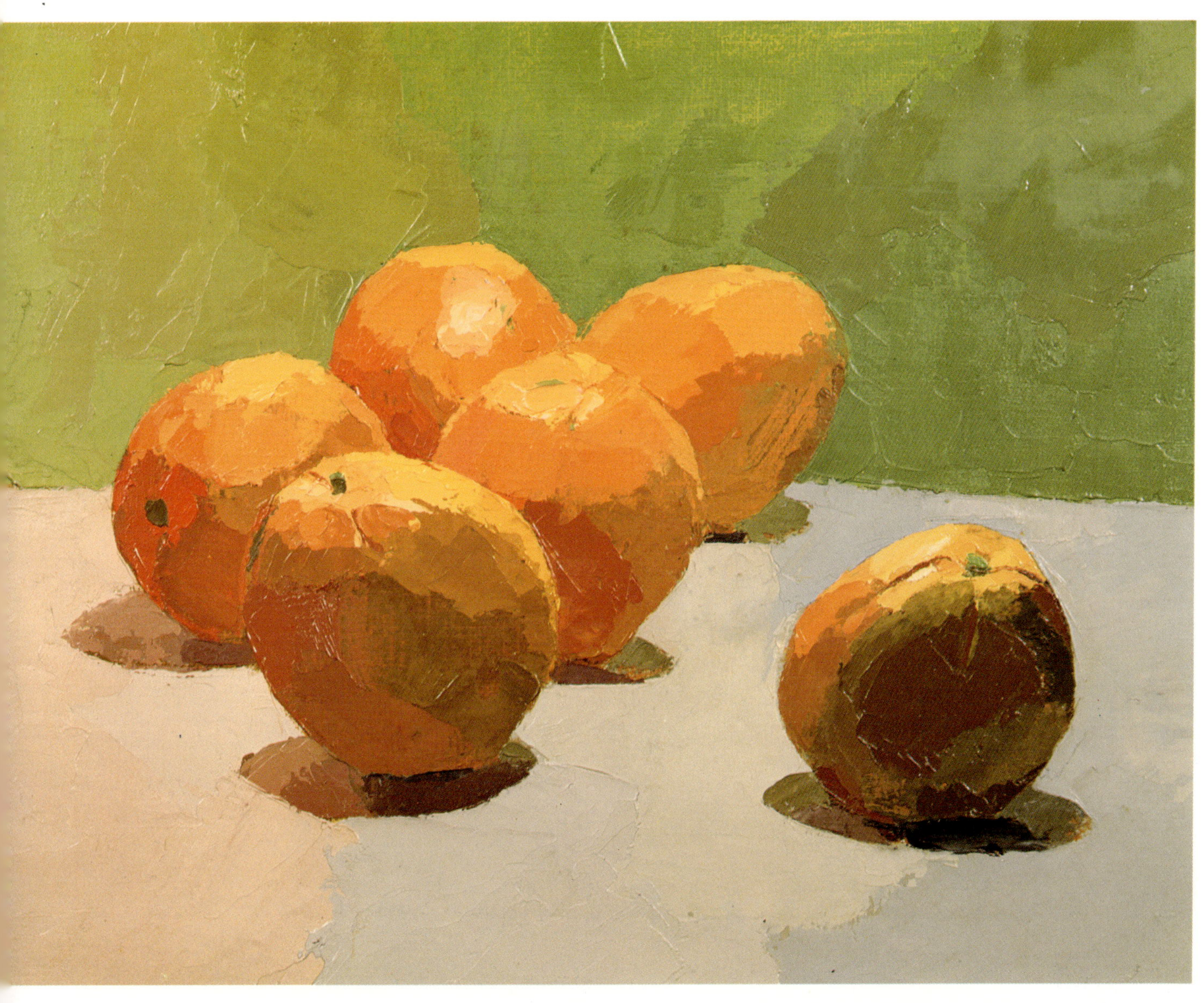

Four Apples, Another Student's Version. Just as the first student was finishing work on his painting of the apples, another student, Jarvis Wilcox, walked into the studio, liked the setup, and decided to paint his own version. As you can see, this second version is far more "aggressive." It was painted from the same physical viewpoint, but from a totally different psychological viewpoint. The second student has used his viewfinder to frame a tense, crowded composition in which the apples press against the edges of the picture and seem to crowd one another as well. The knife work is also turbulent and impulsive.

Six Oranges. Like the apple paintings, when you compare this study of oranges by Richard Gleason, to the one Alfred Tyrol painted in Project 10, you can also see the results of two distinct personalities interpreting the same setup. These differences provoked an observer, admiring the two paintings hung side by side in my studio, to remark that Gleason's oranges looked as if they were commissioned by an orange grower's association or chamber of commerce, while Tyrol's oranges (page 65), looked so tough that they had to come from New York! It is an interesting observation—particularly because Gleason comes from California and Tyrol is a native of New York state. The experiences and backgrounds of both artists may have unconsciously been reflected in their art.

PAINT CHALLENGING SURFACES

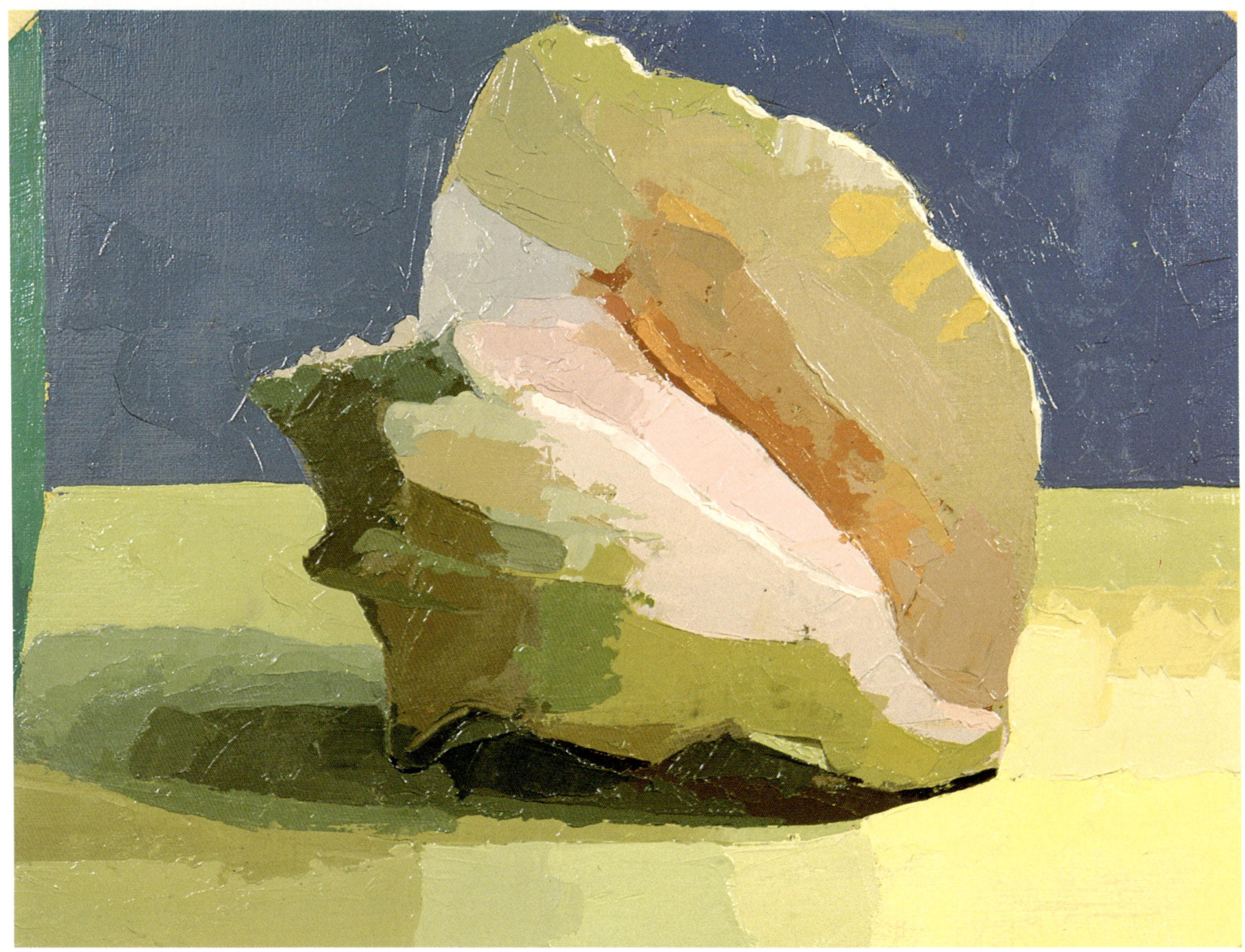

Conch Shell. If you've ever gone to the seashore, you've probably come back with a souvenir like this shell. It may look like a forbidding subject because it's shiny, iridescent, and sometimes translucent, with that peculiar sensation of inner light that makes seashells so extraordinary. But remember how you mastered subjects that presented similar problems, such as the translucent plastic jug, the paper bag with the light coming through, and the other glass and metallic objects that seemed so difficult until you looked at them hard and really *saw* them. Just forget that you're painting a seashell and lay down those color spots without consciously trying to render that magical, inner light. Soon enough, the shell will begin to glow, as it does here. This study is by Richard Gleason.

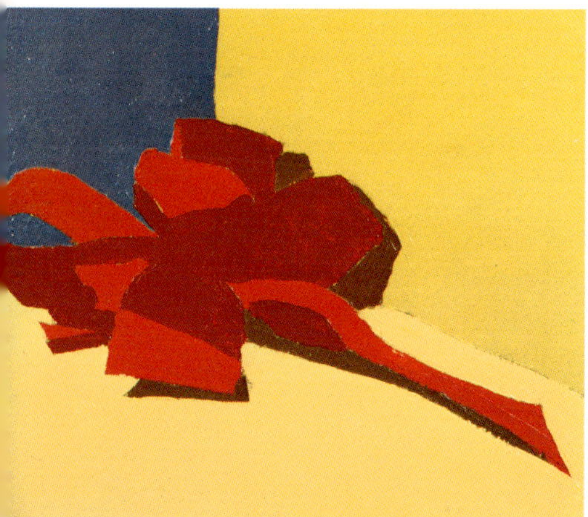

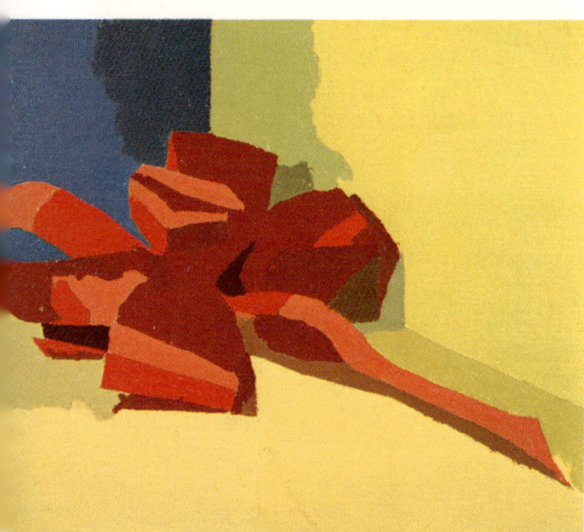

First Statement, Satin Bow. Some cloths, like satin—with its glossy face and dull back—tend to intimidate students. But if you can paint a scoured aluminum saucepan, a brass or copper bowl, ceramic cups and glass, you can also handle a shiny satin bow, with its matte underside. The student, Richard Gleason, began by reducing the number of problems the model presented. He drastically eliminated, for the moment, the subtle play of light over the surface of the cloth and, instead, concerned himself only with major divisions of light and shade. He also treated the bow as a single large silhouette, reserving the details for a later statement. Thus he was able to produce this statement in six colors distributed among fourteen spots. Interestingly, the two colors that state the ribbon are laid down in only seven spots.

Second Statement, Satin Bow. Here is the result of a second look at several smaller silhouettes within the single large area of the bow. Notice that each of these silhouettes has a unique size, shape, and position—as well as its own hue, luminosity, and intensity. The same holds for the color spots that make up the three planes of the setup box. This statement has begun to disclose how all the parts of the setup interpenetrate.

Third Statement, Satin Bow. This final statement is still simple and yet complete. Viewed at arm's length through half-closed eyes, the model looks like what it is—a red satin ribbon bow, the kind found on candy boxes and Christmas wreaths. Again, by concentrating on color spots alone, the entire object and its surface quality is rendered.

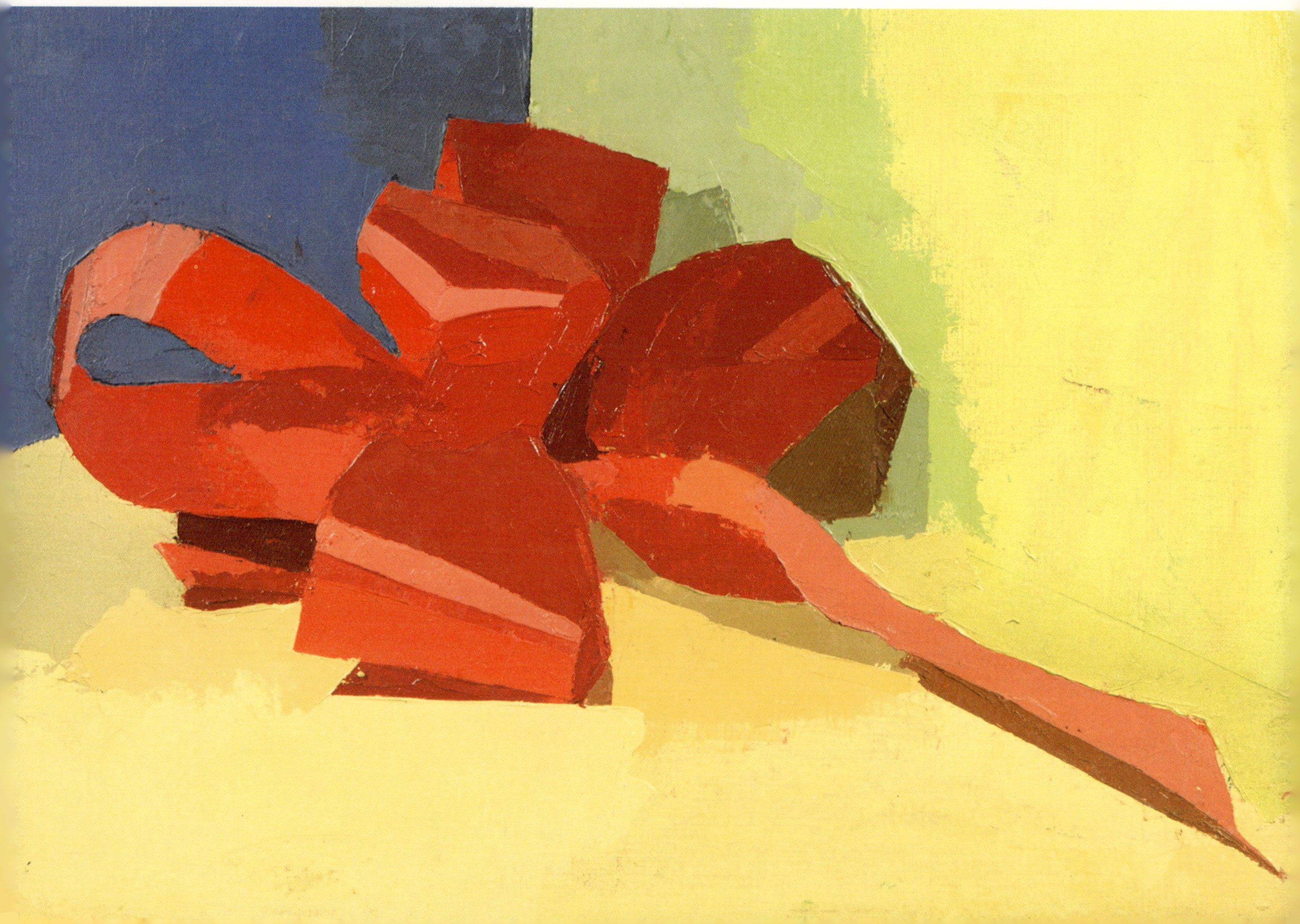

PAINT GLASS

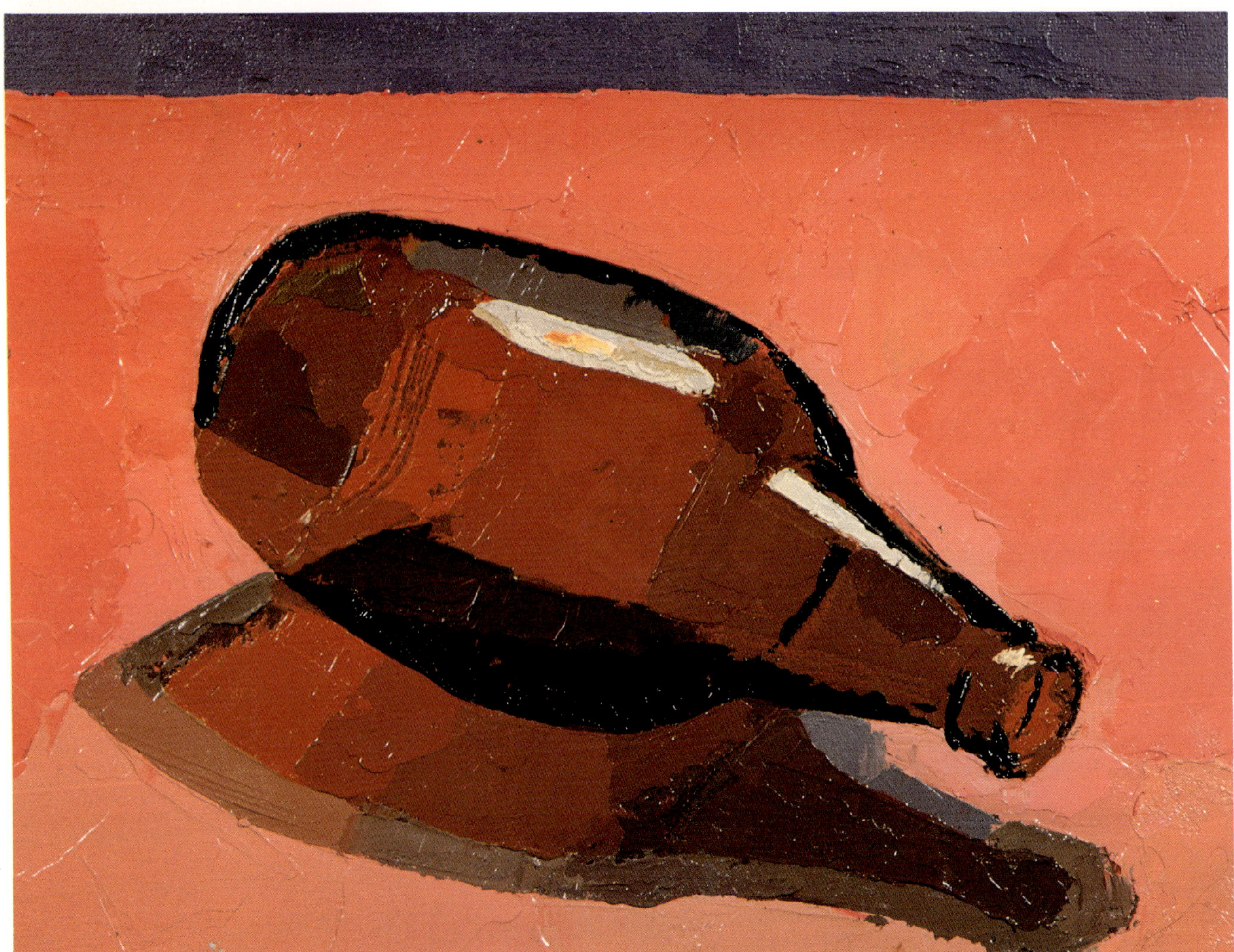

Amber Bottle. Another common household object is the colored glass bottle that contains beer, wine, fruit juice, or some other drink. This student, Richard Gleason, has taken an empty beer bottle and placed it on its side in order to create a big cast shadow that's full of color. Having painted the beer bottle with warm colored paper on the floor of the setup box and cool-colored background, you might try reversing the setup box colors so that the bottle rests on a blue-violet surface, while the background is a hot color like pink or red. You might see some dramatic changes in the color spots within the bottle and its shadow. Perhaps the most interesting color areas in the picture are the segment of shadow we see through the underside of the bottle and the color of its cast shadow. No one could have predicted the sudden change in the shadow color as it passes beneath and behind the bottle.

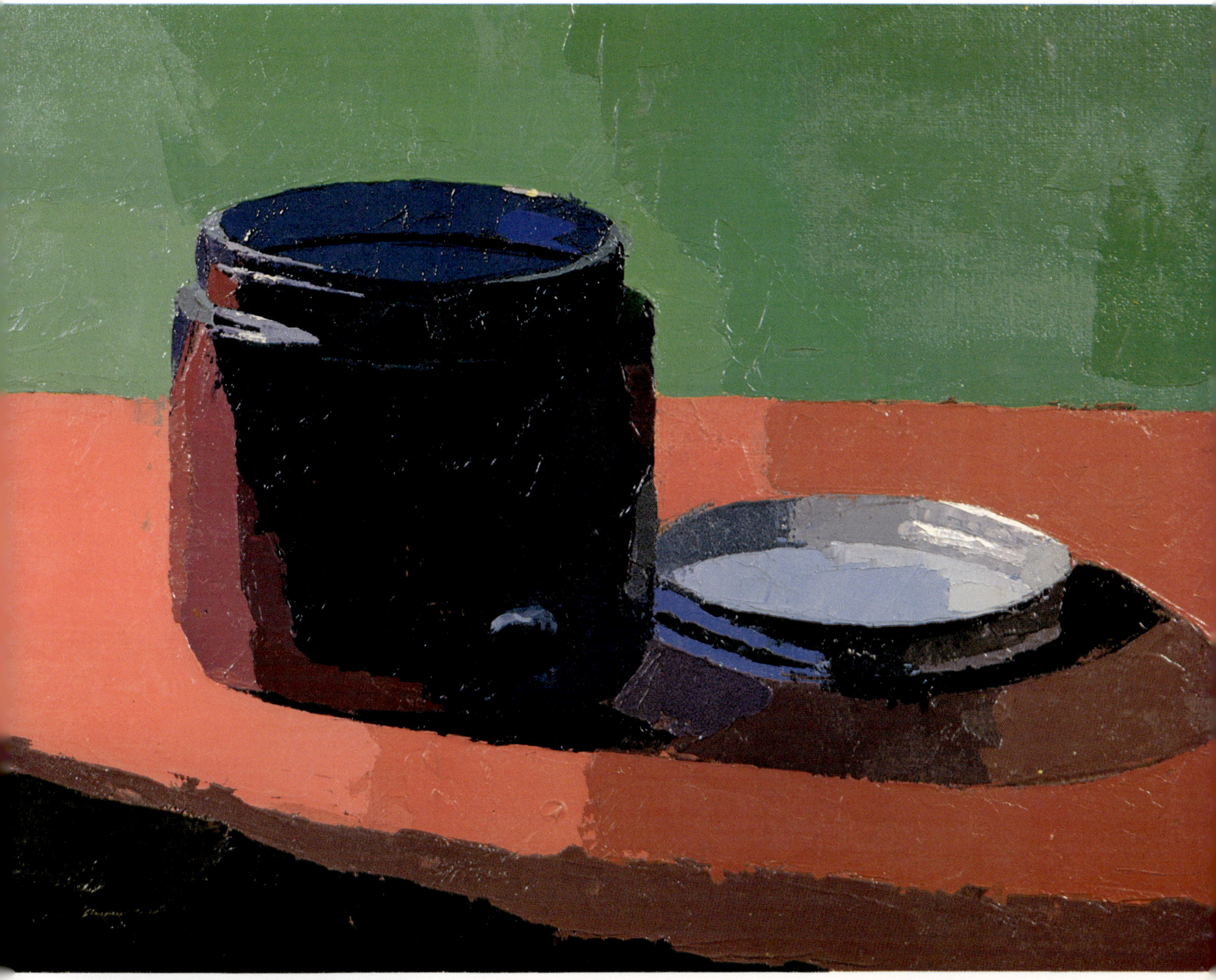

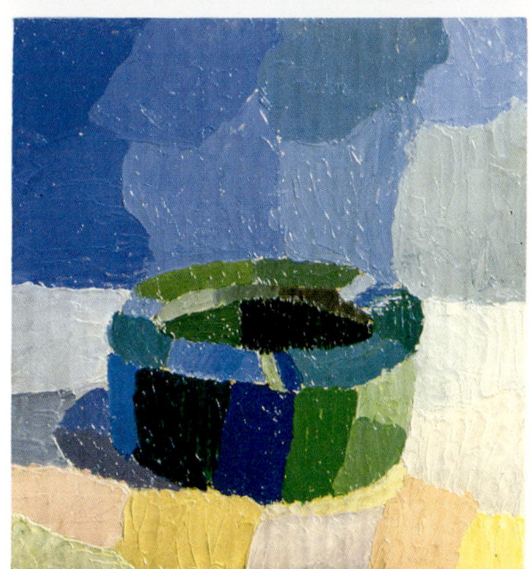

Blue Jar. Skin creams and lotions often come in a squat, blue glass jar like this one. Thus, such a jar is a common object in many households. To extract the maximum number of color possibilities from this simple subject, the student, Richard Gleason, has unscrewed the cap and set it beside the jar so he now has two objects to paint. He has also placed two strongly contrasting, yet harmonious, colors on the wall and floor of the setup box. Like the blue glass plate you painted earlier, this jar reveals astonishingly little blue—but we still read it as blue and as glass! Its metal cap is considerably easier to paint than the metal saucepan of Project 11. The finished picture is an interesting study in contrasts: the glossy, translucent glass of the jar and the satiny, opaque metal of the cap.

Glass Ashtray. Discerning each item and its object color—a green ashtray, white tablecloth, and blue background—is easy. What is hard is trying to pinpoint just which color spot exactly matches the object color of each of the three components. That is because *all* of the color spots in this study influence each other. The painter, Roger Stevens, ignoring what he knew and expected, painted only what his eyes actually saw. (The study was done on corrugated board and its ridged surface has affected the overlying paint.)

PAINT ORDINARY OBJECTS

Mug of Coffee. As you turn the pages of this "gallery" of ideas, you can certainly see that any household object is a potential painting subject. Yet notice this simple, dynamic design. It is an ordinary mug, filled with coffee, but the handle of the mug counterpoints the direction of its shadow, creating a strong movement. This study by Jarvis Wilcox in just five colors is so complete and satisfying that it doesn't need a second statement, let alone a third. This recalls Charles Hawthorne's dictum that if you can paint a study well in five color spots, you can paint it well in fifty or five hundred—but five thousand won't help if the five you began with weren't correctly seen and painted.

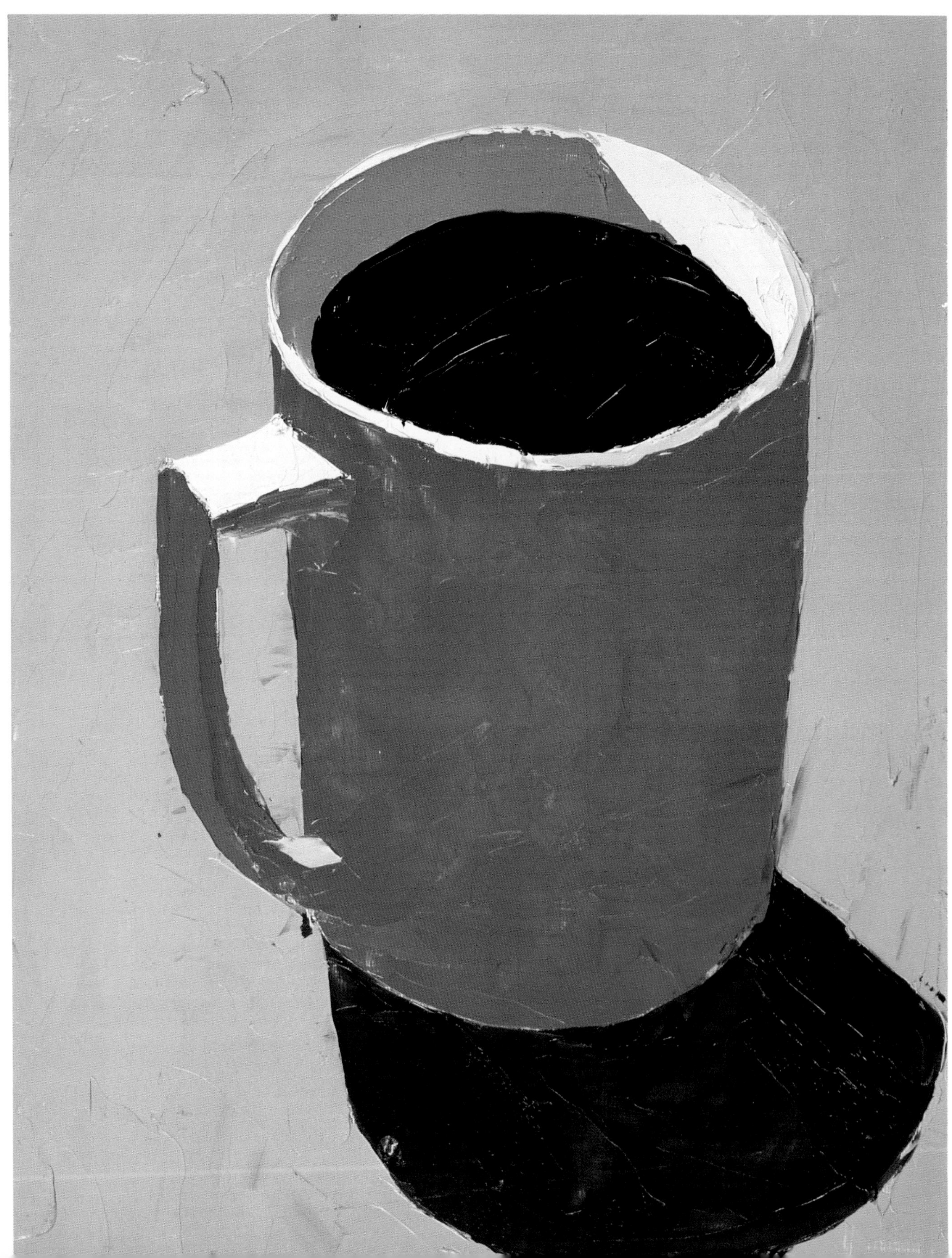

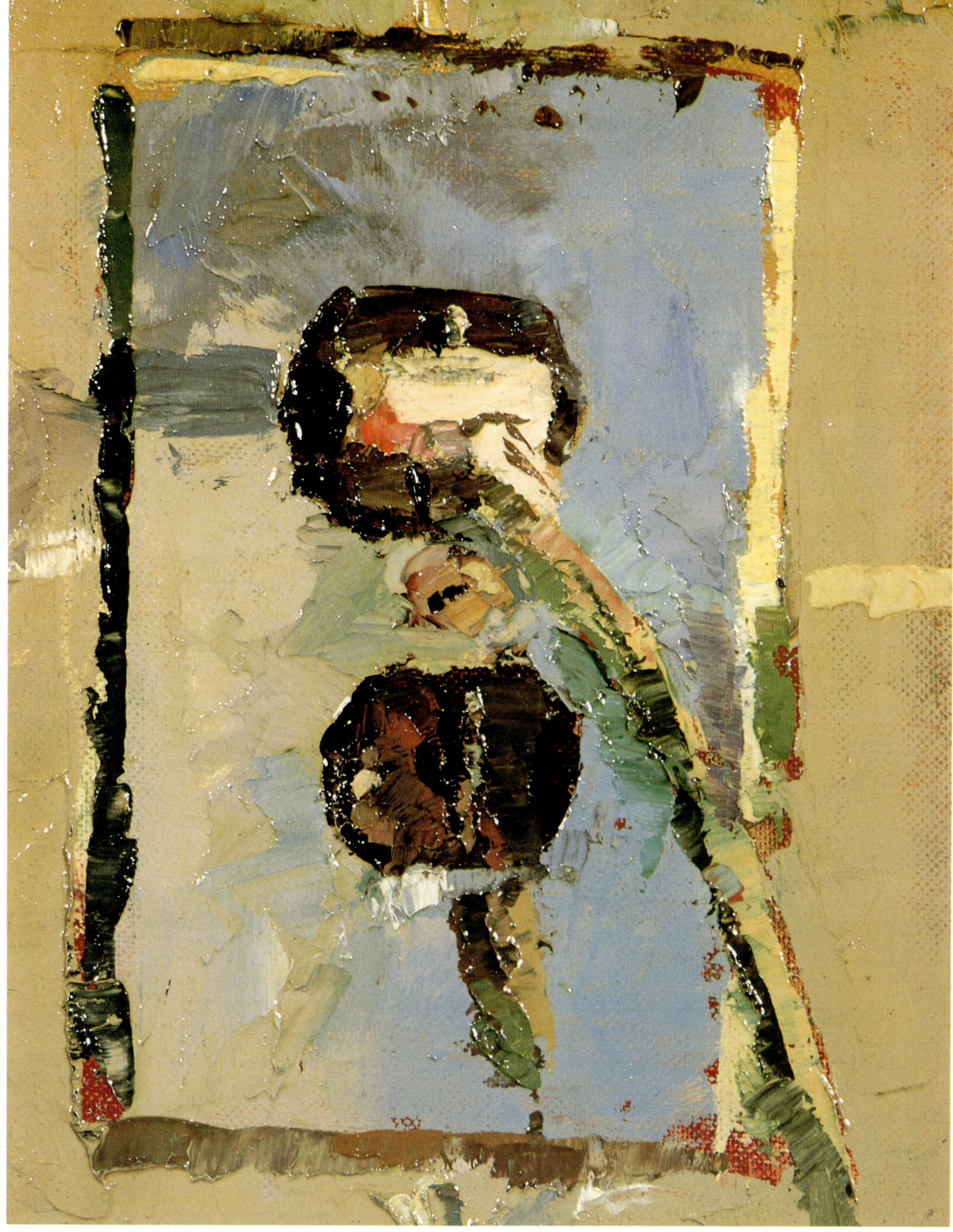

Electrical Outlet. Just to prove that we're surrounded by subjects that we normally ignore—despite the fact that they're filled with interesting color—here's a tiny study of an ordinary electrical outlet with a plug and an electrical cord. The metal plate that covers the outlet is filled with rich reflected color. So are the edges of light and shade that surround the plate. And the rough, spontaneous handling of the paint is full of personality. The fixture in the painting is the actual size of a typical electrical outlet. We once hung the painting on a wall as a kind of optical prank. From a distance, the study was amazingly—and amusingly—convincing. The student, Kenneth Krug, was in his mid-teens when he painted this study, which is in the collection of Georgina d'Eustachio.

REPEAT SIMILAR OBJECTS

Window Still Life. Why not try a natural setting for a still life—like your windowstill. Daylight, flooding through the window, creates wonderful color spots on living plants and their flowerpots, and also creates vivid color *on* and *within* the transparent bottles. If possible, try to arrange for the same natural light that falls on your subject to fall on your painting surface. Martin Myman, the student who painted this picture, knew exactly when to stop. There are just enough bold color spots to communicate the beauty of the subject, but not enough to make the painting too busy or overfinished. (The painting is in the collection of Dr. and Mrs. E.H. Shatzkin.)

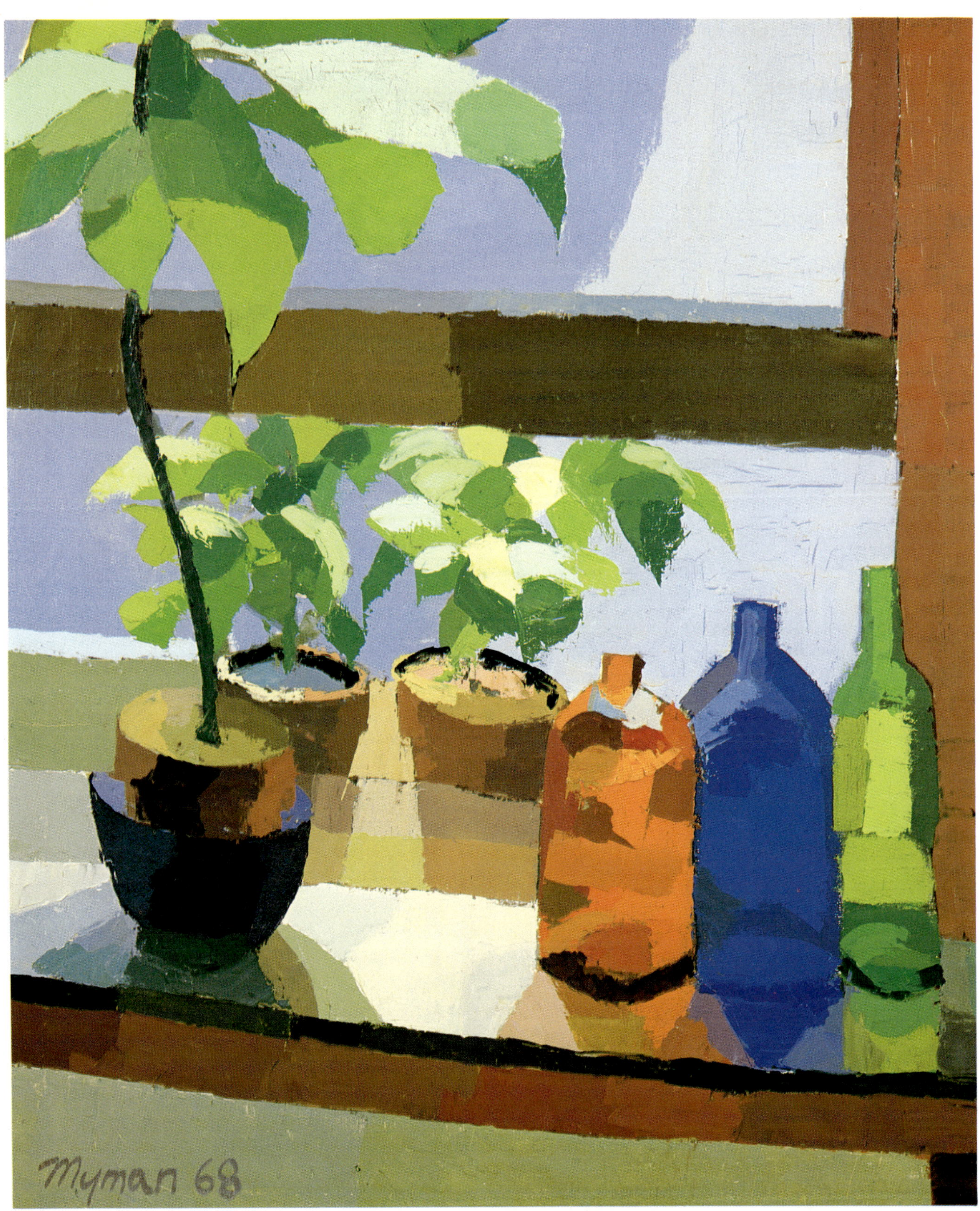

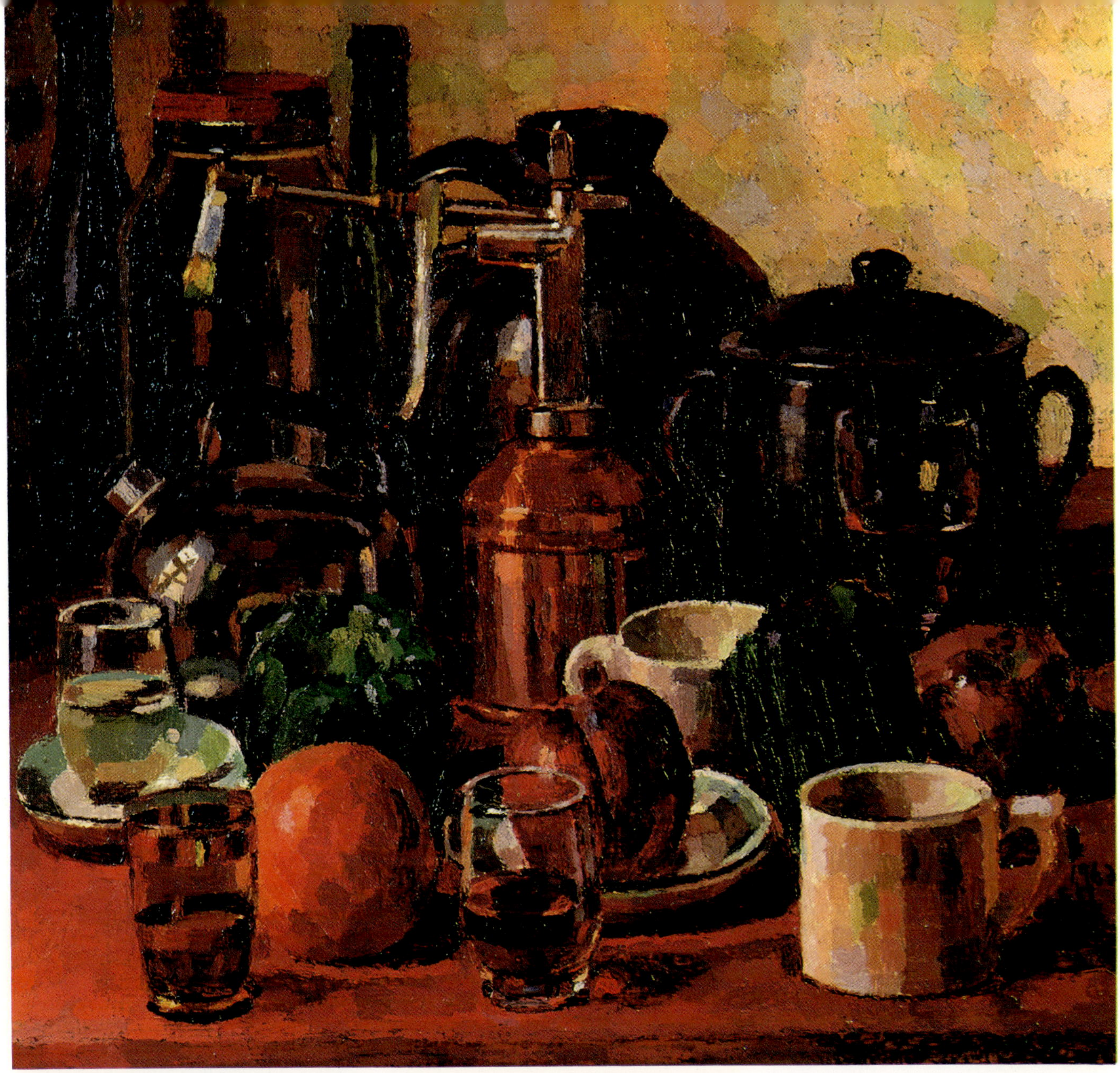

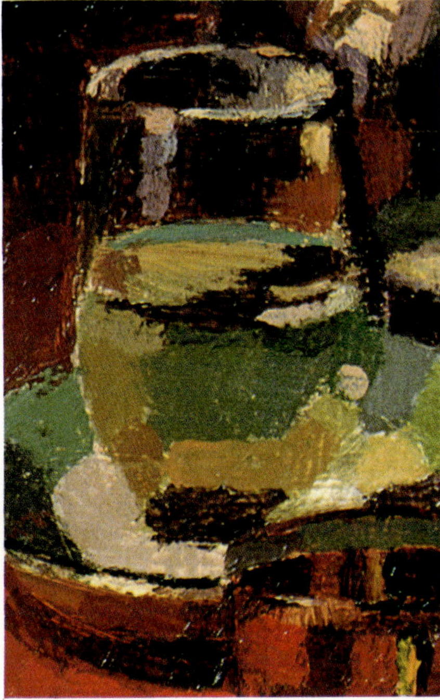

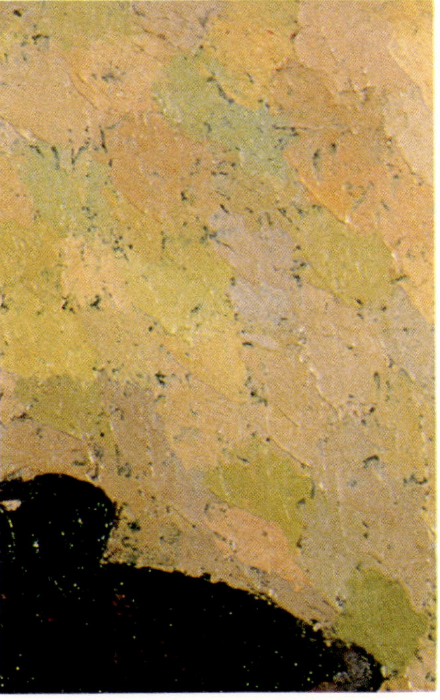

Still Life with Copper Spray Gun. By arranging and painting the same objects in many different positions, Frederic Henderschott has managed to crowd twenty different items onto a fairly small canvas. The painting also serves as a dramatic example of how a still life can unconsciously express the artist's point of view. Upon seeing this work, a fellow-painter remarked, "This is really a landscape—a cityscape—not a still life at all." And years later, a little girl looking at the same painting observed, "It looks just like New York, it's so crowded."

Closeups of Wine Glass and Wall. These closeups of opposite corners of the painting reveal the artist's unusual approach. The half-full wine glass in its saucer is painted with a minimum of color spots, while the seemingly blank wall is so rich in color and light to him that he has crammed it as full of as many color spots as he can fit.

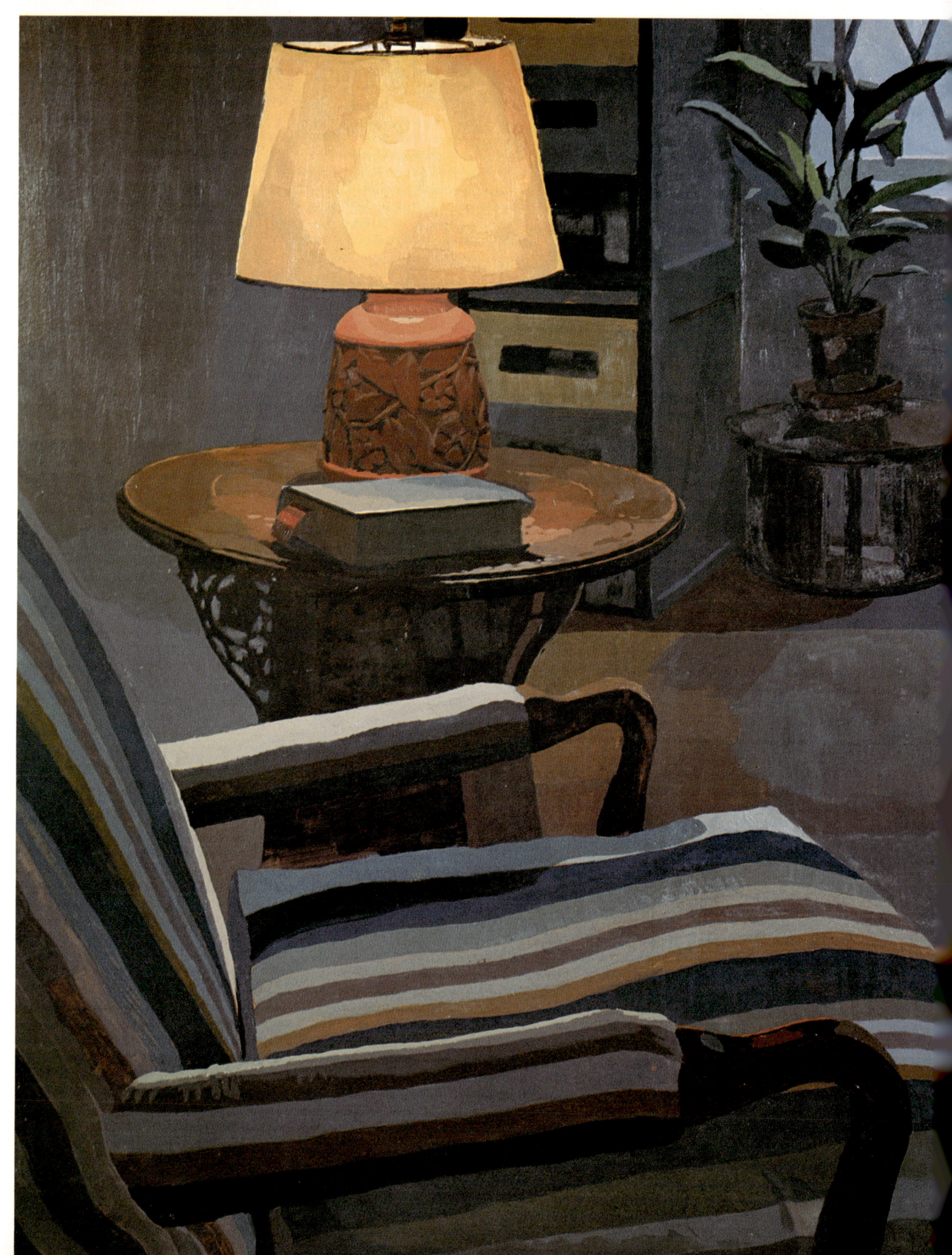

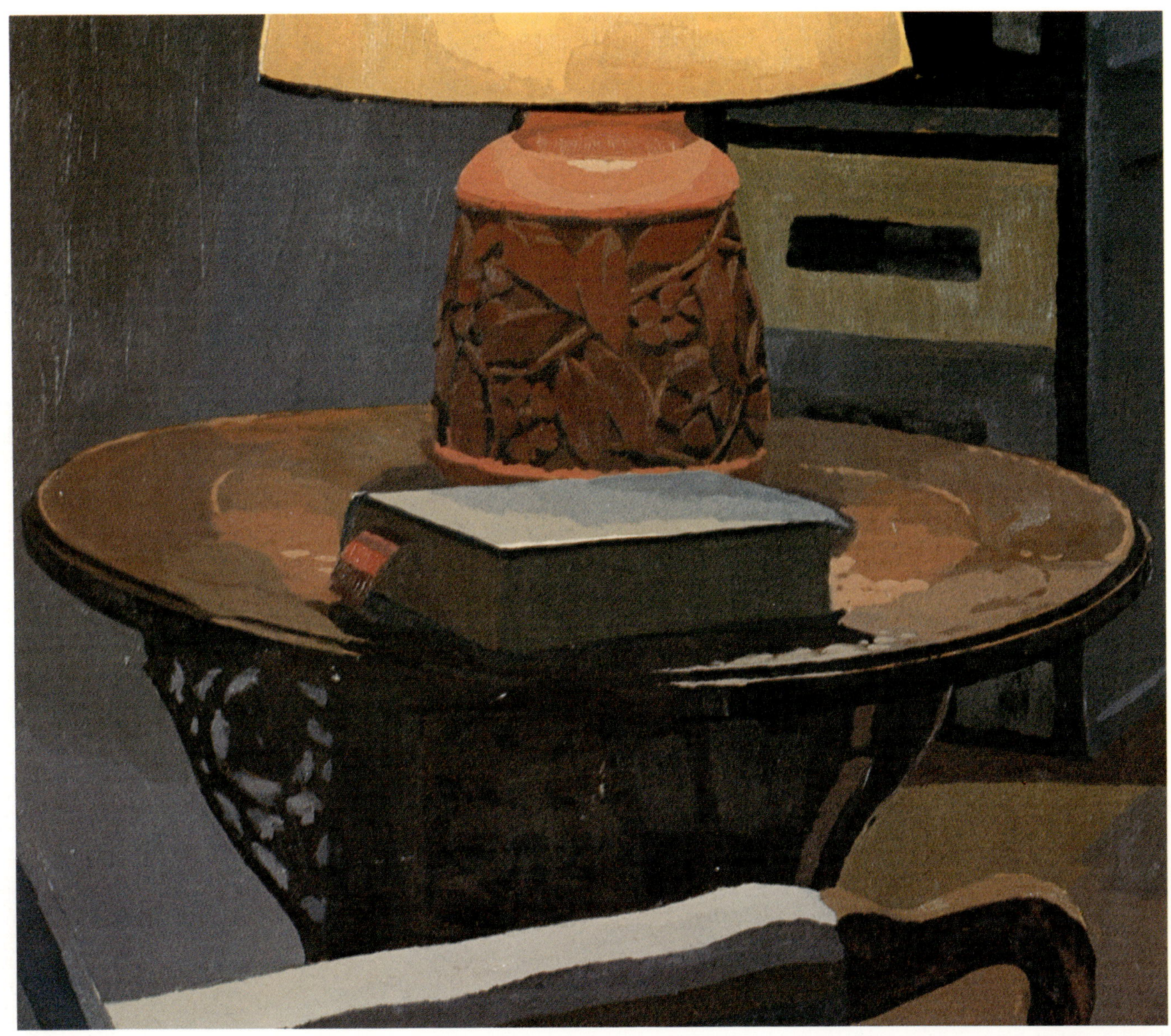

Closeup of Tabletop. Here are three objects of different materials and forms: a carved ceramic lampbase, a closed book, and a wooden tabletop. Yet the essential differences of these objects has been conveyed from the basic, economic patterning of color spots. Notice how the complex fretwork on the table's underside is stated as a silhouette of a single color.

"Portrait." Without painting the person who lives in this room, enough information has been conveyed about his interests, tastes, lifestyle, and habits to be called a portrait. Pictured is a favored spot, a comfortable chair, an unfinished book, and a lighted lamp—as though the room had been momentarily vacated just long enough to be painted. Beyond, a fancy file cabinet and common houseplant stand before a gated urban window. The scene is illuminated by both artificial and natural light, one warm and the other cold.

PAINT ARCHITECTURAL SUBJECTS

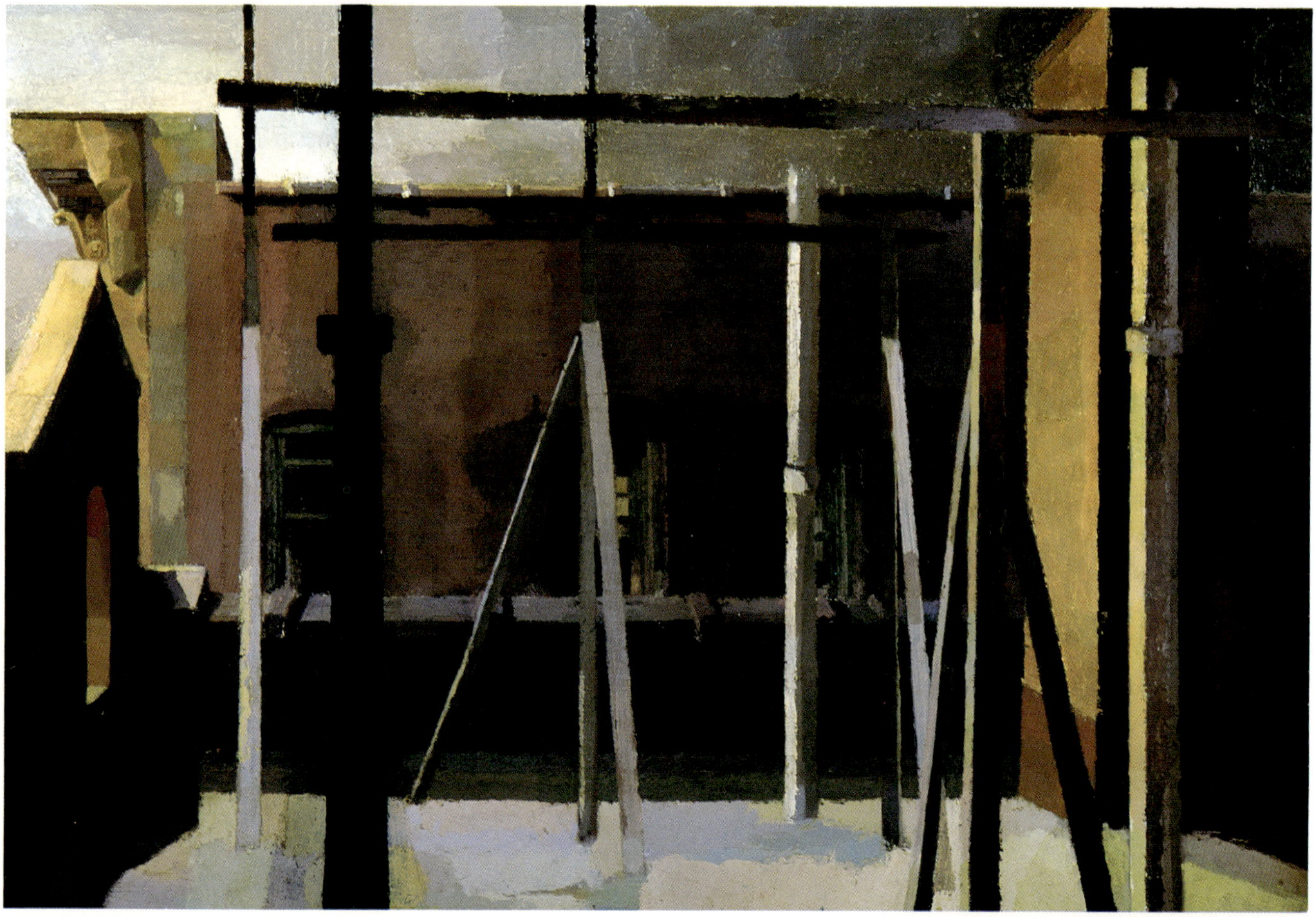

Rooftop Still Life. A still life can also be extended out of doors. Here the painter, Frederic Henderschott, found his setup on an apartment house rooftop. Why not? Nothing here moves but the clouds! The tall steel structures and their oblique props are evidence of former days, when washlines were strung from one vertical post to another. Today there are driers. (This painting is in the collection of Charles Singer.)

Details of Cornice and Window. Compare these two details on the adjacent building. They are different architecturally, and yet they are captured, as always, as spots of color, simply seen and carefully placed.

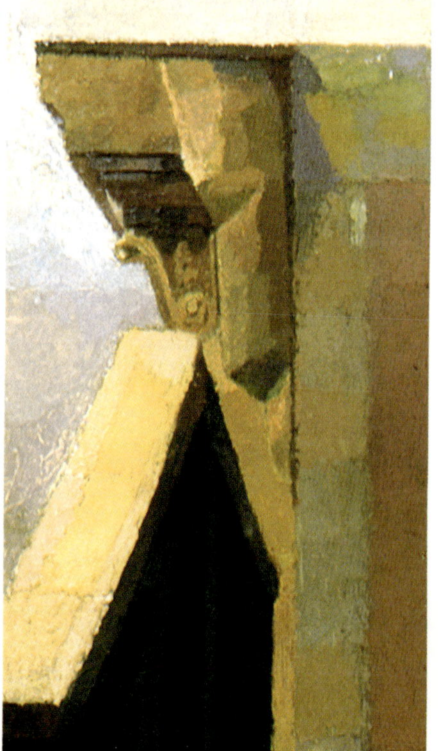

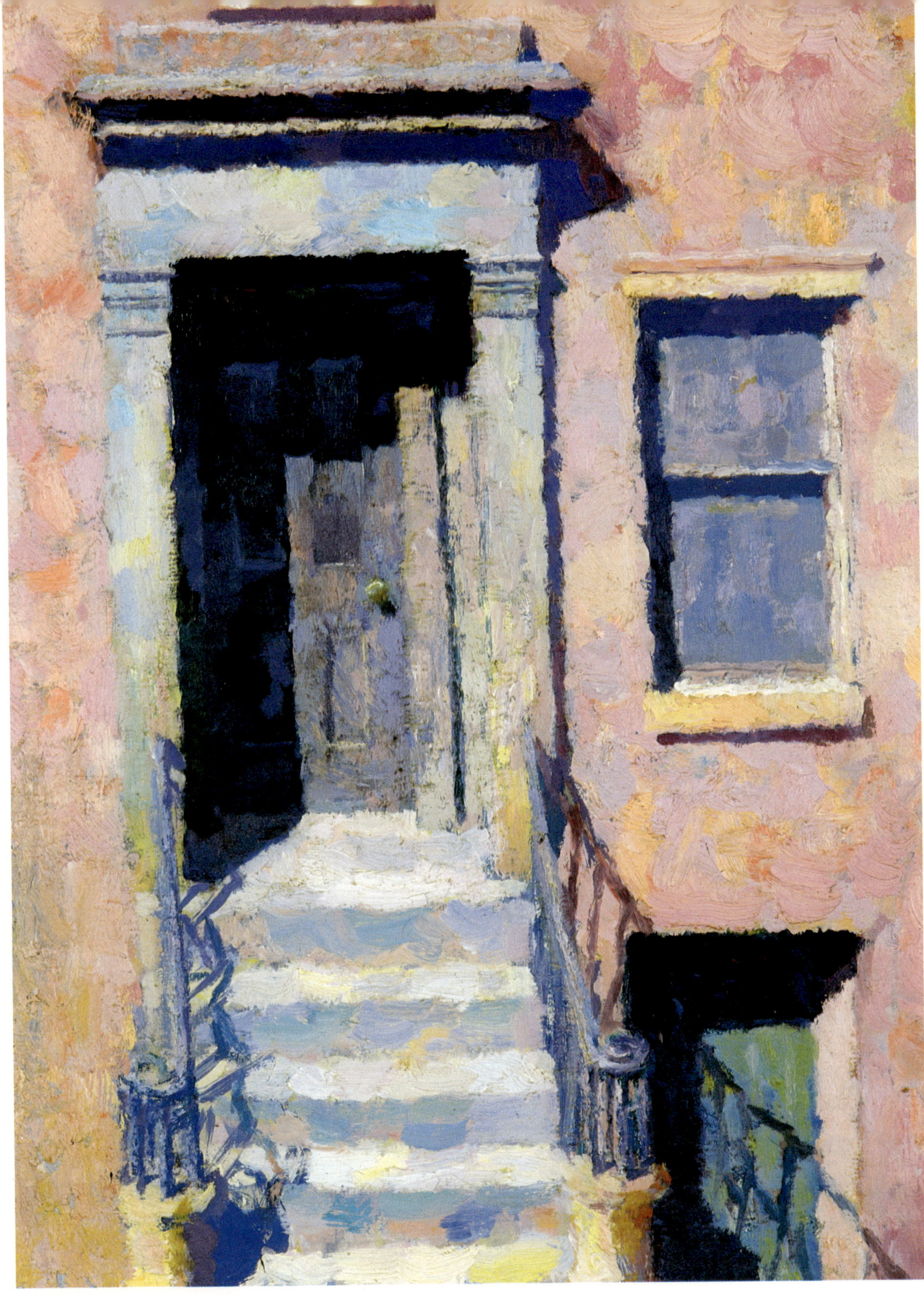

Pink House on Prince Street is a finished painting by John C. Russell, in the collection of Dr. George Edington. Here's another beautiful architectural "still life" that goes beyond the method of this book to a sensitive, personal painting style. The artist uses stiff bristle brushes and thick paint to develop a surface that's entirely his own. He still sees color spots, but they're his own kind of color spots, built up with brushstrokes. He makes no attempt to blend the strokes, but a shimmering effect of broken color emerges as he places one wet stroke over or beside another. This is no longer the work of a student, but the personal statement of an independent artist. While so many of the details of this painting bear careful scrutiny, the color of this cast shadow is exceptional. Notice that it never jumps out at you, but holds its place in the painting.

PAINT A LANDSCAPE

First Statement, Sumac. Landscapes are no more difficult to paint than still lifes if, armed with a viewfinder to crop out all but the essentials and with a palette knife to prevent you from fussing over details, you reduce the scene to the simplest, most basic color spots. But like the "unstill life" of Project 22, there is the problem of movement. Everything in nature is in a state of flux: fields, trees, clouds, water—and especially the light. How to solve this? As with flowers and fish, you must paint quickly—a study shouldn't exceed an hour. Then, you must select the simplest and smallest area you can find—you can always include more once you get the hang of it. Look for a minimum of color spots for your first statement—perhaps even as few as four. See the land—road, water, grass, sky, woods—as horizontal bands. Later, in the second statement, you can break them down into verticals and horizontals.

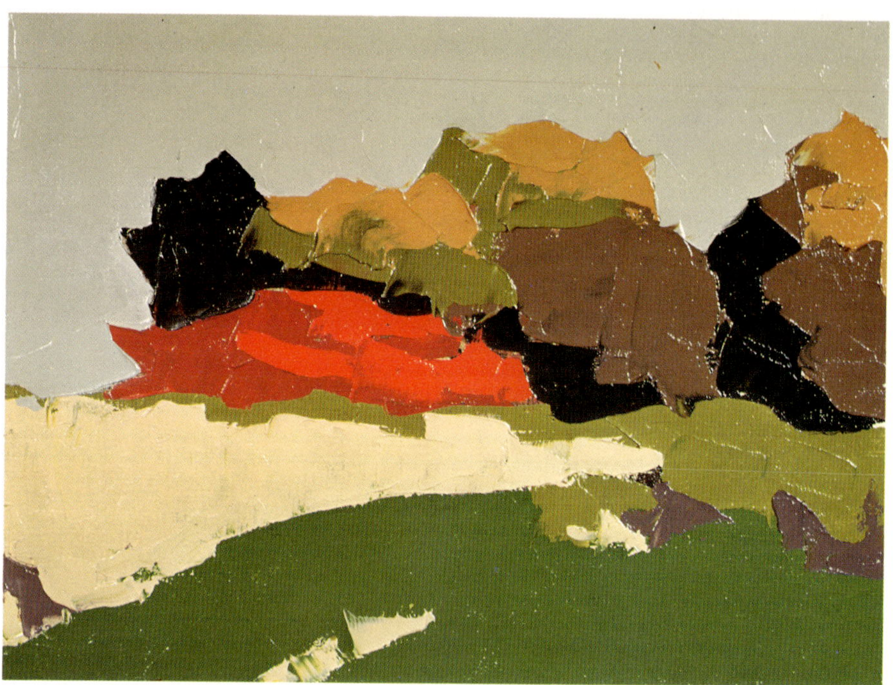

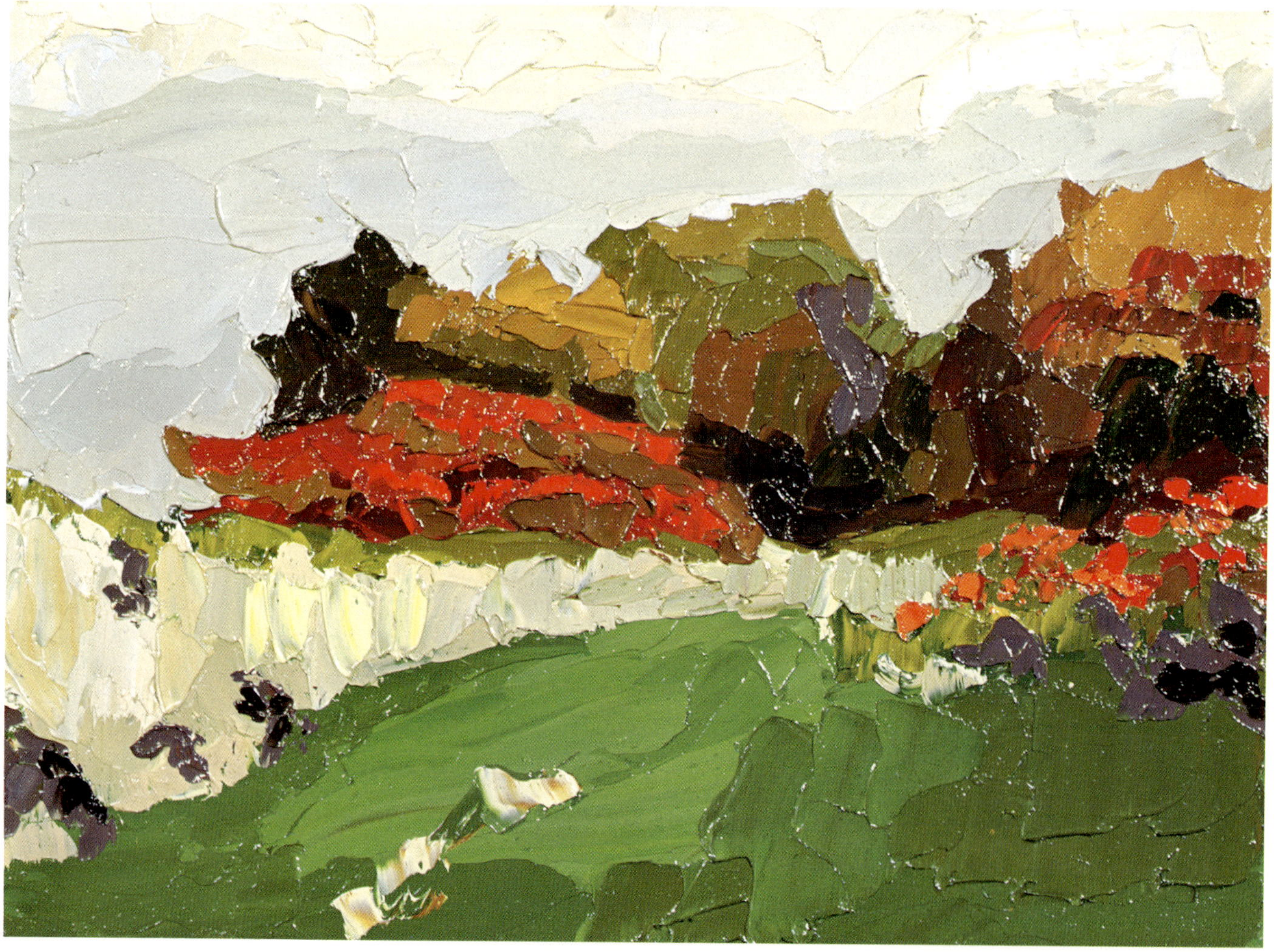

Third Statement, Sumac. Notice how the simple color spots of the first statement have been expanded into smaller and more complex shapes. Look, too, at the colors Jarvis Wilcox saw, both in sunlight and in shade, and at the strong, precise handling of the painting knife—single strokes of color, placed with assurance and without fuss. (Wilcox's painting is in the collection of Joseph Roth.)

PAINT A PORTRAIT

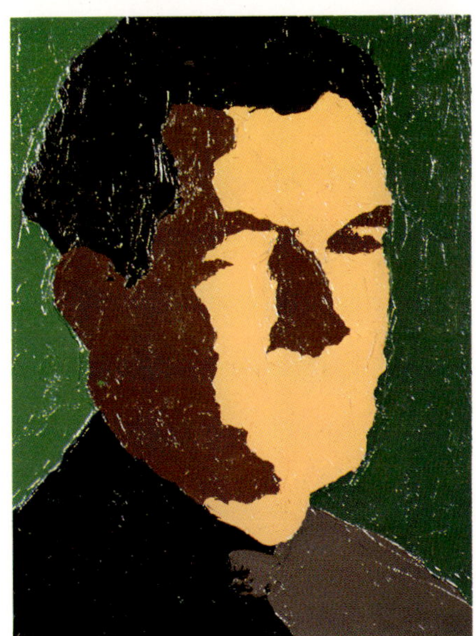

First Statement, Frank. Exactly what color is flesh? Apart from the obvious differences between the races, within one race, and even on the same person, fleshtones can run the gamut of the spectrum. To study flesh, ask a sitter (perhaps a friend)—to model for about three hours, with ten-minute breaks every half hour or so. Have your model wear a solid-colored shirt or sweater, one that contrasts in color temperature with the background. For example, a red shirt against a blue or green background; or a blue sweater against a yellow wall. Arrange the lighting to come from one side so that half the head and the background is in light, and the other half is in shade. Then look for a total of eight color spots: one for the light and one for the shade—of the flesh (face, throat, and neck), hair, clothing, and background. But don't lay down your colors in pairs; paint the color spots at random; or do all the shaded sides first, then all the lighted areas, so you see the work as a whole. Remember, you are not painting a person; you are painting a group of color spots of a particular size, shape, and position.

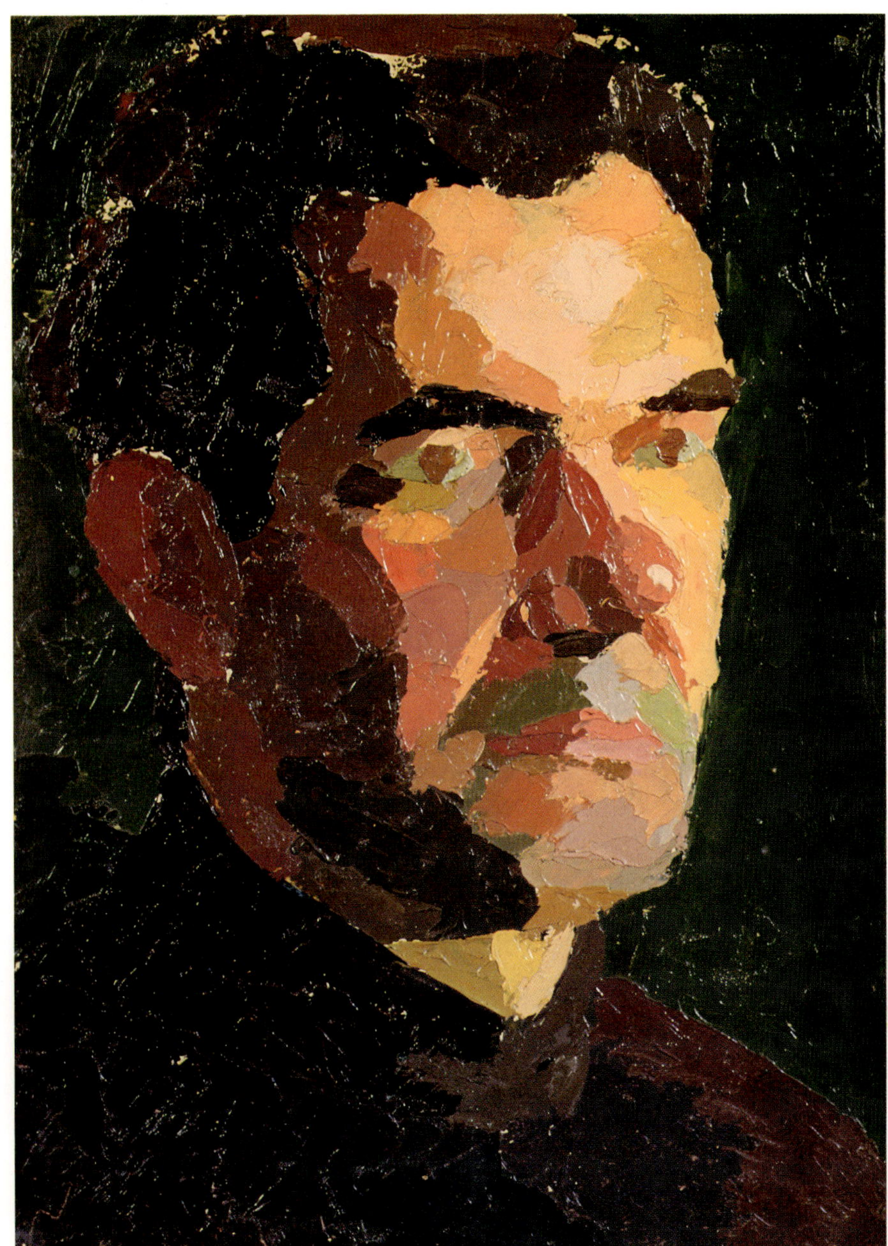

Third Statement, Frank. To paraphrase the question posed by Project 5, "When is the skin flesh-colored—and where?" Although this model's flesh matches the dictionary definitions of Caucasian fleshtones—light pink with a little yellow, neutral red-yellow, pale orange-yellow, light dull pink—in reality, as you can see, the color of the flesh runs the gamut of the entire rainbow! Yet despite the variety of colors—there are about 50 color spots here—the portrait still holds together as a unit, and we know we are looking at flesh! Notice how the background has affected the colors on the model as it reflects onto the skin. (This painting is by Alexander J. Yow.)

PAINT WITH A BRUSH

"Study." Here's a particularly beautiful painting in which the artist has absorbed the lessons of this book, but has applied the paint with a brush rather than a knife. He applied fluid paint with soft, smooth brushstrokes. The color spots are precisely observed and recorded, but then blended at the edges when the artist wants to create subtle gradations. Note the picture by Vermeer on the wall—a tribute to a master famed for beautiful interiors. Don Stern, who painted "*Study*," summarized the message of this book in five memorable words: "Trust—but train—your eye." (The painting is in the collection of Erik Falkensteen.)

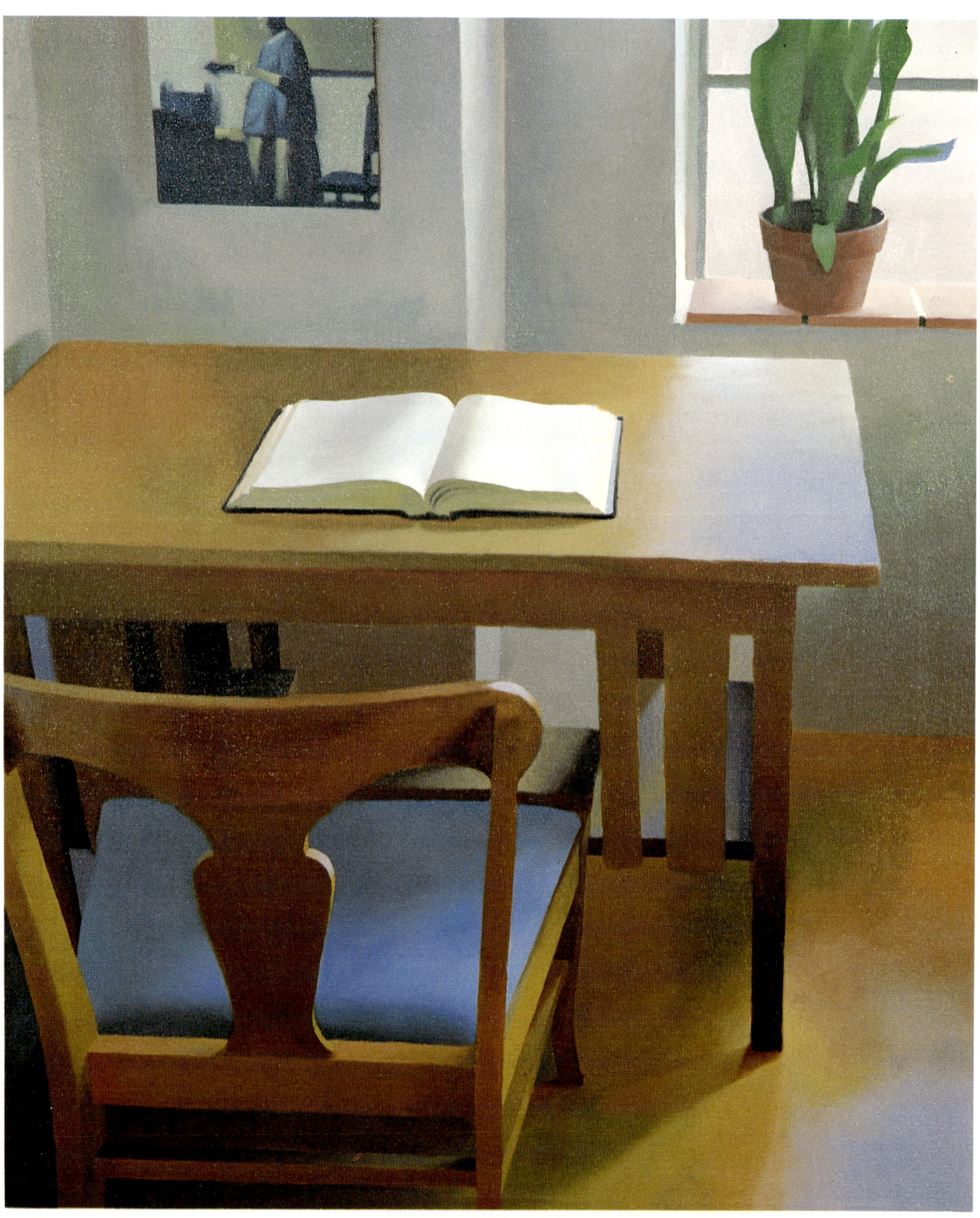

BIBLIOGRAPHY

Cary, Joyce. *Art and Reality*. New York: Harper, 1958.

Churchill, Sir Winston. *Painting as a Pastime*. New York: Whittlesley House, 1950.

Da Vinci, Leonardo. *Treatise on Painting*. Princeton: Princeton University Press, 1956.

Delacroix, Eugene. *The Journal of Eugene Delacroix*. Oxford: Phaidon, and Ithaca: Cornell, 1980.

Eastlake, Charles L. *Materials of Painting of the Great Schools and Masters*. New York: Dover, 1960.

Goldwater, Robert, and Treves, Marco (eds.). *Artists on Art*. New York: Pantheon, 1974.

Grosser, Maurice. *The Painter's Eye*. New York: New American Library, 1963.

Hawthorne, Charles W. *Hawthorne on Painting*. New York: Dover, 1960.

Hazlitt, William. "On the Pleasure of Painting" and "On Gusto" in *Selected Essays of William Hazlitt*. London: Nonsuch Press and New York: Random House, 1948. (Essays appear also in Hazlitt's *Criticisms on Art*. Check your library or local bookstore for newer editions of these classics.)

Hyde, Lewis. *The Gift—Imagination and the Erotic Life of Property*. New York: Vintage, 1983.

Mayer, Ralph. *The Artist's Handbook*. New York: Viking, 1981.

Mayer, Ralph. *The Painter's Craft*. New York: Viking, 1979.

Protter, Eric (ed.). *Painters on Painting*. New York: Grosset & Dunlap, 1971.

Rood, Roland. *Color and Light in Painting*. New York: Columbia University Press, 1941.

Ruskin, John. *The Elements of Drawing*. New York: Dover, 1971.

Sterling, Charles. *Still Life Painting*. New York: Harper & Row, 1981.

Van Gogh, Vincent. *The Letters of Vincent Van Gogh*. Greenwich: New York Graphic Society, 1958.

INDEX

Aluminum saucepan, 66–69
Amber Bottle (Richard Gleason), 131
Anenomes (Don Stern), 119
Apples, green, 78–81
Architectural subjects, 138–139

Baucheron, Geneviève, painting by, 124
Black
  color within, 37, 56
  cube, 36–37
  forbidden name, 24
  how light it can be, 34
  in light and shade, 54–57
Blue, 22
Blue-green, 21–22
Blue Jar (Richard Gleason), 130
Blue paper, 86–89
Blue-violet, 22
Bowl, Spoon, and Tangerine (Jarvis Wilcox), 125
Bread, 82–85
Brown, 24, 71, 96
Brush, 15
  painting with a, 142

Canvas board, 15
Canvas paper, 15
Cardboard, 15
Ceramic mug, 74–77
Chair, 17
Chroma, 24
Cleanup, 17, 30–31
Closeups, 134–135, 137
Clothing, 18
Color
  applying with palette knife, 19–20
  areas influencing each other, 41, 60
  classifying and naming, 23–24
  controlling, 22–23
  and distance of light, 63
  environmental influences on, 89
  finding the average, 40
  forbidden names, 24–25
  and form, 44
  hue, 23
  influences on, 10, 62–65
  intensity, 24
  of light and shade, 58–61
  lightening with white, 22–23
  local, 88, 101
  and location of object, 64
  luminosity (value), 23–24
  making a chart, 23
  matching, 25–26, 27
  of metal, 68–69
  mixing, 19, 20–22, 36–37
  neutralizing with complements, 22
  object, 10
  preconception, 25
  producing true, 21–22
  of shadows, 43
  transitional, 65, 80–81, 93
  variable and unpredictable, 10, 40
  of wall and floor influencing one another, 45
  of wood, 70–73
Colored paper, 17
"Colorless" object, 102–105
Color spots, distinguishing, 10, 34, 37, 39, 40, 41, 43, 44, 47, 50, 51, 54, 56, 59, 60, 63, 67, 68, 71, 72, 75, 76, 79, 80, 83, 84, 87, 88, 91, 93, 95, 99, 103, 107, 108, 111
Color wheel, 20–21
Conch Shell (Richard Gleason), 128
Contour
  adding color spots to define, 49
  lack of, 47–48
Corners, color changes of, 41
Corrugated board, 15
Cube
  black, 36–37
  green, 38–39
Cylinder, 34–35

Daffodils in a Can (Jarvis Wilcox), 118

Easel, 17
Electrical Outlet (Kenneth Krug), 133
El Greco, 10
Elliptical form, 71–73
Equipment, *see* Materials and equipment

Fiberboard, 15
Flowers, 110–113, 116–119
Foam board, 17
Form, 44
Four Apples (Richard Gleason), 126
Four Apples (Jarvis Wilcox), 126
Four Sardines (Don Stern), 121
Frank (Alexander J. Yow), 141

Glass, 98–101, 130–131
Glass Ashtray (Roger Stevens), 130
Glass dish, 98–101
Glass of water, 102–105
Glass Pitcher (Richard Gleason), 33
Gleason, Richard, studies by, 32–33, 68, 71–73, 91–93, 95–97, 126–131
Grapefruit, 46–49, 51, 53
Gray, 24
Green, 21
  cube, 38–39
  seen as red, 39
Greenery, 106–109

Hawthorne, Charles, 10, 132
Highlights, 65, 105
Houseplant, 106–109
Hue, 23

Intensity, 23, 124

Interiors, 136–137

Kennedy, Kevin, studies by, 50–53, 78, 81, 87–89, 105, 107, 109, 111, 113
Kitchen objects, 124
Krug, Kenneth, painting by, 133

Lamp, 18
Landscape painting, 16, 109, 140
Leonardo, 50, 87
Light, *see also* Reflected light
as color, 58–61
comparative, 50
distance from it influences color, 63
effects on similar objects, 78–81
greater, 50, 57
lesser, 50, 57, 65
natural, 18
primary source, 52
secondary source, 52
and shade, 61
on shadows, 50–53
source, 10, 18
studio lighting, 18
Lightening color with white, 22–23
Luminosity (value), 23–34

Materials and equipment
brushes, 15
chair, 17
cleanup paper, 17
clear glass, 15
clothing, 18
colored paper, 17
easel, 17
foam board, 17
lights, 18
mixing surfaces, 15
oil paints, 14
painting surfaces, 15
palette, 15
palette knife, 11, 15
pencil, 17
setup box, 16
solvents and mediums, 14–15
spot screen, 16
storage box, 17
tables, 18
tape, 17
viewfinder, 16
waste receptacle, 17
Metal, 66–69
Mind influences the eye, 9
Mineral spirit, 14
Mixing surfaces, 15
Modeling, 76
Mug of Coffee (Jarvis Wilcox), 132
Myman, Martin, painting by, 134

Neutralizing color with complements, 22

Oil paint, 14
Orange, 10, 21, 42–45, 50–53, 62–65

Painting medium, 14–15
Painting surfaces, 15
Painting what you see, 9–11
Palette, 15, 16
Palette knife, 11, 15
working with, 19–20
Paper bag, 94–97
Pear, 74–77
Pencil, 17
Personal judgment, 104
Pheasant (Geneviève Baucheron), 124
Pink House on Prince Street (John C. Russell), 139
Planes, influencing color of each other, 40–41
Plastic jug, 90–93
Plywood, 15
Point of view, 126–127
"Portrait" (Don Stern), 136–137
Portraiture, 141
Primary light source, 10
Projects, how they work, 28–30

Quartered Pomegranate (Jarvis Wilcox), 123

Rainbow Trout (Alexander J. Yow), 121
Rectangular box, 54–57
Red, 21
Red-orange, 21
Red-violet, 22
Reflected color
aluminum, 69
glass, 103–105
planes, 41
sun and sky, 52
Reflected light, 34, 57
Rincón, Fabio, studies by, 40, 41
Riverside Park, 9
Rooftop Still Life (Frederic Henderschott), 138
Round object, 42–45
Rubens, 10
Russell, John C., painting by, 114–115, 139

Safety, tips on, 30–31
Salad bowl, 70–73
Satin Bow (Richard Gleason), 129
Secondary light source, 10
Setup box, 16
Shadow
color of, 50–53, 58–61
cool, 52
new light on, 50–53
outdoors, 52
Six Oranges (Richard Gleason), 127
Sky, 117
Sliced Bread (Jarvis Wilcox), 122
Solvents, 14–15
Spot screen, 9, 16, 26, 37, 40
Squeezing paint from tube, 16
Stern, Don, paintings by, 12–13, 69, 99–101, 119, 120, 121, 136–137, 142
Stevens, Roger, paintings by, 130
Still lifes, 114–138
Still Life with Copper Spray Gun (Frederic Henderschott), 135
Storage box, 17
Striped Bass (Don Stern), 120
"Study" (Don Stern), 142
Sumac (Jarvis Wilcox), 140
Surface textures, 74–77, 128–129

Tables, 18
Tape, 17
Terracotta flowerpot, 78–81, 106–109
Textures, *see* surface textures
Tintoretto, 10
Titian, 10
Translucency, 90–93
Transparency, 98–101
Turpentine, 14
Tyrol, Alfred, studies by, 37, 39, 55–57, 59–61, 63, 65, 75, 77, 83, 85

Unstill life, 110–113

Velasquez, 10
Value, 23–24
Vermeer, 10, 142
Veronese, 10
Viewfinder, 16
Violet, 22

Waste disposal, 17
Water, 102–105
White
colors of, 56, 58–61
cylinder in shadow, 34–35
forbidden name, 24
how dark it can be, 34
in light and shadow, 54–57
lightening colors with, 22–23
White napkin, 58–61
White Tulips (Don Stern), 12–13
Wilcox, Jarvis, studies by, 43, 45, 47–49, 118, 122, 123, 125, 126, 132, 140
Window Still Life (Martin Myman), 134
Wine Bottle and Apples (John C. Russell), 114–115
Wood, 70–73

Yellow, 21
Yellow-green, 21
Yellow-orange, 21
Yow, Alexander J., paintings by, 121, 141